MORALITY AND POLITICS

MORALITY AND POLITICS

Edited by

**Ellen Frankel Paul, Fred D. Miller, Jr.,
and Jeffrey Paul**

CAMBRIDGE
UNIVERSITY PRESS

Published by the Press Syndicate of the University of Cambridge
The Pitt Building, Trumpington Street, Cambridge CB2 1RP, England
40 West 20th Street, New York, NY 10011, USA
10 Stamford Road, Oakleigh, Melbourne, Victoria 3166, Australia

First published 2004

Printed in the United States of America

Library of Congress Cataloging-in-Publication Data

Morality and Politics / edited by Ellen Frankel Paul,
Fred D. Miller, Jr., and Jeffrey Paul.   p.   cm.
Includes bibliographical references and index.
ISBN 0-521-54221-9
1. Political ethics.
I. Paul, Ellen Frankel.   II. Miller, Fred Dycus, 1944-   III. Paul, Jeffrey.   IV. Title.
JA79.M59   2004
172–dc22   2003065292
CIP

The essays in this book have also been published,
without introduction and index, in the semiannual journal
Social Philosophy & Policy, Volume 21, Number 1,
which is available by subscription.

CONTENTS

INTRODUCTION

Since the ancients, philosophers, theologians, and political actors have pondered the relationship between the moral realm and the political realm. Complicating the long debate over the intersection of morality and politics are diverse conceptions of fundamental concepts: the right and the good, justice and equality, personal liberty and public interest. Divisions abound, also, about whether politics should be held to a higher moral standard at all, or whether, instead, pragmatic considerations or *realpolitik* should be the final word. Perhaps the two poles are represented most conspicuously by Aristotle and Machiavelli. For Aristotle, the proper aim of politics is moral virtue: "politics takes the greatest care in making the citizens to be of a certain sort, namely good and capable of noble actions." Thus, the statesman is a craftsman or scientist who designs a legal system that enshrines universal principles, and the politician's task is to maintain and reform the system when necessary. The science of the political includes more than drafting good laws and institutions, however, since the city-state must create a system of moral education for its citizens. In marked contrast, Machiavelli's prince exalted pragmatism over morality, the maintenance of power over the pursuit of justice. Machiavelli instructed that "a prince, and especially a new prince, cannot observe all those things which are considered good in men, being often obliged, in order to maintain the state, to act against faith, against charity, against humanity, and against religion."

The fourteen contributors to this collection are predominantly arrayed on the Aristotelian end of the continuum, although several moral skeptics and pragmatists do enter the fray. Our authors address questions that have become ever more pressing in our era of global interconnectedness counterbalanced by global terrorism. Should politics be an extension of moral/religious teachings or should the two keep to their own realms: "Render unto Caesar what is Caesar's and unto God what is God's"? Should politics play a meliorative role and attempt to surmount popular morality and replace it with something better, or should politics take humankind as it is? Is there something about the political stage that permits elected officials to act in ways that would be considered morally objectionable in private citizens? Does the statesman's art permit lying for a good cause, concealing the truth from citizens in the name of a lofty purpose of state, or simply lying to preserve one's power or reputation? If so (or not), what standards of morality must politicians be held to if a democracy is to thrive? Does the private morality of politicians matter to our assessment of their fitness for office or of their political achievements? Does the operation of a liberal democracy depend upon agreement about public (or political) morality when private morality is irredeemably plu-ralistic? When is a democratic state justified in intervening in the affairs of other nations for humanitarian reasons? How can pluralistic societies make moral distinctions of the gravest importance, such as that between freedom fighters and terrorists?

Our first two contributors reflect on internationalist themes and how democratic societies ought to assess and respond to international terror-ism and state-sponsored atrocities. In her essay, "What's Morality Got to Do With It? Making the Right Distinctions," Jean Bethke Elshtain chal-lenges the idea that morality and politics are not mutually constitutive, a presumption shared by the positivist epistemology of "value-free" social science and scientific neorealism in the study of international relations. Neorealism claims that international relations is really all about power, and that morality and ethics are dragged in only as "cover." A supposedly value-free social science claims that description and evaluation are two entirely separate activities. Description is neutral and yields no evaluative implications; what we value we "layer on" to our description of actions or events, doing so more or less arbitrarily, based on our own biases. Elshtain challenges such presumptions by showing how getting the de-scriptions right is often morally charged, and doing so enables us to make important distinctions and, then, evaluations. For example, getting the description right allows us to call what transpired on September 11, 2001, an "unspeakable horror" not a "glorious victory." Elshtain emphasizes that distinctions—such as that between combatants and noncombatants, justice and revenge—anchor any decent political world. Only by getting our descriptions right about terrorism and genocide can we prevent a slide into a world of indiscriminate horror.

Whether the use of force by one state against another constitutes an act of aggression or a legitimate humanitarian intervention, observes Mark S. Stein, often hinges on the interpretation of hotly debated terms such as 'political independence', 'territorial integrity', and 'authorized force'. In his essay, "Unauthorized Humanitarian Intervention," Stein explores the legal and ethical issues raised by state-sponsored humanitarian efforts conducted by one or more countries against another country without the explicit approval of the United Nations Security Council. Legal analysis leads Stein to conclude that virtually no respected international body would interpret the UN Charter as permitting unauthorized humanitar-ian intervention. Legal analysis does not, however, answer the ethical question of whether states should avoid unauthorized intervention. This question recalls enduring debates in moral theory about act-utilitarianism, rule-utilitarianism, and the place of institutions in utilitarian theory and practice. While some of these debates involve implausible hypothetical scenarios, Stein considers real-world examples of unauthorized human-itarian intervention—the establishment of no-fly zones in northern and southern Iraq, the NATO bombings of the Bosnian Serbs, and NATO's

Kosovo intervention against Yugoslavia—as a means of gaining practical insight on balancing rule adherence against the minimization of human suffering.

The next four contributors explore various connections between morality and politics in democratic societies. In "Thinking Constitutionally: The Problem of Deliberative Democracy," Stephen L. Elkin critiques the quest, spawned by the work of John Rawls, for an ideal, rational deliberative democracy. The many advocates of such a moralized politics envision a legislative process of public deliberation abstracted from narrow, group-interested motivations. Legislators must be free from self-interest, political ambition, and the crude desire to exercise political power. Instead, they will be conscientious and desirous of pursuing the principles of justice. Not for them the bargaining, the horse-trading of our familiar interest-group democracy. Relying on insights about factionalism and constitutionalism from Madison and about human nature and politics from Machiavelli and Hobbes, Elkin focuses on the importance of institution and constitution building to secure the best regime practicable. He peoples his politics with humans in their flawed state, and his democracy does not depend upon ideal men and women pursuing a selfless public good. Elkin's legislators aim at creating institutions that will secure the good enough, rather than the best. In institution building, it must be recognized that morally ambiguous and even worse motives cannot be avoided altogether in political life. "There is a sense in which politics is precisely what ideal theory seeks to avoid," Elkin remarks. In contrast to ideal theorists, Elkin offers a messy politics that tries to harness ambition, power lust, and the rest of human nature's unseemly qualities.

While Elkin is concerned with constructing a democratic regime that suits humans' flawed nature, Russell Hardin in his essay, "Representing Ignorance," wonders how we might assess the morality of elected officials who govern citizens who are largely ignorant of political issues. Hardin's strategy is to analyze politics as a profession. Thus, just as lawyers and doctors have their respective role moralities, elected officials have theirs, which must be functionally defined by the purpose that they are to fulfill once in office. Hence, the role morality of elected officials will largely be determined by our theory of representation and how it deals with the problem of voter incompetence. Hardin isolates three major and distinct theories of representation: a quasi-Madisonian theory that sees legislators as agents of their constituents, a political party theory that makes elected officials agents of their parties, and an audience democracy theory that views officials as basically agents of themselves rather than others. In our era of media savvy politicians, Hardin sees little room for discerning a distinctive role morality for representatives of the third type, while in earlier eras the first two theories generated much clearer role moralities. In audience democracy, unlike its two predecessors where citizens' interests coincided with their moral expectations for their representatives, no such assumption can be made today. Personality and success in dealing with the media trump other qualities, and what we have are representatives who don't know much about their constituents trying to represent constituents who know little about policies or officials. A well-defined role morality for elected officials remains elusive in light of diverse theories of representation and the actual electoral choices of citizens in democratic regimes today—wherein voters do not seem to have in mind any role morality, conventional or otherwise, for the leaders they put in office. Borrowing from David Hume, Hardin proposes that we define the morality of elected officials as "artificial" duties, defined by their functional fit with the institutional purposes of their profession.

Hardin's attention is directed at the consequences of voter ignorance in crafting a role morality for elected officials, while Stanley A. Renshon focuses on another defect in the citizenry of some democratic societies, particularly in the United States: the lack of national identity and attachment. Political theorists, observes Renshon in "Dual Citizenship and American Democracy: Patriotism, National Attachment, and National Identity," repeatedly remind Americans that they live in an increasingly interdependent world in which traditional understandings of sovereignty are becoming obsolete. Americans are urged to shed their parochial outlook in favor of more inclusive connections to other cultures. In this spirit, Americans welcome people with dual citizenship, that is, individuals who are citizens of two or more countries and hold allegiance to each. At the same time, Americans are being asked to show greater cultural sensitivity to increasingly diverse racial and ethnic groups. Americans are urged to welcome immigrants, to respect their beliefs, and to adjust to their needs. None of this is regarded as a significant issue, as long as everyone believes in the American creed. Yet how the two trends of multiculturalism and dual citizenship accord with the requirements of republican democracy has not been carefully considered, nor fully debated, in the United States. The ethics of dual citizenship and how to balance rights, responsibilities, and obligations ought to be fully examined. Such a discussion must place ethics in the context of the actual practices specific to American democracy and the psychology that underlies them. According to Renshon, this requires us to pay close attention to the nature of American national identity and its largely overlooked importance in providing a foundation for citizenship.

If Renshon's dual citizens can be described as having bifurcated loyalties between "here" and "there," then Tyler Cowen's policymakers might well be described as facing moral dilemmas between serving the public "now" or "later." In "Policy Implications of Zero Discounting: An Exploration in Politics and Morality," Cowen asks, "What are our political obligations to future generations?" As Cowen notes, most plausible moral theories have a strong consequentialist element and must somehow compare present well-being to future well-being. Applying the economist's tools to the question of present versus future, Cowen considers the policy consequences of weighting future societal interests as heavily as current interests. This is what economists call "zero discounting," and, Cowen relates, its policy implications cut across the traditional "Left-Right" divide. Cowen finds that the present generation has strong obligations to save and invest, but not strong obligations to redistribute wealth toward the very poor. To ameliorate poverty in the long term we should pay more attention to increasing the rate of economic growth. Persistent environmental problems become more important according to a zero discount model, but transient or "one-shot" environmental problems become less important. Overall, a zero rate of discount shifts the balance toward consequentialist rather than deontological considerations in public policy-making, underscores the importance of a free society, and explains, in part, why it may be hard to adhere to rule-based prescriptions either in politics or in one's personal life.

Descending into the cave, our next three contributors confront the seamier realities of government and politics, including politicians who lie to cover up personal scandals or to deceive their constituents, and citizens who betray their countries to abet foreign tyrannies. While politicians have long been accused of lying by ordinary skeptics and professional pundits alike (and while many a politician has been caught in a fib or flat-out scandal), in at least one area of national life, secrecy, subterfuge, and deception are essential tools of the trade: the realm of espionage. In his "Reflections on Espionage," Harvey Klehr observes that debate about the morality of espionage emerged almost as soon as the ancient practice itself. Because it requires duplicity and betrayal, espionage has been condemned by idealists, but realists acknowledge that it is unavoidable. Klehr finds that the moral status of spies varies, depending on several factors, including who the spy is. For example, is he a foreign national serving as an "agent in place" in his target country, or a disgruntled "Judas," willing to betray his own country and the lives of his fellow citizens? A moral calculus that justifies espionage must also take into account the nature of a spy's employer, as well as the spy's motives, tactics, and targets. Klehr then examines persistent efforts to first deny, and later justify, the extensive espionage that was committed by Americans working on behalf of the Soviet Union during the 1930s and 1940s. He argues that the attempts at justification of the American Communists who spied for the Soviet Union are clearly flawed and increasingly unpersuasive, particularly since revelations from Soviet and Eastern bloc archives have made the guilt of many indisputable. Indeed, Klehr offers a compelling rebuttal to the ex post facto rationalizations that have been offered either by the spies themselves or by their biological or ideological offspring. Protestations about serving the interests of peace or providing a balance of terror in the nuclear arms race prove hollow when compared against the spies' own words from their KGB files and against the actions that they took to benefit Stalin's USSR, actions that helped to prolong and worsen the Cold War.

Whereas espionage has made a science out of secrecy and subterfuge, the more cynical observer might be inclined to quip that it is politicians who have made an art form out of lying. As Robert Weissberg demonstrates in his delightfully droll essay, "Mr. Pinocchio Goes to Washington: Lying in Politics," serious analytical problems beset those who would attempt to expose or eradicate lying in politics. After all, many falsehoods are not necessarily lies (i.e., intent to deceive is necessary) and different cultures construe truthfulness differently. Mental illness or some other condition may render an individual unable to separate truth from fiction. A falsehood uttered under coercion cannot be deemed a lie, while spoken lies may be admitted or qualified when accompanied by a nonverbal gesture such as a wink or a nod. Specialized terminology can convert seeming fabrication into convoluted truth, and today's truth may become tomorrow's lie, thanks to the unearthing of new information. Moreover, there can be no such thing as a lie if there is no such thing as truth. In attempting to analyze what lying is and when it matters, Weissberg finds that recourse to the great philosophers, such as Plato, Augustine, Machiavelli, and Kant, among others, produces little in the way of clear judgment. Each offers countless loopholes. The United States legal code deals extensively with lying, but lying is not always a crime, and proving perjury in court is an arduous task. After wrestling with the difficulties of identifying and proving lies, Weissberg argues that, ultimately, democratic elections may provide our best defense against political mendacity.

In recent years it has become increasingly common for newspapers and other media to expose problematic aspects of the private lives of political (and other public) figures and to make them the subject of commentary. John Haldane's "A Subject of Distaste; An Object of Judgment" asks the question: How should one judge these revelations? Any reasonable answer will have to take account of circumstance, form, and content. Some methods of acquiring information violate norms of justice. Some styles of exposure or public presentation are so gross and gratuitous as to be beyond principled defense. Some matters are so far removed from a public figure's office that no case for revelation can be made from the side of public interest. Equally, while some matters may be relevant in evaluating the conduct of public figures, and the means of acquiring the information are not unjust, and the proposed manner of presentation would not be gratuitously sensational, it may well be the case that other interests (including the interests of others) are such that it would be wrong to damage them, even as unintended but foreseen secondary effects of otherwise legitimate exposure. Haldane favors a traditional conservative approach to analyzing these issues, also drawing upon moral theology to expound the idea of fraternal correction. He wonders, however, whether these ways of thinking are applicable to contemporary pluralistic societies and, if they are not, to what extent these societies are in any sense moral communities.

The last five essays in this volume address various tensions in modern democratic societies and how to defuse or lessen them. In "Against Civic Schooling," James Bernard Murphy observes that both liberals and conservatives agree that civic education must go beyond civic knowledge and skills to include proper civic motives and dispositions; that is, both sides agree that civic education must aim at civic virtue, even if they disagree about which virtues ought to be learned. Unfortunately, both liberals and conservatives also agree that such an education in civic virtue is the responsibility of public schools. But just because civic virtues must be learned, argues Murphy, does not mean that they can be taught—let alone that they can be taught in the classroom. Murphy assesses the best empirical studies on the effectiveness of civic education in schools and shows that schooling aimed at instilling civic virtue is, at best, ineffective and often counterproductive. Advocates of civic schooling nevertheless argue that schools need a compelling moral purpose and that civic education is the most appropriate such purpose in a diverse, democratic society. Yet, as Murphy demonstrates, these normative arguments fail to grasp that academic schooling already has a compelling moral purpose, namely, to impart the intellectual virtues—those dispositions that make us conscientious in the pursuit of truth. Civic schooling is either irrelevant to the intrinsic moral purpose of schooling or positively subversive of it. Murphy shows that the history of civic schooling is a history of the subordination of truth-seeking to some civic agenda, leading to the whitewashing and distortion of academic knowledge. Indeed, civic schooling aimed at "instilling civic virtue" is inherently partisan and thereby violates the civic trust that underpins vibrant public schools.

Norman Barry observes that for much of the twentieth century, the influence of logical positivism and linguistic philosophy had reduced political and moral theory to a mainly analytical role in ethics and politics. But the publication of John Rawls's *A Theory of Justice* in 1971 prompted a plethora of articles and books on the traditional concerns of political philosophy: principally justice, equality, and rights. In his contribution to this volume, "Political Morality as Convention," Barry argues that much of this work has increased the divisiveness in society. He suggests that political theory should be much more concerned with exploring the conventions and practices of the market and the rule of law that make a society stable, prosperous, and predictable. Hume exemplifies the approach to social philosophy that Barry favors. Although in some ways Hume was the ancestor of logical positivism, Barry emphasizes that Hume did not share its subjectivism and relativism. Barry applies the lessons of Hume's indirect utilitarianism to contemporary law and business: the current "moralism" in law is rejected in favor of a form of legal positivism derived from H. L. A. Hart. Barry claims that constitutionalism and legal decentralization are the keys to harmony, and he argues that the current imposition of ethical duties on business should be replaced with the cultivation of conventions derived from the practice of commerce.

Michael Slote, in "Autonomy and Empathy," develops a welfare-oriented approach to morality and politics that builds on recent feminist work in the ethics of caring. While critics have charged that caring theorists cannot account for such "masculine" principles as justice and autonomy, Slote shows that an empathic approach can ground respect for the autonomy of the person. Drawing, too, on work by developmental psychologists, he sees empathy as crucial to ethics. A caring approach to ethics, explains Slote, must be reconfigured so that it appraises the rightness of human actions and the justice of laws and institutions, depending on whether they express relevant empathic concern. We can then say that parents who impose their own agendas on their children lack empathy for the desires, fears, and aspirations of their children, and thus express a morally criticizable lack of respect for their children's autonomy. Similarly, religious intolerance invariably can be attributed to an absence of real empathy for the point of view of those who are persecuted or denied their religious freedoms (often, ironically, "for the sake of their souls"). Such intolerance, too, involves a morally invidious denial of autonomy. However, paternalism of this invidious sort contrasts with the kind of state paternalism that merely imposes fines on motorists who do not wear their seatbelts. This latter form of paternalism, while it injects moralism into politics, does not necessarily express a lack of empathy or respect for the autonomy of others.

In his essay, "God's Image and Egalitarian Politics," George P. Fletcher argues that secular philosophies are hard pressed to ground their claim that all human beings should be treated with equal concern and respect. "This is simply a postulate of American liberalism," argues Fletcher, and while few today would question the idea of human dignity and equality, less clear is its historical provenance. Fletcher rejects claims that the principle of equality emerged in the natural law of the ancient Romans or in Stoic philosophy. He traces the modern conception of human equality to the biblical account of creation, yet he acknowledges certain contradictory elements in the Book of Genesis. Contradictions in the Hebrew text may reflect the difference between normative and anthropological approaches to equality, observes Fletcher. Nevertheless, they are instructive today as jurists and elected officials wrestle with competing interpretations of the Constitution and Bill of Rights. While equality remains the ideal, the pursuit of a successful and satisfactory egalitarian politics remains, in many ways, a work in progress.

In his essay, "Should Political Liberals Be Compassionate Conservatives? Philosophical Foundations of the Faith-Based Initiative," John Tomasi examines the relationship between liberal egalitarianism and the vision of American welfare reform known as "compassionate conservatism." Compassionate conservatives call for a substantial mixing of church and state; in particular, they call for public funding to be directed freely to religious organizations that provide social services. Political liberals wish to justify the use of political power in a way that accepts the fact of reasonable value pluralism; in particular, they are committed to treating citizens of faith as political equals. Tomasi shows that an argument for the compassionate conservatives' vision of welfare reform can be formulated in public reason terms. Accordingly, political liberal egalitarians, to be true to their own deepest principles, should advocate principles of justice that would be welcoming to the compassionate conservatives' model of church-state relations. Ultimately, Tomasi suggests, the dominant contemporary idea of liberalism, unlike classical conceptions, is incompatible with any strong notion of separation between church and state.

The essays that comprise this volume address perennial concerns in political and moral theory, from the meaning of citizenship to the proper role of the legislator, from the legitimacy of the state's use of force to the warrant for acts of terror by zealots against civilians, from espionage and deceit to the cultivation of religious and civic virtue. These essays underscore the rekindled yearning of many to hold the political realm to a higher standard, despite the skepticism of the dissenters who question the likelihood or even the desirability of success.

ACKNOWLEDGMENTS

The editors gratefully acknowledge several individuals at the Social Philosophy and Policy Center, Bowling Green State University, who provided invaluable assistance in the preparation of this volume. They include Mary Dilsaver, Terrie Weaver, and Assistant Director Travis S. Cook.

We thank Publication Specialist Tamara Sharp for her essential contributions to a smooth and timely production process, Editorial Assistant Carrie-Ann Khan for her indefatigable attention to detail, and Managing Editor Teresa Donovan.

CONTRIBUTORS

Jean Bethke Elshtain is Laura Spelman Rockefeller Professor of Social and Political Ethics at the University of Chicago. She is the author or editor of twenty books, including *Just War against Terror: The Burden of American Power in a Violent World* (2003). She is a Fellow of the American Academy of Arts and Sciences and a member of the Board of Directors of the National Endowment for Democracy. She has published more than six hundred essays in scholarly journals and journals of civic opinion.

Mark S. Stein is a Visiting Assistant Professor in the Department of Government at Dartmouth College. He has published articles in numerous journals, including *Accountability, Bioethics, Chicago-Kent Law Review, George Mason Law Review, Polity,* and *Social Theory and Practice.* His first book, *Disability and Distributive Justice,* is forthcoming.

Stephen L. Elkin is Professor of Government and Politics at the University of Maryland. He has been a Visiting Fellow at the Australian National University and Beijing University. He is the editor of the journal *The Good Society,* chair of the executive board of the Committee on the Political Economy of the Good Society (PEGS), and a principal of the Democracy Collaborative. He is the editor, with Karol Edward Soltan, of *A New Constitutionalism: Designing Political Institutions for a Good Society* (1993), *The Constitution of Good Societies* (1996), and *Citizen Competence and Democracy* (1999). Elkin is also the author of *City and Regime in the American Republic* (1987) and *Constituting the American Republic* (forthcoming).

Russell Hardin is Professor of Politics at New York University and Professor of Political Science at Stanford University. He was for many years the editor of *Ethics* and has published widely in other scholarly journals, including *Journal of Political Philosophy, European Review, Boston University Law Review, University of Virginia Law Review, Social Research,* and *Ethics and International Affairs.* He is the author of *Collective Action* (1982); *Morality within the Limits of Reason* (1988); *One for All: The Logic of Group Conflict* (1995); *Liberalism, Constitutionalism, and Democracy* (1999); *Trust and Trustworthiness* (2002); and *Indeterminacy and Society* (forthcoming).

Stanley A. Renshon is Professor of Political Science at the Graduate Center, the City University of New York, and a certified psychoanalyst. His book on the Clinton presidency, *High Hopes* (1996), won the 1997 Richard E. Neustadt Award of the American Political Science Association for the best book published on the presidency. *High Hopes* was also the winner of the 1998 Gradiva Award of the National Association for the Advancement of Psychoanalysis for the best published work in the category of biography. His recent books include *America's Second Civil War: Dispatches from the Political Center* (2002) and *The 50% American: National Identity in a Dangerous Age* (forthcoming).

Tyler Cowen is Holbert C. Harris Professor of Economics at George Mason University. He also serves as Director of the Mercatus Center and the James Buchanan Center for Political Economy. He has published widely in the economics of culture and rational choice ethics and is the author of *In Praise of Commercial Culture* (1998), *What Price Fame?* (2000), and *Creative Destruction: How Globalization Is Changing the World's Cultures* (2002).

Harvey Klehr is Andrew W. Mellon Professor of Politics and History at Emory University. He has published widely in both scholarly journals and popular periodicals, including *The New Republic, The Weekly Standard,* and the *New York Review of Books.* He is the author, coauthor, or editor of ten books, including *The Secret World of American Communism* (with John Earl Haynes and Fridrikh Igorevich Firsov, 1995) and *Venona: Decoding Soviet Espionage in America* (with John Earl Haynes, 1999; Russian documents translated by Timothy D. Sergay). His newest book is *In Denial: Historians, Communism, and Espionage* (2003).

Robert Weissberg has taught Political Science at Cornell University and is Professor of Political Science at the University of Illinois at Urbana-Champaign. He has published articles in the *American Journal of Political Science, Journal of Politics, Public Opinion Quarterly, Critical Review, Political Behavior, The Public Interest,* and many other scholarly journals and anthologies. His recent books include *Political Tolerance: Balancing Community and Diversity* (1998); *The Politics of Empowerment* (1999); *Democracy and the Academy* (editor, 2000); and *Polling, Policy, and Public Opinion: The Case against Heeding the "Voice of the People"* (2002). He has also written for general audiences through *The Weekly Standard, Chronicles, Society,* and other popular publications. He has earned grants from the Earhart and Sarah Scaife Foundations, and he is currently working on two book projects: the first will assess the impact of political activism, while the second will examine the United States government's effort to expand wealth by encouraging personal debt.

John Haldane is Professor of Moral Philosophy at the University of St. Andrews and Director of the Center for Ethics, Philosophy, and Public Affairs there. He is widely published in several areas of philosophy, in particular history of philosophy, metaphysics, philosophy of religion, philosophy of mind, and philosophy of value. He is the editor of *Reality, Representation, and Projection* (with Crispin Wright, 1993) and *Mind, Meta-*

physics, and Value in the Thomistic and Analytical Traditions (2002). He is the author of *Atheism and Theism* (with J. J. C. Smart, 2d ed., 2003), *Faithful Reason* (2003), and *An Intelligent Person's Guide to Religion* (2003). He also contributes to newspapers, radio, and television.

James Bernard Murphy is Associate Professor of Government at Dartmouth College. He earned his Ph.D. in Philosophy and Political Science from Yale University and has been awarded grants and fellowships from the National Endowment for the Humanities, the American Council of Learned Societies, the Earhart Foundation, and the Pew Charitable Trusts. He has published articles in *Political Theory, The Review of Politics, The Review of Metaphysics, Semiotica, The Thomist, The American Journal of Jurisprudence,* and *The American Catholic Philosophical Quarterly.* He is the author of *The Moral Economy of Labor: Aristotelian Themes in Economic Theory* (1993) and *The Philosophy of Positive Law: Misadventures in Legal Theory* (forthcoming). He is an editor of *Aristotle and Modern Law* (with Richard O. Brooks, 2001) and is currently working on a book about intellectual virtue as the academic and moral aim of schooling.

Norman Barry is Professor of Social and Political Theory at the University of Buckingham. He has taught at the University of Exeter and Birmingham Polytechnic. He specializes in political philosophy, welfare theory, and business ethics. His books include *Hayek's Social and Economic Philosophy* (1979), *An Introduction to Modern Political Theory* (1981), *On Classical Liberalism and Libertarianism* (1986), *The New Right* (1987), *Welfare* (1990), and *Business Ethics* (2000). He has published widely in academic journals, including *Political Theory, The British Journal of Political Science,* and *Political Studies.* He is a member of the Academic Advisory Councils of the Institute of Economic Affairs (London) and the David Hume Institute (Edinburgh).

Michael Slote is UST Professor of Ethics and Professor of Philosophy at the University of Miami. He is a member of the Royal Irish Academy and a former Tanner Lecturer. He has authored many articles on ethics and political philosophy, as well as several books, including *Three Methods of Ethics: A Debate* (with Marcia W. Baron and Philip Pettit, 1997) and *Morals from Motives* (2001). His present work focuses on integrating virtue ethics with the ethics of caring and with moral sentimentalism more generally.

George P. Fletcher is Cardozo Professor of Jurisprudence at Columbia Law School. Fluent in numerous languages, he has addressed and trained lawyers and judges throughout the world, including the legal staff of the International Criminal Tribunal. In 2001 he delivered the prestigious Storrs lectures at Yale Law School, and in 2003 the *Notre Dame Law Review* published a special issue devoted to commentary about his work. He has published more than one hundred articles in academic journals, as well as pieces in the *New York Times*, the *Washington Post*, *The New Republic*, the *New York Review of Books*, and other popular media. He is the author of *Rethinking Criminal Law* (1978), *A Crime of Self-Defense: Bernhard Goetz and the Law on Trial* (1988), *Loyalty: An Essay on the Morality of Relationships* (1993), *With Justice for Some: Victims' Rights in Criminal Trials* (1995), *Our Secret Constitution: How Lincoln Redefined American Democracy* (2001), and *Romantics at War: Glory and Guilt in the Age of Terrorism* (2002).

John Tomasi is Associate Professor of Political Science at Brown University. He has taught in the philosophy department at Stanford University, and has held research appointments at Princeton University, Harvard University, and the Social Philosophy and Policy Center, Bowling Green State University. He is the author of *Liberalism Beyond Justice: Citizens, Society, and the Boundaries of Political Theory* (2001). His articles have appeared in *Ethics*, the *Journal of Philosophy*, and, more recently, in a *NOMOS* volume on civic education. He is currently writing a book on the relationship of political power to territorial space in an era of global capitalism.

WHAT'S MORALITY GOT TO DO WITH IT?
MAKING THE RIGHT DISTINCTIONS

By Jean Bethke Elshtain

I. Introduction

I will be arguing against a school of thought and an epistemology. The school of thought is 'scientific neorealism', as it is called in the study of international relations. This perspective is shaped by the insistence that ethics and international politics have nothing to do with one another, save insofar as morality is brought in as window dressing in order to disguise what is really going on: the clash of narrowly self-interested powers. The world of international relations is construed as a zone of self-help in a Hobbesian clash of a war of all against all. For more than twenty-five years now, I have argued that, to the contrary, ethics does not stop at the water's edge and morality is not silent during war.

The epistemology that I will contest is not so much argued against up front as challenged by a narrative that makes an antipositivist case. Contrary to the presuppositions of the political science in which I was trained, description and evaluation are not entirely separate activities. We do not layer evaluations onto a neutral description; rather, moral evaluation is embedded in our descriptions. How we describe is itself often a moral act. This is a case made eloquently in a book that seems to have disappeared from view, Julius Kovesi's *Moral Notions*.[1] The argument against positivism is also an argument against an account of moral evaluation named 'emotivism', which holds, roughly, that our moral evaluations are not rationally defensible and bear no serious cognitive content. Each of these contentions will be taken up in the context of a treatment of the current international crisis, specifically the struggle against terrorism.

II. Emotivism, Evaluation, and Description

There is a classic line associated with Sergeant Joe Friday, leader of the detective team that investigated and solved crimes on the classic television series *Dragnet*. At one point or another in every episode, stony-faced Sergeant Friday would turn to a witness or a suspect and intone flatly: "Only the facts, ma'am," or "Just give us the facts, sir." There is no substitute for the facts, nor for an attempt to achieve a description of

---

[1] Julius Kovesi, *Moral Notions* (London: Routledge & Kegan Paul, 1967).

events or phenomena that is as accurate and complete as possible. If we get our facts—hence, our descriptions—wrong, then our analyses and our ethics will be wrong, too. There are deep moral principles involved in this claim. Many heated debates in ethics and moral philosophy swirl around such matters. But most of us understand intuitively what is at stake. When Pope John Paul II described the September 11, 2001, attacks on the World Trade Center towers and the Pentagon as an "unspeakable horror," we nodded our heads: Yes, that seems right. Noncombatants, hence innocents under the international war convention, were attacked as they chatted with colleagues, drank the day's first cup of coffee, or called home to say they had arrived safely at work.

It follows from my characterization that we would be obliged to say the same thing if someone had flown commercial jetliners loaded with fuel and civilian passengers into crowded buildings anywhere in the world with the explicit aim of killing as many civilians as possible. It would be an "unspeakable horror" whether it happened in New York City or Moscow or Tokyo or Delhi or Karachi or Riyadh. But it happened in the United States. Americans bear a special burden to pay attention and to get the facts right. Our depiction of an event carries our moral evaluation of that event. "Unspeakable horror" is not a neutral description of what happened on September 11. The pontiff's words convey the viciousness of the perpetrators and the miserable fruits of their labor.

By contrast, a madman or the ideological fanatic who looks on September 11 as a glorious victory begins by misdescribing what happened. His words aim to draw our attention away from desperate people who plunged like birds with broken wings to their deaths in order to escape a certain death by fire, or from buildings imploding and shattering thousands of human beings into minute bits of rubble and dust. Innocent civilians will not be represented as who they were on September 11: human beings from more than eighty-six countries at work in the World Trade Center towers as well as in the Pentagon. Instead, the madman or the fanatic will represent these innocent people as "infidels" and revel in their destruction. He will strip them of their status as noncombatants and hence of the protection that this status affords in the laws of war and their provisions against intentional targeting and assault.

One description, the Pope's, condemns an intentional attack that used instruments of peaceful travel—commercial airliners—against buildings in which commerce was being conducted and people were working to support their families. The other description, the ideological fanatic's, revels in the attack. The fanatic's description is not just another way of saying the "same thing" as does a person whose description embeds a condemnation of the attacks. Instead, it is a strategy of exculpation, a way to let terrorists off the hook, or even to glorify what they have done. What of the hijackers themselves? How do we get the description right where they are concerned? Were they martyrs to their faith, as some claim? To be a 'martyr', in ordinary language, is to be one who dies for one's faith. A person who kills wrongly, meaning a person who kills outright and intentionally in a civilian context, is not usually called a martyr but a murderer—rightly so. To glorify those whose primary aim is to murder thousands of unsuspecting civilians is to perpetuate an odious view of the world. The *Oxford English Dictionary* defines a 'martyr' as one who "voluntarily undergoes the penalty of death for refusing to renounce the Christian faith or any article of it." In the classic understanding, a martyr is a witness. A martyr is, therefore, one who undergoes death "in behalf of any religious or other belief or cause." Nowhere is a martyr defined as one who "tries to kill as many unarmed civilians as possible and, in the process, meets his or her own end." Why should one accept a radical redefinition of an old and noble term? When we think of a martyr we rightly think of an unarmed individual who meets death bravely because he or she will not recant the faith. If we extend the use of the term 'martyr' from brave victims of unearned suffering to perpetrators of mass murder, we traffic in a distortion of language that leads to contortions of moral meaning.

Here is another example of what I have in mind. In a talk at Columbia University in 1946, Albert Camus characterized the crisis "in human consciousness" forced upon humanity by World War II. He illustrated that crisis through four vignettes, spare descriptions of events. One vignette went like this:

> In Greece, after an action by the underground forces, a German officer is preparing to shoot three brothers he has taken as hostages. The old mother of the three begs for mercy and he consents to spare one of her sons, but on the condition that she herself designate which one. When she is unable to decide, the soldiers get ready to fire. At last she chooses the eldest, because he has a family dependent on him, but by the same token she condemns the two other sons, as the German officer intends.[2]

Here Camus locates us in the heart of darkness. He laid the crisis he described on the doorstep of an unchecked will to power. From an untrammeled will flows the terrible notion that one can remake the world in precisely the way that one wants, purge it of all that is undesirable and unclean in one's eyes, cleanse it, and reconstitute it. Camus' vignette forces us to look evil in the eye and not to deflect our gaze. Given his deep and abiding moral concerns, Camus would have resisted with all his might any description of this event from World War II that attempted to make the horror look good, or exemplary, or like a fine day's work.

[2] Albert Camus, "The Human Crisis," *Twice a Year* 1, no. 16–17 (1946–47): 21. Lecture delivered at Columbia University, Spring 1946.

There are those who would disagree, claiming, as they do, that description is a more or less arbitrary thing. There is no such thing as getting 'right' right because we are simply imposing our own subjective opinions when we claim that we are doing so. It follows that John Paul II's language of "unspeakable horror" and Osama bin Laden's language of a glorious deed are both descriptions of what happened on September 11. Each description comes from a purely subjective point of view. There is no compelling way to distinguish between them. There is no ground of truth on which to stand in such matters.

Thus, philosopher Richard Rorty, a leader of a dominant tendency of contemporary thought that holds that our descriptions are more or less arbitrary, argues that one could describe the German officer in Camus' vignette in ways that make his compulsion of the mother look not only acceptable but heroic. Rorty asks us to imagine that the German officer and his friends were college students before the war who had learned to "rise above slave morality" and to "outdo each other in scorn for the weak ... and a concomitant contempt for everything stemming from Platonism and Christianity. Home on leave, the officer tells his friends the story of how he broke a Greek mother's heart. . . . His friends, hearing his story, are envious of the robustness of his moral stance. . . . They swear to themselves that, when they return to their posts, they will imitate the good example their friend has set." Everybody, Rorty continues, "tries to whip up a story according to which he or she did the right thing," and nobody "knowingly does evil." (He says that this is a bit of truth derived from Socrates, with whom he otherwise disagrees.)[3]

Let us grant Rorty one of his points, namely, that many people, at least some of the time, try to "whip up" stories according to which they did the right thing. But surely we are obliged to call them on it when they do, otherwise we are in a world in which nothing can be definitively distinguished from anything else. Let us take this one step further and ask: What are the implications of calling Camus' description of that horrid tale from World War II and Rorty's reconstruction in which the German officer tells friends that he did a noble day's work, just two different descriptions of the same event?

It means, first, that we treat the German officer, driven by ideological certainty, and Albert Camus, a moralist who prizes lucidity and insists on humility in moral judgments, as equally reliable describers of the world. Each is self-interested, whipping up a story to make himself or a cause look good. What finally settles the matter is not whether one description is apt and the other a distortion, but, rather, whoever has the biggest guns

[3] Richard Rorty, "Robustness: A Reply to Jean Bethke Elshtain," in Daniel W. Conway and John E. Seery, eds., *The Politics of Irony: Essays in Self-Betrayal* (New York: St. Martin's Press, 1992), 219–20. Rorty was responding to my essay, "Don't Be Cruel: Reflections on Rortyian Liberalism," which likewise appeared in *The Politics of Irony* and was critical of his work (199-217).

or the most clout. There is no way to get it right, for all of us arbitrarily pick and choose as we see fit in order to make ourselves or our cause look good. Literary scholar and academic gadfly Stanley Fish illustrates this point nicely, if chillingly: "The moral vision of Hitler is a moral vision. We have to distinguish between moralities we approve and moralities we despise. A morality simply means that someone who has one has a world view in which certain kinds of outcomes are desired and certain kinds of strategies are necessary." [4]

As distinguished constitutional scholar Stephen Carter puts it, at the end of this line of thinking "lies a pile of garbage." Here are Carter's words in full, in the context of African-Americans confronting directly the crimes that some among their number commit:

> We must never lose the capacity for judgment, especially the capacity to judge ourselves and our people. We can and should celebrate those among us who achieve, whether in the arts or in the professions, whether on the athletic field or the floor of the state house, whether publicly fighting for our children or privately nurturing them; but we must not pretend that they are the only black people who make choices. Standards of morality matter no less than standards of excellence. There are black people who commit heinous crimes, and not all of them are driven by hunger and neglect. Not all of them turn to crime because they are victims of racist social policy. . . . We are not automatons. To understand all may indeed be to forgive all, but no civilization can survive when the capacity for understanding is allowed to supersede the capacity for judgment. Otherwise, at the end of the line lies a pile of garbage: Hitler wasn't evil, just insane.[5]

The important point here at the outset is not that we more or less arbitrarily describe events and then decide which morality applies, but that the moral point is embedded in the description. As theologian Robin Lovin puts it:

> To say that a person or a state of affairs is morally good, to conclude that an action is the right thing to do, to identify a goal as better than the existing conditions—all these moral statements express our understanding that a particular constellation of facts links aspirations and limitations in that peculiarly satisfying way that we call "good." *If we get the facts wrong, we will be wrong about the ethics, too; for the*

---

[4] Said during Fish's television appearance on *The O'Reilly Factor*, October 17, 2001; as cited by *The New Republic*, November 5, 2001, 12.

[5] Stephen L. Carter, *Reflections of an Affirmative Action Baby* (New York: Basic Books, 1991), 144–45.

> *reality to which moral realism refers is not a separate realm of moral ideas,*
> *independent of the facts. Moral realities <u>are</u> facts about the world, properties*
> *that we judge persons, actions, and situations to have precisely because they*
> *have identifiable factual characteristics that link up in appropriate ways*
> *with other sets of facts and possibilities.*[6] (Emphasis added.)

This is not so mysterious. Let me offer one final example to clarify my point before we turn to the hotly contested question of what it means to call someone a terrorist. Imagine that a group of people is gathered around listening to a speaker's description of an event in which young children were tortured systematically by sadistic adults. The account is replete with details of the desperate pleas of the children and the imperious cruelty of their torturers. One listener, who believes there is no relationship between descriptions of events and how we evaluate them, insists, when the speaker is finished, that he then tell the group whether he is sympathetic to the plight of the children or to the actions of the torturers.

Would such a demand make sense? The speaker has already characterized the situation on the basis of those features that are most relevant. These include the details of the suffering of the children at the hands of their torturers, and one knows from the simple recounting of what happened that these persons are remorseless, brutal, and sadistic. The description of events embeds a moral claim. A speaker devoid of a moral compass would have described the torture of the children in another, and wildly incorrect, way. Or, enchanted perhaps by the supposed arbitrariness of the original description, the speaker would have said, "Of course, I don't want children to be tortured. But a sadist would describe this differently, so we can't go by the speaker's description." Again, would this make sense? As with the tale of the German officer's actions as "heroic," accepting the sadist's description makes evil a co-equal interlocutor. *Why would one do that?*

All of us evaluate descriptions of events depending, in part, upon the past deeds and descriptions of whoever is doing the describing. If I have a friend who specializes in hyperbole, then I am going to discount a good portion of what she says. If, sadly, I have an acquaintance who is an inveterate liar, then I am going to discount all of what he says. If I am in the presence of a known fanatic who disdains any distinction between combatants and noncombatants and argues that Americans to the last man, woman, and child should be killed wherever they are found, I am not going to put his depiction of September 11 on a par with the characterization of it by John Paul II, an ecumenist who has opened up a dialogue between Christianity and Islam, and a near-pacifist who has often

---

[6] Robin W. Lovin, *Reinhold Niebuhr and Christian Realism* (Cambridge: Cambridge University Press, 1995), 106–7. It is a version of moral and political realism on which this book rests. This will become clearer as we go along.

criticized U.S. military action. So when John Paul II calls September 11 an "unspeakable horror," and I add this to what I witnessed with my own eyes, heard with my own ears, and read in dozens of magazines and newspapers, here and abroad, an unspeakable horror it is.

III. What Is a Terrorist?

Why have I been belaboring the matter of getting our descriptions right? For the simple reason that there are many among us who resist calling things by their right names, and such distortions are deeply damaging to political life, which begins with trying to get the facts right. There were those during the Cold War who proclaimed a moral equivalence between the United States and the Soviet Union. These proclamations began with a wildly inaccurate characterization of the two respective systems. Brave dissidents in the Soviet Union and the occupied satellite states of Central Europe did not do that.

On my pre-1989 trips to behind the Iron Curtain, I was struck by the fact that none of the dissidents I spoke with had a problem with President Ronald Reagan's characterization of the Soviet Union as an "evil empire." Of course, they knew about America's racial problems and the debacle in Vietnam. They also knew that democratic protest against Jim Crow laws led to the 1964 Civil Rights Act and a profoundly altered American social and political system. They knew that American political leaders had to take the language of rights seriously because that was the lingua franca of American political culture. You cannot keep talking about rights and systematically deny a minority of your population those rights on the arbitrary basis of skin color. Americans had a way to put things right.

In his 1985 essay, "Anatomy of a Reticence," Vaclav Havel, Czech dissident, playwright, and later president of the Czech Republic, noted the irony that representatives of Western peace groups tracked him down to gain his support for their cause, yet they uttered views that indicated that they were suspicious of dissidents, including Havel himself. The dissidents were regarded as "suspiciously prejudiced against the realities of socialism, insufficiently critical of Western democracy and perhaps even sympath[etic] . . . with those detested Western armaments. In short, for peace activists the dissidents tended to appear as a fifth column of Western establishments east of the Yalta line."[7]

The Western visitors were unmoved when Havel tried to explain how even the word "peace" had been drained of its meaning and corrupted in empty, official slogans like the "struggle for peace" against "Western imperialists." The dissident, "unable to protect himself or his children, suspicious of an ideological mentality, and knowing firsthand where ap-

---

[7] Vaclav Havel, from *Open Letters: Selected Writings 1965–1990*, ed. Paul Wilson (New York: Knopf, 1991), 292.

peasement can lead," positioned himself against "the loss of meaning," including a diminution in the meaning and power of words. Draining words of meaning is a mark of what Havel called "pseudoideological thinking," which separates the words we use from the realities they purport to describe. As a consequence, "evasive thinking" has "separated thought from its immediate contact with reality and crippled its capacity to intervene in that reality effectively."[8]

This pertains directly to how we talk about 'terror' and 'terrorist'. Just as the language of 'martyr' and 'martyrdom' is distorted when it is applied not to those who are prepared to suffer, even to die, as witnesses to their faith but, instead, to those who are prepared to kill as many civilians as they can while killing themselves in the process, so 'terrorist' is twisted beyond recognition if it is used to designate anyone anywhere who fights for a cause.

The word 'terror' first entered the political vocabulary of the West during the French Revolution. Those who guillotined thousands in the Place de la Concorde in Paris and called it "justice" were pleased to speak of revolutionary terror as a form of justice. 'Terrorist' and 'terrorism' entered ordinary language as a way to designate a specific phenomenon: killing directed indiscriminately against all ideological enemies and outside the context of a war between opposing combatants. A 'terrorist' is one who kills because someone is an "objective enemy," no matter what that person may or may not have done. If you are a bourgeois, or a Jew, or a religious nonconformist—the list of victims of terror is long—you are slated to die in revolutionary violence. And as long as you are an enemy, you can be killed, no matter what you are doing, no matter where you are, no matter whether you are two years old or ninety.

A complex, subtle, and generally accepted international language emerged to make critical distinctions where violence and its use are concerned. Combatants are distinguished from noncombatants. A massacre is different from a battle. An ambush is different from a firefight. When Americans look back with sadness and even shame at the Vietnam War, it is horrors like the My Lai *massacre* that they have in mind. People who called the slaughter of more than three hundred unarmed men, women, and children a *battle* were regarded as having taken leave of their senses, perhaps because they were so determined to justify anything that Americans did during the Vietnam War that they had lost their moral moorings. To be sure, it would only be fair to point out that the Vietnam War was a terrible one in part because it was often difficult to distinguish combatants from noncombatants, and because noncombatants often harbored, willingly or not, combatants who lay in wait to ambush American soldiers. The soldiers at My Lai were inflamed, having just lost comrades.

---

[8] This quotation of Havel is drawn from my essay, "Politics without Cliché," *Social Research* 60, no. 3 (1993): 433–44.

But none of this exculpates or mitigates what happened. Massacre it was. Anyone who claimed a glorious victory over My Lai villagers and chortled at their suffering would rightly be regarded as a moral monster.

A 'terrorist' is one who sows terror. Terror subjects its victims or would-be victims to paralyzing fear. In the words of political theorist Michael Walzer,

> [terrorism's] purpose is to destroy the morale of a nation or a class, to undercut its solidarity; its method is the random murder of innocent people. Randomness is the crucial feature of terrorist activity. If one wishes fear to spread and intensify over time, it is not desirable to kill specific people identified in some particular way with a regime, a party, or a policy. Death must come by chance. . . .[9]

Remember this: 'terrorism' is the random murder of innocent people. Those who died in Stalin's Great Terror were victims in this sense. One must add another terrible word—purge—to characterize the killing of high party, government, and military officials. These officials were not innocent in the sense of being nonculpable for the crimes of the Stalin regime, though they were certainly innocent by any decent legal standard of the concocted crimes of espionage and conspiracy with which they were charged. 'Innocence' in a context of terrorism is best reserved for "people in no position to defend themselves." The designation is not a reference to moral innocence, for none among us is fully innocent in that way, but to the fact that civilians going to work, taking a trip, shopping, or riding a bus are not armed to the teeth and ready to defend themselves. In other words, they are not combatants.

Terrorists are not interested in such distinctions, nor in the subtleties of diplomacy, nor in compromise solutions. Terrorists have taken leave of politics.[10] They are ready to kill anyone simply because he or she is an American or a Jew or a Kurd or a Kosovar.

IV. WHY MAKING THE RIGHT DISTINCTIONS IS SO IMPORTANT

Needless to say, the designation of terrorism is contested because terrorists, and their apologists, would prefer not to be depicted accurately. It is important to distinguish between two cases here. In some hotly contested political situations in which each side has a lot at stake and each resorts to force, it may be in the interest of one side to try to label its opponents as "terrorists" rather than "combatants" or "soldiers" or "fight-

---

[9] Michael Walzer, *Just and Unjust Wars: A Moral Argument with Historical Illustrations* (New York: Basic Books, 1977), 197.

[10] That terrorism, then and now, has always had its apologists says nothing about how one accurately defines the phenomenon.

ers." But one must ask who such men (and women) attack. Do they target soldiers at outposts and in the field? Do they try to disable military equipment, killing soldiers in the process? As they carry out such operations, are they open to negotiation and diplomacy at the same time? If so, then it seems reasonable to resist any blanket label of "terrorist" or "terrorism" for what they do.

Contrarily, in a situation in which noncombatants are *deliberately* targeted and the wholesale murder of noncombatants is the *explicit* aim, labelling the perpetrator a "fighter" or "soldier" or "noble warrior" is language that is not only beside the point, but also pernicious. It collapses the distance between those who plant bombs in cafes or fly civilian aircraft into office buildings filled with innocent people and those who fight other combatants, taking the risks that are inherent to such forms of fighting. There is a nihilistic edge to terrorism: it aims to destroy. Period. War, by contrast, presents specific political aims. This does not mean that fighting in a legitimate war may not descend into moments of terrorism. It can and it has.

The distinction between war and terrorism is vital to observe. It is the way we assess what is happening when force is resorted to. It is a distinction marked in historic moral and political discourses about war and in the norms of international law. This is why those who call the attacks of September 11 acts of "mass murder" rather than terrorism under international law, and then go on to claim that the United States has also engaged in "mass murder" in its legally authorized counteroffensive, are guilty of serious factual distortion. To equate removing the Taliban from power in Afghanistan and disrupting the al Qaeda network and its training camps to the knowing mass murder of civilians perpetrates a moral equivalence that amounts to the "pile of garbage" that Stephen Carter noted.[11] (If we could not distinguish between an *accidental* death, say, resulting from a car accident, and an *intentional* murder, then our criminal justice system would fall apart.)

If we cannot distinguish combatants who fight other combatants while assiduously trying to avoid noncombatant casualties from those who deliberately target civilians and sow the maximum amount of terror among them, then we are in a world in which everything reduces to the same shade of gray. In fact, the United States military trains its soldiers in strict rules of engagement that compel them to practice the principle of discrimination, separating combatants from noncombatants and never knowingly and deliberately putting civilians in harm's way. That the U.S. military operates in this way is known by its adversaries, who have tried to use this compunction to their advantage. For example, in the 1991 Persian Gulf War, occasioned by Iraq's invasion of Kuwait, the Iraqis put their

---

[11] On some international debates about terrorism, see Todd S. Purdum, "What Do You Mean 'Terrorist'?" *New York Times*, Sunday April 7, 2002, sec. 4, p. 1, col. 5.

own civilians in harm's way by deliberately locating, even relocating, them near or within legitimate military targets. They understood America's moral concern for civilians. Were American forces not averse to killing innocent noncombatants, no moral regret would ever be expressed when unintended casualties occur—as they do in any war. Instead, the U.S. military would just say, "Tough, it's a war, anything goes," thus tacitly underwriting the view that I am explicitly contesting; namely, that the moral law is silent during war.

V. Conclusion: Democratic Argument Requires Getting the Distinctions Right

America's war against terrorism would collapse into a horror if the nation failed to distinguish between combatants and noncombatants in its response. It is both strange and disheartening, therefore, to read the words of those distinction-obliterators for whom, crudely, a dead body is a dead body and never mind how it got that way. Only if there is a distinction that marks a moral difference between the intentional murder of non-combatants and the wartime deaths of combatants can one simultaneously attempt to hold one's own forces to certain norms and to demand the same of others. The war convention, as it is routinely called, turns on such recognized distinctions. These distinctions turn, in the first instance, on getting basic descriptions right. Our evaluations follow and these evaluations mark vital normative claims.

Let us put one final important distinction in place, that between 'justice' and 'revenge'. These are not the same and any attempt to equate them adds to that "pile of garbage" of which Carter writes. In President George W. Bush's speech to the nation on September 20, 2001, he distinguished carefully between Islam as a great world religion and terrorists who are "trying, in effect, to hijack Islam itself." He pointed out that Americans are despised because of their freedoms and rights, for these are anathema to radical Islamic fundamentalists, in contrast to "all who believe in progress and pluralism, tolerance and freedom."[12] One could argue that the president's call for a war against terrorism and those who harbor terrorists does not articulate sufficiently the limits to be observed in such an effort, although such limits were embedded in the care that the president took in his speech to distinguish combatants from noncombatants as legitimate targets. A 'just cause' is one that responds proportionately to a grievous harm to oneself or others. 'Just means' require that the response be restrained, that it, too, partake of justice rather than slide over into revenge.

[12] President George W. Bush, "Address to a Joint Session of Congress, September 20, 2001," in "Our Mission and Our Moment: Speeches Since the Attacks of September 11" (Washington, DC: White House Printing Office, 2001) PREX 1.2: M69, 11, 12.

We all have a rough-and-ready sense of the distinction at stake here. 'Revenge' conjures up a desire to inflict harm for a real or imagined harm that one has sustained. 'Revenge' does not involve deliberation or care. It does not incorporate a notion of limits. The vengeful spirit is one that knows no rest until harm has been exacted to the ultimate degree. At the conclusion of Clint Eastwood's great film *Unforgiven*, protagonist William Munney promises to return and to kill all of the "sons of bitches" in the town of Big Whiskey (as well as their wives and children) and to burn down their houses and otherwise destroy them, should they fail to bury or should they in any way deface the body of his best friend, who has been murdered and put on display. This threat is vengeance, pure and simple. 'Justice', by contrast, is measured. This is why justice is iconographically represented as a blindfolded figure holding balanced scales.

'Justice' has to do with equity, with putting things right when an injustice has been committed. One contrasts justice to injustice and asks what might be done to right the balance and to restore the scales of justice. But what is the contrast to revenge? It is hard to think of one. Perhaps this is one reason why revenge tends to run riot: it is not framed by a recognition of some alternative. Moreover, the harm that triggers revenge can be something as slight as a knowing glance or a verbal insult. 'Justice', by contrast, has to do with proportion and prevention. How can we stop another grievous harm from occurring? Can justice slide over into revenge? Yes, the distinction can be obliterated in practice and this is why caution is always in order. But to do nothing as people are slaughtered makes one complicit in injustice. Only by maintaining the vital distinction between justice and revenge—a distinction that begins by offering up concrete descriptions that any reasonable person recognizes as belonging to one category or the other—can clarity be approximated. One also must realize that some descriptions will blur the difference: the matter is not so clear. So we try as best we can, through law and through moral norms that assign degrees of culpability, to sort out the matter fairly. We could do no such thing were critical distinctions impossible or unnecessary.

Justice implies responsibility. What is our responsibility when we have sustained a violent attack and egregious harm? What is at stake? How do we assess the central issues in a measured way? You cannot respond robustly to any of these questions if you separate politics from morality and description from evaluation. So-called scientific neorealism spends a great deal of time looking at concrete cases of war, hardball diplomacy, negotiation, and compromise, but denies that any of its descriptions of situations yield normative or evaluative conclusions. Scientific neorealists, and the positivist epistemology that underwrites so-called value-free social science, deny that we are always implicated in what philosopher Charles Taylor has called a "value slope": values are always enmeshed in our characterizations of events. This, in turn, undercuts the idea of the realm of politics as a form of practical reason that must always function, if it is to function responsibly, by obtaining the best data (the basic facts) and then by getting the descriptions right. We know too much about the horrors that follow when accurate descriptions are ignored because we want to avoid the implications if we pay attention. Refugees from Nazi Germany were ignored, as were dissidents from the Soviet Union. Shall we now ignore the testimony of Iraqi exiles who suffered under the systematic brutality of Saddam Hussein's regime? During the ethnic cleansing perpetrated against Bosnian Muslims by Bosnian Serbs in the early 1990s, word came down in the Clinton Administration that the term 'genocide', although an accurate description of what was going on, was not to be used because *normative implications follow*. These implications, taking the form of political pressure, might have forced the hand of the Clinton Administration when it did not want its hand forced.[13] In insisting that words have meaning, that signifiers do not just float aimlessly, that there is a 'there' there in the world, and that we had best be about the business of getting things right (or at least as right as we can), my position does not permit us to let ourselves off the hook as easily as we might if we just adjusted the facts to suit a pregiven ideology or attitude. Insisting that description and evaluation are not entirely separate activities is the only way to do either responsible politics or responsible moral thinking.

Social and Political Ethics, University of Chicago

---

[13] On this question see Samantha Power, *"A Problem from Hell": America and the Age of Genocide* (New York: Basic Books, 2002).

UNAUTHORIZED HUMANITARIAN INTERVENTION*

By Mark S. Stein

I. Introduction

In this essay, I offer a utilitarian perspective on humanitarian intervention.[1] There is no generally accepted precise definition of the term 'humanitarian intervention'. I will provisionally, and roughly, define humanitarian intervention as the use of force by a state, beyond its own borders, that has as a purpose or an effect the protection of the human rights of noncitizens or the reduction of the suffering of noncitizens.

From a utilitarian perspective, there is likely to be a deficit of humanitarian intervention in any state-based system, just as there is likely to be a deficit of foreign aid. Political organizations such as states care far more about the welfare of their own members than they care about the welfare of nonmembers. States often have the opportunity to reduce massive suffering among foreigners at comparatively small cost to their own citizens, but they fail to do so.

Besides this inevitable particularism, another factor works to limit humanitarian intervention: anti-intervention norms in international law and international politics. Even if a state were willing to spend its treasure and risk the lives of its citizens for the sake of foreigners, it might refrain from doing so because of these norms.

There is an exception to the anti-intervention norms in international law and politics. Any humanitarian intervention that is authorized by the United Nations Security Council has enormous legal and political legitimacy. The Security Council and the other organs of the United Nations can even, potentially, help to counteract the problem of particularism. The UN can help states to pool the costs and risks of humanitarian intervention and can provide a forum through which international suffering is made more salient to the people and leaders of states. The current UN secretary-general, Kofi Annan, has attempted to

* I acknowledge with thanks the comments of James Bernard Murphy, who is more distrustful of unauthorized humanitarian intervention than I am. For illuminating discussions of humanitarian intervention, I thank the contributors to the American Society of International Law Listserve, including Anthony D'Amato, Jason Beckett, Andre de Hoogh, Jorg Kammerhofer, Francisco Martin, Iheke Ndukwe, Jordan Paust, and Alfred Rubin.
[1] For another utilitarian discussion, see Peter Singer, *One World: The Ethics of Globalization* (New Haven, CT: Yale University Press, 2002), 106–49.

use his office to relieve international suffering and promote international human rights. As he said in his much-quoted *1999 Annual Report to the General Assembly*, "[T]he genocide in Rwanda will define for our generation the consequences of inaction in the face of mass murder." [2]

Since the end of the Cold War, the Security Council has authorized forcible humanitarian intervention a number of times. Rwanda in 1994 was actually one of those instances.[3] The failure of the international community to stop the genocide in Rwanda was not due to the resistance of what are considered the usual recalcitrant suspects on the Security Council (Russia and China), but to lack of will by those countries that could have intervened immediately in Rwanda, including France and the United States.[4] Other instances of Security Council-authorized intervention were Bosnia in 1992–94,[5] Somalia in 1992–95,[6] Haiti in 1994,[7] and East Timor in 1999–2002.[8]

Given the increased willingness of the Security Council to authorize humanitarian intervention, should states continue to undertake humanitarian interventions that are not authorized by the Security Council? During the 1990s, even as the Security Council was increasingly willing to authorize humanitarian intervention, the United States and its allies took military action on at least three occasions, for express humanitarian purposes, when the specific action was not authorized by the Security Council. I refer to the establishment of no-fly zones in Northern and Southern Iraq in 1991 and 1992;[9] the bombing of the Bosnian Serbs by NATO in 1995;[10] and NATO's Kosovo campaign against Yugoslavia in 1999.[11]

---

[2] *1999 Annual Report of the Secretary-General*, UN GAOR, 54th Sess., UN Doc. SG/SM/7136/GA/9596; available on-line at http://www.un.org/News/Press/docs/1999/19990920.sgsm7136.html [accessed December 4, 2002].

[3] S/Res/929, UN SCOR, 49th Sess., 3392nd mtg. (June 22, 1994). For accounts, see Inger Österdahl, *Threat to the Peace: The Interpretation by the Security Council of Article 39 of the UN Charter* (Uppsala, Sweden: Iustus Forlag, 1998), 59–65; Fernando R. Teson, *Humanitarian Intervention: An Inquiry into Law and Morality*, 2d ed. (Irvington, NY: Transnational Publishers, 1997), 258–62; and Sean D. Murphy, *Humanitarian Intervention: The United Nations in an Evolving World Order* (Philadelphia: University of Pennsylvania Press, 1996), 243–60.

[4] Few performed well during this crisis, and Annan himself has much to regret.

[5] For accounts, see Österdahl, *Threat to the Peace*, 47–52; Teson, *Humanitarian Intervention*, 262–66; and Murphy, *Humanitarian Intervention*, 198–217.

[6] For accounts, see Österdahl, *Threat to the Peace*, 52–58; Teson, *Humanitarian Intervention*, 241–49; and Murphy, *Humanitarian Intervention*, 217–43.

[7] For accounts, see Österdahl, *Threat to the Peace*, 65–70; Teson, *Humanitarian Intervention*, 249–57; and Murphy, *Humanitarian Intervention*, 260–81.

[8] This was with the acquiescence of Indonesia. S/Res/1272, UN SCOR, 54th Sess., 4057th mtg. (Oct. 25, 1999).

[9] For an account, see Murphy, *Humanitarian Intervention*, 165–98.

[10] For accounts, see Teson, *Humanitarian Intervention*, 264–65; and Murphy, *Humanitarian Intervention*, 212–13.

[11] A brief and admirably objective account of the background of the Kosovo campaign, from one of its supporters, is given in Ruth Wedgwood, "NATO's Campaign in Yugoslavia," *American Journal of International Law* 93, no. 4 (1999): 828–34, at 828–29.

In all three cases, there was some argument that intervention had been authorized by a prior Security Council resolution.[12] The Kosovo intervention gave rise to considerable controversy and commentary, and most commentators, regardless of whether they supported the intervention, agreed that it was not authorized by the Security Council.[13] The no-fly zones over Iraq were, in my opinion, also unauthorized.[14] I believe that the bombing of the Bosnian Serbs was in fact authorized under prior Security Council resolutions, but others disagree.[15] It is clear, in any event, that the specific actions would not have been authorized by the Security Council at the time that they occurred, as they were strongly opposed by Russia and China, two veto-bearing permanent members of the Security Council.

The 2003 invasion of Iraq also had humanitarian aspects. In the run-up to the war, the humanitarian justification was perhaps not predominant, but it became so after the war began. Here, too, there was some argument that Security Council resolutions authorized the invasion of Iraq and the overthrow of the Saddam Hussein regime, but a resolution explicitly authorizing the war would not have been approved by the Security Council.

The propriety of unauthorized humanitarian intervention is a major issue of international ethics and international law. In Section II of this essay, I discuss the legal issues surrounding humanitarian intervention. I spell out, in more detail than is usual, the major arguments based on the text of the UN Charter. I also focus on the legal consequences of intervention: the likely response of international bodies—such as the Security Council, the International Court of Justice (ICJ), and the International Criminal Court (ICC)—to arguments that might be presented to them.

In Section III, I discuss some of the ethical and policy issues surrounding humanitarian intervention. I describe my own utilitarian approach, discuss some nonutilitarian alternatives, and attempt to apply utilitarian theory to the problem. An ideal application of utilitarian theory would resolve all major empirical issues, such as whether the Kosovo intervention or the 2003 invasion of Iraq had good consequences overall, and whether alternative approaches would have produced better conse-

---

[12] On the general problem of ambiguous Security Council authorizations, see Jules Lobel and Michael Ratner, "Bypassing the Security Council: Ambiguous Authorizations to Use Force, Cease-Fires, and the Iraqi Inspection Regime," *American Journal of International Law* 93, no. 1 (1999): 124–54.

[13] Commentaries by leading international law scholars are collected in "Editorial Comments: NATO's Kosovo Intervention," *American Journal of International Law* 93, no. 4 (1999): 824–62; available on-line at http://www.asil.org/ajil/kosovo.htm [accessed December 14, 2002].

[14] In accord with this view are Lobel and Ratner, "Bypassing the Security Council," 126, 132–33. See Murphy, *Humanitarian Intervention*, 184–98, for a more equivocal view.

[15] NATO was authorized to protect the safe havens, and Bosnian Serb forces were violating the safe havens. This was sufficient authority, even though NATO also had the broader purpose of compelling the Bosnian Serbs to agree to a settlement. For a contrary view, see Teson, *Humanitarian Intervention*, 265.

quences. I do not aspire to such an ideal. I offer opinions on some issues, but often I am content merely to describe the issues and map them onto utilitarian moral theory.

II. The Legal Status of Humanitarian Intervention

A. Authorized intervention

It is generally though not universally agreed that the Security Council has the authority, under Chapter VII of the UN Charter, to conduct or authorize humanitarian intervention.[16] The keystone of the Security Council's authority is Article 39 of the Charter, which states: "The Security Council shall determine the existence of any threat to the peace, breach of the peace, or act of aggression and shall make recommendations, or decide what measures shall be taken in accordance with Articles 41 and 42, to maintain or restore international peace and security."[17]

When authorizing humanitarian intervention, the Security Council typically determines that a humanitarian crisis poses a threat to the peace. Since the end of the Cold War, the Security Council has interpreted the term 'threat to the peace' broadly.[18] Humanitarian crises do have international consequences—in particular, the flow of refugees across borders—but in general such crises do not pose the threat of armed conflict across borders. Hence, there is some question whether humanitarian crises can be called threats to the peace. Nevertheless, Article 39 states: "The Security Council shall determine" the existence of a threat to the peace; it does not say, for example, that "in the event of a threat to the peace," the Security Council shall take action. The language of Article 39 expressly gives the Security Council the authority to determine what is a threat to the peace.

Article 2(7) of the UN Charter states that the Charter does not authorize the United Nations "to intervene in matters which are essentially within the domestic jurisdiction of any state."[19] This might seem to rule out authorized humanitarian intervention. However, Article 2(7) has a proviso: "[T]his [nonintervention] principle shall not prejudice the application of enforcement measures under Chapter VII."[20] In view of this proviso, Article 2(7) is generally not taken to limit the Security Council's authority under Chapter VII of the Charter. Also, it is questionable whether the violation of human rights can be considered a matter "essentially within the domestic jurisdiction" of states. Since the founding of the United Nations, there has been a progressive development of human

---

[16] Louis Henkin, "Kosovo and the Law of 'Humanitarian Intervention'," *American Journal of International Law* 93, no. 4 (1999): 824–28 (humanitarian intervention is lawful if authorized by the Security Council).

[17] UN Charter art. 39.

[18] See generally Österdahl, *Threat to the Peace.*

[19] UN Charter art. 2, para 7.

[20] Ibid.

rights law, starting with the Universal Declaration of Human Rights (1948)[21] and the Convention on the Prevention and Punishment of the Crime of Genocide (1948),[22] and unfolding through the International Covenant on Civil and Political Rights (1966);[23] the International Covenant on Economic, Social, and Cultural Rights (1966);[24] and other multilateral conventions. Human rights law arguably takes humanitarian intervention outside the prohibition of Article 2(7), so that, once again, the Security Council's authority under Chapter VII of the Charter is unimpaired.

B. Unauthorized intervention

If humanitarian intervention is not authorized by the Security Council, its status under the Charter is considerably more dubious. Most attention focuses here on Article 2(4), the Charter's prohibition of the threat or use of force in international relations. Article 2(4) states: "All Members shall refrain in their international relations from the threat or use of force against the territorial integrity or political independence of any state, or in any other manner inconsistent with the Purposes of the United Nations."[25]

Some interpret Article 2(4), in the context of the Charter as a whole, as prohibiting all use of force in international relations, with only two exceptions: (1) as authorized by the Security Council, and (2) in exercise of the right of self-defense recognized in Article 51 of the Charter.[26] Others disagree with this broad interpretation. They point out that the language of Article 2(4) imposes not a general prohibition, but three specific prohibitions.[27] They argue that unauthorized humanitarian intervention is permitted under the Charter if it (1) does not constitute the use of force against territorial integrity, (2) does not constitute the use of force against political independence, and (3) is not otherwise inconsistent with the purposes of the United Nations.

With regard to the specific terms of Article 2(4), some interpret the term 'territorial integrity' broadly; in their view, every territorial incursion is a

[21] G.A. Res. 217 (1948), available on-line at http://193.194.138.190/udhr/lang/eng.htm [accessed March 10, 2003].

[22] G.A. Res. 260 (1948), entered into force 1951, available on-line at http://193.194.138.190/html/menu3/b/p_genoci.htm [accessed March 10, 2003].

[23] G.A. Res. 2200 (1966), entered into force 1976, available on-line at http://193.194.138.190/html/menu3/b/a_ccpr.htm [accessed March 10, 2003].

[24] G.A. Res. 2200 (1966), entered into force 1976, available on-line at http://193.194.138.190/html/menu3/b/a_cescr.htm [accessed March 10, 2003].

[25] UN Charter art. 2, para 4.

[26] Bruno Simma, "NATO, the UN, and the Use of Force: Legal Aspects," *European Journal of International Law* 10, no. 1 (1999); available on-line at http://www.ejil.org/journal/Vol10/No1/ab1.html; and Oscar Schachter, *International Law in Theory and Practice* (Dordrecht, The Netherlands: Kluwer, 1991), 128–29.

[27] See Anthony A. D'Amato, *International Law: Process and Prospect* (Irvington, NY: Transnational Publishers, 1995), 56–72. D'Amato offers an exhaustive history of the terms 'political independence' and 'territorial integrity'.

violation of territorial integrity. This interpretation of 'territorial integrity' would once again turn Article 2(4) into a general prohibition. Under a more narrow interpretation of 'territorial integrity', a state violates the territorial integrity of another state only if it seizes part of the second state's territory.

It should be noted that even the more narrow interpretation of 'territorial integrity' poses a problem for humanitarian intervention on behalf of secessionist minorities. The Kosovo intervention ousted the state of Yugoslavia from its Kosovo province for the indefinite future, and the Northern no-fly zone over Iraq ousted the state of Iraq from the Kurdish areas in Northern Iraq for the duration of the Saddam Hussein regime. In both cases the intervenors ultimately disclaimed the intention of redrawing international boundaries, but some find it hard to see these interventions as anything other than the use of force against territorial integrity.

The term 'political independence' in Article 2(4) is also contested, particularly in the context of pro-democratic intervention. Under a broad interpretation of the term 'political independence', intervenors violate the political independence of a state when they change its political path in any way—for example, from dictatorship to democracy.[28] Some would disagree, claiming that the restoration or installation of democracy respects and indeed increases the political independence of a state.[29]

The import of the third prohibition in Article 2(4)—proscribing force otherwise inconsistent with the purposes of the United Nations—is also contested. Article 1 of the Charter lists "The Purposes of the United Nations." The first-listed purpose, and by nearly all accounts the primary purpose, is "To maintain international peace and security."[30] Seeing this as an overriding purpose, some aver, once again, that Article 2(4) prohibits all nondefensive force not authorized by the Security Council. However, the promotion of human rights is also listed as a purpose of the Charter, in Article 1(3).[31] As the threat of wide-ranging interstate war has receded, the promotion of human rights should arguably take on greater importance. This, essentially, is the position of Secretary-General Annan.

Also relevant to the legality of humanitarian intervention is Article 2(3) of the Charter, which states: "All Members shall settle their international disputes by peaceful means in such a manner that international peace and

---

[28] As noted below in Section II D, this may be the position of the International Court of Justice.

[29] This position is particularly identified with W. Michael Reisman. See W. Michael Reisman, "Haiti and the Validity of International Action, " *American Journal of International Law* 89, no. 1 (1995): 82–84; and W. Michael Reisman, "Sovereignty and Human Rights in Contemporary International Law," *American Journal of International Law* 84, no. 4 (1990): 866–76.

[30] UN CHARTER art. 1, para 1.

[31] "To achieve international cooperation in . . . promoting and encouraging respect for human rights and for fundamental freedoms for all without distinction as to race, sex, language, or religion. . . ." UN CHARTER art. 1, para 3.

security, and justice, are not endangered."[32] The requirement that disputes be settled so that "justice" is not endangered may leave some room for unauthorized humanitarian intervention under Article 2(3). At the very least, however, force could not be the first resort; there would have to be a genuine attempt to achieve a peaceful resolution in order to comply with Article 2(3). The Kosovo intervention arguably violated even this minimal requirement, as NATO presented rather extreme demands to Yugoslavia, on a "take it or leave it" basis, in the run-up to war. NATO's ultimatum would have required Yugoslavia to agree to allow NATO troops to operate anywhere in Yugoslavia (not just Kosovo) and would have set the stage for a referendum on independence by the Kosovars, to be held within three years. Both of these demands were dropped in the settlement that ended NATO's campaign.[33]

In addition to Charter law, the legal status of humanitarian intervention may be affected by the somewhat mysterious body of law known as customary international law. It is generally though not universally agreed that international custom can rise to the level of law if (1) it is sufficiently widespread, and (2) it is regarded as binding by states. Article 38 of the Statute of the International Court of Justice lists several sources of international law. The first-listed source is "international conventions" (including, of course, the UN Charter). The second-listed source is "international custom, as evidence of a general practice accepted as law."[34] There is great controversy over the content of customary international law, in the area of humanitarian intervention as in other areas.[35] Some find a strong prohibition against intervention in customary international law;[36] others find no prohibition against intervention.

A number of commentators believe that the Charter can, in effect, be amended through the processes of customary international law.[37] In theory, repeated humanitarian intervention without the authorization of the Security Council could establish a right to humanitarian intervention or even a general permission to use force in international relations. It has even been suggested that Article 2(4)'s prohibition on the use of force has already been abrogated through the processes of customary international law.[38] This is a minority position, to say the least.

[32] UN CHARTER art. 2, para 3.
[33] "Messy War, Messy Peace," *The Economist*, June 12, 1999, 15–16.
[34] ICJ STATUTE art. 38, para 1.
[35] For a discussion of some of the controversies, see Anthea Elizabeth Roberts, "Traditional and Modern Approaches to Customary International Law: A Reconciliation," *American Journal of International Law* 95, no. 4 (2001): 757–91; available on-line at http://www.asil.org/ajil/roberts.pdf [accessed March 10, 2003].
[36] As noted below in Section II D, this was the position of the ICJ in the *Nicaragua* case.
[37] Henkin, "Kosovo and the Law of 'Humanitarian Intervention'," 828; and Michael J. Glennon, *Limits of Law, Prerogatives of Power: Interventionism after Kosovo* (New York: Palgrave, 2001), 37–65.
[38] Michael J. Glennon, "How War Left the Law Behind," *New York Times*, November 21, 2002, sec. A, p. 37, col. 2.

There are many opinions as to the meaning of the Charter and the content of customary international law. While I have expressed some of my own opinions, I am not primarily interested in whether humanitarian intervention is legal or illegal in the abstract. I am interested in the possible legal consequences of humanitarian intervention. I will explore these consequences by considering what would happen if a target of intervention attempted to challenge the intervention as a violation of international law. The target state might try to press its case in a number of different forums, but each of these forums would present problems for it.

C. UN Security Council

Under Article 24(1) of the UN Charter, the Security Council has primary responsibility for the "maintenance of international peace and security."[39] A target of unauthorized humanitarian intervention might theoretically appeal to the Security Council, requesting it to take action against intervening states. But an appeal to the Security Council would fail if, as is likely these days, one or more of the intervening states was a veto-bearing permanent member of the Security Council, or if one or more of the intervening states was protected by a permanent member. The permanent members of the Security Council are the United States, the United Kingdom, France, Russia, and China.

During the Kosovo intervention, the Security Council was presented with a draft resolution that would have condemned the NATO bombing campaign against Yugoslavia.[40] The resolution was defeated, 12–3. Two permanent members, Russia and China, voted in favor of the resolution. Three permanent members, the United States, the United Kingdom, and France, voted against.

In the case of Kosovo, the veto power of permanent members was not necessary to the defeat of the proposed resolution condemning intervention. Things were different in the case of Nicaragua in 1984. The United States was then seeking to overthrow the Sandinista regime in Nicaragua. The motives of the United States were geopolitical rather than directly humanitarian, though one could say that the geopolitical goal of containing Communism was indirectly humanitarian in that Communism causes suffering.

In seeking to overthrow the government of Nicaragua, the United States mined Nicaraguan ports and conducted several naval attacks on Nicaraguan ports, oil installations, and a naval base. These operations were conducted or organized by the CIA. In addition, the U.S. armed and

---

[39] UN CHARTER art. 24, para 1.
[40] Belarus, India, and Russian Federation: Draft Resolution, UN Doc. S/1999/328 (Mar. 26, 1999).

trained the Nicaraguan "Contra" rebels who were seeking to overthrow the government of Nicaragua.[41]

Nicaragua sought to challenge U.S. intervention as a violation of international law, and its efforts still hold lessons for any target of intervention, humanitarian or otherwise. Nicaragua first sought relief from the Security Council against American military intervention. All of the members of the Security Council except the United States voted for (or abstained on) a mild resolution in favor of Nicaragua, one that did not take any enforcement action against the United States. However, the United States exercised its veto, and the resolution did not pass.

Nicaragua next sought relief from the ICJ. It achieved somewhat better results there, as discussed below.

D. *International Court of Justice*

The ICJ is the court of the United Nations; its statute is a part of the UN Charter.[42] Fortunately for "intervenees," the ICJ has shown that it is willing to enforce, or to attempt to enforce, prohibitions on the use of force contained in the Charter and in customary international law. Unfortunately for intervenees, the ICJ will not exercise jurisdiction over every claim that one state seeks to bring against another. The ICJ will only exercise jurisdiction over a state if that state has consented to jurisdiction in some way. This consent may be expressed in a treaty. The Genocide Convention, for example, gives the ICJ jurisdiction over claims arising under that treaty. The other significant way in which a state can consent to the ICJ's jurisdiction is to issue a declaration under Article 36(2) of the ICJ Statute (the 'optional clause'),[43] stating that it recognizes the jurisdiction of the court over future claims by another state that has accepted the same obligation under the optional clause.

Article 96 of the Charter provides that the General Assembly or the Security Council may request an "advisory opinion" from the ICJ on "any legal question." Conceivably, even if the ICJ could not exercise jurisdiction over a case against the intervenor state, the intervenee could persuade the General Assembly to request an advisory opinion on legal questions relating to the intervention. It is not certain that the ICJ would agree to deliver such an opinion, however.

There is very little likelihood that the ICJ will ever brand as illegal a humanitarian intervention authorized by the Security Council. There is a

---

[41] The facts regarding U.S. intervention in Nicaragua are laid out (accurately, in my view) in the ICJ's decision on the merits in the *Nicaragua* case: *Military and Paramilitary Activities in and against Nicaragua (Nicar. v. U.S.)*, Merits, 1986 ICJ 14.

[42] UN CHARTER art. 92.

[43] ICJ STATUTE art. 36, para 2.

very large likelihood that the ICJ will brand as illegal any humanitarian intervention *not* authorized by the Security Council, if the ICJ ever squarely addresses the legality of such an intervention.

In the Kosovo dispute, Yugoslavia sought relief from the ICJ. Yugoslavia brought cases against ten of the NATO countries, seeking, among other things, a provisional measure (what in the United States would be called a preliminary injunction) ordering the NATO countries to cease their attacks. The ICJ refused to order the NATO countries to stop bombing. The NATO countries had raised jurisdictional objections, and the ICJ decided that it was not sufficiently persuaded that it had jurisdiction over any of the cases brought by Yugoslavia.[44] However, the ICJ did throw something of a bone to Yugoslavia in its decisions. The ICJ stated: "[T]he Court is profoundly concerned with the use of force in Yugoslavia . . . . [U]nder the present circumstances such use raises very serious issues of international law. . . ."[45]

The ICJ also retained all but two of the cases on its docket (it dismissed the ones against the United States and Spain). This left open the possibility that Yugoslavia could ultimately prevail on the merits after convincing the ICJ that it had jurisdiction. In the interim, of course, the NATO campaign was successful in ousting Yugoslavia from Kosovo, and there was a change of government in Yugoslavia. As of March 2003, the eight remaining cases filed by Yugoslavia are in a kind of limbo; possibly Yugoslavia will withdraw them.[46]

It is interesting to speculate on what would have happened if the ICJ had ordered the NATO countries to stop participating in the attack on Yugoslavia. My own view is that some of the European countries would have obeyed the ICJ's order.

In the *Nicaragua* case that began in 1984, the ICJ did issue a preliminary injunction and then a final judgment against the United States.[47] For complicated jurisdictional reasons, the ICJ in the *Nicaragua* case did not apply the prohibition on the use of force in Article 2(4) of the Charter; instead, the ICJ applied customary international law on the use of force, which it found to be essentially identical to Charter law. In its 1986 decision on the merits, the ICJ held that the United States had violated customary international law by using force against Nicaragua and had

---

[44] See Peter H. F. Bekker and Christopher J. Borgen, "World Court Rejects Yugoslav Requests to Enjoin Ten NATO Members from Bombing Yugoslavia," American Society of International Law, *ASIL Insights* (June 1999); available on-line at http://www.asil.org/insights/insigh36.htm [accessed December 14, 2002].

[45] *Yugoslavia v. Belgium*, Order of June 2, 1999, para. 17; available on-line at http://www.icj-cij.org/icjwww/idocket/iybe/iybeframe.htm [accessed March 10, 2003].

[46] As indicated and further explained on the ICJ website: http://www.icj-cij.org/icjwww/ipresscom/ipress2002/ipresscom2002-10_yugo_20020322.htm [accessed March 10, 2003].

[47] *Military and Paramilitary Activities in and against Nicaragua* (*Nicar. v. U.S.*), Request for Provisional Measures, 1984 ICJ 169 (Order of May 10); and *Military and Paramilitary Activities in and against Nicaragua* (*Nicar. v. U.S.*), Merits, 1986 ICJ 14.

also violated customary international law by intervening in Nicaragua through military assistance to the Contra rebels.

The ICJ's 1986 decision on the merits of the *Nicaragua* case contains a number of passages that are hostile to the concept of humanitarian intervention:

> [T]he United States Congress . . . expressed the view that the Nicaraguan Government had taken 'significant steps towards establishing a totalitarian Communist dictatorship'. However the regime in Nicaragua be defined, adherence by a State to any particular doctrine does not constitute a violation of customary international law. . . . Nicaragua's domestic policy options, even assuming that they correspond to the description given of them by the Congress finding, cannot justify on the legal plane the various actions of the [United States]. . . . The Court cannot contemplate the creation of a new rule opening up a right of intervention by one State against another on the ground that the latter has opted for some particular ideology or political system. . . .
>
> In any event, while the United States might form its own appraisal of the situation as to respect for human rights in Nicaragua, the use of force could not be the appropriate method to monitor or ensure such respect. With regard to the steps actually taken, the protection of human rights, a strictly humanitarian objective, cannot be compatible with the mining of ports, the destruction of oil installations, or again with the training, arming and equipping of the contras. . . .[48]

Under the ICJ statute, decisions of the ICJ are theoretically nonprecedential; a decision "has no binding force except between the parties and in respect of that particular case."[49] In practice, the ICJ follows precedent rather closely, perhaps more closely than does the U.S. Supreme Court. The *Nicaragua* case in particular has been cited and followed numerous times. It has become the leading case on the use of force under the UN Charter, even though, strictly speaking, the Court did not apply Charter law.

Despite the *Nicaragua* decision, advocates of unauthorized humanitarian intervention might still entertain some hope that the ICJ will some day drop or moderate its opposition to such intervention. First, the world has changed since 1986. At that time, two contending political systems were in equipoise: democracy and Communist dictatorship. Now democracy is ascendant, and this development may influence the ICJ (more of whose judges now come from democratic countries). Second, the government in Nicaragua was by no plausible account a particularly horrible

---

[48] *Nicaragua* (merits), 1986 ICJ at paras. 263, 268.
[49] ICJ STATUTE art. 59.

regime, in the context of its time and place. Possibly a truly repellent regime would receive less sympathy from the ICJ.

   1. Territorial integrity and political independence, revisited. It will be recalled that a major issue bearing on the legality of unauthorized humanitarian intervention is the proper interpretation of the terms 'territorial integrity' and 'political independence' in Article 2(4) of the Charter. In the *Nicaragua* decision, the ICJ held that the United States had violated a customary-law obligation that was essentially identical to Article 2(4). The ICJ did not clearly specify whether the United States had violated Nicaragua's territorial integrity, or political independence, or both. However, in its opinions on provisional measures and on the merits, the ICJ did twice admonish the United States as follows:

> The right to sovereignty and to *political independence* possessed by the Republic of Nicaragua, like any other State of the region or of the world, should be fully respected and should not in any way be jeopardized by any military and paramilitary activities which are prohibited by the principles of international law, in particular the principle that States should refrain in their international relations from the threat or use of force against the territorial integrity or the political independence of any State, and the principle concerning the duty not to intervene in matters within the domestic jurisdiction of a State. (emphasis added)[50]

This passage suggests (to me, at least) that the United States had used force against Nicaragua's political independence, but had not necessarily used force against Nicaragua's territorial integrity. Hence, the ICJ did not endorse, in the *Nicaragua* case, the expansive definition of 'territorial integrity' mentioned above, according to which every territorial incursion is a violation of territorial integrity.

   In 1996, the ICJ issued a closely divided advisory opinion on the legality of using or threatening to use nuclear weapons.[51] In that opinion, in the course of expounding on the meaning of Article 2(4), the ICJ made the following statement: "[I]t would be illegal for a State to threaten force to secure territory from another State, or to cause it to follow or not follow certain political or economic paths."[52] This once again suggests a broad interpretation of 'political independence' and a possibly narrow interpretation of 'territorial integrity'. While most commentators see the Kosovo campaign as more clearly a violation of territorial integrity than political independence (assuming it is a violation at all), the ICJ could potentially

---

[50] *Nicaragua* (provisional measures), 1984 ICJ 169, Order B(2); and *Nicaragua* (merits), 1986 ICJ at para. 288.
[51] *Legality of the Threat or Use of Nuclear Weapons*, Advisory Opinion, 1996 ICJ 226.
[52] *Nuclear Weapons* case, 1996 ICJ at para. 47.

rely on the 'political independence' prong of Article 2(4) if it ultimately declares the Kosovo campaign to be unlawful.

2. *Enforcing a decision of the ICJ.* The UN Charter provides that a state that obtains a favorable decision from the ICJ can appeal to the Security Council for enforcement of the ICJ's decision.[53] In the Nicaragua dispute, Nicaragua appealed to the Security Council to enforce the ICJ's decision against the United States. The United States, of course, vetoed enforcement of the ICJ decision.

Does this mean that the whole ICJ procedure is meaningless, that it offers a target of intervention no more than a simple appeal to the Security Council? Not really. Decisions of the ICJ have a political effect even if enforcement is blocked by a veto in the Security Council, and states may comply with ICJ decisions even if they are able to block enforcement.

Because the United States vetoed enforcement, the *Nicaragua* case is sometimes seen as illustrating the problem of enforcing decisions of the ICJ, and more generally the problem of enforcing international law. Be that as it may, there is substantial evidence that the ICJ proceedings did affect the policy of the United States toward Nicaragua. As noted above, the ICJ issued a preliminary injunction against the United States in the *Nicaragua* case; it ordered the United States to stop mining Nicaragua's ports. In response to this preliminary measure, the U.S. State Department announced that the United States had stopped its naval attacks on Nicaragua the previous month (after Nicaragua's application with the ICJ had been filed), and that the attacks would not resume.[54] Moreover, the ICJ proceedings figured in the decision of Congress to cut off aid to the Nicaraguan Contra rebels in October 1984.[55]

E. International Criminal Court

A target of intervention might also seek relief from the new International Criminal Court. The ICC came into existence in July 2002, despite opposition from the United States.[56] While the ICJ can only hear cases against states, the ICC will hear cases against individuals, some of whom may be leaders of states.

[53] UN CHARTER art. 94.

[54] "Court's Ruling Acceptable, State Department Declares," *New York Times*, May 11, 1984, sec. A, p. 8, col. 1.

[55] Daniel Patrick Moynihan, *On the Law of Nations* (Cambridge, MA: Harvard University Press, 1990), 141–47; and Hendrick Smith, "Reagan Fighting to Win Aid for Anti-Sandinistas," *The New York Times*, May 7, 1984, sec. 1, p. 12, col. 1. (The dispute over aid "reached a climax in early April with revelations that the C.I.A. had directed the mining of Nicaraguan ports, reinforced by a subsequent ruling of the International Court of Justice that called for a halt in the mining and asserted that Nicaragua's independence 'should not be jeopardized by any military or paramilitary activities.'") The Reagan Administration's attempt to obtain aid for the Contras in spite of the Congressional cutoff led to the Iran-Contra affair.

[56] See Curtis A. Bradley, "U.S. Announces Intent Not to Ratify International Criminal Court Treaty," American Society of International Law, *ASIL Insights* (May 2002); available on-line at http://www.asil.org/insights/insigh87.htm [accessed March 10, 2003].

Under its constitutive treaty (the "Rome Statute"), the ICC is supposed to exercise jurisdiction over four kinds of international crimes: genocide, crimes against humanity, war crimes, and the crime of aggression.[57] The crime of aggression is most relevant here. Unfortunately for intervenees, the ICC is not yet exercising jurisdiction over the crime of aggression, and may never do so. The parties to the Rome Statute could not reach agreement on issues surrounding the crime of aggression; they decided to defer those issues, hoping to resolve them by later amendment to the treaty. Such an amendment could become effective, at the earliest, in 2009.[58]

One outstanding issue is how to define the crime of aggression. Most definitions proposed for inclusion in the Rome Statute are based on the General Assembly's 1974 "Definition of Aggression" resolution, which in turn is based on Article 2(4) of the Charter, the Charter's prohibition on the threat or use of force.[59] Simplifying greatly, it appears likely that if the crime of 'aggression' is ever defined under the Rome Statute, a serious use of force in violation of Article 2(4) will be a crime of aggression.

Another outstanding issue regarding the crime of aggression is whether, as a precondition to any prosecution for the *crime* of aggression, the Security Council must determine that an *act* of aggression has occurred. Some believe that such a prior determination by the Security Council is required by the UN Charter; they point to Article 39 of the Charter, which states that the Security Council "shall determine the existence of any threat to the peace, breach of the peace, or act of aggression."[60] If the Security Council shall determine the existence of aggression, then arguably no other body may determine the existence of aggression. Others argue that the Security Council's power to determine the existence of aggression is not exclusive, at least in the context of international criminal proceedings.

If there can be no prosecution for the *crime* of aggression until the Security Council has determined the existence of an *act* of aggression, then the ICC will not be of much help to targets of intervention. However, there is great resistance, among parties to the Rome Statute, to allowing the veto of one permanent member of the Security Council to preclude a prosecution for the crime of aggression. Several proposals now under

[57] Rome Statute of the International Criminal Court, art. 5, para 1.

[58] Art. 5, para 2 of the Rome Statute provides: "The Court shall exercise jurisdiction over the crime of aggression once a provision is adopted in accordance with articles 121 and 123 defining the crime and setting out the conditions under which the Court shall exercise jurisdiction with respect to this crime. Such a provision shall be consistent with the relevant provisions of the Charter of the United Nations."

[59] For recent proposals, see "Discussion Paper on the Definition and Elements of the Crime of Aggression, prepared by the Coordinator of the Working Group on the Crime of Aggression," in *Report of the Preparatory Commission for the International Criminal Court*, 10th Session, UN Doc. PCNICC/2002/2/Add.2 (July 24, 2002); available on-line at http://www.un.org/law/icc/prepcomm/jul2002/english/pcnicc2002_2_add2e.doc [accessed September 29, 2002].

[60] UN CHARTER art. 39.

consideration would give the Security Council an initial opportunity to determine the existence of aggression, but in the case of a veto would allow final determination to be made by the ICC, or the ICJ, or the General Assembly.[61] My own compromise proposal (which I do not expect to be adopted) is that there can be a prosecution without Security Council approval up to the confirmation of charges against an accused party (similar to an indictment in the United States), but further proceedings would require the approval of the Security Council.[62]

If there could be any proceedings before the ICC on a prosecution for the crime of aggression, without the prior approval of the Security Council, targets of intervention would have a major new legal avenue. It would be very embarrassing for leaders of an intervening state to be the subjects of an ICC prosecution, even if the likelihood is small that they would ever fall into the custody of the ICC. It would also be easier for intervenees to confer jurisdiction on the ICC over a claim of aggression than it is for intervenees to bring a claim of unlawful force that is within the jurisdiction of the ICJ.[63] If the ICC ever begins to exercise jurisdiction over the crime of aggression, the possibility of being prosecuted for aggression may deter some unauthorized humanitarian interventions, for good or ill.

F. Charter law is not plastic

I previously noted the view of some scholars that Charter prohibitions on the use of force could be abrogated through the processes of customary international law. The Charter plasticity view has widely different normative implications, depending on whether force prohibitions are assumed to be (1) vulnerable but not yet abrogated, or (2) already abrogated. If force prohibitions are assumed to be vulnerable but not yet abrogated, Charter plasticity could be an additional reason to avoid humanitarian interventions, lest they lead to a general abrogation of prohibitions on the use of force between states. If force prohibitions are assumed to be already abrogated, Charter plasticity could *remove* international-law impediments to humanitarian intervention.

In any event, neither version of the Charter plasticity view is realistic, given the institutional framework I have described above. Anyone can make a grand pronouncement that the law is now "Y" rather than "X." But the ICJ, which is governed by the Charter, will never say that the Charter's prohibitions on the use of force are void. All of its decisions

---

[61] See Coordinator's Discussion Paper, available on-line at http://www.un.org/law/icc/prepcomm/jul2002/english/pcnicc2002_2_add2e.doc [accessed September 29, 2002].

[62] Mark S. Stein, "The Role of the Security Council in Prosecutions for the Crime of Aggression," *Accountability: Newsletter of the American Society of International Law, International Criminal Law Interest Group* 1, no. 1 (2002): 8–10.

[63] See Rome Statute, art. 12. By conferring jurisdiction on the ICC, intervenees would also subject their own leaders to possible prosecution before the ICC.

tend in the other direction; since the *Nicaragua* case, the ICJ has issued a number of decisions demonstrating that it takes a narrow view of the permissibility of the use of force under the Charter. There is not the tiniest cloud hanging over Article 2(4) in the ICJ's decisions.

The Security Council, similarly, will never give up its role in enforcing Article 2(4). All of the Security Council's resolutions on Iraq, from 1990 to 2002, grew out of Iraq's violation of Article 2(4) by its invasion of Kuwait. While the veto of permanent members prevents enforcement against them and their allies, the Security Council will never agree that Article 2(4) has been nullified so that all states are now free to use force in international relations.

And similarly, if the crime of aggression is ever defined as part of the Rome Statute, the ICC will never determine that the provisions of the Rome Statute as to the crime of aggression have become instantly obsolete, and that aggression is not a crime after all. As noted, the definition of the crime of aggression is likely to be based on Article 2(4) of the Charter.

The idea that Charter law can be modified in a way that would never be accepted by the ICJ or the Security Council reflects an anachronistic, pre-Charter view of international law. At one time, the behavior of states was almost the exclusive material of international law, but we now have respected international institutions. It is almost pointless to suggest that something is or could be law if these institutions will never accept it as law.

And if we look at the behavior of states, we would have to conclude, once again, that Charter law on the use of force is alive and well: it has considerable weight as a political norm. When the United States was moving toward a war with Iraq in 2002, most states expressed the view that such a war, if not authorized by the Security Council, would be a violation of the UN Charter. Faced with this opposition, the United States drew back, temporarily, from launching an unauthorized attack on Iraq. There could hardly be any greater proof of the viability of an international norm than if the most powerful state in the world prepares to violate that norm and then draws back, even temporarily, in the face of opposition from other states. Certainly there have been times, since the founding of the United Nations, when permanent members of the Security Council launched nondefensive military interventions with far less concern for the approval of the Council.

As long as the United Nations lasts, international law will never again permit the free use of force by states. There may be a small possibility that an exception to the law on force will develop for unauthorized humanitarian intervention—an exception some claim already to find in international law. Such an exception is possible because there are plausible interpretations of Article 2(4) that permit it. Given the ICJ's decisions on the use of force, however, it seems unlikely that the ICJ will smile on unauthorized humanitarian intervention in the foreseeable future.

I hasten to add that international law should not be the last word in international political morality. Perhaps states should undertake unauthorized humanitarian intervention even if such intervention is contrary to international law. I now turn to such issues of morality and policy.

III. Utilitarianism and Humanitarian Intervention

I take a utilitarian approach to humanitarian intervention: interventions, or rules concerning intervention, are right in proportion as they reduce the suffering of all concerned. I also believe it would be best to employ a utilitarian definition of 'humanitarian intervention': humanitarian intervention is the use of force by a state, beyond its own borders, that has as its purpose or effect the reduction of suffering among all concerned, including noncitizens of the intervening state.

Many would define humanitarian intervention in terms of action to protect human rights, and I have accommodated this view in my earlier, provisional definition of humanitarian intervention. I do not object to talk of human rights, especially if such talk contributes to the reduction of suffering. Nevertheless, the reduction of suffering should be the fundamental object. I note, for what it is worth, that a suffering-based definition of humanitarian intervention seems more consistent than a rights-based definition with the dictionary definition of the word 'humanitarian',[64] and with the generally accepted meaning of terms such as 'humanitarian aid', 'humanitarian organization', and even 'humanitarian law'.

A. Alternatives to utilitarianism

Many others also take a generally utilitarian approach to humanitarian intervention, whether or not they use the term 'utilitarian'. However, there are alternatives to a utilitarian approach. For example, a number of thoroughgoing deontological or rights-based positions are possible. Such positions are sometimes suggested by the rhetoric of some participants in the debate over humanitarian intervention.

It might be argued, on deontological grounds, that intervenors should be willing to pay any price to secure human rights abroad. Thus, the United States and NATO should have intervened in Chechnya, even if the result were a bloody war with Russia—even if the result were a bloody *nuclear* war with Russia.

A deontological position with nearly opposite consequences would be that intervention is prohibited unless the motives of the intervenor are pure: if the intervenor is partly or primarily motivated by geopolitical

---

[64] "[A] person promoting human welfare and social reform," *Merriam-Webster OnLine*, s.v. 'humanitarian'; available on-line at http://www.m-w.com/cgi-bin/dictionary [accessed December 5, 2002].

rather than humanitarian considerations, it must hold back. This position would rule out most if not all interventions, whether or not they are authorized by the Security Council. As political philosopher Michael Walzer and others have suggested, intervenors rarely if ever have purely humanitarian motives; most beneficial interventions occur when the geopolitical interests of the intervening state fortuitously coincide with the interests of humanity.[65] Examples often given are Vietnam's overthrow of the Khmer Rouge regime in Cambodia (1979) and Tanzania's overthrow of Idi Amin's government in Uganda (1979). Possibly America's overthrow of governments in Grenada (1983), Panama (1989), and Iraq (2003) also fits this pattern.

Another deontological position would be that intervenors must avoid inconsistency and hypocrisy with respect to the seriousness of human rights violations that they are seeking to remedy. This position would in effect require that we intervene everywhere (e.g., war with Russia over Chechnya, war with China over Tibet) or nowhere. And the likely choice of nowhere would be bad for all victims of oppression, not just those whom the intervenor otherwise would have helped. Humanitarian intervention shines a light on abuses that are similar to those committed by the intervenee, especially if failure to suppress these similar abuses seems hypocritical. The Kosovo intervention spawned charges of hypocrisy as to NATO's failure to intervene in Turkey (treatment of the Kurds), Indonesia (East Timor), and India (Kashmir). All three of these states have now improved their treatment of their respective minorities or breakaway groups. There are, of course, local factors in all three cases, but perhaps a part was played by additional publicity and additional pressure from allies generated as a result of the Kosovo campaign. To the old saw that hypocrisy is vice's tribute to virtue, we can add: hypocrisy shines virtue's light on vice.

There are also egalitarian alternatives to a utilitarian position on humanitarian intervention. Egalitarians would like to give more weight to the interests of those who are worse off than to the interests of those who are better off (at least, that is how utilitarians view the matter).[66] Egalitarians would prefer to see a larger amount of suffering by those who are or have been better off than a smaller amount of suffering by those who are or have been worse off.

In the area of humanitarian intervention, egalitarianism (at least, of the cosmopolitan variety) would require intervenors from wealthy countries to accept more casualties than would any variant of utilitarianism. Thus, on an egalitarian analysis, it might be right for the United States to sacrifice the lives or limbs of one thousand of its soldiers in order to save the

[65] Michael Walzer, "The Argument about Humanitarian Intervention," *Dissent* 49, no. 1 (2002): 29–37.
[66] John C. Harsanyi, "Rule Utilitarianism, Equality, and Justice," *Social Philosophy & Policy* 2, no. 2 (1985): 125–26.

lives or limbs of five hundred badly off young people in another country, even without considering the other benefits of intervention. This would be sacrificing a greater amount of utility for a more equal distribution of utility, a trade-off that egalitarians typically claim to favor.

Another possible alternative to utilitarianism is ethical nationalism, the view that states should give absolute priority to the interests of their own citizens. Under this view, it would be wrong to sacrifice the welfare of even one citizen in order to save the lives or relieve the suffering of any number of foreigners. An advocate of ethical nationalism would see humanitarian intervention as an immoral impulse.

Of course, it is also possible to have a mixed view, one that combines utilitarianism with other approaches. Legal scholar Fernando Teson, for example, delves very deeply into the rhetoric of deontology and trots out some stock arguments against utilitarianism, but ends up concluding that "other things being equal, humanitarian interventions that are likely to cause substantially disproportionate additional suffering should not be initiated."[67] Utilitarianism seems to be so large an element in Teson's mixed view that I am not sure it is possible to distinguish his view from utilitarianism in practice.

I will not defend here my utilitarian approach to humanitarian intervention (other than through the foregoing discussion of the alternatives). In what follows I will view the problem of unauthorized humanitarian intervention through the lens of utilitarian moral theory, but some of what I say may be of interest to devotees of other approaches.

B. Act or rule?

The debates about humanitarian intervention recall debates in moral theory about rule-utilitarianism, act-utilitarianism, and the place of institutions in utilitarian theory. Most discussions of humanitarian intervention are rule oriented: Under what conditions should a state (such as the United States) intervene? The most prominent possible rule, and one that arguably already exists, is that states should intervene only with the authorization of the Security Council. I will refer to this as the 'authorization rule'.

Suppose one thought, as the Kosovo intervention was about to be launched, that it would have good effects overall. One might still oppose the Kosovo intervention, based on the authorization rule. This would be similar to a rule-utilitarian approach, and if one's reasons for supporting the authorization rule were utilitarian, it would in fact be a rule-utilitarian approach.

---

[67] Teson, *Humanitarian Intervention*, 123.

Rule-utilitarians are vulnerable to embarrassment by situations in which obeying a generally beneficial rule would have disastrous consequences. Some such hypothetical examples conjured up by moral theorists are a little silly, but in the area of humanitarian intervention, the problem seems more realistically acute. Should states observe the authorization rule at the cost of allowing hundreds of thousands of people to die?[68] (Of course, if this is going to be a consequence of the rule, then it is hard to believe that the rule is beneficial overall.)

The same problem can beset adherents of other rules that have been suggested in the area of humanitarian intervention. Numerous writers have attempted to specify the conditions under which humanitarian intervention should take place. If these conditions take the form "Intervene only if X, Y, and Z," they are also vulnerable to attack by way of difficult realistic examples. For example, three worthy suggestions are that (1) intervening states should act through regional organizations; (2) intervening states should subject themselves to the jurisdiction of the ICJ and the ICC for all claims arising out of their intervention; and (3) intervening states should not bomb from high altitudes if doing so makes it difficult to distinguish between military and civilian targets. Suppose now that the United States had been prepared to intervene against genocide in Rwanda, but had not been able or willing to meet these and other worthy conditions. After all, the humanitarian impulse is a fragile thing, likely to be overridden by national interest, and such conditions would give the United States additional reasons not to intervene. Would it be better not to intervene in a Rwanda-like situation than to intervene without meeting the conditions?

Many theorists, following philosopher David Lyons, believe that rule-utilitarianism is always in danger of collapsing into act-utilitarianism. In the area of humanitarian intervention, such a merger would be effected by the rule: intervene so as to cause the best consequences, or intervene so as to minimize suffering overall.

Lyons suggests that while utilitarians can support institutions that limit by rules the direct pursuit of utility, they will behave in an act-utilitarian manner once they are inside those institutions.[69] There is some truth to this view, but there are reasons why utilitarians can sometimes be effec-

---

[68] To quote Annan again:

> To those for whom the greatest threat to the future of international order is the use of force in the absence of a Security Council mandate, one might ask—not in the context of Kosovo—but in the context of Rwanda: If, in those dark days and hours leading up to the genocide, a coalition of States had been prepared to act in defence of the Tutsi population, but did not receive prompt Council authorization, should such a coalition have stood aside and allowed the horror to unfold?

1999 Annual Report of the Secretary-General (details at note 2).

[69] David Lyons, *Rights, Welfare, and Mill's Moral Theory* (New York: Oxford University Press, 1994). For a utilitarian response, see William H. Shaw, *Contemporary Ethics: Taking Account of Utilitarianism* (Oxford: Blackwell, 1999), 192–96.

tively committed to institutions even if they are not fundamentally committed to them. One such reason would be a continuing lack of trust in the ability of agents, including themselves, to deviate from institutional rules in a utility-maximizing way.

In the area of humanitarian intervention, one's commitment to rules, and in particular to the authorization rule, is likely to be affected by one's attitude toward the United States. The United States is the country most able to project force beyond its borders. Is the United States a benevolent, huggable hegemon or a malevolent, reckless rogue? Doubtless the truth is somewhere between these two poles. I am disposed to believe that the effects of American intervention will likely be good; I know that others disagree.

C. Danger of abuse

Opponents of a humanitarian exception to the authorization rule fear that such an exception will be abused. It is important to distinguish between two different ways in which such abuse can occur. First, a perceived right of humanitarian intervention could lead states to label as 'humanitarian' wars that they undertake for other-than-humanitarian motives, and that they would have undertaken in any event. This would not be an unfortunate result. Of course, it is unfortunate when states launch bad wars, that is, those having bad consequences overall. But given that a state will launch a bad war, it is preferable that the state claim to be undertaking humanitarian intervention rather than offer some other pretext, such as self-defense. A state that claims to be undertaking humanitarian intervention has pledged, however hypocritically, to promote the well-being of people beyond its borders. Such a pledge can be held up to it by other states, and may even moderate its behavior.

The second possibility is that a perceived right of humanitarian intervention could lead states to wage bad wars that they would *not* have waged if they could not claim to be acting from humanitarian motives. This is the true danger of abuse. Consider a hypothetical brutal dictatorship in State X. The dictatorship, let us suppose, is hostile to the United States, which desires to replace it with a friendlier and more benevolent regime. A U.S. military intervention to overthrow the dictatorship would have humanitarian aspects. The people of State X would probably be better off under a replacement regime (at least, those who remained alive would be better off). However, military intervention would also be motivated by nonhumanitarian considerations, which might be paramount for American policymakers. Hypothetically, the nonhumanitarian objectives could lead the United States to start a war that would predictably cause far more suffering than it would cure, a war that the United States would not start if it could not claim a humanitarian objective and *also* would not start if it were acting solely from humanitarian motives.

Accordingly, those who mistrust the United States (and, presumably, every other state) could advocate adherence to the authorization rule even while conceding the argument I made at the beginning of this essay, that there is a deficit of humanitarian intervention because of the particularism of states. A perceived right of humanitarian intervention could lead states to launch interventions that have some humanitarian aspect, but that have bad consequences overall because they are primarily motivated by geopolitical considerations.

One does not need bad motives, of course, to get bad consequences. Mistakes can also lead to bad consequences, and there are plenty of mistakes in war.

Even if we trust our own country (e.g., the United States), we might mistrust other countries. In that event we might support the imposition of a globally effective authorization rule. Suppose we sat in a world parliament that could somehow enforce its laws. As utilitarians, we might support the authorization rule, even though we thought that our own country could produce good consequences by deviating from it, if we thought that all unauthorized force, considered together, would have bad consequences. And once we succeeded in passing the authorization rule, we would not be able to deviate from it.

Of course, we are not sitting in a world parliament. If our country refrains from using unauthorized force, this will not necessarily prevent other countries from using unauthorized force. Our country might just be giving up "good" wars only to see other countries continue to make "bad" wars.

If we are seeking political realism, it may even be a mistake to view the issue as whether unauthorized force by our country, or unauthorized force under a claim of humanitarian intervention, would have good or bad consequences overall. Citizens interested in a moral foreign policy may be able to affect some uses of force better than others. My own view, as I have said, is that the humanitarian impulse is fragile: the more purely humanitarian an intervention, the more likely it is to be a marginal case, one in which policy can be swayed. Conversely, where a state has a strong geopolitical interest in war, it is less likely to be held back. Therefore, if we support the authorization rule because of its generally beneficial effect, we may be more likely to impede good interventions than bad interventions.[70] I must admit, however, that the current American administration was dissuaded in 2002, at least temporarily, from using unauthorized force against Iraq, by the combined opposition of the American public and most of the world, in a situation where many members of the administration saw a strong geopolitical interest in attacking Iraq immediately.

---

[70] Not that strong geopolitical interests mean that the use of force should necessarily be opposed. Self-defense is a strong geopolitical interest.

D. The rules we have

We do not have an effective authorization rule that makes deviation impossible and so makes it unnecessary to calculate the consequences of deviation. But we do have a somewhat ambiguous authorization rule, as part of international law and international politics, and violating this rule can have some consequences.

As a political norm, the authorization rule varies in effectiveness depending on the political support that it receives in any given situation. In the period leading up to Security Council Resolution 1441 on Iraq,[71] the authorization rule received enormous political support, leading the United States to abandon, at least temporarily, its plan to attack Iraq without authorization. In the period leading up to the Kosovo intervention, the authorization rule received less political support. The difference was not a matter of law, in my opinion: the unauthorized Kosovo intervention was just as clearly a violation of international law as the unauthorized attack on Iraq. Or so it seems to me.

Sometimes the authorization rule has specifically legal consequences, which in turn have political consequences. Some states are reluctant to violate what they consider to be international law, even if it is naked law, unsupported by any judicial decision. And once law is applied by an international court, it gains greater and wider credibility. In the case of forcible intervention, the ICJ may brand the use of force as illegal and order the intervening state to stop, as in the *Nicaragua* case. And the ICC prosecutor may bring charges against the leaders of an intervening state, if the ICC ever begins to exercise jurisdiction over the crime of aggression.

Ultimately, such legal consequences will be political consequences only to the extent that they have political credibility with states. But international judicial and prosecutorial decisions do have political credibility—at least, they have greater credibility than naked law. The ICJ's decisions in the *Nicaragua* case may have helped to end direct American military operations against Nicaragua, and if the ICJ had ordered NATO countries to halt their participation in the Kosovo campaign, such an order may also have had a political effect.

Thus, the political and legal force of the authorization rule can affect the behavior of states in the area of humanitarian intervention. As a matter of prudence, in light of legal and political consequences, states might not intervene because of the authorization rule we now have—though they would intervene if there were no authorization rule.

A different question is whether the legal consequences of the authorization rule should be morally significant beyond their effect on the na-

---

[71] S/Res/1441, UN SCOR 57th Sess., 4644 mtg. (Nov. 8, 2002). For an explanation of this resolution, see Frederic L. Kirgis, "Security Council Resolution 1441 on Iraq's Final Opportunity to Comply with Disarmament Obligations," *ASIL Insights* (November 2002); available on-line at http://www.asil.org/insights/insigh92.htm [accessed March 7, 2003].

tional interest of potential intervenors. In act-utilitarian terms, this question becomes: Do the legal consequences of a particular humanitarian intervention make the total consequences of that intervention bad (not just for the intervenor, but for all people), where absent the authorization rule the total consequences would have been good?

If each humanitarian intervention eroded the authorization rule, making more likely the nonhumanitarian and nondefensive use of force, that would indeed be a negative consequence. I have already expressed my view that such erosion will not occur, and that it has not occurred as a result of previous humanitarian interventions. The ICJ will not hold that Charter prohibitions on the use of force have been abrogated, and the ICC will not hold that the Rome Statute provisions on the crime of aggression have been nullified before the ICC has even begun to exercise jurisdiction over that crime.

The idea that humanitarian interventions will lead to nonhumanitarian wars has been somewhat overtaken by events. In preparing the way for a war against Iraq, the United States advanced a very broad interpretation of the concept of 'anticipatory self-defense'. Under this novel view of self-defense, the United States was entitled to attack Iraq and overthrow its government because Iraq might pose a threat to the United States at some time in the nebulous future. This doctrine, if universalized, truly would signal the end of any effective prohibition on the use of force in international relations: in every conflict, it is always possible that one side will someday pose a threat to the other. Here there is a possibility of like cases leading to like cases; this seems more realistic than the possibility, feared by opponents of unauthorized humanitarian intervention, that like cases will lead to unlike cases.

Humanitarian intervention will not erode the authorization rule so as to permit the free use of nonhumanitarian and nondefensive force. It is more likely that any change in the law caused by humanitarian intervention will relate specifically to humanitarian intervention. On the one hand, if repeated cases of unauthorized humanitarian intervention establish a humanitarian exception to the authorization rule, that could be a positive development. On the other hand, there is the danger that humanitarian intervention in borderline cases can strengthen the authorization rule, as applied specifically to humanitarian intervention, so that it becomes more difficult to intervene in the future even when intervention is enormously beneficial. The *Nicaragua* case, in which the ICJ announced that force is not an acceptable means of promoting human rights, was at the very best a borderline case for humanitarian intervention. While there was a risk that Nicaragua would slip into Cuba-style totalitarianism, the human rights situation in Nicaragua was far better than in many other countries in Central and South America. The Kosovo case, in which the ICJ remarked that the intervention "raises very serious issues of international law," was also something of a borderline case. Yugoslavia confronted an armed secessionist movement, and its response, while brutal, was not so brutal as to set it apart from other states confronting armed secessionism.[72]

Soft cases, I suggest, make bad law on humanitarian intervention. Probably the ICJ would not have been so quick to brand humanitarian intervention illegal, as in the *Nicaragua* case, if the intervenee was a state that was killing tens of thousands or hundreds of thousands of people. Fortunately, the ICJ has not yet addressed the merits of the Kosovo case and may never have to do so. If there is any possibility that the fall of Communism and other changed circumstances will cause the ICJ to moderate its position on humanitarian intervention, we should not foreclose that possibility by presenting it with another borderline case. So the broader legal consequences of unauthorized intervention may, after all, be a reason to err on the side of the authorization rule.

IV. CONCLUSION

Like many authors, I have discussed the authorization rule as an either-or proposition: comply or violate. Such an approach makes analysis simpler, but we should also remember that international politics as practiced is often ambiguous. It is not always clear whether an intervention is authorized.

Ambiguities aside, I might be asked: After all of this theorizing, do I support the authorization rule? Not as a hard-and-fast rule. States should sometimes intervene without authorization, if intervention would clearly reduce suffering.

Government, Dartmouth College

---

[72] The more serious brutality imputed to Yugoslavia, fairly or unfairly, was the brutality of the Bosnian Serbs against the Bosnian Muslims. The Bosnian tragedy colors the attitude of many toward the Kosovo intervention, including possibly some ICJ judges.

THINKING CONSTITUTIONALLY:
THE PROBLEM OF DELIBERATIVE DEMOCRACY

By Stephen L. Elkin

I. Introduction

A variety of arguments have been advanced that deliberation should be at the center of any good political regime in which there is popular self-government. Deliberation is to be the basis for lawmaking, that is, for the making of the collectivity's binding decisions. Thus, John Rawls says, "[O]f course, actual constitutions should be designed as far as possible to make the same determinations as the ideal legislative procedure." This procedure, in turn, is defined as having laws that result from "rational legislators . . . who are conscientious, trying to follow the principles of justice as their standard." These legislators "are not to take a narrow or group-interested standpoint."[1] Joshua Cohen broadly agrees with Rawls and characterizes Rawls's view as one that argues for a democratic politics that is built around public deliberation.[2] Cohen says (agreeing with Rawls) that "an ideal pluralist scheme, in which democratic politics consists of fair bargaining among groups each of which pursues its particular or sectional interest, is unsuited to a just society."[3] John Dryzek shares these views and comments that the "essence of democratic legitimacy should be sought . . . in the ability of all individuals subject to a collective decision to engage in authentic deliberation about that decision."[4] Others have argued along similar lines, including James Bohman,[5] Amy Gutmann and Dennis Thompson,[6] David Gauthier,[7] and Jurgen Habermas.[8]

In this essay, I want to argue that there are two temptations to avoid in theorizing about deliberation in democracy, especially when the argu-

---

[1] John Rawls, *A Theory of Justice* (Cambridge, MA: Harvard University Press, 1971), 360.

[2] Joshua Cohen, "Deliberation and Democratic Legitimacy," in James Bohman and William Rehg, eds., *Deliberative Democracy: Essays on Reason and Politics* (Cambridge, MA: MIT Press, 1997), 67–92.

[3] Ibid., 68. Cohen points to Rawls's statement on the matter in *A Theory of Justice*, 360–61.

[4] John S. Dryzek, *Deliberative Democracy and Beyond: Liberals, Critics, Contestations* (New York: Oxford University Press, 2000), v.

[5] James Bohman, *Public Deliberation: Pluralism, Complexity, and Democracy* (Cambridge, MA: MIT Press, 1996).

[6] Amy Gutmann and Dennis Thompson, *Democracy and Disagreement* (Cambridge, MA: Harvard University Press, 1996).

[7] David Gauthier, "Constituting Democracy," in David Copp, Jean Hampton, and John E. Roemer, eds., *The Idea of Democracy* (New York: Cambridge University Press, 1993), 314–34.

[8] Jurgen Habermas, "Popular Sovereignty As Procedure," in Bohman and Rehg, eds., *Deliberative Democracy*, 35–66.

ment concerns building a whole regime around deliberative ways of lawmaking. These temptations are as follows:

1. The belief that deliberation itself—the exchange of reasons—is what is valuable, not reasoning about particular matters that must be addressed if the political regime is to be maintained.

2. The belief that the primary concern of political action in a good regime is to foster the virtues and motives that make deliberation possible, and that the more effort that is put into promoting these virtues and motives and the political processes that revolve around them, the more likely that popular self-government will flourish. These virtues and motives include the ability and desire to set out clear arguments, rhetorical ability, the ability and desire to listen carefully to others, and a willingness to show respect for other deliberators.[9] Political processes that rest on other motives, notably bargaining and the exercise of political power, are to be kept to a minimum. Moreover, in the more radical formulations, they should, if possible, be eliminated. In this view, to the degree that democratic politics revolves around bargaining and the exercise of power, it is badly flawed. A good regime is held together by good motives.[10]

Both of these beliefs are problematic if we are to have a well-designed form of popular self-government. But aspects of these beliefs are not uncommon in works on deliberative democracy. The source of such weaknesses in deliberative theory, or so I will argue, is a lack of deep engagement by theorists with the question of how a political order that revolves around deliberation (although it is generally agreed that none does so at present) will actually work. Even more importantly, there is too little thought given to what will make it work in the required fashion. Once we think about the institutional workings of such a political order—and especially about what is necessary to secure and maintain its crucial institutions—we are likely to have a different view from the one held by those who share the beliefs I have just described. In particular, we are likely to view differently what the role of deliberation in a democracy should be, and how to evaluate what might be called "morally ambiguous" motives and political processes. In other words, once we think constitutionally about these matters—that is, once we think about what is necessary to constitute an attractive and enduring form of popular self-

[9] See Benjamin Barber, "An American Civic Forum," *The Good Society* 5, no. 2 (1995); and Iris Marion Young, *Inclusion and Democracy* (New York: Oxford University Press, 2000), especially chaps. 2–3.

[10] Cf. Harvey Mansfield's comment that "the good . . . think goodness is enough." Harvey C. Mansfield, *Machiavelli's Virtue* (Chicago, IL: University of Chicago Press, 1996), 29.

government—we will likely end up with a theory of how this might be done that is substantially different from the theories set out or implicit in the work of many deliberative democrats. We will also find ourselves drawn into a discussion of the problem of political evaluation, especially regarding the place of morally ambiguous political motives and processes in good political regimes.

Much of the latter discussion will emerge out of an examination of the mode of theorizing engaged in by John Rawls. A significant portion of the work on democratic deliberation has been influenced by Rawls's manner of theorizing, which he terms 'ideal theory'. Rawls is quite clear that he proceeds in his theorizing by putting aside any consideration of morally ambiguous motives and the political processes that are built on them. These are viewed as matters that get in the way of realizing justice. They are to be discussed only under what Rawls terms 'partial compliance theory', as things that prevent strict or full compliance with the substance of justice that ideal theory is meant to elaborate, and which is his principal subject. Rawls thus explicitly sets out a mode of theorizing, echoed in the work of many deliberative theorists, and he asserts that unattractive motives, skills, and political processes can be laid aside while we concentrate on ideal motives and processes. Moreover, Rawls believes that we can do so without any damage to our understanding of how to create and maintain a good regime of popular self-government. Indeed, proceeding in this manner, Rawls suggests, is the preferred way to theorize. My concern here, then, is not only substantive: the question of how to achieve deliberative lawmaking in a democracy. I am also concerned, through an examination of ideal theory, with the question of how to do political theory. Given the link between Rawlsian ideal theory and much deliberative theory, the two issues are, in fact, interconnected: criticism of one has a bearing on the attraction of the other.

My basic contention is that if we treat political theory as an examination in concrete and institutionally specific detail of how to constitute a regime of popular self-government, then we will value deliberation as such rather less, and value morally ambiguous motives and the political processes built on them rather more, than does much of deliberative theory. Thus, how we do political theory, I will contend, has a significant effect on what evaluation we give to important features of democratic political life and the attendant political practices. Moreover, we are more likely to succeed in creating and maintaining an attractive democratic regime if our actions are guided by what may be called 'constitutional thinking'.

Since what is missing in much deliberative democratic theory is a substantial account of the workings of crucial institutions and what will make them work in the required way, and since a similar account is needed for constitutional thinking, I will develop my argument by considering a particular polity—the United States—and what would be necessary if it is to have deliberative lawmaking. I will focus on the United States because, from the nation's beginnings, the value of deliberative lawmaking has been a constant theme.[11]

II. DELIBERATIVE LAWMAKING AND THE AMERICAN REGIME

We can start by considering what public deliberation or, more precisely, deliberative lawmaking entails. To the degree that a regime of popular self-government engages in deliberative lawmaking, it makes its collectively binding decisions not through the exercise of power or through bargaining, but through reasoning. For such deliberation to occur, there must be political institutions that put lawmakers in a deliberative relation with one another. The legislative process and the institutions that compose it must work deliberatively.

What does it mean for the legislative process to work deliberatively? Crucial is a disposition on the part of lawmakers to think about public matters in terms of how they might affect the public interest, instead of solely in terms of each lawmaker's own interest or the interest of some particular group in the society.[12] As Arthur Maass says, legislators must have "breadth of view."[13] Lawmakers must try to answer the implicit question posed by any piece of legislation, Is it in the public interest? by *discussing* it. Accordingly, they must argue, adduce evidence, point to comparable cases, etc.[14] General ideas about "what constitutes good public policy" will be "important in determining the results of the process."[15] As William Galston says, lawmakers must possess "deliberative excellence."[16]

---

[11] See *Federalist No. 10* (J. Madison), in Clinton Rossiter, ed., *The Federalist Papers* (New York: New American Library, 1961); Cass Sunstein, "The Enduring Legacy of Republicanism," in Stephen L. Elkin and Karol Edward Soltan, eds., *A New Constitutionalism: Designing Political Institutions for a Good Society* (Chicago, IL: University of Chicago Press, 1993); Joseph M. Besette, *The Mild Voice of Reason: Deliberative Democracy and American National Government* (Chicago, IL: Chicago University Press, 1994); and Stephen L. Elkin, *Constituting the American Republic* (forthcoming), esp. chaps. 2–4, 9–10.

[12] Some theorists have doubted whether deliberation must or ought to be directed at giving content to the public interest. See, e.g., Young, *Inclusion and Democracy*, chap. 1. As will become apparent, I think it must. At this point in the argument, however, the reader need not decide the matter, since I will show below in the text that even deliberative theorists who deny that there is a public interest must believe that there is one if their theory is to be compelling. Otherwise said, the presumed difference between theorists who affirm or deny that deliberative lawmaking ought to serve the public interest collapses once we understand what is required for such lawmaking to work.

[13] Arthur Maass, *Congress and the Common Good* (New York: Basic Books, 1983), 18.

[14] Cf. Karol Edward Soltan, "What Is the New Constitutionalism?" and "Generic Constitutionalism," in Elkin and Soltan, eds., *A New Constitutionalism.*

[15] Steven Kelman, *Making Public Policy* (New York: Basic Books, 1987), 208.

[16] William Galston, "Liberal Virtues," *American Political Science Review* 82, no. 4 (1988): 1284.

In deliberative ways of lawmaking, lawmakers understand that their views of the public interest and any interpretations of it that they have offered to voters are their initial positions. These are partial viewpoints that will be subject to expansion and revision, especially as lawmakers attempt to reconcile their positions with those of other members of the legislative body. Their policy positions are not to be considered mere counters in a trading game, but partial, tentative answers to the question, What is in the public interest? Thus, lawmakers who stand in relation to one another as deliberators will have a disposition to reach beyond their initial positions and to revise them in light of argument and evidence. Deliberative lawmakers will offer *reasons* for their positions, but lawmaking is not analogous to a debating society where great speeches are delivered by one modern-day Pericles after another. Because widespread agreement on important legislative measures is not likely to emerge quickly or easily, but must be built up from diverse initial positions, the premium for deliberatively minded lawmakers will be less on oratory and more on drawing out, making concrete, and reconciling various interpretations of the public interest.

Obvious questions follow. Will the institutions that make possible the kind of deliberation just described work over time in the necessary ways, without any special attention given to maintaining them? Will they be relatively free of corruption, as political actors who would gain from preventing deliberative lawmaking attempt to undercut them? And, in the face of strong incentives to focus on short-term interests and concerns, will many people be willing to invest the resources needed to maintain these institutions? The answer to all these questions is almost certainly no. This, in turn, means that if lawmakers are to engage in deliberation, then a number of conditions must be met. First, they must be free to deliberate about these matters, and not be prevented by various political pressures from considering the public interest. But being free to consider the public interest is one thing, being motivated to consider it is another. Thus, a second requirement is that the legislature be so organized that lawmakers not only find it possible to turn to the public interest but also have some incentive to do so. Third, and similarly, lawmakers will need to believe that there are political rewards for concerning themselves with the public interest, that is, there must be a citizenry with the ability and the inclination to reward lawmakers whose legislative activity is directed at serving the public interest. If we assume that Americans aspire to realize a political regime in which deliberative lawmaking plays a central role,[17] then we can explore how these three conditions might be met in the American context. On the basis of what we discover, we can also say

---

[17] For evidence and argument that this is so, see Elkin, *Constituting the American Republic*, chap. 1.

something about the value of deliberative lawmaking generally, and what is at stake in efforts to create it. I shall discuss the first condition in subsection A below and the related conditions two and three in subsections B and C.

A. Preventing faction: The first condition

A useful way to understand the problem of preventing lawmakers from being captured by forces that would turn them away from a deliberative inquiry into the meaning of the public interest is provided by James Madison. For Madison, this is the problem of 'faction', and preventing faction is the key to republican, that is, to limited, popular government. If lawmakers are not free of factional influence, they will be unable to concern themselves with securing the public interest. By 'faction', Madison means "a number of citizens, whether amounting to a majority or minority of the whole, who are united and actuated by some common impulse of passion, or of interest, adverse to the rights of other citizens, or to the permanent and aggregate interests of the community." [18] Factional government is unlimited government, since factions recognize no legitimate barrier to serving their own interests. In Madison's language, factions lead to disregarding "the public good" and to matters being decided "not according to . . . the rights of the minor party, but by the superior force of an interested and overbearing majority." [19]

Madison extends the traditional worry that government itself endangers individual liberty to include the idea that the people, when wielding political power, also present a danger. As Madison observes, "Had every Athenian citizen been a Socrates, every Athenian assembly would still have been a mob." [20] The problem of majority faction is particularly difficult, Madison argues. A popular regime is especially vulnerable to the passions of majorities since, in significant ways, such a regime must work according to majoritarian principles if it is indeed to be the rule of the people. Majority factions, that is, can claim the cover of law for their actions. Conversely, minority factions pose less of a problem since ma-

---

[18] *Federalist No. 10* (J. Madison), in Rossiter, ed., *The Federalist Papers*, 78.

[19] Ibid., 77.

[20] *Federalist No. 55* (J. Madison), in Rossiter, ed., *The Federalist Papers*, 342. Jack Rakove, a careful student of Madison's thought, writes:

> For most 18th century liberals, the problem of rights was to protect the whole people against the coercive power of monarchy. Madison was the first to realize that this formula was irrelevant to the American republic, where real power lay with popular majorities, who would use legislative power to burden whichever minorities they disliked.

Jack Rakove, "A Nation Still Learning What Madison Knew," *New York Times*, March 11, 2001, sec. 4, p. 15, col. 1.

jorities can "defeat [their] sinister views by regular vote." The "republican principle" is enough to prevent factional rule by a minority.[21]

Madison is clear that faction cannot be eliminated on any grounds consistent with republican government. Factions could be prevented from forming by destroying liberty, but this remedy is "worse than the disease." To save republican government by subverting its very purpose does not commend itself.[22] Alternatively, an attempt might be made to give every citizen "the same opinions." But this, writes Madison, is "as impracticable as the first [approach] would be unwise." For faction is "sown in the nature of man."[23] It is also possible, supposes Madison, that every citizen might simply *have* the same opinion, thus eliminating factional disputes, but this is only likely in a small republic where people live much the same way, and where those who have heterodox opinions would find it expedient to move to a more congenial place. Here Madison shares Alexander Hamilton's view that a multiplicity of small republics on American soil would be a recipe for weakness and conflict, an environment in which republican government would be unlikely to flourish.

In general, Madison argues that instead of trying to eliminate faction, it is better to work to control its effects. And, indeed, if factional interests could be multiplied, faction would actually indirectly help to create and maintain a well-ordered republican government. Thus, Madison argues that the way to limit factional strife and to prevent factional government—to control the effects of faction—is (1) to create a system of representation; (2) to divide power and tie this division to ambition so that ambition could be made to counter ambition; (3) to extend the sphere of the republic to encompass multiple interests; and (4) to stimulate commerce, which would create the multiplication of interests.[24]

First, representation would cool passion by placing an agent between a people given to faction and the content of the laws. Representatives would "refine and enlarge the public views," leading to laws "more consonant to the public good." However, representation is no cure-all. It could, and more than likely would, produce as representatives some men of "factious tempers" given to "local prejudices."[25]

Madison also argues that, while a "dependence on the people is, no doubt, the primary control on government," and thus the system of representation is crucial for securing republican government, there must also be "auxiliary precautions."[26] One such precaution, the second way to control faction, is to divide the powers of government, thus reducing the

[21] *Federalist No. 10* (J. Madison), in Rossiter, ed., *The Federalist Papers*, 80.
[22] Ibid., 78.
[23] Ibid., 78 and 79.
[24] Ibid., 82–84.
[25] Ibid., 82.
[26] *Federalist No. 51* (J. Madison), in Rossiter, ed., *The Federalist Papers*, 322.

chances that a majority faction could gain control. The likelihood of this occurring would be reduced simply because of the division itself: a faction might, for example, gain a majority in one house of the legislature, but not control the presidency. The difficulties for a faction would be multiplied by requiring that each branch of government—and within Congress, each house—be elected or selected in a different fashion and for a different period of time.

Perhaps even more important, the separation of powers would be strengthened—indeed, would only work—through the harnessing of ambition. As Madison explains, "Ambition must be made to counteract ambition. The interest of the man must be connected with the constitutional rights of the place."[27] The problem is how to motivate each branch of government to resist the incursions of the others. It is important that each branch have the inclination and the capacity to resist what it understands to be incursions by the others. What will provide the motivation? Madison answers: ambition. What will provide the capacity? Madison answers: "the constitutional rights of the place." Thus, Madison supposes that members of each branch, or at least many of them, will not wish to become the lackeys of another branch, doing the president's bidding, for example, simply because it is his bidding, or the Supreme Court's bidding, simply because it has decided some matter in a particular way. No one, Madison thinks, will welcome serving in a branch of government that is widely perceived to be subordinate and puny. Ambition and the desire for recognition will lead members of the various branches to employ the powers that the Constitution awards their branch. The results will be a separation of powers that is not a mere "parchment barrier"[28] and a decrease in the likelihood that any faction can gain control of the full powers of government.

Third, an extended republic is also an advantage in controlling faction, Madison argues. In contrast to the older view popularized by Montesquieu that republican government could only succeed in a relatively small and homogeneous country where there is a commonality of interests, it is precisely the multiplicity of interests that would emerge in a large country that is useful for republican government because this multiplicity would make it less likely for a single large faction to form. An extensive republic would also make it harder for a large faction to form, given that communication would be costly and the resources required would be substantial. Moreover, Madison explains, majorities would "seldom take place on any other principles than those of justice and the general good."[29] Further, a large republic would also mean large constituencies if the number of representatives were to be small enough to prevent "the confusion

[27] Ibid.
[28] *Federalist No 48* (J. Madison), in Rossiter, ed., *The Federalist Papers*, 308.
[29] *Federalist No. 51*, p. 325.

of a multitude."[30] Large districts would reduce the likelihood that the practice of "vicious arts" would decide elections and would favor the election of men of "the most diffusive and established characters."[31]

Fourth and finally, as Martin Diamond has argued,[32] Madison believed that multiplication in the number of economic interests would make it less likely that there would be only one major economic fault line, between property-owners and the propertyless, around which political conflict would organize. The principal vehicle for multiplying interests would be a vibrant commercial society in which those who pursue their livelihood in shipping, for example, would have different interests than those who work in finance.[33] The size of the country would also increase economic diversity. As important, those involved in these various economic pursuits who are not property-holders but are recipients of wages might be expected to see their interests tied as much to the flourishing of the shipping or banking trade as to the fact that they hold little or no property. One way to understand Madison here is to contrast a commercial society to an agrarian society in which there is a small landholding class and a mass of agricultural laborers who are dependent on the landed class for work. The latter society is an inhospitable environment for popular self-government because the interests of the two classes conflict and define all other relationships, and because the laborers are too economically dependent to be the kind of independent citizens that republican government requires.

Madison's overall view, then, is that auxiliary precautions would (1) increase the number of interests, making it less likely that two great opposing factions would emerge; (2) divide governmental power, lessening the possibility that any faction could control the entire government; and (3) create through representation a class of political leaders of independent character and outlook, who would be accountable to the citizenry but sufficiently removed by distance—and in the case of the Senate, by indirect election—that they will be relatively insulated from the passions that will inevitably roil the citizenry from time to time. These leaders would then be in a position to consider the public interest. The regime would be popular, but so arranged that any passionate majority would need to persist over long periods if it were to hold sway, and perhaps in the process it would become cooler in outlook.

[30] *Federalist No. 10*, p. 82.

[31] Ibid., 82–83.

[32] Martin Diamond, "Democracy and the Federalist: A Reconsideration of the Framers' Intent," in William Schramba, ed., *As Far As Republican Principles Will Admit: Essays by Martin Diamond* (Washington, DC: AEI Press, 1992).

[33] Cf. Judith Best's comment that the "promotion of commerce will foster heterogeneity. This axiom is implicit in Madison's recognition that this protection [of diverse talents] results in 'different degrees and kinds of property.' " Here Best is quoting *Federalist No. 10*, p. 78. Judith Best, "Fundamental Rights and the Structure of Government," in Robert A. Licht, ed., *The Framers and Fundamental Rights* (Washington, DC: AEI Press, 1991), 43.

It is worth emphasizing here that in recommending the harnessing of interest and ambition, Madison is not suggesting that these are the only motives of humankind. He is clear that human beings are also capable of concern with a larger good. The problem is that this sort of motive is neither strong nor widespread enough to be used as the only building block for republican government. Something more reliable is called for, and Madison believed he had found it in the related motives of self-interest and ambition.[34]

B. Organizing the legislature: The second condition

Will lawmakers who are free to deliberate in fact concern themselves with the public interest? Many will show that modicum of attachment to the public interest that is characteristic of all decent people in not completely wretched regimes. But for these lawmakers, such attachment to the public interest is unlikely to be sufficient to generate a consistent and ample disposition to engage in deliberative ways of lawmaking. These lawmakers are not, after all, likely to be Solons. More inducement to serve the public interest will be needed. Some of the incentives to legislate in the public interest can come from the organization and leadership of the legislature itself. Additional, and crucial, incentives for deliberative ways of lawmaking must come from the citizenry. Its members must reward through reelection those who evidence a disposition to deliberate. The citizens of a commercial republic must be, in their way, as capable as its lawmakers. They must have qualities of judgment that allow them to discern which prospective lawmakers understand lawmaking to be, in significant part, a deliberative process, and have either the skills necessary to participate in the process or the inclination to develop such skills. The hope for deliberative lawmaking in a republic lies in the combination of what might be termed the 'legislature as school' and the capacities for judgment by the citizenry.

At present in the United States, noted legislative careers do not require any great talent for legislation, that is, for the arts of hammering out how the public interest is to be brought to bear in particular policy decisions. That a keystone of republican government is a legislature adept at deliberating about the public interest seems to be remote from the concerns of most present members of Congress. The possibility and importance of such a great

---

[34] See *Federalist No. 55*. See also Alexander Hamilton's comment (*Federalist No. 76*, p. 458):

> The supposition of universal venality in human nature is little less an error in political reasoning than the supposition of universal rectitude. The institution of delegated power implies that there is a portion of virtue and honor among mankind, which may be a reasonable foundation of confidence.

Cf. Samuel Johnson's comment: "I know, Madam, how unwillingly conviction is admitted when interest opposes it" (quoted in James Boswell, *Everybody's Boswell: Being the Life of Samuel Johnson*, ed. Frank Morley [London: Bell & Hyman, 1980], 74).

role for the legislature seems to be lost on those who think of themselves as servants of the interests of their home districts. Moreover, many members of Congress appear drawn to the idea of a political career that is graced by regular appearances on television, enjoyment of the perks of office, and indulgence in the pleasures supplied by those who finance campaigns. More wholesomely, but of not much greater assistance to the public interest, legislators also pursue happy careers attending to the concerns of private and public interest groups focused on single policy issues.

If there are few lawmakers whose ambitions are to be great legislators, paladins of the public interest, then the separation of powers cannot do its work as the vehicle for giving concrete meaning to the public interest. For the separation of powers is designed not only to prevent faction; it is also meant to promote wide-ranging and broad discussion of the appropriate content of the laws. It may not be the case that the greater the number of voices the better, but it almost surely is the case that to have all the voices coming from a single institution with a concomitantly limited set of concerns, history, and tradition is not a good bet for those who want the public interest served. The separation of powers widens the discussion because each branch of government needs the cooperation of others to make laws: the branches *share* power as well as have separate powers. There is then a push toward cooperation among the branches. For a republican government to flourish, we might say, it must have a deliberative core, and for present purposes it is important to see that essential to there being such a core is a legislature that can act as a deliberatively minded interlocutor. Such a body will draw the other branches into deliberative argument: deliberation within the legislature will promote deliberation among the branches.

What will make the legislature work in the ways necessary? Part of the answer is a legislature with a certain kind of leadership. The overwhelming number of lawmakers are not likely to be great statesmen but ordinary people who in the end will act in deliberative ways, if at all, for the same reasons that most people do—because it will be personally rewarding to do so. These lawmakers will, in significant part, be self-interested. But, for many, their self-interest is unlikely to be narrowly understood, and will thus probably include a desire to be held in esteem by their colleagues for exhibiting knowledge of public matters and a concern for the public interest. In addition, lawmakers will likely be motivated by fear of being exposed by their legislative adversaries as ignorant and in the pocket of special interests. Lawmakers will find satisfaction in the prospect of political advancement that comes with a reputation for being devoted to the public interest and knowledgeable about public affairs.[35] Moreover, some lawmakers will harbor a deep and abiding desire to be

---

[35] Cf. John Locke's comment that "Esteem and Disgrace are, of all others, the most powerful Incentives of Mind, when once it is brought to Relish them." John Locke, *Some Thoughts Concerning Education*, 1693, ed. John W. Yolton and Jean S. Yolton (Oxford: Clarendon Press, 1989), sec. 56.

famous, to go down in the history of the country as a lawmaker of great distinction who was devoted to the well-being of its citizenry.[36] As Gouverneur Morris, a signer of the U.S. Constitution, put it, "The love of fame is the great spring to noble and illustrious actions."[37] It is in the motives just canvassed that part of the hope for deliberative ways of lawmaking lies. For these motives can be built upon and extended in ways that bring lawmakers to a regular concern for the public interest. The legislature as an institution can teach. The motives of the pupils can be harnessed, and the legislature can become a school for learning the arts of deliberative lawmaking.[38]

To be sure, as I will argue below, something more must be present than pupils who come to the legislative school with motives of self-interest and ambition if the legislature as school is to succeed. Surely, if the legislature does not have the right pupils, it will ultimately fail in its teaching. But just as important, it cannot be the proper sort of school without the right teachers—both to build on the motives just described and to foster inclinations toward public-spiritedness on the part of lawmakers, if they are elected by a citizenry similarly inclined. Who then might the teachers be? Not surprisingly, they will be legislative leaders who are willing to organize a legislature that encourages a deliberative concern with the public interest. These leaders will include, most notably, those who hold its formal positions of leadership, such as majority leader and committee chairs. But informal leaders who have reputations for knowing how the business of legislation works and should work will also be important. A legislature that is more or less entirely composed of abject mediocrities, that is, one lacking such leadership, cannot by some hidden hand miraculously turn itself into a lawmaking body of great distinction. John Stuart Mill tartly remarked in this regard that

> a school of legislative capacity is worthless, and a school for evil, instead of good, if through want . . . of the presence within itself of a higher order of character, the action of the body is allowed, as it so often is, to degenerate into an equally unscrupulous and stupid pursuit of self-interest of its members.[39]

What will attract persons of great ambition and competence to pursue their ambitions through a political life anchored in leading the legisla-

---

[36] For a classic account of such motives as they applied to the framers of the Constitution, see Douglass Adair, "Fame and the Founding Fathers," in Douglass Adair, *Fame and the Founding Fathers*, ed. Trevor Colburn (Indianapolis, IN: Liberty Fund, 1998).

[37] As quoted in James Madison, *Notes of Debates in the Federal Convention of 1787* (1840; reprint, with an introduction by Adrienne Koch, Athens, OH: 1966), 323.

[38] See the marvelous discussion by William K. Muir, Jr., in his *Legislature: California's School for Politics* (Chicago, IL: University of Chicago Press, 1982).

[39] John Stuart Mill, *Considerations on Representative Government* (1861), in John Gray, ed., *On Liberty and Other Essays* (Oxford: Oxford University Press, 1991), 417.

ture? What will dispose them to see politics as a place where things can be done that will win them lasting acclaim? Why will they give up a quiet life of large offices and staffs, modest prestige, and modest power for the rigors of leadership? The work of a leader in a deliberatively minded legislature will bring with it fame, but not necessarily in a day-to-day way, and probably not of a kind that will make the leader an attractive companion for movie stars and pop singers. Otherwise said, legislative leaders in a republican regime must see the connection between their own ambitions and a great and powerful role for the legislature in carrying on the business of republican government. Lackeys of presidents are comparatively easy to come by.

Again, what might prompt the ambitious and the competent to undertake the burdens of leadership? The answer—leaving aside for the moment any inclination of the citizenry to elect public-spirited lawmakers—is likely to be a heightened form of what motivates ordinary lawmakers to consider moving beyond the narrow interests of their constituents and their own self-regarding desires. A prospective leader wishes for the fame that goes along with having a reputation for being a great lawmaker. Therefore, if there are to be leaders who will work to create a legislative school, then it must at least be possible for persons of high ambition to realize their desire for widespread public esteem through a career running the legislature. If the organization of the legislature and the manner of choosing its members is such that even those with the greatest concern for the public interest cannot expect to shape the legislature into a mighty engine of the public interest, then persons with the requisite appetite for fame will look elsewhere—and the legislature will be dominated by nonentities and by those whose appetite for fame requires no more than holding public office. The ambitious and the talented are no different from their more ordinary counterparts. They are more or less rational and are unlikely to waste their energies in fruitless pursuits. To realize their ambitions, therefore, those who wish to be great legislative leaders will need the help of a substantial proportion of their colleagues—and it must be possible to gain this help without enormous cost. This will depend, in significant part, on what kind of people are elected to the legislature, a matter I will turn to in a moment. But first, something must be said about what legislative leaders who wish to promote deliberative lawmaking must do in order to make the legislature work as a school that teaches and reinforces the arts of legislating by deliberating.

As I suggested at the outset of Section II, a deliberatively minded legislature is not a big debating society in which legislators assemble in a large room, and those who wish to persuade the body of lawmakers of the rightness of their views employ rhetorical devices to carry the day. If the legislature is to do the work of deliberating about the public interest, it must be able to build on a good deal of careful argument and analysis of information. A debating society is one of the least likely forms of organization to accomplish much of anything, except to hone the skills of debaters and to provide either delight or boredom for their audience.[40] How, then, shall the legislature be organized?

Of fundamental importance, leaders must devise ways for those with the inclination to enlarge their purview and that of their constituents to do so without being punished at election-time or in public opinion polls. Leaders must also find ways to reward such lawmakers both inside and outside the legislature. Their rewards inside will include positions of influence in the legislative organization and attention to the projects that are closest to the hearts of these lawmakers' constituents. Outside of the legislature, leaders must look for ways to emphasize that these lawmakers are persons of integrity and acumen who deserve seats at the tables of the momentarily mighty. Meaningful opportunities to appear in the public eye in ways that will please the folks back home are also important. Lawmakers must be given the opportunity to be *seen* to deliberate. To some degree, however, this is in tension with actual deliberation, since deliberation cannot usefully be done through the whole chamber meeting in floor debate. Thus, the real task of leaders is to ensure that deliberation occurs in committees, where it will be both easier to prompt and more fruitful in result, and to make the course and outcome of such deliberation widely available to anyone who is willing to pay modest attention. The organization of the legislature must be such as to allow publicity, so that voters may judge the deliberative qualities of their lawmakers and thus reward those who make the effort. But this must be accomplished without making it impossible for lawmakers to move beyond their initial commitments to their constituents insofar as these reflect relatively narrow and particular interests.

How might all this be done? Among other things, a leader must be adept at sounding out the views of members of the legislative body. This means listening carefully, trying to see where each lawmaker feels strongly, particularly where his or her views are based on a strong grasp of the matter at hand. Where they are not—perhaps the lawmaker does not care very much, or he or she does care but the opinion is rooted in very little information—the leader may present arguments and data. Or, more likely, the leader will facilitate contact with someone who may convince the lawmaker of the error of his or her ways. ("See Jones, she's a genius at this stuff and she will set you straight.") The leader may also give the member a reading of support for his or her position as an exercise in backbone-strengthening if the legislator is fearful of being too far out in front of popular opinion. Probably most important of all, the leader will convene those who seem to be the most articulate and persuasive advocates of a viewpoint, and who also show some affinity for one another, and get

---

[40] Consider here the British House of Commons: its debates are fun to watch, but no one supposes that much in the way of lawmaking is actually going on.

them to argue out a common position.[41] The leader will then dispatch these advocates to other legislators to teach them the merits of the proposed legislation.

The leaders—now with the help of friends of the bill—will also spend a good deal of time arguing to the faint of heart that they need to show courage, that they will be widely admired for taking a stand, that they will go down in history, and, if necessary, their pet projects will be given loving attention. Making good law requires patience and hard work. The heart of it is a process by which those with broad vision talk to one another and find ways to bring along enough of their colleagues of fainter heart, more limited purview, and tight political situations at home in order to push the legislation through its various stages. The crucial thing in all of this is that the leadership and its helpers run the legislature in such a manner that there are incentives for doing the hard work of making good law, including listening to arguments, offering concrete suggestions for amendments to those who are worried about a bill, and so forth. In short, the legislature must be an elaborate system for rewarding those who work at lawmaking—as compared to those who work at getting on television, doing the bidding of powerful constituents and campaign contributors, or sitting in their offices admiring the look of the pictures on the walls.

Leaders who can manage all of this over time—and who have built up a stable of lawmakers who are willing and able to take the lead on specific pieces of legislation—will develop an aura about them. They can be trusted; they should not be double-crossed; they should be fought with only when something of great moment is at stake and there is no way out; and they should be applauded in public as great lawmakers on whose shoulders others are willing to stand.

Can we expect such leaders to be in evidence? If what is required is a deep and sophisticated grasp of the public interest—call people who have such a talent 'statesmen'—then Madison gave the answer long ago. We probably cannot do without them, but we cannot build a regime around their regular and continuing presence either.[42] But lesser mortals may well be enough, since all that leaders will probably need beyond the kind of ambition that I have sketched, which is unlikely to be rare, is some sense that there *is* a public interest and some interest in discerning its contours. This they can have, if what they learn in school, imbibe from the common culture, and read in the newspaper does not regularly convince

---

[41] The bill "will be amended by its friends," as Jefferson said. See Edwin Haefele, "Toward a New Civic Calculus," in Lowdon Wingo and Alan Evans, eds., *Public Economics and the Quality of Life* (Baltimore, MD: Johns Hopkins University Press, 1977). Haefele is quoting Thomas Jefferson, *A Manual of Parliamentary Practice*, in Wilbur Samuel Howell, ed., *Jefferson's Parliamentary Writings*, 2d ser. (Princeton, NJ: Princeton University Press, 1988), 353 *ad passim*.

[42] See *Federalist No. 10* (J. Madison), in Rossiter, ed., *The Federalist Papers*, 80.

them that they are chumps to believe in any such thing. It would, of course, be even better if all leaders were statesmen, but, again, fortune is unlikely to be so bountiful. Still, if there are to be regular displays of deliberative lawmaking, the odds need to be high for the emergence of leaders of the kind that I have just described. What forces must be at work for this to happen? Similarly, if the leaders of the legislature are to succeed, they will need, as I have suggested, a significant number of lawmakers who share their inclinations, colleagues who will take on a part of the burden of crafting legislation. What will increase the odds that there will be many of this sort of lawmaker? Of critical importance is a citizenry attentive to whether there is deliberative lawmaking in the public interest.

C. A public-spirited citizenry: The third condition

However unsettling the thought, the citizens of a commercial republic must be, in their own way, as capable as its lawmakers. A republic will stand or fall on the qualities of its citizens. They must have a significant measure of public-spiritedness. Even the best legislative school cannot overcome the problems presented by a large contingent of legislators who are without talent and without concern for broad interests. No amount of institutional contrivance can overcome a citizenry that regularly chooses for office time-serving, self-interested mediocrities who lack "due acquaintance with the objects and principles of legislation."[43] If there is to be deliberative lawmaking, then there must be processes at work that foster a citizenry with the ability to judge which legislators will be up to republican lawmaking. The citizens of a republican regime must have the experience of deliberating and struggling over the content of the public interest themselves if they are to judge the inclinations and capacities of their lawmakers. There is, however, good reason to suppose that the ability to make the necessary judgments about lawmakers is not to be found widely distributed among citizens in the absence of experiences that promote it.

Public-spiritedness is a disposition to give significant weight to the public interest. It consists of the not very demanding belief that there is a public interest and that political life should at least partly revolve around an effort to give it concrete meaning. A principal expression of public-spiritedness is the inclination to judge lawmakers by whether they show both a concern for the public interest and its necessary corollary, deliberative ways of lawmaking. If voters cannot make such judgments, then lawmakers will easily recognize that as long as they *say* they are concerned with the public interest, despite providing little evidence of wanting to reason about its content, the avowal alone will do the trick: voters will not be able to tell a huckster from a good lawmaker.

---

[43] *Federalist No. 62* (J. Madison), 379.

The citizenry of a republican regime will likely have some measure of public-spiritedness as a result of living in a free society with free political institutions. But this measure is likely to be insufficient. Where shall we look to foster this spirit? John Stuart Mill provides one important answer, namely, that "free and popular local and municipal institutions" are part of "the peculiar training of a citizen, the practical part of the political education of a free people." [44] Mill's formulation suggests that local politics affords an opportunity for citizens to consider a wide range of public matters, and thus to develop the skills and outlook necessary to be effective participants in the larger political life of the regime. We may say that local political life can help to form the character of the citizenry. Again, it is in the combination of the legislature as school and the capacities for judgment by the citizenry that the hope for deliberative lawmaking lies. To this we can now add that these capacities can be developed in local political life.

Properly structured, local government makes plain that there is no easy escape from our fellow citizens. They are in close enough proximity so that their travails and successes become ours to some degree. If even the most powerful and lucky among us cannot insulate themselves by creating through legal walls their own enclaves, then the message that we are all in this together—that there is something more than the interests of me and mine, that there is a common or public interest—becomes not an abstraction, but a fact of everyday life. A nation, or even a state or region within it, is too big to make this point in any concrete and regular way. And when the point is made in these larger contexts, the ability to respond to it is impeded by the sheer size and complexity of the larger political system. Local government is also the only context in which (1) matters of direct and compelling interest to the mass of citizens are decided and the interconnections among them not easily dismissed, (2) the skills can be honed for weighing up the claims of various interests in light of the larger interests of the local community, and (3) the citizens' ability to judge those who claim that they are speaking in the public interest can be sharpened.

If citizens of a republican regime are to make such judgments of the inclinations and capacities of their lawmakers, then an essential feature of local government must be that it affords citizens the experience of deliberating and struggling over the content of the public interest. They must have some firsthand experience of trying to answer the question, What is the public interest in this case? Since this is always a complicated matter to assess, and the incentive on the part of present and aspiring lawmakers to dissimulate will be great, without experience the citizenry will be easily misled. As V. S. Naipul says, "When men cannot observe they don't

---

[44] John Stuart Mill, *On Liberty*, ed. Gertrude Himmelfarb (1859; reprint, London: Penguin Books, 1982), 181.

have ideas: they have obsessions."[45] If we substitute "participate in deliberative processes" for "observe," the possibility for mischief and worse is apparent. Walter Lippmann simply said that "the kind of self-education which a self-governing people must obtain can only be had through its daily experience."[46]

Tocqueville summed up the crucial point about the relation between local political life and republican government when he argued that the most powerful way, and perhaps the only way, in which to interest men in their country's fate is to make them take a share in its government.[47] We may extend the thought by saying that for citizens to have any concern for the public interest of the regime, they must have the experience of grappling with its elements. For any significant number of citizens this can only happen through local political life.

What must local political institutions look like? I have suggested that, first and foremost, local political institutions must place citizens in relation to one another as deliberators, as people who think that a crucial feature in decisions about public choices is the giving of reasons. Where possible, the making of public choices should elicit arguments about what is beneficial to the members of the community, and not just reflect the summation of wants and interests. It follows that local political institutions must be relatively open in their operations and participative, because each citizen must be a prospective deliberator. In a word, local political institutions must be heavily legislative in form.

However, it is one thing to say that institutions must emphasize deliberation and reason-giving, but quite another to get them actually to work in this way. They are, after all, not bits of machinery but forms of human interaction, and so we must consider what kinds of motives need to be at work if these institutions are to function in the desired ways. In the context of a commercial republic, we must look to the harnessing of powerful private motives, as against some abstract concern for the public good. Thus, for ordinary citizens, political argument about the public interest must concern things such as neighborhood matters, schools, the land use patterns of their localities, and public safety. Most citizens are

---

[45] Quoted in Roger Shattuck, "The Reddening of America," *New York Review of Books*, March 30, 1989, 5.

[46] Walter Lippmann, *The Good Society* (Boston, MA: Little, Brown, 1943), 263.

[47] See Alexis de Tocqueville, *Democracy in America*, ed. J. P. Mayer, trans. George Lawrence (Garden City, NY: Anchor Books, 1969), vol. 1, chap. 5. See also Stephen Elkin, *City and Regime in the American Republic* (Chicago, IL: University of Chicago Press, 1987), especially chap. 6. Mill says that without the habits of mind learned through participation in local political life—specifically the inclination to act from "public or semi-public motives"—a "free constitution can neither be worked or preserved." Mill, *On Liberty*, 181. Tocqueville also said that "municipal institutions constitute the strength of free nations. Town meetings are to liberty what primary schools are to science: they bring it within the people's reach, they teach men how to use and enjoy it. A nation may establish a free government, but without municipal institutions it cannot have the spirit of liberty." Tocqueville, *Democracy in America*, vol. 1, chap. 5.

unlikely to accept that something is in the public interest unless it is connected to their private interest. Under free, popular government, there probably cannot be any other starting point in public matters than my interest in my own safety and well-being and that of those dearest to me. What would make a free citizen start from any other place, at least in noncalamitous times? It is from such natural concerns that a conception of the public interest must grow, and it is from such motives that citizens participate in local politics. Anything else is very likely cant and will be widely seen to be so. As J. A. W. Gunn writes, "[T]he raw materials for discovering the public interests are the concerns of private men as understood by those men themselves."[48]

If they are to be public-spirited, citizens must find it a reasonable use of their time to engage in a politics that broadens their concerns by fostering deliberation. The arena must be one that deals with some of their most important day-to-day concerns and that is not so large as to be, on its face, irrational for most people to participate in—hence the importance of local political life. Nor should this be surprising since it is in localities that most of us carry on much of the activity that is central to our lives. Some people may be able to live with little or no concern about what happens in their local communities. Their children go to private school someplace else; their work takes place in cyberspace; and their homes are protected by private security measures. They in effect wall themselves off from their neighbors. But most of us still live without such walls, in the old-fashioned way. What rolls up to our door, what happens around the corner, and what occurs in other parts of the community all have direct effects on us that we cannot easily escape. Local community life is still sufficiently important to most people so that it can provide the foundation for a public-spirited citizenship.

One key to the design of republican local politics, then, is a set of institutional arrangements that can harness the citizens' concern for promoting their own good and for securing their own interests in matters that concern their neighborhoods and schools.[49] Private interests will be used to draw citizens into local decision-making, and these interests can be stretched through a deliberative politics that has as its principal concern the attempt to answer the broad questions of the public interest. Citizens will be drawn into a process in which they will have to do more than argue that some proposal is beneficial to them or to people like them. They will have to give reasons.

[48] J. A. W. Gunn, *Politics and the Public Interest in the Seventeenth Century* (Toronto: Routledge & K. Paul/University of Toronto Press, 1969), 139–40.

[49] William James once commented that one of the secrets of popular government was to ensure that "common habits [are] carried into public life." Cf. Shelly Burtt's comment that in commercial republican regimes citizens will not "engage in politics for abstractly public reasons." Shelly Burtt, "Virtue Transformed: Republican Argument in Eighteenth Century England," unpublished ms, 1992, chap. 7, p. 21. See also Shelly Burtt, "The Politics of Virtue Today: A Critique and a Proposal," *American Political Science Review* 87, no. 2 (1993): 360–68.

The story of private interest and its relation to deliberation and the public interest cannot, however, stop here. The collective choice literature teaches that purposes or goals by themselves are unlikely to be sufficient motivation, even if they have some direct connection to self-interest.[50] This means that additional motives are necessary to get republican citizens involved in giving content to the public interest. Once again, these motives must be private-regarding. For example, citizens can be drawn to reason-giving and deliberation out of their desire to enjoy the esteem of others. Concern for the esteem of others, as Tocqueville pointed out, is a powerful motive in all popular regimes.[51]

Concern for the esteem of others and a connection to vital day-to-day interests thus are motives that can be harnessed to promote deliberative participation in local political life. Indeed, this is probably the only context in which such private-regarding motives can be systematically employed in ways that will lead citizens to engage in a deliberative politics that will, in turn, make them able to judge the deliberative inclinations of their national lawmakers. If this can be done, then a significant number of citizens will be able to judge how prospective lawmakers talk about public matters. Does the aspiring lawmaker try to make it appear that there are no costs other than monetary ones to major policy proposals, that there is, in short, no conflict among our values such that securing more of one means having less of others? Conversely, does the candidate speak of the public interest as real, thus requiring choices and sacrifices? Candidates who speak about public questions without attending to conflicts among values or the need for sacrifices are likely to be either fools or demagogues, or both. In any case, citizens with experience of a properly constituted local political life will likely know them for what they are. Citizens who have themselves participated in deliberative ways of lawmaking not only will expect to see lawmakers struggling to give concrete definition to the public interest at the local level but will also expect it in national lawmaking. They will expect of their lawmakers what they expect of themselves. Not only will they expect reasoned arguments, but they will be in a position to judge whether they are hearing such arguments. They will act on the first law of social science: it takes one to know one.

III. AN INSTITUTIONAL CONCEPTION OF THE PUBLIC INTEREST

We are now in a position to answer one of my opening questions: Does the substance of deliberation matter in a regime of popular self-government? Or is it enough that the heart of such government is simply

---

[50] Mancur Olson, *The Logic of Collective Action* (Cambridge, MA: Harvard University Press, 1965).

[51] Tocqueville, *Democracy in America*, 1:69.

deliberation, the substance of it being of little importance? My answer should now be apparent. If there is going to be deliberative lawmaking, it must and should concern itself with such substantive matters as controlling faction, keeping open opportunities for ambitious legislative leadership, and encouraging forms of local political life that will foster a public-spirited citizenry. Deliberative lawmaking must have a substantive focus of this kind if it is to survive and flourish. Lawmaking must be reflexive, taking as its subject its own processes and what makes them possible. A political regime that revolves around deliberation must first reason about how to secure and maintain the institutions that make that reasoning possible.[52]

This effort by deliberatively inclined lawmakers to secure deliberative institutions can best be understood as an attempt to serve the public interest. It is an effort to secure an important element in an institutional conception of the public interest. Such lawmaking is aimed at securing and maintaining the deliberative institutions that help to constitute the political order and give it its characteristic manner of working. Deliberative lawmaking, then, must have as its central concern a substantive public interest. Thus, to say that deliberative lawmaking should concern itself with the public interest is not an empty phrase—as it often is in discussions of deliberative lawmaking where it is meant only to reinforce the idea that lawmaking should not concern itself with group interests or simply be an exercise of political power. Instead, my point, again, is the reflexive one. For deliberative lawmaking to exist, it must concern itself with particular substantive matters, namely, those things that help to secure and maintain deliberative lawmaking itself. There is a public interest, and lawmaking must concern itself with it.

An important advantage of this kind of institutional conception of the public interest is that it enables us to make sense of the common intuition that politics is less about getting to some destination than about how we stand in relation to others wherever we are going. Many political observers sense that defining particular destinations for a whole society is difficult to do: the world is too uncertain and we differ too much to agree on anything very detailed. What seems more important is that we are related to one another in durable and attractive ways. Such a view also draws on a deep sense on the part of many people living in liberal societies that too much insistence that we must seek to secure shared social purposes undercuts liberty: individuals should be the principal holders of purposes. An institutional focus also draws upon the sense that society-wide planning has been shown to be very unattractive and unmanageable: after all,

---

[52] Since by definition this is a bootstrap operation, there is the question of how things get started in the first place and how each step reinforces the preceding one, that is, how increasing attention being given to securing deliberative institutions increases the ability of the legislative process to think about these same matters. For a discussion of this and related questions, see Elkin, *Constituting the American Republic*, chaps. 8 and 9.

if there really is a public interest composed of a comprehensive set of particular social ends, then our politics should be an exercise in planning to serve those ends. But it is precisely this we cannot do and should not attempt.[53]

In similar fashion, an institutional conception of the public interest does not carry the divisive freight of a morally insistent conception of the ends of politics and their relation to the good life. As many have argued, we are unlikely to agree much about such matters, given our ethnic, religious, and racial lines of division. The "substance" of the public interest as I have set it out is, in fact, largely procedural, focused as it is on securing institutional forms through which a variety of purposes may be sought. Being procedural in this sense, the public interest is more likely to be widely accepted.[54]

Finally, an institutional view of the public interest makes sense of the idea that, if we desire a certain political way of life, then we must put a good deal of effort into creating and maintaining the institutions at its core. Something as complex as a political way of life is unlikely to come into being by itself, and it is not very likely that it will maintain itself through its ordinary, nonlegislative institutional workings. If we value a regime, we must value the efforts of lawmakers to secure its crucial institutions, which is to say we must have a conception of the public interest. Not to value these efforts is to belie our commitment to that regime, and to render ourselves foolish and feckless.

A similar institutional conception of the public interest has been offered by Samuel Huntington, Bernard Crick, and John Finnis. Huntington comments that "the capacity to create political institutions is the capacity to create public interests."[55] Crick says that the public interest is simply a way of "describing the common interest in preserving the means of making public decisions politically."[56] Finnis, more cumbersomely, defines the public interest (which he terms "the common good") as a set of conditions that "enables the members of a community to attain for them-

[53] See, most notably, David Braybrooke and Charles E. Lindblom, *A Strategy of Decision: Policy Evaluation As a Social Process* (New York: Free Press of Glencoe, 1963); Charles E. Lindblom, *Politics and Markets: The World's Political Economic Systems* (New York: Basic Books, 1977); Friedrich A. Hayek, *The Road to Serfdom* (London: G. Routledge & Sons, 1944); and Friedrich A. Hayek, *Law, Legislation, and Liberty*, vol. 2, *The Mirage of Social Justice* (Chicago, IL: University of Chicago Press, 1978), 1–100.

[54] See Bruce Ackerman, *We the People* (Cambridge, MA: Harvard University Press, 1991), esp. chaps. 1 and 2; and John Rawls, *Political Liberalism* (New York: Columbia University Press, 1993).

[55] Samuel P. Huntington, *Political Order in Changing Societies* (New Haven, CT: Yale University Press, 1968), 24.

[56] Bernard Crick, *In Defense of Politics* (New York: Penguin, 1964), 177. By making decisions "politically" Crick means employing a form of nonviolent political rule in societies where a large variety of wills must be concerted. The concerting of those wills in a nonviolent fashion is the essential political act. See also Robert Dahl's discussion of the public interest in *Democracy and Its Critics* (New Haven, CT: Yale University Press, 1991), chap. 21.

selves reasonable objectives, or to realize reasonably for themselves the value(s), for the sake of which they have reason to collaborate with each other . . . in a community."[57]

It would be odd indeed if something very much like what has just been described were not the public interest of a good political regime. If the regime is good, so must be the institutions that give it its character. To wish for one is to wish for the other. It would be equally odd if regimes did not have any public interest: what it takes to realize a good regime is surely its public interest, and thus all good regimes must have one.

Deliberative lawmaking is essential, then, not in and of itself, but because it provides the possibility of giving concrete meaning to the public interest—which is to say, of working out how to secure and maintain the constitutive institutions that make the regime what it is. Deliberation is not intrinsically valuable in a design for republican government. It is instead necessary to republican government because it is the best way to do something, namely, to give concrete meaning to the public interest. The test of republican government, then, is not whether there is deliberation, but whether the public interest is served.

Given that deliberative lawmaking must concern itself with serving an institutionally defined public interest, what will increase the odds that deliberation will occur? After all, deliberating about such complex matters is costly, while the benefits of deliberative lawmaking in the form of a flourishing regime of popular self-government are long term and diffuse. To this we may add that deliberative lawmaking makes it more difficult for powerful groups to serve their interests. Public discussion characterized by extensive reasoning is likely to expose the self-interest that powerful actors are anxious to hide and, given their power, would plausibly be able to serve if there were no deliberative lawmaking. Thus, if there is to be deliberative lawmaking concerned with securing deliberative institutions, lawmakers will need political support to resist pressures from self-interested actors.

I have already identified some likely sources of support. Public-spirited citizens will not only wish for deliberative lawmaking, but also likely judge their lawmakers on whether they make any effort to strengthen its foundations. Such citizens, in short, will wish for deliberation in the public interest to have a clear purpose, namely, to help constitute a regime where deliberative lawmaking institutions play a central role. We may doubt whether this will be sufficient, but rather than pursuing this question further, it will be more useful to consider what else deliberative lawmaking must focus on, and from where political support for such a focus might come.

---

[57] John Finnis, *Natural Law and Natural Rights* (Oxford: Oxford University Press, 1980), 155.

IV. The Social Basis of the Regime

If there is to be deliberative lawmaking, it must not only be concerned with strengthening the "political" foundations of public deliberation— preventing faction, making it possible for legislative leaders to promote deliberation, fostering a public-spirited citizenry, and so forth. It must also have "economic" concerns: in particular, whether the citizens have sufficient economic independence and security, as well as that measure of economic equality that is necessary if they are to be public-spirited. People who are seriously worried about surviving economically and who, because of gross economic inequality, think of themselves as subordinates in some kind of hierarchy are unlikely to take a great interest in public affairs. Nor are such people likely to think that they have a right to do so. They are also unlikely to feel confident that they can hold lawmakers accountable to any standard, including that of a deliberative engagement with the public interest.

Some proponents of democratic deliberation have looked to a form of socialized ownership of property as the best and, perhaps, the only way to provide the economic foundations for deliberation.[58] This is not the place to settle the debate over what kind of system of ownership of capital would best serve deliberative lawmaking. Since we are discussing the United States, I will simply stipulate that Americans aspire to realize a *commercial* republic, that is, one whose economic base consists of a significant measure of private ownership of large-scale productive assets.[59] If I am wrong here, and Americans aspire or ought to aspire to some socialized form of ownership, the character of the problem for deliberative theorists remains the same: lawmaking will still have to maintain a set of economic institutions that help make deliberative lawmaking possible, in this case institutions of socialized ownership.

With this stipulation in mind, we can say that deliberative lawmaking, in its concern for the public interest—that is, in its aim to maintain institutions that give life to deliberation itself—must look at the organization and results of productive life. How successfully it does so will substantially affect the possibility of deliberative lawmaking. What will make this focus probable in light of the likelihood that pressure from a public-spirited citizenry to attend to these matters will not be sufficient?

Again, Madison is helpful. While he gives a good deal of weight to institutional contrivances—valuing them over the "parchment barriers" of a written constitution—Madison also holds that the regime must have a foundation in self-interest. This means, for Madison, to begin with, that self-interest is to be checked by self-interest as multiple and competing interests would be drawn into the complex and divided machinery of

---

[58] David Miller, *Market, State, and Community: Theoretical Foundations of Market Socialism* (Oxford: Oxford University Press, 1990).

[59] See Elkin, *Constituting the American Republic*, chap. 1.

government in such a fashion that each would check the other. In addition, Madison understands that a regime is a set of institutions harnessed to the realization of a certain conception of justice, and that this conception must at least be consistent with the one held by the most powerful social strata of the regime.[60]

Madison himself looks to the self-interest of the propertied class to provide the foundation for the regime's operation. The political activities of this class would increase the odds that what he calls the permanent interests of the regime would be given due attention.[61] The design of government is meant not only to protect property rights, but also to have institutions so arranged that men of property will have political advantages in the struggle to define the content of the laws. Moreover, the design will provide incentives for the propertied to broaden their conception of their own interests so that there will be an overlap between their interests and the permanent or public interest. Thus, there will be two principal sources of energy in this new government: nonfactional majorities and a propertied class with broad interests.

Madison therefore believes that the propertied class can be relied upon to play a crucial role in giving concrete meaning to the public interest. Perhaps not all men of property will be equally disposed to have their self-interest broadened; still, many might, including, most notably, those of landed property. He thinks that public-spirited majorities will give government some of the needed energy, but doubts that the concerns of temporary majorities would be sufficient to keep lawmaking on the path of securing all rights and the permanent interests of the community. To shape lawmaking in this fashion, Madison relies heavily on the possibility that through a combination of the private interests of the propertied in seeing that property is secure and their holdings increased, and through institutional design, the propertied might be induced to look further than the narrowest conception of their interests, and in doing so be instrumental in giving direction to government.

However, it is unlikely, certainly at present, that the propertied have any deep and abiding interest in promoting through legislation the economic security, economic independence, and (a modest degree of) equality of the less well off. Each policy would undercut the material interests of the propertied: economic security would drive up wages as labor mobility decreased; economically independent workers could more easily

---

[60] For more discussion of this point, see Elkin, *Constituting the American Republic*, chap. 6.

[61] For a very useful discussion on this point—a discussion I have learned much from—see Jennifer Nedelsky, *Private Property and the Limits of American Constitutionalism: The Madisonian Framework and Its Legacy* (Chicago, IL: University of Chicago Press, 1990), esp. chaps. 2 and 5. See also Lance Banning, *The Sacred Fire of Liberty: James Madison and the Founding of the Federal Republic* (Ithaca, NY: Cornell University Press, 1995), 83–84. Hamilton said (in *Federalist No. 35*, p. 216) that "the representative body, with too few exceptions to have any influence on the spirit of the government, will be composed of landholders, merchants, and men of the learned professions."

organize to gain various perquisites from owners, not least of which would be higher wages; and a measure of equality would likely mean a more politically active citizenry, thus reducing the political influence of the propertied. In short, the propertied are unlikely to be a reliable source of support for the economic foundations of deliberative lawmaking. Indeed, the political advantages that the Madisonian constitution gives to the propertied make it likely that they will be regularly successful in defending their interests. We need to look elsewhere for a major stratum or class whose self-interest would lead it to support efforts aimed at strengthening the economic foundations of deliberative lawmaking. There is reason to suppose that a secure and confident middle class might do the job,[62] but enough has been said to indicate the importance of the whole problem. It is unlikely that public deliberation can flourish without an overlap between the self-interest of a class or stratum and the economic underpinnings needed for deliberative lawmaking. Thus, we must look to divisions within society, even if on other grounds they might be objectionable. Class and social stratification generally are perhaps not desirable for their own sake, but they probably are ineluctable, and, it would seem, highly useful in creating a self-governing, deliberative regime.

V. The State of Deliberative Theory

Where does all this leave us with regard to deliberative theory? Two conclusions stand out, each pointing to a significant weakness in much deliberative theory.

First, while there is possibly a case to be made for deliberation as such, it must be part of a larger argument that distinguishes between deliberation focused on securing the constitutive institutional foundations of a regime of popular self-government—its public interest—and deliberation concerned with other matters. The first is preeminent: any case for deliberation as such must be subordinated to the one concerning the need for deliberation to secure and maintain constitutive institutions. There cannot be general deliberation without there also being deliberation reflexively aimed at strengthening deliberative institutions. This, in turn, means that lawmaking must concern itself with such matters as how to foster a public-spirited citizenry and how to make a citizenry economically secure.

Second, we can now see the importance of morally ambiguous or worse motives—and the political processes built on them—for sustaining a regime of popular self-government built around deliberation. Harnessing self-interest, political ambition, and the desire to exercise political power, as well as political processes resting on these motives, is crucial to realizing a regime of deliberative lawmaking. Accordingly, a case can be

---

[62] See Elkin, *Constituting the American Republic*, chap. 11.

made that motives such as self-interest, ambition, and the desire to wield power over others are "good." Or, stated differently, a good regime must rest in no small part on morally ambiguous or even bad motives. One task of a political theory concerned with strengthening a deliberative democracy is thus to praise these morally ambiguous or worse motives, to show why they must be cultivated, and to explain how this might be done. We are a long way from much contemporary deliberative theory here—especially the more radical kind that aims at building a whole regime around deliberative lawmaking and keeping to a minimum, or eliminating, other processes and the motives on which they rest. If my argument here is correct, then the road to deliberative lawmaking looks rather different from how it is pictured in much deliberative theory. It is a road by which we attempt to foster much that is at variance with deliberation, with regard both to motives and to political processes. If the American case is indicative, then the multiplication of interests, the ensuing bargaining that makes factional rule less likely, the play of ambition among officeholders, and the exercise of political power by a major social class, are all necessary to achieving a significant measure of deliberative democracy. Certainly, the road does not seem to be the straight and simple one contemplated in many deliberative theories, where all we need is to pile good motives and political processes on top of one another in a kind of orgy of goodness.

Some will accept what I have been arguing here but still insist that instead of making use of such motives as self-interest and ambition, indeed praising and fostering them, we would be better off if we minimized them. Even assuming that it would be wise to attempt to reduce significantly the importance of such motives, what likely would be required to do so? Wouldn't we need to eviscerate the liberty that is one of the foundations of deliberation and one of its fundamental purposes? This would be worse than the problems such motives present for a regime of deliberative democracy; the cure will be worse than the disease.[63]

We may go further. It is now possible to see that a regime built around deliberative lawmaking not only has deep roots in morally ambiguous or worse motives. In addition, it will almost certainly be held together and be widely felt to be legitimate, not only because its laws are the product of reasoning and have a claim to reasonableness, but also because of self-interest and the exercise of power—not least because it is anchored in a particular class.[64] This last point suggests, once again, that the justice at which the regime aims in its efforts to serve the public interest can only be a partial justice, not the full justice that much deliberative theory assumes.

---

[63] Cf. Madison in *Federalist No. 10*, p. 78.

[64] See the discussion below in the text on the problem of stability in Rawls's theory of justice.

It seems clear, then, that if we wish for a deliberative democracy, we should be suspicious of advice to focus our political practice on the cultivation of only good motives and the political processes built on them. The point can be made in a different manner. We will better understand the role of deliberation in popular self-government and how to secure it if we start our theorizing with what might be called the 'circumstances of politics'.[65] The circumstances of politics may be defined as a state of affairs in which there is a large aggregation of people who have conflict-ing purposes that engender more or less serious conflict, who are given to attempts to use political power to further their own purposes and those of people with whom they identify, who are inclined to use political power to subordinate others unlike themselves, and who are sometimes given to words and actions that suggest that they value limiting the use of political power by law and harnessing it to public purposes. We would be better off starting from what might be termed the 'political whole'—to give these circumstances a different name—rather than focusing on the parts of political life that we find attractive, and then implicitly or explic-itly arguing that the key to a good regime of popular self-government lies in expanding these elements as much as possible.

We should start from the circumstances of politics because they define the problem of how we can secure a good political order. We must first prevent the worst before we can achieve the good enough, let alone the best. Any plausible account of human motives will posit that human beings are capable of the grossest cruelty, of a desire to tyrannize over their fellows, and of a whole host of lesser evils. If we do not prevent these motives from being acted upon, then there is little reason to suppose that citizens and those who speak for them will have leeway to pursue even the good enough. This is not only Madison's point, but also the fundamental premise of all liberal theory, and it means that, contrary to Rawls's claim,[66] we do not best grasp the nub of partial compliance theory by focusing on ideal theory. I will turn in a moment to this issue in a more complete way, but here I want to insist that we can best un-derstand partial compliance when we grasp that there can only *be* partial compliance, and that what we need to do to achieve even this modest state of affairs is daunting. Thus, Madison teaches that we cannot have republican government if it is necessary that men act like angels.[67] The circumstances of politics are, to an important degree, irremediable, and

---

[65] Quite independently, Jeremy Waldron has arrived at much the same conclusion, even to the use of the term the 'circumstances of politics'. See Jeremy Waldron, *The Dignity of Legislation* (New York: Cambridge University Press, 1999), 49 and 154.

[66] I do not mean to say here that Rawls was not a liberal. He was and certainly thought of himself as one, not least because his first principle of justice concerns the securing of rights. But his attachment to ideal theory made it difficult for him, and for those who follow his lead, to see the way in which starting from preventing the worst calls into question his theory of justice. I will say more about this in the next section, where I discuss the costs of doing ideal theory.

[67] *Federalist No. 51* (J. Madison), in Rossiter, ed., *The Federalist Papers*, 322.

our account of good political regimes should be tempered by this knowledge. We either build our institutions upon reliable and plausible motives or they will fail—and with them, our hopes for realizing an attractive political order.

More generally, we can say that the road to the good regime probably does not coincide with the road to the ideal regime, as a kind of stop along the way. This is, in fact, the point behind the theory of the second best,[68] and behind the phrase "the best is the enemy of the good." Thus, the pursuit of the ideal, which is by definition beyond us, may bring out the worst in us: consider the political consequences of some of humankind's efforts to find unity with God. Moreover, effort expended on the ideal is effort lost to seeking the good enough. Additionally, pursuit of the ideal, which *must* fail, is also likely to be dispiriting.

Finally, and most important for the present discussion, if we shape institutions with an eye to moving toward the ideal, then there is little reason to suppose that these institutions will be of much use in securing a good regime, which is, in fact, all we can hope to achieve. With a little exaggeration, we can say that the ideal is something best avoided in attempting to constitute an attractive political life.[69] The task of a political constitution is to take what cannot be changed—or changed only at prohibitive cost—and make the best of it. We need ideals to help us identify the various kinds of good regimes, but we also need to have our political constructions informed by a clear-eyed understanding of the circumstances in which we are going to carve out our constitution. Getting our ideals clear will not solve the political problem.[70]

VI. IDEAL THEORY

Insofar as deliberative theorists work by laying aside morally ambiguous motives and processes, they are engaged in ideal theory. If ideal theory has significant weaknesses, then this is important in its own right,

---

[68] R. Lipsey and K. Lancaster, "The General Theory of the Second Best," *Review of Economic Studies* 24, no. 1 (1956): 11–32.

[69] Cf. David Hume's comment:

> Here, I would frankly declare, that though liberty be preferable to slavery, in almost every case; yet I should rather wish to see an absolute monarch than a republic in this island. For let us consider what kind of republic we have reason to expect. The question is not concerning any fine imaginary republic of which a man forms a plan in his closet. There is no doubt but a popular government may be imagined more perfect than an absolute monarchy, or even than our present constitution. But what reason have we to expect that any such government will ever be established in Great Britain, upon the dissolution of our monarchy?

David Hume, *Essays Moral and Political*, ed. Eugene F. Miller (Indianapolis, IN: Liberty Fund, 1987), 66. I owe this citation to Peter Levine.

[70] Cf. David Schaefer's comment: "One can say that Rawls's conception of political philosophy is the mirror image of modern positivistic social science: whereas the latter aspires to be value-free, the former is fact-free." David Schaefer, *Justice or Tyranny?: A Critique of John Rawls's "Theory of Justice"* (Port Washington, NY: Kennikat Press, 1979), 85.

but it also points to deep difficulties for deliberative theorists who look to ideal theory as the prototype of the kind of political theory that they are doing.

As is well known, Rawls, the principal proponent of ideal theory, offers a theory of justice anchored in an account of the organizing principles for a whole society that rational people would choose if they made their choices behind what he calls the "veil of ignorance." Behind this veil, people do not know what their position will be in a society designed to serve these principles. The rest of the theory is devoted to developing the implications of what Rawls calls these principles of justice for the organization of various important elements of a society. Rawls sees this effort as an exercise in ideal theory; that is, his concern is with "the form a just society would take in a world in which, for theoretical purposes, everyone is presumed to act justly."[71] As Rawls puts it, ideal theory assumes

> that (nearly) everyone strictly complies with . . . the principles of justice. We ask in effect what a perfectly just . . . constitutional regime might be like, and whether it may come about and be made stable . . . under realistic, though reasonably favorable, conditions. . . . [J]ustice as fairness is realistically utopian . . . [that is, it concerns] how far in our world (given its laws and tendencies) a democratic regime can attain complete realization of its appropriate political values.[72]

These reasonably favorable conditions are what Rawls terms "the circumstances of justice." These are features of the social world that those choosing the principles of justice behind the veil of ignorance will know. These features include the following: that this world makes cooperation possible and necessary, that individuals are roughly similar in physical and mental powers, that they have conflicting claims on the resources available, and that there is moderate scarcity. In the circumstances of justice there is a veil of ignorance and no problem of compliance once the con-

---

[71] Ian Carter, "A Critique of Freedom as Non-Domination," *The Good Society* 9, no. 3 (1999): 43–46. Cf. Jeremy Waldron's view, as quoted by Ferdinand Mount, that the question Rawls poses is, "[W]hat would institutions look like if they were designed by people who were already agreed on a set of principles of justice?" Mount goes on to say that Waldron "argues fiercely . . . that this isn't an interesting question. If such an agreement existed already or could come after exhaustive deliberation, then political institutions would soon become fairly unimportant 'dealing as they would with only minor or technical matters'." Ferdinand Mount, "Against Smoothness," *Times Literary Supplement*, September 24, 1999; reviewing Waldron, *The Dignity of Legislation*. For Waldron's criticism of Rawls in this book, see especially 70–73. Waldron notes that he has "found it extremely difficult to persuade colleagues to reproduce, or at least recognize, *within* their philosophical theories of politics, law and constitutionalism, the existence and significance" of controversies about fundamental political matters (49). Cf. Michael Zuckert's comment that Locke saw that "the conditions for the existence of rights . . . and the conditions for effectual securing of rights are not the same." Michael P. Zuckert, *Launching Liberalism: On Lockean Political Philosophy* (Lawrence: University Press of Kansas, 2002), 328.

[72] John Rawls, *Justice As Fairness: A Restatement*, ed. Erin Kelly (Cambridge, MA: Harvard University Press, Belknap Press, 2001), 13.

tent of justice is known. What is at issue is what a political order should look like among people who are already committed to a common sense of justice. The problem, therefore, is to work out what is contained in this conception of justice and the structure of politics and society that is consistent with it.

Let us suppose that an important aim of political philosophy is to help create the best political regime of which we are capable. This seems to be a view that Rawls shares, as the quotation above indicates. Moreover, Rawls is clear[73] that he is concerned not only with a "strict compliance theory" of justice, where everyone is assumed to act justly, but also with a "partial compliance theory," which concerns "how we are to deal with injustice."[74] Indeed, he says that "the reason for beginning with ideal theory is that it provides the only basis for the systematic grasp of" the "more pressing problems," such as "weighing one form of institutional justice against another"—and he goes on to say that "I shall assume that a deeper understanding can be gained in no other way."[75]

In short, Rawls lays aside morally ambiguous or worse motives and processes and argues that, in doing so, there is no loss in understanding of how to construct a just and stable form of popular self-government. Indeed, there is a possible gain (namely, "a deeper understanding"). My preceding section suggests reasons to doubt this, but we can go further. If we lay aside how deliberative lawmaking is to be brought about, then we also put to one side morally ambiguous motives and processes. In doing so, we are led to misunderstand the role of deliberation in an actual regime of popular self-government, even one of a broadly Rawlsian kind. Similarly, we are unlikely to understand the role that morally ambiguous

---

[73] Rawls, *A Theory of Justice*, 9.

[74] Ibid., 8.

[75] Ibid., 8–9. Whether this can be "assumed" is, in effect, the subject under discussion here. It is worth emphasizing that in *Political Liberalism*, the book that followed *A Theory of Justice*, Rawls still pursues ideal theory. It is easy to mistake Rawls's intention in *Political Liberalism* (see, e.g., his comment on page xvii that the theory of justice in the earlier book is unrealistic), since one of his starting points is that people in a society like the United States will not share a comprehensive philosophical doctrine that leads to a particular conception of justice. A society like the U.S. will be pluralistic, with a variety of comprehensive but reasonable religious, philosophical, and moral doctrines. Rawls's discussion in *Political Liberalism* is not meant to be empirical, however, in the sense of considering, in light of what we know about political behavior, what conception of justice will prove workable. Rather, he is engaged in the same exercise as he was in *A Theory of Justice*, namely, what should a society look like if all its citizens are committed to a particular conception of justice. In *Political Liberalism* Rawls complicates the problem by stipulating the fact of moral and philosophical pluralism. If it can be shown that it is possible that a conception of justice much like "justice as fairness" can emerge in "the best of foreseeable circumstances" (xvii), then we can still go on to ask what the institutions of the society would look like if they were designed by people committed to this conception of justice. Rawls's realism is not the realism of someone wondering whether and how it is possible to create a just society, given people as they are or might plausibly become. The realism, if that is what it is, consists of demonstrating that it is, in principle, possible for a certain conception of justice to be held, given one ineluctable and thus realistic feature of modern democratic societies—their pluralism. There is no claim that people will behave in the stipulated way. Indeed, it is far from clear that they will, or, in fact, even can do so.

and worse motives and processes must play if we are to have such a regime. Thus, we may ask whether Rawls's mode of theorizing makes it more difficult to understand the broadly empirical question of how to make stable a just regime of popular self-government. It is clear that the problem worries him, and is, in fact, a principal reason why he wrote *Political Liberalism*.[76] However, if my argument is correct, then a strong attachment to justice and an overlap of the political principles of the various groups that compose a pluralistic, democratic society—the conditions to which Rawls looks—are not sufficient to create a stable regime (something Rawls would likely agree with). Not only that, but we are traveling the wrong path if our focus is on these factors. Much more likely, it is the morally ambiguous motives and processes, and deliberative lawmaking that attempts to secure its own foundations, that must carry the principal burden of creating a stable and reasonably just regime. Ideal theory makes it less likely that we will see this and more likely that we will not take the full measure of how self-interest, ambition, and the like do their work in a good democratic regime.[77]

This in itself should make us uneasy about ideal theory, but there is more to say about the way in which it is flawed. It is worth going further, moreover, to deepen our critique, because a whole generation of political theorists has been influenced by ideal theory. And, of course, any additional criticism of it weakens the claims of the kind of deliberative theory that I have been criticizing. To see what is at issue, I need to extend what I have already said about how ideal theory works.

In its efforts to develop a theory of how to constitute a good political regime, ideal theory proceeds by defining an ideal and spelling out how such an ideal might work. Only afterward does it consider—if they cannot be eliminated—less attractive motives and processes. This means that the destination we aim for in our political practice and the road to get there are defined by ideal theory. The destination to which political activity is to bring us is understood as being as close as possible to the ideal; the road to reach it is defined as putting as much effort as possible into fostering the motives and processes defined by ideal theory. The assumption here seems to be that the more effort that is exerted, the closer we will get to the regime envisaged by ideal theory. Insofar as other motives and processes emerge that threaten to block progress down the road, we

[76] See the introduction to that volume.

[77] One is tempted here to say that Rawls, having looked at the world and having noted the existence of value pluralism, should have looked at it more comprehensively. Similarly, why stop at "accept[ing] the facts of commonsense political sociology" (*Political Liberalism*, 193) as they bear on whether liberal regimes can be neutral with regard to conceptions of the good? Why *those* facts, and not the "facts of political sociology" as they bear on what is necessary to actually secure a regime in which the exercise of public reason is a crucial component of its workings? Indeed, why not the facts of commonsense political sociology all across the board? Of course, to take these into account would call into question whether ideal theory is really useful, or whether we must have some sort of mix of normative and empirical analysis, which is, in effect, what I am arguing here.

should deal with them as necessary. Otherwise said, ideal theory defines the destination that political action is to aim at in terms of strict compliance, as a state where only morally attractive motives and processes are at work. It thus defines the road to this destination in terms of devoting all of our effort to strengthening these motives and processes except as problems of partial compliance emerge. By contrast, the kind of analysis that I have engaged in here, concerning how to secure deliberative lawmaking and what its content should be—call it 'constitutional thinking' or 'constitutional theory'—defines our destination from the beginning as one in which there is at work a mixture of good, morally ambiguous, and even bad motives and processes. The road to reach our destination then is, accordingly, also different from that in ideal theory. From the viewpoint of constitutional theory, we must put as much or nearly as much effort into nonideal, morally ambiguous, and worse motives and processes as ideal ones in order to reach our destination.[78]

The fundamental question is, which manner of proceeding is more likely to bring into being an attractive and stable regime of popular self-government? That is, should we conceive of the ideal as less than the ideal? This is partly an argument about political practice—how best to act[79]—but this argument is linked inextricably to different understandings of what the essential problems of political life are and of how we are to face them in our efforts to create attractive political regimes. The difference may be put as whether we should view morally ambiguous motives and processes as ancillary to our essential political task or as integral to it. Repeating a term that I used above, should we start from the 'political whole', from the full array of motives and processes at work in political life; or should we take as central to the theoretical task an intellectual division of labor in which some of us are specialists in the good, some in the bad, and some in the ugly mix of good and bad that I have termed morally ambiguous? On the basis of the discussion of deliberation, we can be more or less certain that which way we start has a significant effect on how we understand deliberation itself. More generally, which we choose will have a profound effect on our understanding of the full array of practical problems that politics poses, including those having to do with deliberative ways of lawmaking.

There is good reason to think, then, that the differences between ideal and constitutional theory are not academic, not least because how we understand political processes and motives will surely affect how we act. This, in turn, will affect how likely we are to succeed in constructing

[78] Cf. Allan Bloom's remark, made in a critique of Rawls's *A Theory of Justice*, that the latter's discussion is "redolent of that hope and expectation for the future of democracy" that is "forgetful of the harsh deeds that preceded it and made it possible, without anticipation of the barbarism" that can and has followed it. Allan Bloom, "Justice: John Rawls Vs. The Tradition of Political Philosophy," *American Political Science Review* 69, no. 2 (1975): 648.

[79] Consider here Edmund Burke's comment that "the circumstances are what render every civil and political scheme beneficial or noxious to mankind." Edmund Burke, *Reflections on the Revolution in France* (1790; reprint, London: Bohn, 1855), 2:283.

political ways of life that are worthy of our affections. There are costs to the intellectual division of labor on which ideal theory rests. At bottom, the essential problem with ideal theory is that, if we take seriously that political theory must start from the full array of political motives and processes at work in the world, by design ideal theory does not do this.

So far, most of what has been said about ideal theory reinforces what has been strongly implied by the discussion of deliberative theory. There is, however, more to say. Ideal theory reinforces an already strong inclination in us to avert our eyes from the possibility that the categories of "good" and "bad" in describing political motives and processes are themselves inadequate. This is, of course, one of the great questions of political theory: Is the morality of good and bad as it applies to individuals appropriate for the evaluation of political life? Nothing said so far indicates that such a vocabulary is completely inadequate. It is unlikely that we can or should do without the vocabulary of moral judgment when it comes to governments that engage in the wholesale murder and torture of their citizens. Whatever else we might want to say in this regard, we surely want to say that such behavior is bad, indeed evil, and our sense of transgression is much the same as when we condemn an individual who tortures or murders someone.

Still, my discussion of deliberation has indicated that, for a significant portion of political life, the vocabulary of good and bad is much less useful, indeed misleading. This discussion suggests that were we to think constitutionally and give a full account of the institutional design of a self-governing republic, we would see that we must rely upon self-interest, ambition, and the like. Additionally, we would see that motives such as pride, greed, fear, and ignorance—and the political processes through which they are expressed and that build upon them—turn out to be necessary for a full realization of a self-governing republic. If good political regimes must rely on morally ambiguous or worse motives, then in what sense, we may ask, are such motives to be characterized as bad? Machiavelli is the great teacher of the ambiguity of good and bad in political life.[80] He makes us ask whether morally unattractive motives are an inevitable feature of political life, part of the necessity that political action must take account of, both constraining and relying on them if it is to succeed.[81] A deeper concern in Machiavelli's thought is whether po-

---

[80] See Niccolò Machiavelli, *The Prince*, ed. [trans] Harvey C. Mansfield (Chicago, IL: University of Chicago Press, 1985); and Niccolò Machiavelli, *Discourses on Livy*, trans. Harvey C. Mansfield and Nathan Tarcov (Chicago, IL: University of Chicago Press, 1996). For extraordinarily helpful accounts of Machiavelli's thought, see Mansfield, *Machiavelli's Virtue*; Harvey C. Mansfield, *Taming the Prince* (New York: Free Press, 1989), chap. 6; and Harvey C. Mansfield, *Machiavelli's New Modes and Orders: A Study of the Discourses of Livy* (Ithaca, NY: Cornell University Press, 1979). See also Judith N. Shklar, "Bad Characters for Good Liberals," in Shklar, *Ordinary Vices* (Cambridge, MA: Harvard University Press, 1984).

[81] Mansfield writes that according to Machiavelli, "men may choose, but the only prudent choice is anticipation of necessity." Mansfield, *Taming the Prince*, 277.

litical good can be produced without what are normally considered to be morally unattractive actions, and thus whether it is right to think of these actions as immoral. Deeper still, Machiavelli's writings present the problem of whether the language of morality is misplaced, or worse, when we seek to understand and evaluate political life. Pierre Manent suggests one possibility when he comments that "Machiavelli did not erase the distinction between good and evil. On the contrary, he preserved it—and he had to, if he wanted to establish the scandalous proposition that 'good' is founded by 'evil'." Manent says that, according to Machiavelli, "the 'good' happens and is maintained only through the 'bad'." [82]

VII. Conclusion

Machiavelli may be too harsh. Indeed, after the twentieth century we may suspect that he has gone too far, but he does teach us that we must look at the political whole if we wish to understand and act with effect in politics. To look at this whole is to take account of the full range of human motives at work in politics. It is to see how these motives need to and can be harnessed to effective political action, to the creation of political institutions that can be fitted together to constitute the same whole but in another form—namely, in the form of a political regime, which is a coming together in a regularized fashion of these motives. To think about the political whole is to think about the human whole. Machiavelli tries to strengthen us, to get us to cease averting our eyes from examining the bad, and to see that some portion of it is essential to achieving the good. What looks to be bad from the standpoint of morality can be good from the point of view of political theory and action if it helps humankind to live freely. If we cannot face the bad and make use of it, then we risk allowing it to do its work, thereby making good regimes impossible to create and destroying those in existence. [83]

That we seemingly must rely on, at best, morally ambiguous motives to serve the justice promised by a republican regime—and presumably by all good regimes—suggests, once more, that justice can only be partial, not ideal. As Harvey Mansfield writes in commenting on Machiavelli, "Every regime has a self-definition that is partisan." A regime is "the organizing form that gives the virtues a partisan bent as they appear in

---

[82] Pierre Manent, *An Intellectual History of Liberalism*, trans. Rebecca Balinski (Princeton, NJ: Princeton University Press, 1994), 14. Cf. Leo Strauss's comment that for Machiavelli "the foundation of justice is injustice." Leo Strauss and Joseph Cropsey, eds., *History of Political Philosophy*, 3rd ed. (Chicago, IL: University of Chicago Press, 1987). If we were to replace the language of morality as applied to politics, what would we replace it with? The language of prudence? Of virtue?

[83] Consider here Machiavelli's comment that it is "more fitting to go directly to the effectual truth of the thing than to the imagination of it." He goes on to say that "many have imagined republics and principalities that have never been seen or known to exist in truth," with the result that they come to ruin. Machiavelli, *The Prince*, 61.

politics." The rulers of a regime are "partisan creatures."[84] As we must have political regimes to achieve any measure of justice or good, all of our efforts to do so will be partisan, unless, stretching credulity, we are somehow able to create a universal, that is, an ideal, regime. The subject of political theory is humankind in motion, men and women propelled by self-interest, eros, rationality, spiritedness, etc. As Machiavelli argues, the things of men cannot stay steady.[85] We may surmise that he means that political theory must be practical, and that we should follow Aristotle in avoiding "the philosopher's mistake of despising what is practical."[86]

We are left with a question. Are these morally ambiguous motives a fixed point of human nature, part of that which must be taken into account if political action in the service of good politics is to succeed? Machiavelli and Hobbes and those influenced by them apparently think so. If such motives are an inextricable feature of humankind in society, then politics—the effort to constrain the reach of such motives while also relying on and fostering them—is as well. There is a sense in which politics is precisely what ideal theory seeks to avoid, or at least to put off to another day. The comment has been made that "the secret dream of liberalism [is] to do away with politics altogether."[87] To which we might add, not all liberals wish to do so, but Rawlsian ones certainly appear to. At its worst, ideal theory reads like nothing so much as the comment of one of the protagonists from William Morris's imaginary society in *News From Nowhere* who, when asked "[H]ow do you manage with politics?" replies "that we are very well off as to politics—because we have none."[88] Ideal theory is the vehicle by which many contemporary philosophers seek to preserve a central role for moral philosophy in talking about political life, without having to face politics. We might say that while ideal theorists such as Rawls take as central "the manyness of minds" and concern themselves with the relation in which persons stand to others,[89] practitioners of ideal theory want these persons to engage in as little politics as possible, to be "ideal" persons. This makes the resulting theory

---

[84] Mansfield, "Machiavelli and the Idea of Progress," in Mansfield, *Machiavelli's Virtue*, 112; and "Machiavelli's Virtue," *op. cit.*, 22.

[85] See, for example, Machiavelli, *Discourses on Livy*, bk. 2, sec. 19.

[86] Mansfield, *Taming the Prince*, 47.

[87] Harvey C. Mansfield, *The Spirit of Liberalism* (Cambridge, MA: Harvard University Press, 1978), 95.

[88] William Morris, *News From Nowhere* (London: Thomas Nelson, 1941), 117–18. I do not mean to claim here that ideal theory as a mode of doing political theory is without merit. I mean only to dispute its usefulness for understanding the kind of political practices that we will need to secure and maintain an attractive regime of popular self-government. Thus, ideal theory can teach us the danger of attempting too much in political life. The distance we would have to travel to create anything approximating an ideal would be great and the dangers of the journey large. Along the same line, ideal theory could be understood as a frankly utopian exercise designed to teach us what our actual condition as human beings is, e.g., by comparing a society where there is no politics to any society that human beings are ever likely to create.

[89] Charles Larmore, "Lifting the Veil," *The New Republic*, February 5, 2001, 32.

ill suited to guiding action in political life, the defining characteristic of which is that its participants are not ideal. This escape from politics can also be found in much work done by economists and legal theorists interested in political life.[90] Many of the former wish to substitute for the pulling and hauling of politics (which they conceive of largely as the play of self-interest) the genuine article, namely, the market, which is revealed in their theorizing to be a giant social-calculating machine that is nonpareil in the aggregation of interests. Too much legal theory has as its underlying point that if only law could replace politics, then the arrival of the good regime would be imminent. The value of such legal theory is nicely captured by Grant Gilmore's comment that in hell there will only be law.[91]

It would be better to have a political theory that is less insouciant with regard to the central features of the world about which it theorizes.[92] Thinking constitutionally, trying to conceive of an attractive political whole out of the complex human whole, at least pays appropriate respect to unattractive features of human conduct in political life that, if we wish to understand politics, we cannot put aside. But even this is not enough if our political theories are to do more than restate our hopes. For, given that these unattractive features will not go away, we must also think about how they can be harnessed in the effort to constitute a good political regime.

Government and Politics, University of Maryland

---

[90] See, for example, Gary S. Becker and Kevin M. Murphy, *Social Economics: Market Behavior in a Social Environment* (Cambridge, MA: Harvard University Press, Belknap Press, 2001); and Herbert Wechsler, "Toward Neutral Principles of Constitutional Law," *Harvard Law Review* 73, no. 1 (1959).

[91] Grant Gilmore, *The Ages of American Law* (New Haven, CT: Yale University Press, 1979).

[92] Cf. Glen Newey's comment that we need "to reinstate politics itself in political philosophy." Glen Newey, "How Do We Find Out What It Means?" *Times Literary Supplement*, June 26, 1998, 29. Cf. also Colin McGinn's comments about a social contract argument that parallels Rawls's: "[W]hat is the point of unity with purely hypothetical others[?]" Colin McGinn, "Reasons and Unreasons," *The New Republic*, May 24, 1999, 37.

REPRESENTING IGNORANCE*

By Russell Hardin

I. Introduction

If we wish to assess the morality of elected officials, we must understand their function as our representatives and then infer how they can fulfill this function. I propose to treat the class of elected officials as a profession, so that their morality is a role morality and it is functionally determined. If we conceive the role morality of legislators to be analogous to the ethics of other professions, then this morality must be functionally defined by the purpose that legislators are to fulfill once in office. Hence, the role morality of legislators will largely be determined by our theory of representation. We will need not a normative account of their role, but an empirical explanatory account. In David Hume's terms, the morality of role holders is one of "artificial" duties, that is to say, duties defined by their functional fit with the institutional purposes of a profession.[1] Our most difficult problem, therefore, is to understand the role of our elected representatives.

This problem is severely complicated by the nature of democratic choice and participation in a modern, complex society. A central problem of democratic theory for such a society is the general political ignorance of the citizens. In *Capitalism, Socialism, and Democracy* (1942), Joseph Schumpeter argues that citizens have no chance of affecting electoral outcomes and, therefore, no reason to learn enough about politics even to know which candidates or policies would serve their interests. He writes, "[W]ithout the initiative that comes from immediate responsibility, ignorance will persist in the face of masses of information however complete and correct."[2] If the problem of knowing enough to judge elected government officials is already hard, the lack of incentive to correct this problem is

* I am indebted to my fellow contributors to this volume, to participants in the Monday Night Theorists at New York University, and to Ellen Frankel Paul for comments on an earlier draft of this essay.

[1] Russell Hardin, "The Artificial Duties of Contemporary Professionals," *Social Service Review* 64 (1991): 528–43. Hume distinguishes "natural" from "artificial" virtues in David Hume, *A Treatise of Human Nature* (1739–40), ed. L. A. Selby-Bigge and P. H. Nidditch, 2d ed. (Oxford: Oxford University Press, 1978), bk. 3, pt. 2, sec. 1. Acting from a natural duty produces a good directly, and more or less immediately. Acting from an artificial duty, such as the duty of justice, produces good only through the mediation of a social institution or norm.

[2] Joseph A. Schumpeter, *Capitalism, Socialism, and Democracy* (1942), 3d ed. (New York: Harper, 1950), 262.

devastating. Indeed, the costs of knowing enough about government to be able to vote intelligently in one's own interest surely swamp the modest costs, for most people in the United States and other advanced democratic nations, of actually casting a vote, at least on commonplace issues of public policy outside moments of great crisis. Therefore, an economic theory of knowledge or "street-level epistemology" weighs against knowing enough to vote well because the incentives cut heavily against investing in the relevant knowledge.[3] The typical voter will not be able to put the relevant knowledge to beneficial use.[4]

One response to the problem of citizens' incompetence to judge how they should be governed is government by Burkean representatives. Throughout his writings, Edmund Burke (1729–97) supposes that only members of an elite are.competent to govern, and the mass of the citizenry ought to turn government over to them to do what they think best.[5] I will suppose that we resort to representative government for a very different, structural reason. It is impossible for the entire polity of a large state to make policy directly or to implement it.[6] We therefore have specialized bodies to do these things. It is this structural fact that wrecks our incentive to know much about the politics that governs much of our lives. Still, we want representative government genuinely to represent us, to adopt the policies that we would adopt if we had relevant knowledge and power. Any actual representative government may have many problems that get in the way of its serving us in such a manner,[7] but I will ignore those problems and focus on the ethics of the representative in trying to

[3] Russell Hardin, "The Street-Level Epistemology of Democratic Participation," *Journal of Political Philosophy* 10, no. 2 (2002): 212–29; reprinted in James Fishkin and Peter Laslett, eds., *Philosophy, Politics, and Society*, vol. 7 (London: Blackwell, 2003), 163–81. The argument here is essentially from the logic of incentives and it casts no blame on anyone. Others hold the political system, the poor educational system, or politicians responsible for the seeming incompetence of voters. See, for example, Matthew A. Crenson and Benjamin Ginsberg, *Downsizing Democracy: How America Sidelined Its Citizens and Privatized Its Public* (Baltimore, MD: Johns Hopkins University Press, 2002).

[4] Martin P. Wattenberg argues that, additionally, there are obstacles even to casting one's vote correctly in the United States, where the act of voting can be almost as difficult as taking a college entrance examination. See Martin P. Wattenberg, *Where Have All the Voters Gone?* (Cambridge, MA: Harvard University Press, 2002), chap. 6.

[5] See, for example, Edmund Burke, "Speech to the Electors of Bristol" (1774), in Hanna Fenichel Pitkin, ed., *Representation* (New York: Atherton Press, 1969), esp. 174–75; and Edmund Burke, "Appeal from the New to the Old Whigs" (1791), in *The Works of Edmund Burke* (London: George Bell & Sons, 1890–1906), 3:85–87. For later views, see Michael Oakeshott, *Rationalism in Politics and Other Essays* (New York: HarperCollins, 1962), esp. Oakeshott's essay, "On Being a Conservative."

[6] Even in a not so modern polity—England and Wales in 1754—the electorate was about two hundred and eighty thousand out of a population of roughly eight million. See Bernard Manin, *The Principles of Representative Government* (Cambridge: Cambridge University Press, 1997), 82. In the United States at the time of ratification of its constitution in 1788, the electorate was about one million out of a population of a little more than three million. Thus, even these relatively small populations, by modern standards, required representative government or some other device for making decisions without involving all citizens at once.

[7] Ibid.

represent others in the face of both gross ignorance on the part of voters and harsh limits on information for the representative.

I will not assume the position of those who view representative democracy as a forum for deliberation on "the truth." In *The Principles of Representative Government* (1997), Bernard Manin states that political scientist Carl Schmitt (1888–1985) holds this view, namely, "that truth must 'make the law,'" and that "debate is the most appropriate means of determining truth, and therefore the central political authority must be a place of debate, that is, a parliament."[8] I will not deal with this vision here, because I think it largely irrelevant. Parliamentary debate does not often approach "truth," and, in any case, politics is far more about interests than it is about truth.[9] If there is a truth to be discovered and demonstrated, then after sufficient debate there should be consensus and each of us should grasp the truth. In that case, the Schmitt thesis would make sense. When there is a conflict of interests, however, there is no truth of the kind Schmitt envisions. Deliberation on interests is as likely to lead to dissensus as to consensus.[10] I should also note that Schmitt's justification of a parliamentary body does not require that the body actually be representative of the various groups in a society, but only that it be the political decision-making body for the society.

In general, the tasks of representatives will be easiest when they merely represent interests of fairly basic kinds on issues, for example, of economic policy or welfare provision. Their tasks might also seem to be straightforward when they deal with hotly contested issues over which public views are relatively forcefully asserted, as with the contemporary debate over abortion in the United States. Indeed, for any controversial matter such as abortion, representatives might often think of themselves as delegates because they would not expect to get reelected if they reneged on their electioneering commitment to take one side or the other on the issue (although there might be intermediate positions on which they could compromise). The most difficult issues for representatives will generally be those for which clarity is lacking, at least in the sense that citizens do not know where they stand or, rather, where their interests lie. As John Stuart Mill says, individuals distort many issues with their idiosyncratic beliefs, and they tend to discount the future, so that individuals' claims of what their interests are can be distorted.[11]

[8] Ibid., 185. See also Carl Schmitt, *The Crisis of Parliamentary Democracy* (1923), trans. Ellen Kennedy (Cambridge, MA: MIT Press, 1988), 35, 43.

[9] Geoffrey Brennan and James M. Buchanan, *The Reason of Rules: Constitutional Political Economy* (Cambridge: Cambridge University Press, 1985); and Russell Hardin, "Deliberation: Method, Not Theory," in Stephen Macedo, ed., *Deliberative Politics: Essays on Democracy and Disagreement* (New York: Oxford University Press, 1999), 103–19.

[10] See Hardin, "Deliberation: Method, Not Theory"; and Cass Sunstein, "Deliberative Trouble? Why Groups Go to Extremes," *Yale Law Journal* 110 (2000): 71–119.

[11] John Stuart Mill, *Considerations on Representative Government* (1861), in John Stuart Mill, *Essays on Politics and Society*, vol. 19 of *Collected Works of John Stuart Mill*, ed. J. M. Robson (Toronto: University of Toronto Press, 1977), 444–45.

II. VOTER IGNORANCE

If, in general, we make the effort to know something in large part *because we think it will serve our interest to know it*, then we cannot expect people to know very much about what their representatives do. In the argument of the "economic theory of democracy," a citizen typically does not have very much interest in voting. One vote has a miniscule chance of making a difference, so miniscule that, even when it is multiplied by the value of making a difference and getting one's preferred candidate or policy, the expected value of the vote is vanishingly slight. Therefore, if there is any real cost involved in casting a vote, this cost swamps the expected benefit to the voter of voting. Hence, there is little point in knowing enough actually to vote well.

Most of the research on and debate over voting since Schumpeter's *Capitalism, Socialism, and Democracy* and Anthony Downs's *An Economic Theory of Democracy* (1957)[12] has focused primarily on the incentive to vote rather than the incentive to know enough to vote intelligently.[13] The latter is at least logically derivative from the former, because it is the lack of incentive to vote that makes knowledge of how to vote well virtually useless, so that mastering such knowledge violates the pragmatic understanding of knowledge. Since my vote has miniscule causal effect on democratically determined outcomes, there is no compelling reason for me to determine how to vote intelligently. Or, to put this the other way around, the fact that I would benefit from policy X does not give me reason or incentive to know about or to understand the implications of policy X unless I can somehow affect whether policy X is to be adopted.

In what follows, I will simply take for granted that typical citizens do not master the facts they need to know if they are to vote their interests intelligently. There is extensive evidence on this claim, although there is, of course, also great difference of opinion on its significance for electoral choices. For example, political scientist Samuel Popkin canvasses problems of voter ignorance in American presidential elections and then refers to "low-information rationality," which is rationality despite abysmal factual ignorance.[14] He also argues for a 'Gresham's law' of political information: bad facts drive out good facts. According to this law, "a small amount of personal information [on a candidate] can dominate a large amount of historical information about a past record."[15] The personal information might be some minor fact that comes up during a campaign. However, the effect of Gresham's law might often run against Popkin's claim for low-information rationality by driving out the little bit of policy-

---

[12] Anthony Downs, *An Economic Theory of Democracy* (New York: Harper, 1957).

[13] Hardin, "The Street-Level Epistemology of Democratic Participation." (Passages in the next two pages are taken from pages 217–19 of this essay.)

[14] Samuel L. Popkin, *The Reasoning Voter: Communication and Persuasion in Presidential Campaigns*, 2d ed. (Chicago, IL: University of Chicago Press, 1994).

[15] Ibid., 73.

relevant information the voter has. If the personal information seems to be politically relevant, however, its dominance over other information might not matter so much. For example, Italy's prime minister, Silvio Berlusconi, has been caught up in an ongoing scandal over accusations that he bribed his way to wealth and, thence, to political power. Sociologist Renato Mannheimer says, "Italians don't understand the contents of the processes against him, so they make their judgments according to their political leanings."[16] But some voters might judge him for his use of office to serve his own interests.[17]

Manin argues that the form representative democracy now takes is "audience democracy."[18] The trouble with the large amount of historical information that is, at least in principle, available is that voters do not typically know much about it because it would be silly for them to invest the time needed to acquire such information. Hence, in this age of media and celebrity, we vote for personalities rather than for policies and thereby give an outsized role to personal information.

As evidence of how seldom voters even seek better information before voting, consider the difficulty that candidates have in getting their message across to voters. Congressional scholar Richard Fenno elegantly portrays the burden that candidates for the U.S. House of Representatives face in merely finding people to talk to.[19] Even professional political scientists, who have a strong interest in knowing more about politics than their mere interest in the outcome of elections would suggest, find it hard to keep up with much of what happens. Weekly tallies of votes in the U.S. House of Representatives and Senate, for example, are reported in some newspapers, but with such brevity that only specialists on a particular issue would find them meaningful.

Results of referenda on even relatively simple issues suggest astonishing misunderstanding by voters. California voters displayed cavalier irresponsibility in a 1994 referendum (Proposition 184) on a so-called three-strikes sentencing law that mandates harsh minimum prison terms for repeat offenders.[20] Consider two early cases to which the law was applied. The first involved a thief with a prior record, who was sentenced to a term of twenty-five years to life, with no possibility of parole before serving at least twenty years, for his "felony petty theft" of one slice of pizza.[21] In the second case, Russell Benson was sentenced to a similar

---

[16] Quoted in Frank Bruni, "Italy, a Land of Tolerance, Even to Prime Ministers," *New York Times*, May 28, 2003, late edition–final, sec. A, p. 4, col. 3.

[17] He pushes legislation that would directly benefit him as an oligopolistic media owner. See "Italian Leader Faces Dissent over Control of the Media," *New York Times*, April 6, 2003, late edition–final, sec. A, p. 4, col. 1.

[18] Manin, *The Principles of Representative Government*, 218–32.

[19] Richard F. Fenno, Jr., *Home Style: House Members in Their Districts* (Boston, MA: Little, Brown, 1978).

[20] Susan Estrich, *Getting Away with Murder: How Politics Is Destroying the Criminal Justice System* (Cambridge, MA: Harvard University Press, 1998).

[21] "25 Years for a Slice of Pizza," *New York Times*, March 5, 1995, sec. 1, p. 21.

term for shoplifting a twenty-dollar carton of cigarettes.[22] The three-strikes referendum was provoked by some truly gruesome crimes, yet it is so badly framed that it brutalizes petty felons.

California voters also apparently displayed complete misunderstanding of a 1998 referendum (Proposition 3) to undo a prior referendum (Proposition 198 of 1996) on open primaries. The prior referendum, passed by the voters in presumable ignorance of its consequences, would stupidly have disallowed California representation at the national Republican and Democratic Party nominating conventions in the year 2000. After the electorate failed to pass Proposition 3, administrative devices were used to enable the state to distinguish Democratic and Republican voters in its presidential primary elections, thereby securing representation at the two party conventions.[23] In this failure to enact Proposition 3, democracy was a charade and, when it failed due to ignorance and widespread misunderstanding, a knowledgeable bureaucrat, California Secretary of State Bill Jones, intervened against the democratic result. (In a subsequent suit by the major parties against the law, the U.S. Supreme Court overturned Proposition 198 as a violation of the constitutional right of the political parties to assemble.)[24]

III. Madisonian Representatives

Edmund Burke supposes that constituents are apt not to understand what would serve the public good and, therefore, he suggests that representatives should act in the true interest of the public rather than as their constituents might want them to act.[25] He further supposes that constituents should recognize the superiority of their representatives to carry out the task of serving the public interest. His view is not contrary to Schmitt's, and it would allow the selection of members of a parliament by criteria other than representativeness of the polity. On this view, all representatives represent everyone, or the public as a whole. Virtually no one supposes this today, however, and from U.S. constitutional debates forward, we generally assume that representatives primarily represent merely the interests of their constituencies and of those who supported their campaigns.

Let us drop two of Burke's views: that representatives ought to be concerned with the overall public good and that representatives are or should be superior individuals, imbued with character and values that only hereditary elites can acquire. A national party or a national executive might claim to fulfill the first, although parties are invariably partisan and national executives are commonly partisan. On the second, contrary to

[22] Elisabeth R. Gerber et al., *Stealing the Initiative: How State Government Responds to Direct Democracy* (Upper Saddle River, NJ: Prentice Hall, 2001), 64.
[23] Ibid., 71–74.
[24] *California Democratic Party v. Jones*, 530 U.S. 567 (2000).
[25] See also Mill, *Considerations on Representative Government*, 511–12.

what Burke wants, what might set legislators apart is that they become competent at politics, legislation, and governance through their specialized roles. Our representatives even tend, in Manin's characterization, to become aristocratic in that they must have relatively high levels of competence and achievement to attain and hold their offices.[26] They clearly do not represent their constituents in the sense of being like them. There are, for example, almost no working-class representatives in modern democratic governments, and lawyers are radically overrepresented in U.S. legislative bodies. Representation of groups must often be through so-called active representation by people who themselves do not directly share the interests of the groups they represent. For example, Senator Ted Kennedy (D–MA) often represents the interests of union members and the poor, although he has no experience of either status in his own life.

An obvious but painful implication of the Schumpeterian world, in which the public exhibits a general political ignorance, is that representatives can take advantage of citizens. This is true not merely in the manner of Italy's Berlusconi, who has used his official power to enact laws that specifically benefit him by helping him avoid trial for bribery, an offense that he has implicitly admitted.[27] It is true more fundamentally in the sense that, even without such overt actions as Berlusconi's, government personnel can be parasitic on the larger society, making themselves wealthier than they otherwise could have been in any other profession, giving themselves prerogatives far beyond their ordinary emoluments, and securing long tenure for themselves and often even their relatives. In a sense well beyond Manin's, they become an aristocratic class apart from the society that they both govern and represent.

Even the slightest Madisonian or Humean view of human nature as self-interested yields this implication. Political sociologist Robert Michels (1876–1936) claims that democratic government within political parties—especially European socialist parties—produced an aristocracy with great power over rank-and-file members.[28] This claim is true more generally of democratic governments, although they may typically be subjected to greater scrutiny that might impede some of the worst excesses of oligarchic power. In Michels's famous slogan, "Who says organization says oligarchy." Perversely, who says representative democracy evidently also says oligarchy.

---

[26] Manin, *The Principles of Representative Government*, chap. 4.

[27] Members of Berlusconi's party in the Italian Parliament introduced legislation to exempt the top five government officials from facing trial while they hold office (Jason Horowitz, "World Briefing/Europe: Berlusconi Immunity Plan," *New York Times*, May 30, 2003, late edition–final, sec. A, p. 8, col. 5). Berlusconi previously pushed through legislation to reform the courts in ways that might have permitted him to avoid prosecution for bribery, complaining that "to search for, and single out, individual culprits [is] disingenuous and inherently unjust" when there is so much suspicious activity to go around (Bruni, "Italy, a Land of Tolerance").

[28] Robert Michels, *Political Parties: A Sociological Study of the Oligarchal Tendencies of Modern Democracy* (1911), trans. Eden and Cedar Paul (Glencoe, IL: Free Press, 1949).

According to the Manin and Michels theses of an aristocracy of leadership, in some sense it is not the individual elected officials but the class of them that is problematic. As John C. Calhoun (1782–1850) writes: "The advantages of possessing the control of the powers of the government, and thereby of its honors and emoluments, are, of themselves, exclusive of all other considerations, ample to divide ... a community into two great hostile parties."[29] As a class, the political aristocracy is parasitic on the society that it ostensibly serves and that has the power of election over it. Although some representatives may be very well grounded in their constituencies, many representatives are far more likely to view their fellow "aristocrats" as their reference group than their respective electorates. The supposedly mighty citizenry with its power of election over officials does not have the power to refuse to elect any of them; it can only turn out the occasional overtly bad apple. The electorate usually does not have the temerity to overcome incumbents' advantage. Burke believes that citizens should be deferential to their aristocratic leaders. Few people would argue for such social deference today, although there is pervasive deference to the power of elected officials and to their celebrity, which is a peculiarly ugly aspect of modern democracies, perhaps uglier and more pervasive in the United States than in other advanced democracies.

The U.S. Constitution does not explicitly say either that elected officials have a special status or that they have a duty to represent their constituents. *It is essentially a social convention that they should represent their constituents.* Social conventions generally are not morally binding except through considerations other than the fact that they are conventions. Moreover, there is no constitutionally determined principle of representation to which elected officials are bound. The range of possible principles is so large and various that all officials could claim to be living up to one or another principle. For example, a legislator could claim to represent some part of a particular geographical constituency and to support whatever the leaders of the relevant interest groups in that constituency want.

Add to various visions of the nature of representation the problem of citizens' ignorance. This is a problem that does not bother a Burkean, because Burke's arguments are grounded in the presumption of citizens' ignorance and their deep incapacity to decide what policies their government should adopt. It is also not a problem for Schmitt's views, because he supposes that the role of the representative body is not to represent but to find truth; that citizens do not know truth is taken for granted in the very structure and purpose of legislative government. In both Burke's and Schmitt's views, elected representatives might suppose that they should do for citizens what citizens do not even know they want done. Indeed, citizens might not even want it done once they had given it some

[29] John C. Calhoun, *A Disquisition on Government and Selections from the Discourse* (1851), ed. C. Gordon Post (Indianapolis, IN: Bobbs-Merrill, 1953), 14–15.

thought because, virtually by definition, they are not in the places of the Burkean or Schmittian representatives who have superior capacities for determining what should be done.

Although Madison's views include some of the elitism of Burke and others, he is, with Manin, more focused on the way things actually work than on a recommendation that we create a deliberately elitist system. Mill stands somewhere between these theorists in that he supposes that elected parliamentarians should be elite in their qualifications but not, as Burke supposes, via birthright. Mill is also less interested in representation per se, so that he would allow extra votes (which he calls plural votes) to such people as fellows at Oxford and Cambridge Universities, because they would likely be better qualified to vote intelligently.[30] He, too, seems more driven by some (extremely vague and underarticulated) sense of the public good than by concern with representation of varied interests. Perhaps it is the fact that Madison is engaged in actually creating a representative government that makes him the most realistic and focused of all these theorists. His realism is driven in part by his concern to deal with the divisiveness of factions that seemed to fracture the political affairs of several of the states in the United States under the Articles of Confederation.

Madison wants representatives to represent moderately large communities, so that they will not be too focused on narrow issues. (In this, he opposes the Anti-Federalists, who want representation down to the small community level.) But he does not have a conception of "the" public good, and he does not expect the legislature to work for any such good. It would, rather, somehow aggregate diverse interests. One might argue that serving constituency interests would be a way of discovering the collective good in a Madisonian system. This good would not be the true good, as Schmitt would want, but only the product of a compromise of interests negotiated by legislators.

Madison is concerned with at least two overriding issues that he might have thought of as part of the public good. One of these is simply order, and the other is a relatively uniform national economic system that would encourage, or at least enable, economic growth and prosperity by facilitating trade, especially by preventing states from placing restrictions on interstate trade and by standardizing tariffs on foreign trade. There were parties who would have preferred to keep the economic system diverse so that they could free-ride on the anticompetitive practices of others. For example, the antinationalists of Rhode Island benefited from the high tariffs that Massachusetts imposed on goods from England and the Caribbean. Traders in Rhode Island imported goods from these places without tariffs, and then transshipped the goods to Massachusetts, where they could undercut the prices of both domestic and imported goods even while making a substantial profit.

[30] Mill, *Considerations on Representative Government*, chap. 8.

Henceforth, I will focus on what we might call 'Madisonian', 'Humean', or 'Schumpeterian' representatives (or, with more criticism for the unreality of his vision, 'Millian' representatives). I will also discuss (in Section VB) the nature of representation in the current era of audience democracy. Although they have intellectual appeal, 'Burkean' and 'Schmittian' representatives are not part of our political world and we need not dwell on their conceptions. Madisonian representatives are strongly driven by their interests, and they work for the interests of their constituents not because they necessarily share those interests, but because they will be rewarded for doing so. Representatives elected by parties have an analogous interest in supporting their parties' positions on behalf of the parties' electorates. There appears to be no analogous sense in which politicians of audience democracy have an interest that mirrors that of their constituents.

IV. Austrian Social Theory

So far the focus has been on the ignorance of citizens. Another similarly pervasive and important problem is that central government and its agents cannot know enough to devise good policies in many realms. Much of the relevant knowledge is decentralized to smaller organizations and to citizens. The knowledge relevant to governing is, therefore, extremely dispersed. There are things I know that you do not know, and so forth, and things that each of us knows that no one in government can know. This fact of the nature of our knowledge is clearly of fundamental importance for the prospect of a centralized economy. Indeed, much of the main debate over socialist economic organization during the first half of the twentieth century was about how demand functions could be determined so that they could be matched with supply that was set entirely by central authorities.

Suppose we do not have a centralized economy in anything like the form that existed in the socialist economies of the former Soviet bloc. We have central fiscal policy, centrally determined regulations for many activities, and central oversight of civil liberties. Many of these central determinations of policy seem not only to work reasonably well, but better than the lack of such central controls. Clearly, central authorities ought to oversee or regulate many activities, but not others.

The nearest equivalent to Madisonian theory in the twentieth and early twenty-first centuries has been Austrian economics, as represented by F. A. Hayek among others.[31] Although it is ostensibly an economic theory, its most cogent insights apply to broader social theory. An especially odd aspect of the current hegemony of Austrian and Madisonian views of politics and society—even without these labels attached—is that they were almost purely theoretical when enunciated. In the past, there was no

[31] Russell Hardin, "Seeing Like Hayek," *The Good Society* 10, no. 2 (2001): 36–39.

way to test Austrian views on the ground. But now they have been and
are being tested, and they seem to be acquitting themselves very well,
although shenanigans at Enron, WorldCom, and so on are attributed by
some to the loosening of government regulation. Madison himself was
not willing to practice his theory once he was in office, and perhaps if
they had gained office, Hayek and others of the Austrian School would
not have been either. But the example of the Soviet world, admittedly a
bad version of socialist statism, compared to the freer but partially tram-
meled markets of the more prosperous West, gave us a chance to see a
crude, perhaps second-best test of the Austrian-Madisonian theses.

Of course, my assessment is made while we are in the midst of extensive changes, and it might turn out to be grossly optimistic, a mere ex-
trapolation from the most positive aspects of current appearances. But for
the moment, the Austrian and Madisonian schools seem to have the right
vision. This is a stunning turn, even more stunning to those on the traditional Left than to Millian libertarians. The most impressive consequence is the reversal of the long historical trend toward ever increasing
state hegemony over the economy, and all else when the state fell into bad
hands, such as Stalin's or Hitler's.

The centerpiece of the Austrian-Madisonian vision is that the knowledge to run a society is widely distributed and most of it cannot become
available to a central government. Hence, a central government should
not attempt to manage society in detail, and it should not attempt a
massive redesign of society. Austrian economists typically worry about
central control of the economy, but they could just as well worry about
central control of social relations more generally. Political scientist James
Scott especially deplores what Hayek calls "Cartesianism" and what Scott
calls the "high modernism" of arrogant redesign of major parts of society,
as in the effort to design cities in supposedly more rational ways,[32] or to
reorganize peasants into collective farms in the Soviet Union or into
Ujamaa villages in Tanzania.[33]

Austrian constraints mean that legislators cannot know in detail what
their constituents want. On average, a member of the U.S. Congress has
a district of nearly six hundred and fifty thousand people, and a senator
from all but a handful of states represents millions of people. These
representatives cannot know their constituents. Survey research at its best
(as it seldom is) cannot determine very clearly what people want from
government or what would benefit them if government acted in relevant
ways. Commonly, when government tries to benefit citizens through attention to their narrow interests, it is not by directly providing benefits,
but only by regulating, prohibiting, or enabling various activities. Of

---

[32] James C. Scott, *Seeing Like a State: How Certain Schemes to Improve the Human Condition
Have Failed* (New Haven, CT: Yale University Press, 1998), chap. 4.

[33] Ibid., chaps. 6 and 7.

course, there are exceptions, as evidenced by the astonishing scale of government largesse toward agriculture both in the United States and the European Union. It is only on relatively big issues that public preferences are likely to be known, and very often even for such issues—for example, health care—understanding is radically defective, so that it is virtually impossible to know what would serve constituents well, much less what would serve them best.

V. Theories of Representation

The two most rigorous accounts of representative government that are relevant to actual practice in modern democracies are those of Mill and Manin. Each focuses much of his discussion on representatives, and each has some sense of the "Austrian" constraints that I discussed above. Let us briefly canvass Mill's and Manin's theories in order to set up an account of what the functions of representatives should be and, from that, infer their role morality. I will not provide a full rendition of the views of Mill and Manin, but only of those aspects that are especially relevant to understanding the role morality of representatives.

A. Mill

In his *Considerations on Representative Government* (1861), Mill supposes that a good government must provide order and progress. For this, a sine qua non is obedience (but not excessive obedience). The requisites of order and progress are much the same, because of the dynamism of the problems that human beings face (387).[34] For government to work well, the most important consideration is the quality of citizens (389). Hence, the most important tasks of government are to promote the virtue and intelligence of citizens (390) and to organize what virtue and intelligence already exist (392). Of course, Mill is a welfarist, and therefore his central claim is that government must enable the people to do well. For this and for progress more generally, liberty and individuality are fundamentally important (396–97).[35]

Mill notes that it is historically commonplace to assert that the best form of government is benevolent dictatorship (chapter 3). He says on the contrary that, for example, the benevolent despotism of Augustus set up Romans for the "more odious" reign of Tiberius (403). Moreover, an autocratic government cannot know enough (399) to run the society well. Mill essentially presumes an Austrian social theory. He also anticipates

---

[34] In this section only, citations to pages and chapters in Mill's *Considerations on Representative Government* will be given in parentheses. See note 11 for complete bibliographic information.

[35] Mill gives a compelling consequentialist justification for liberty, without which progress is eventually stifled.

Schumpeter's main point, that a voter's incentive is to be ignorant because, as Mill puts it, "a person must have a very unusual taste for intellectual exercise in and for itself who will put himself to the trouble of thought when it is to have no outward effect" (400). Mill holds an essentially pragmatic view of knowledge. He also reinforces this view when he says that no one will take an interest in government who cannot participate (469). This suggests that almost no one will take much interest in government, because almost no one can participate to any significant extent. But Mill's point in this passage seems to have been intended to suggest that people could be motivated to participate through education. Unfortunately, education might sooner lead one to understand just how massive are the obstacles to real participation most of the time. Mill himself concludes that there is very little opportunity for holding office in the central government (chapter 15). Local government, with its smaller scale and higher proportion of office holding, helps (535–36), but even local government in modern democracies is commonly carried out by representatives who have constituencies numbering in the thousands and even hundreds of thousands, so there cannot be very much participation even here.

In a continuation of his quasi-Austrian views, Mill says that what a legislative body is competent to do is quite limited (chapter 5). It can adopt not very precise legislation—for example, in our time, tax policy or environmental regulation. To do much more, it must delegate such things to expert advisers and to committees (430). Even then, laws will tend to become inconsistent over time because no one will have massive oversight of the whole body of law (a task performed by the Nomothetae in ancient Athens [431]). Hence, the proper function of a legislature is the very limited one of watching and controlling the administrative branches of government (432).

Mill famously claims that it is especially useful to engage in debate (433). This is not the "deliberative democracy" of current visions, although Mill's authority is often invoked in its support. His claim may partly suggest Schmitt's concern with deliberation as a device for finding the truth. Against Schmitt, however, Mill thinks that genuine representativeness is required, because it enables the legislature "to indicate wants, to be an organ for popular demands, and a place of adverse discussion for all opinions relating to public matters . . . ; and, along with this, to check by criticism, and eventually by withdrawing their support, those high public officers who really conduct the public business" (433).

Mill attributes the infirmities of representative government to two general causes (chapter 6). First, there is the quasi-Austrian general ignorance and incapacity of government and its agents; second, there is the danger of being under the influence of interests not identical to the general welfare of the community (436). He supposes that the main comparison to be made is between government by bureaucracy and government by representative democracy (438–39). Autocracy and aristocracy are too obviously flawed to merit consideration.

Against the danger of class legislation, Mill optimistically supposes that the few individuals who are public-spirited combined with those whose own interest happens to coincide with the public interest can collude in a majority to carry the day for the public interest (446–47). This is Panglossian. He should have read Madison more attentively. Indeed, he should have read himself more attentively.

In chapter 8 Mill discusses the extent of the suffrage and his view that it should generally be extended and should include women (479–81). Mill argues that fully representative democracy is the only true democracy (467). In keeping with his general view that citizens must be required to be intelligent enough to see their own interests if they are to gain the franchise, he proposes educational requirements on suffrage, because voters must be able to read, write, and do arithmetic if they are to vote intelligently on their own interests. For him this seems to be little more than a definitional implication of the idea of democracy: universal teaching must precede a universal franchise (470).

Mill especially worries about the fact that the large majority of citizens in his England are manual laborers. He supposes that they might abuse their power through their democratic majority to enact class legislation. He was largely wrong about this empirical point, because manual workers in his time were a diverse lot with conflicting interests. Manual laborers included farmers as the largest group, factory workers (who only became the bare majority of the English work force several decades after Mill wrote), and a miscellany of service workers, especially in urban areas. (In the United States in his time farmers were the overwhelming majority of all workers.) These quite diverse groups had little in common. Indeed, the only interest that they might have shared was in redistribution from the middle and upper classes, which in any case was not a viable political program in Mill's day. (Madison, too, worries about the possibility that the poor majority could combine to dispossess the wealthy of their property, a worry that made some sense empirically in his time, but not in ours, when evidence says it does not happen.)

Mill advocates universal but unequal suffrage (473–74). Uniquely among democratic theorists up to his time, he proposes intelligence, not property, as the qualification for extra weight (478). He grants, however, that unequal suffrage may not be a practical suggestion (476). He is also inclined to contrive devices that give greater weight to some voters over others, as through the use of gerrymanders to block workers from achieving a parliamentary majority by concentrating their votes in certain districts that they would win overwhelmingly while diluting their strength elsewhere (477). (This is what he calls a "fully representative democracy.") He gives a not very convincing causal claim in support of such voter inequality. He says that the best incentive to the growth of intelligence is rising to power, not having achieved it (479). This claim is a pointless fallacy of composition: the class might rise to power but almost none of its members would. Thus, although the class of workers might rise to power, individual workers generally cannot. Mill thinks that a constitution should not declare ignorance to be entitled to as much political power as knowledge—as the U.S. Constitution virtually does declare (478). He therefore excoriates the American system.

B. Manin

In the first two chapters of his *The Principles of Representative Government*, Manin gives an account of the great transformation from direct to representative democracy.[36] In Athens, there was general representation of all by all in certain bodies of government, coupled with selection by lot of people to serve in more restrictive bodies. Now democracies are with rare exception systems of elected representative bodies. For Madison and Emmanuel-Joseph Sieyes, the great constitutional thinkers of the American and French democratic revolutions, respectively, representative democracy was a new and, for its time, preferable form of government.

Manin's main thesis on the development of representative government is that it inherently tends toward aristocracy of an odd and familiar kind. Membership in the class of aristocrats is determined by citizens through elections, and the characteristics that earn entry into this class have changed over time, from something like social distinction in Madison's time and earlier in colonial America and England, to something more nearly like celebrity today. This aristocratic tendency of elected representative government was already foreseen by the ancient Greeks, who preferred to select officeholders by lot, considering it more genuinely representative (27). By lot, even the lowliest citizen could be selected for a government position. Montesquieu famously observed that there is a close link between lot and democracy and between election and aristocracy (70). Manin says that rotation in office and selection by lot reflect deep distrust of the professionalism that would follow from specializing in holding office over a long period. Madison and Sieyes, however, want professionalism (32). They worry that democracy could entail putting power in the hands of amateurs (33). They believe that officeholders should be more distinguished than the ordinary run of citizens (94). In actual democracies, wealth, property, and the payment of taxes have often been employed as qualifications for running for office (97–98), and wealth in our time is often still very useful for gaining office by spending lavishly on one's campaign.

---

[36] In this section only, citations to pages and chapters in Manin's *The Principles of Representative Government* will be given in parentheses. See note 6 for complete bibliographic information.

In the Constitutional Convention of 1787, and in the state ratifying conventions and the debates leading up to them, the Anti-Federalists held that representatives should fairly closely mirror their constituents (109). Representation was not a matter of giving representatives mandates but of having the diverse U.S. population represented by their own types (109). Anti-Federalist Samuel Chase pointed out that the great majority of the population—farmers and ordinary workers—could never be elected (112). Before early fascist or corporatist guilds, the Anti-Federalists were probably the only true advocates of genuinely representative democracy by station in life rather than by geographical location, and there has been no further debate on the aristocratic nature of election after the Anti-Federalist arguments of 1787–88 (132). Manin concludes that, for solid causal reasons, "election cannot, by its very nature, result in the selection of representatives who resemble their constituents" (149). In the end, however, power is not earned by distinctive traits or capacities but by agreement among the electorate about what traits constitute superiority (158). Apart from his being the son of a former president, one would be very hard pressed to account for the traits that put George W. Bush in the presidency, but one can give an account of how support coalesced around him at various stages in the 2000 election cycle. Still, Manin notes that the principles of distinction and salience that make for election do not violate norms of equality and political right, although the constraint of wealth does (159). Mill thought that American political leaders in his time were woefully undistinguished.[37]

In the traditional view, members of the British Parliament represented the nation as a whole and not merely their constituencies (163), as in the views of Burke and, to some extent, Mill. This view has given way, first to party democracy, in which a party gains control of parliament and governs for its term (206–18), and then to what Manin calls "audience democracy" (218–32), which is substantially formed by the media and the capacity of individual candidates to appeal to the voters.

Against Schmitt's view that deliberation is valued for giving us access to truth, Manin concludes, "It is the collective and diverse character of the representative organ, and not any prior or independently established belief in the virtues of debate, that explains the role conferred on discussion" (187). What makes some resolution of legislative debate a law is some form of consent, not discussion of it or its truth value (189). Moreover, the requisite consent is typically merely majority agreement, whereas truth should command unanimous consent once it is established.

In keeping with Manin's thesis on audience democracy and "celebrity," the great playwright Arthur Miller (1915–) analyzes the acting abilities of

---

[37] John Stuart Mill, "De Tocqueville on Democracy in America, II," in John Stuart Mill, *Essays on Politics and Society*, vol. 18 of *Collected Works of John Stuart Mill*, ed. J. M. Robson (Toronto: University of Toronto Press, 1977), 175.

modern American presidents, going back to Franklin Roosevelt.[38] Miller
evaluates the acting ability of these presidents as he would assess how
and why an actor succeeds on the screen or on the stage. He especially
notes the peculiar differences between live and screen performances; in
the latter, close-up cameras could turn more intense expressions into
something baroque or rococo. In the television age, candidates must be
flat; they cannot be orators in the grand style of, say, William Jennings
Bryan. Miller argues that successful politicians tend to master performing
before the camera and that we the voters value them in part for this
success. Miller's analysis is far more sophisticated in its appreciation of
the theatricality of politics than we are accustomed to from pundits, who
typically lack his professionalism. Miller himself came to appreciate the
difference between screen and stage from participating in the filming of
The Misfits (1961). Clark Gable, the film's star, explained to Miller that he
had to play his part very low key. Roosevelt might partly be Miller's
favorite from the cast of modern presidents because he politicked in the
era before television, which allowed him a florid acting style, rather than
the flat affect favored by presidents in the television era.

VI. THE ROLE MORALITY OF REPRESENTATIVES

Carl Schmitt holds that democracy is the identity of ruler and ruled,
and this is not compatible with representation; Rousseau believes that
representative democracy is slavery.[39] Schmitt's is merely a definitional
move. If we suppose Schmitt's identity, it is pointless for us to talk about
the role morality of the rulers with respect to the ruled. The issue only
arises because there is not an identity between the ruler and the ruled in
a representative democracy. Similarly, if representative democracy is a
form of slavery, it is silly to speak of a role morality for the overseers of
the slaves. Against both these views, elected officials are, by a complex
formula, both the agents and the rulers of the citizenry.

My purpose is to analyze the role morality of elected representatives in
the light of the more credible theories of representation that I have canvassed: Madisonian constituency representation, party representation, and
representation in Manin's audience democracy. I propose that we define
the morality of representatives as artificial duties derived from their roles.

There are two other ways that we might proceed. We might apply
something like conventional morality to the roles of representatives.
Apart from intuitionists, no moral philosopher would do this, but we
might suppose that, empirically, there is a broadly expected—therefore
conventional—morality for elected officials. One measure of such a con-

---

[38] Arthur Miller, *On Politics and the Art of Acting* (New York: Viking, 2001).
[39] Manin, *The Principles of Representative Government*, 151, 1. Rousseau specifically discusses England in the eighteenth century. He wrote, of course, before the rise of representative democracy in its fuller forms.

ventional morality might be gleaned from surveys on why people vote against someone whom they previously supported. I doubt that there is a standard, widely accepted conventional morality for elected officials, but there might be, or there might have been in some eras. Insofar as there is such a conventional morality, it seems likely to be related to the functional role moralities that I will canvass below.

Although it seems unlikely that there is even the hint of a consensus on any broad conventional morality for elected officials in modern democracies, there might be nearly a consensus that our officials should not use their offices to work for their private benefit against the interests of their constituencies or of the larger public. There is a standard moral constraint on agency relationships in general, which bars the agent from taking any action that would be a conflict of interest. Agents should not use their position of acting on the authority of others to take advantage of them. While this principle is seemingly simple in the contexts of many agency relationships—in our dealings with lawyers, doctors, accountants, and so forth—articulation of such a principle for elected officials is complex, as I shall argue below.

A. Functionally determined morality

The role morality of a doctor is to see to the patient's health because this is the function for which the doctor's services are sought; the role morality of a lawyer is, analogously, to see to winning the client's case or giving beneficial legal advice. If we wish to determine what the role morality of elected officials is—by analogy to professional ethics—we must first settle on what the function of an elected official is in relation to a constituent. This depends on our explanatory (not normative) theory of representation. Clearly, there cannot be a generally correct role morality for political representatives in the way that there is for doctors, because there are many theories of representation and these require different principles of action by elected officials.

We have at least three practical theories of representation that are quite distinct from one another. First, there is the *quasi-Madisonian theory* that focuses on individual legislators as agents of their constituencies. Second, there is the *political party theory* that makes elected officials the agents of their parties, and parties the agents of their partisan constituencies, which typically are broadly defined classes rather than geographical constituencies. Third, there is *Manin's audience democracy*, in which it is not clear that elected officials are agents of anyone other than themselves. The first two theories yield relatively straightforward principles of role morality for representatives. Historically, the role morality that seems most commonly stipulated by citizens in many democracies is that representatives be seen as agents of their constituents or as party loyalists. Given that representatives cannot know in detail what their constituents' wants are, representatives can knowledgeably only address their constituents' interests as fairly broadly conceived. Therefore, the role morality of an elected lawmaker is to see to the broadly defined interests of his or her constituents. We can call this the 'Madisonian role morality' of elected legislators, which had its greatest influence in the early United States. We can call it 'party role morality' in systems organized by parties, although in a party system, service to one's constituency is rendered indirectly through service to one's party, which serves all relevant constituencies.

If we consider the current stage of development of representation, Manin's audience democracy, we may wonder whether any role morality still applies to elected officials. One might assert a role morality, but the voters are unlikely to be concerned with it, except perhaps when a representative is grossly out of line. Suppose we do not elect our officials on the ground of how we expect them to handle their role in office, but primarily on the ground of who they are, including whether they happen to be celebrities. Then they would seem to have no mandate beyond continuing to be themselves. If media mastery is the route to election, then it might also be the route to renown while in office. It would be perverse for the electorate to complain that their officials are very good at precisely the skills that got them elected.

We might still think that the role morality of representatives is to represent, to work as agents for their constituents' interests, sometimes to seek the larger public good, and sometimes to defend civil liberties. But in America our moral expectations evidently do not explain or even correlate with how we vote to select our representatives. It was a happy fact of both Madisonian individual and later party systems that our interests coincided with our moral expectations for our representatives. In audience democracy, they do not correlate well.

Voters sometimes do hold candidates accountable for lack of media appeal, as in the case of Al Gore and George Bush in 2000, or for loss of it, as in the case of Gary Condit in 2002. Gore was often ridiculed for his stiff, dull manner (with at least one popular comedian comparing him to a wooden cigar store Indian). Bush, who barely won a close election over Gore, had likewise been satirized for his frequent verbal clumsiness. Prior to 2002, Condit had been reelected several times, even though his legislative impact was nil throughout his time in office. When he became the furtive man who refused to speak to the press about his reputed affair with his murdered former intern, his career was doomed, even if it could have been shown that he had played no role in her murder, and even though mere revelation of his affair, had the woman not been murdered, might not have blocked his continued reelection. By appearing indifferent, if not sinister, he simply lost much of the personal appeal that had repeatedly won him reelection.

If personality and media success are the grounds for election, then the electorate is likely to be divided on most politicians just because different personalities are likely to appeal to different voters. It seems probable, for example, that the astonishing divergence of views on Bill Clinton had much to do with divergent responses to his personal style. Even as he shifted the Democratic Party toward the center of American politics, he was detested by the American Right as perhaps no one since Franklin Roosevelt. In keeping with Manin's thesis on the evolution from Madisonian to audience democracy, Roosevelt seems to have been despised for his political positions, Clinton for being Clinton.

The development of audience democracy raises the question of whether personality might correlate with political positions to a sufficient degree as to yield the cues that Popkin and others need for their argument that voters base their votes on low-information rationality. There are two interlocking sets of correlations: first, on the side of the candidates and, then, on the side of the voters. Candidate personality must correlate with candidate position, and, given this correlation, candidate appeal must correlate with the voters' positions on issues. These correlations are tenuous reeds for us to hold onto in the hope for rational politics, if we have indeed entered an era of audience democracy. Against even such a slim hope for rationality, it seems likely that audience democracy is a response to the combination of voter ignorance of policy and government and of politicians' ignorance of voters' interests other than in broad terms. If we put the Schumpeterian vision of the limited capacities of voters together with the Austrian vision of the limited capacities of the state, we have representatives who cannot know much about their constituents trying to represent constituents who do not even know their interests in many areas and who, in any case, know very little about their government, its policies, and its officials.

B. Conventionally determined morality

Beyond any role morality that is functionally determined by our theory of representation, we might insist on several other "moral constraints" (that derive from conventional morality) on what our representatives do in office. There is one fairly broad, general concern that representatives are commonly expected to address: the political equality of citizens. This is a concern that seems to follow from the nature and purpose of democracy. We might fundamentally disagree about the extent to which economic inequality is good (as in the theory of justice of John Rawls, who allows inequalities— which might be extreme—that redound to the benefit of the worst off), but we do not generally argue in public that political inequality is good, although some, including Mill and Texas oilman H. L. Hunt, are notable exceptions. Exactly what it takes to make individuals politically equal is not easily determined, but some elements seem clear enough.[40] Anything that is an obstacle to political participation, such as extremely poor education, and that might be affected by public policy is an issue that we might ex-

---

[40] For discussion, see Thomas Christiano, *The Rule of the Many: Fundamental Issues in Democratic Theory* (Boulder, CO: Westview Press, 1996).

pect our representatives to take on, even though it goes beyond our own interests and beyond their representation of our interests.

As noted earlier, Mill supposes that two of the most important tasks of government are to promote the virtue and intelligence of citizens, and to organize what virtue and intelligence already exist.[41] These two functions are of such salience for him because he supposes that the most important consideration in creating and running government is the "quality" of citizens,[42] which might be partly a concern with political equality. (Against such generosity of interpretation, however, we know that Mill strongly defends inequality of political power grounded in intellectual qualifications.) If we thought that citizens played a substantial and active role in government, then we might agree with this claim, but it is prima facie false that citizens play a great role. They might occasionally mobilize effectively and bring about a change in government policy, as may have happened in the civil rights and anti–Vietnam War movements in the United States. But such activism is surely a rare activity for citizens, who generally attend to their own lives, acquiesce in government's discretion to determine and carry out public policy, and even acquiesce to the extreme as millions are sent off to fight and die in "great" wars.

One might contrive an argument that, say, broader education would redound not only to the benefit of those educated by this new policy, but also to the benefit of more or less all citizens through the creation of a more productive or otherwise more appealing society. But in general, it seems likely that a representative who works for such an egalitarian policy for the whole society will risk harming the interests of his or her constituents, who may not directly benefit from, but may directly pay for, the programs that enhance educational equality. Some things that a representative might seek for his constituents can most readily be attained if they are provided for all those in the relevant class. For example, the best way to guarantee a minimum wage for my constituents might be to legislate it for the entire nation. Hence, I might act in a way that is similar to the actions of a Burkean or Millian representative concerned with the general welfare and not merely with the welfare of my own constituents.

We could stipulate other "moral constraints" on representatives, such as seeing to the constituents' moral development or their religious beliefs. These two purposes were ruled out by the American constitutionalists, although they have been stipulated to be a large part of the mandate of government by many other regimes. In American politics there have been major movements that advocate the use of government for other purposes, for example, the social-agenda crowd that wants regulation of values, the mercantilist-statist Right that wants government to protect business interests, or the socialist-statist Left that wants government to restructure society to achieve greater economic equality.

---

[41] Mill, *Considerations on Representative Government*, 390, 392.
[42] Ibid., 389.

Additionally, we can probably claim that part of the role morality of some government officials in the United States is to defend individual liberties, such as those defined in the Bill of Rights. For many officials, such as legislators, the defense of liberties requires merely refraining from infringing them, although, on occasion, legislators might be called upon to devise new protections, and other officials, especially those in the justice system, might be expected to defend liberties against official abuse. It is primarily the judiciary that has the function and, therefore, the role morality to defend civil liberties. Elected officials and appointed officials, such as the U.S. Attorney General, frequently find civil liberties an annoyance.

Finally, we might wish to press upon legislators as part of their role morality the more general purpose of working for the interest of the entire public, and not merely for their constituents. In a variant on my example of education, many legislators who represent districts in which education meets reasonably high standards might be expected, nevertheless, to vote for legislation mandating such standards for the entire nation, not in order to enhance political competence (as in my original example), but to enrich the life prospects of those who would benefit from the new programs. The votes of these legislators would serve not the interests of their own constituents, but only, in some sense, the broader public good or even only the interests of other citizens outside their constituency, possibly even at a substantial cost to their own constituents. If the policy were seen as a public good, then support for it could easily be justified on Burkean or Millian grounds, but it might sometimes also be argued on the ground of concern for political equality, in which case it would be an outgrowth of a conventional morality.

Clearly, none of these conventional moral principles for legislators is strongly backed by the electorates of many democratic nations. These are in many cases idiosyncratic views endorsed by activists of various stripes, not views inferred from the logic or nature of representation. Some of them might be backed by particular moral theories, such as utilitarianism, which might also back the institutions of representative government, but the principles are still not inherent in the nature of representation.

C. Conflicts of interest

Finally, we ought to consider one aspect of the role morality of anyone who acts as an agent for anyone else. All agents must avoid conflicts of interest that could lead them to benefit themselves at the expense of their principals. If our elected officials are our agents, then they must adhere to this constraint. The problem of conflicts of interest raises what is apparently the most striking difference between traditional professional ethics and any plausible ethics for elected officials: both the traditional professional and the elected official are agents on our behalf, and we want them to act in our interests, but the politician's position is far more complex than that of the traditional professional. For example, every doctor to whom I go as a patient should be my agent. But a representative can be seen as my agent and not yours in a meaningful and important sense if I voted for this representative while you voted against her. You cannot claim that she should work for your interests in the same way that I can, because she should act for the majority who elected her, including me, more than for those who opposed that majority.

Moreover, you might want to have her removed from office if she engages in practices that seem to benefit herself at public expense. I might not want her to be removed because I suspect that any replacement would be less committed to serving my interests. Consider the complications that might factor into opposition or support for a politician aside from the merits of any charges against him. As a real-world example, consider the positions of those who supported or opposed the impeachment of President Clinton and his removal from office. (The concern in his case was not over any abuse of office for his own interest.) Obviously, there was a substantial correlation between one's position on these moves and one's interest in having Clinton continue in office. Similarly, supporters of Berlusconi and his Northern League have argued that court actions to try him for bribery are politically motivated and opportunistic and, as I previously noted, they support legislation that would protect him from prosecution.[43]

If we are legislating in advance, when there is no political valence to corruption, then we might all agree that acting from certain classes of conflict of interest should be punished by removal from office. When there is an actual case, you might favor removal while I do not, because your interests are served by removal and mine are not. The role morality for the officeholder will then be whatever we have stipulated by law and will not be colored by our own interests in removal or retention of a particular person in office. We could sensibly say that there is a public interest in blocking certain classes of conflict of interest.

VII. Conclusion

If democracy were strictly representative, then government would be an epiphenomenon determined by the wants and interests of citizens, as in the view of political scientist Arthur Bentley (1870–1957).[44] It is not merely an epiphenomenon, though, because citizens' interests and demands are only weakly determinative. Government takes on a life of its own that has much to do with the elevation of political leaders to a peculiar aristocracy. This aristocracy is not the oligarchy of Michels, because its members are far more subject to election, and they can occasionally be unelected by the larger public. Michels's oligarchs were subject to control only within their organizations, not by the larger public.

[43] Bruni, "Italy, a Land of Tolerance."
[44] Arthur F. Bentley, *The Process of Government* (Chicago, IL: University of Chicago Press, 1908).

A saving grace of aristocratic representative democracy is that, in any case, democracy works at all only where there is fairly broad consensus on political order and, commonly, civil liberties. This consensus means that most citizens need merely acquiesce in allowing government to run or intrude into large parts of their lives. As political scientist Robert Dahl says, "In a sense, what we ordinarily describe as democratic 'politics' is merely the chaff. It is the surface manifestation, representing superficial conflicts. [These] disputes over policy alternatives are nearly always disputes over a set of alternatives that have already been winnowed down to those within the broad area of basic agreement."[45] This is roughly Tocqueville's view as well: "When a community actually has a mixed government—that is to say, when it is equally divided between adverse principles—it must either experience a revolution or fall into anarchy."[46]

We should qualify Dahl's claim with the note that "the broad area of basic agreement" need only be an area in which the politically effective groups are in agreement. Indeed, it need merely be an area in which the aristocratic political class is in agreement while the rest of the population basically acquiesces.[47] We might revise the Dahl and Tocqueville view to fit current conditions and say that much of the chaff of politics today is more nearly a part of the image than of real policy-oriented concern in its own right. For example, the chaff of Gary Condit's life dominated the media for weeks until it was reduced to its properly trivial status by the terrorist attacks of September 11, 2001.

Finally, note the irony that it is only because citizens began to be somewhat educated that representative democracy could arise in a large state (although the state's capacity to take a census and its technological capacity to collect votes have also played roles).[48] Yet it is the limits of citizens' understanding that makes it difficult for us to assess the quality of the very representatives we elect and, in particular, to determine whether they live up to any role morality we might assign to them. In the face of current trends in electoral motivations, it seems unlikely that the electorate consistently has in mind any role morality, either conventional or functional, for the media masters we put in office.

Politics, New York University, and Political Science, Stanford University

[45] Robert A. Dahl, *A Preface to Democratic Theory* (Chicago, IL: University of Chicago Press, 1956), 132–33.

[46] Alexis de Tocqueville, *Democracy in America*, 2 vols. (1835, 1840; reprint, New York: Knopf, 1945), 1:260.

[47] Russell Hardin, *Liberalism, Constitutionalism, and Democracy* (Oxford: Oxford University Press, 1999), chap. 4.

[48] Scott argues that a state's capacity to keep records on us or, in his term, to make us 'legible' allows the state to control us in various ways, such as by raising taxes and armies. This capacity also makes it possible to determine just who is to be represented in a modern democracy. Indeed, the U.S. Constitution requires a periodic census primarily for the purpose of allocating seats in the House of Representatives according to state populations so that representation is relatively equal.

DUAL CITIZENSHIP AND AMERICAN DEMOCRACY: PATRIOTISM, NATIONAL ATTACHMENT, AND NATIONAL IDENTITY*

By Stanley A. Renshon

I. Introduction

Until recently, with one historical exception, America was able to take for granted a coherent national culture and identity. Successive waves of immigrants entered a country that assumed that their ultimate assimilation was a desirable, not an oppressive, outcome. The United States did not prove equally hospitable to everyone: some groups endured enormous hardships on their way to a fuller realization of America's great promise of opportunity and freedom. Yet, throughout U.S. history, the dream of common purpose and community propelled the collective desire to live up to this promise and provided the framework within which progress was understood and made.[1]

Only the Civil War really tested the cultural and civic bonds that united America's disparate interests. Now, however, for the second time in its history, the United States faces a real question of how to fulfill its motto, *E pluribus unum*, that is, "Out of many, one." Specifically, the U.S. faces the challenge of how to maintain a stable and effective relationship between this *unum* (the single American polity) and *pluribus* (the plurality of racial, ethnic, and religious groups that constitute America's citizenry). Unlike the first, the "Second Civil War" does not pit commerce against agriculture, urban centers against rural traditions, or North against South. Rather, the new danger lies in conflicts among people of different racial, cultural, and ethnic heritages, and between those who view America's cultural and political traditions as impediments to liberal democracy and those who think that preserving these traditions, while reforming them, is the best route to an improved society.

Unlike the first Civil War, this "Second Civil War" is not pitting one section of the country against another, but, rather, it is being waged in *every* section of the United States. This 'culture war' is, in reality, a series

* I would like to thank my fellow contributors to this volume and the editors for helpful comments.
[1] Arnold Rose, *The Negro in America*, the condensed version of Gunnar Myrdal's *An American Dilemma* (New York: Harper & Row, 1964).

of wars: history wars, language wars, military culture wars, family definition wars, and so on. As a result, unlike the opposing camps of the first Civil War, today's antagonists cannot take refuge in the primary institutions in their part of the country, that is, their families or their religious, social, cultural, or political organizations. These are precisely the places where the battles are being fought.

The consequences of these conflicts are not to be found in the number of killed or wounded. Rather, they are to be found primarily in the retreat from common ideals, in basic cultural values abandoned or under siege, and in institutions floundering in a sea of shrill and conflicting demands. While America is undeniably more diverse than at any time in its history, it is also undeniably more fragmented, alienated, and polarized. At issue is whether it is possible or desirable to preserve the strengths of a common heritage in the face of insistence from some quarters that America's past has resulted in a culture that should be torn down in order to be built over, rather than one that is worth keeping and building upon.[2] It is a conflict over the viability of American culture and identity itself.

---

[2] Stark illustrations of this viewpoint are found in the responses of some to the September 11, 2001, terrorist attacks on the United States, which resulted in the loss of thousands of human lives. Susan Sontag had this to say:

> The disconnect between last Tuesday's monstrous dose of reality and the self-righteous drivel and outright deceptions being peddled by public figures and TV commentators is startling, depressing. The voices licensed to follow the event seem to have joined together in a campaign to infantilize the public. Where is the acknowledgment that this was not a "cowardly" attack on "civilization" or "liberty" or "humanity" or "the free world" but an attack on the world's self-proclaimed superpower, undertaken as a consequence of specific American alliances and actions? How many citizens are aware of the ongoing American bombing of Iraq? And if the word "cowardly" is to be used, it might be more aptly applied to those who kill from beyond the range of retaliation, high in the sky, than to those willing to die themselves in order to kill others.

In other words, the terrorists' attacks were America's fault.

Sontag is not alone. Michael Lerner opined:

> We live in a society that daily teaches us to look out for No. 1, to keep our focus on our own bottom line and to see others primarily as instruments to help us achieve our goals and satisfactions. . . . And that same insensitivity is institutionalized in the global system whose symbolic headquarters have been the World Trade Center and the Pentagon. Yet we rarely look at our lives in these larger terms. We don't feel personally responsible when a U.S. corporation runs a sweatshop in the Philippines or crushes efforts of workers to organize in Singapore. It never occurs to us that when the U.S. (with 5% of the world's population and 25% of the wealth) manages over the course of several decades that shape global trade policies, that increase the disparity between rich and poor countries, this directly produces some of the suffering in the lives of 2 billion people who live in poverty, 1 billion of whom struggle with malnutrition, homelessness and poverty-related diseases.

In other words, there is poverty in the world. The U.S. as a nation and Americans as individuals have not eradicated it; therefore, the chickens have come home to roost and Americans have experienced the understandable (and just?) consequences of their neglect. See Susan Sontag, "The Talk of the Town," *The New Yorker*, September 24, 2001, 32; and Michael Lerner, "The Case for Peace," *Time*, October 1, 2001, 77.

II. American National Identity and Dual Citizenship

In 1782, the Frenchman Crèvecoeur asked, "What does it mean to be an American?" [3] This has never been an easy question to answer, although many have tried over the two-hundred-plus years of the country's existence. It is much less easy to answer now. Indeed, during the past three decades, new and more troubling questions have emerged.

Some ask: What is American national identity? Others ask: Should there be one? Some worry about how Americans can maintain and further develop common understandings and purpose in a diverse country. Others ask: What useful purpose do such worries serve when Americans live in a "postmodern" era and when their allegiances ought to be global?

The implications of these issues are well illustrated by the increasing incidence of dual citizenship by United States citizens. What, exactly, is dual citizenship? At its most basic level, dual citizenship involves simultaneously holding more than one citizenship or nationality.[4] The two terms, though often confused, are not synonymous. 'Citizenship' is a legal term and refers to the rights and responsibilities that become attached to a person by virtue of his or her formal membership in a political

---

[3] J. Hector St. John de Crèvecoeur, *Letters from an American Farmer* (1782), ed. Susan Manning (New York: Oxford University Press, 1997).

[4] A person in the United States may acquire multiple citizenship in any one of five ways:

1. He or she may be born in the United States to immigrant parents. All children born in the United States are U.S. citizens regardless of the status of their parents (*jus soli*).
2. A person may be born outside the United States to one parent who is a U.S. citizen and another who is not (*jus sanguinis*). A child born in the United Kingdom to an American citizen and a British citizen, for example, would be a citizen of both countries.
3. A person may become a naturalized citizen of the United States and this act may be ignored by his or her country of origin. This can occur even if the country of naturalization requires, as the United States does, that those seeking naturalization "renounce" their former citizenship and nationality. In the case of the United States, a new citizen's failure to take action consistent with renunciation carries no penalties, and other countries can, and often do, simply ignore the new oath of allegiance.
4. A person may become a naturalized citizen of the United States and, in doing so, lose her citizenship in her country of origin, but the individual may regain it at any time and still retain U.S. citizenship.

These are the traditional sources of multiple citizenship. Yet, there is now a fifth and potentially far-reaching method of obtaining multiple citizenship, namely, 'cluster citizenship'. Increasingly, some regions of the world are working toward common citizenship, even while specific countries within these groupings retain the right to regulate citizenship. So, for example, a citizen of Germany and France now shares a common citizenship in the European Union, even though both countries retain a legal right to regulate their own citizenship standards. This follows a similar practice between South American nations and Spain, whereby a number of countries in South America recognize dual citizenship with the latter. Or an Algerian can have dual French citizenship and if he then becomes a naturalized American citizen he would then hold citizenship in three countries.

society. 'Nationality' is, at base, a psychological term that refers to the emotional and epistemological understandings about the world that bind members of a group to each other and to the institutional and cultural forms that reflect such understandings. The basic dilemma of dual citizenship is that, in the modern world, passports and attachments are increasingly separated from each other.

The United States does not formally recognize dual citizenship, but neither does it take any effective stand, politically or legally, against it. Thus, a person can have all, or many, of the rights and responsibilities that adhere to a U.S. citizen while doing the same in each of the several countries in which she also holds a passport, regardless of the limited length of time or actual absence of residence in the U.S., and regardless of the nature of her economic, cultural, political, or emotional ties to the other countries.

Many people are surprised to learn that an American citizen cannot be deprived of citizenship even if he or she holds elective office in another country, serves as an advisor to a foreign government, votes in another country's elections, or serves in its armed forces—even if that country is actively engaged in hostilities against the United States or its allies. John Walker Lindh, also known as "Suleyman al-faris," an American who took up arms with the Taliban against the United States in Afghanistan, could have been tried and convicted of treason without ever having had his U.S. citizenship stripped from him. (He pleaded guilty to two lesser charges and received a twenty-year prison sentence.)

The attacks of September 11, 2001, have made Americans more aware of the issue of allegiances and attachments, but this awareness primarily has been focused narrowly on Middle Eastern and South Asian immigrants. The national security implications of immigration and national attachment are real, but they are not my concern here.[5] The issue of national attachment, cohesion, and integration is a problem that goes well beyond any specific group of immigrants, and it is this larger issue that I would like to address in this essay.

This issue comes into sharper focus by looking at some basic numbers. There are now ninety-two countries that recognize, and many of which encourage, dual citizenship for their nationals. This number grew dramatically during the 1990s and is expected to continue to grow.

The numbers involved are quite striking. Historically, of the more than twenty-two million immigrants legally admitted into the United States between 1961 and 1997, almost seventeen million arrived from countries that allow dual or multiple citizenship. Official figures from the U.S.

---

[5] I take up the national security implications of dual citizenship and multiple attachments elsewhere. See Stanley A. Renshon, *The 50% American: National Identity in a Dangerous Age* (Washington, DC: Georgetown University Press, forthcoming).

Immigration and Naturalization Service for 1994 through 1998 show that seventeen of the "top twenty" immigrant-sending countries (85 percent) allow some form of multiple citizenship. Of the slightly more than 2.6 million immigrants who arrived during this period, some 2.2 million (86 percent) are multiple-citizenship immigrants. And these represent only the "top twenty" immigration sources. Historically, of the more than twenty-two million immigrants legally admitted into the United States between 1961 and 1997, some 16.3 million, or almost 75 percent, are from countries that allow dual or multiple citizenship. A conservative estimate of the number of individuals living in America with, or entitled to, multiple citizenship is well over forty million and rising.

One might ask, So what? My answer is this: The psychological implications and political consequences of having large groups of Americans holding multiple citizenship has rarely, if ever, been seriously considered. It is yet another example of how American political institutions often "make" policy by not paying attention. Yet, the issues raised by these facts go to the very heart of what it means to be an American and a citizen. These facts also hold enormous implications for the integrity of America's civic and cultural traditions, as well as for domestic national security.

Is it really possible to be a fully engaged and knowledgeable citizen of several countries? Is it possible to follow two or more different cultural traditions? Is it possible to have two, possibly conflicting, core identities and associated attachments? And, even assuming that such things are possible, from the standpoint of democratic and cultural functioning, are they desirable?

A. Unlimited identities: A narcissistic conceit

Consider the question of multiple loyalties and American national identity. Most advocates of multiple citizenship subscribe to the "Why not one more?" theory.[6] They remind us that we are, as in my own case, sons, husbands, and fathers. We are labeled as "Caucasian" and Western. We might be working class by background but slightly upper-middle class by socioeconomic status (SES) categories. We are Jewish and reformed, New Yorkers, Manhattanites, and Upper West Siders. We are professors, scholar/ writers, psychologists, psychoanalysts, and neo-Freudians. Economically we are progressive capitalists; we are politically moderate and culturally conservative. And we are Americans and Northerners.

---

[6] See, for example, Randolph S. Bourne, "Trans-National America," *Atlantic Monthly* 118 (1916): 86–97; T. Alexander Aleinikoff, "A Multicultural Nationalism?" *American Prospect* 9, no. 36 (1998): 80–86; and Peter J. Spiro, "Dual Nationality and the Meaning of Citizenship," *Emory Law Journal* 46, no. 4 (1997): 1412–85.

Postmodern theorists see us as comprising a virtually unlimited and replaceable set of selves that can be enacted or abandoned at will. Liberal political theorists and their allies count up all of the categories by which we may be understood and conclude that adding one more, even a different nationality, will make little, if any, difference.

The first basic fallacy underlying these arguments is the notion that the elements that comprise a person's core identity are infinitely malleable. They are not. The second basic fallacy is that all identifications have equal weight. They do not.

The "Why not one more?" position fails to distinguish between the elements of personal identity that form the central core of one's psychology and those that are more peripheral. I am much more a father than a Caucasian, much more a political moderate than an Upper West Sider. And, I am definitely more of an American than most of the other categories in my list.

B. Dual citizenship and American democracy

The idea that individuals can integrate multiple, conflicting basic orientations toward life may well prove a form of cultural conceit. Apparently, it is easy for some in the privileged elite to disregard the primary attachment to their country that other citizens feel and that is crucial to American civic life. In so doing, the elite appear to have confused "sophistication" with a new form of rootlessness. Such people may go anywhere, but belong nowhere.

Such rootlessness is the opposite of civic engagement. The American ideal of civic republicanism is, after all, grounded upon the citizen, not the subject. It has been well understood in political theory that democracy makes many demands on its citizens. They need to be informed about the issues that their societies face, temperate in their deliberations on them, and restrained in actions designed to further their preferred solutions. Living in a country that faces complex and divisive issues arising from its increasing diversity and the threat of catastrophic terror requires even more from its citizens.

Yet, advocates of dual citizenship consistently minimize the difficulties of being a fully engaged, knowledgeable, and effective citizen in one political system, much less two. Some endorse Michael Sandel's view that whether one chooses to carry out one's commitments as an American citizen or as a responsible citizen of another country is a matter of personal moral reflection and choice.[7] Sandel and his supporters combine a profoundly robust view of citizens' entitlements with an equally pro-

---

[7] Michael J. Sandel, *Democracy's Discontent: America in Search of a Public Philosophy* (Cambridge, MA: Belknap Press, 1996).

found, but narrow, view of their responsibilities. This combination has significant ramifications for America's commitment to the foundation of republican democracy upon an informed and engaged citizenry. At a time when Americans' civic connections and institutions are, by almost any measure, depleted,[8] is it wise to argue in favor of making the responsibilities of citizenship wholly optional?

C. Knowledge of two cultures?

The informed citizen is the basic integer of the democratic process. If citizens do not or will not know or cannot understand their country, then a linchpin of democratic government has been lost. Advocates of multiple citizenship assume that it is possible—indeed, desirable—for citizens to be well versed in the culture, history, language, and political debates of more than one country.

Regretfully for those who make this assumption, however, the American public fails badly on indicators of deliberative knowledge. In a 1996 poll, the Pew Research Center for the People and the Press found that "a quarter of those surveyed said they learned about the presidential campaign from [television comedians Jay] Leno and David Letterman, a figure rising to 40 percent among those under 30."[9]

Not surprisingly, perhaps, in view of the above, U.S. schools appear to be losing ground in what might well be considered the most basic element in preparing young persons for their role as citizens, that is, having a foundation of knowledge about the country in which they live and the political institutions that undergird its freedom and way of life.[10] A nationwide survey conducted by the National Constitution Center found that "only 6 percent [of Americans surveyed] can name all four rights guaranteed by the First Amendment; 62 percent cannot name all three branches of the Federal government; 35 percent believe the Constitution

---

[8] See, for example, Robert D. Putnam, *Bowling Alone: The Collapse and Revival of American Community* (New York: Simon & Shuster, 2001), and the literature related to his argument.

[9] Cited in Howard Kurtz, "Americans Wait for the Punch Line on Impeachment: As the Senate Trial Proceeds, Comedians Deliver the News," *Washington Post*, January 26, 1999, A1. See also Michael X. Delli Carpini and Scott Keeter, *What Americans Know about Politics and Why It Matters* (New Haven, CT: Yale University Press, 1996).

[10] See, for example, John J. Patrick, "Political Socialization and Political Education in Schools," in Stanley Allen Renshon, ed., *Handbook of Political Socialization: Theory and Research* (New York: Free Press, 1977), 190–222; and Judith Torney-Purta, "Psychological Theory As a Basis for Political Socialization Research: Individuals' Construction of Knowledge," *Perspectives on Political Science* 24, no. 1 (1995): 23–33; Judith Torney-Purta, "Education in Multicultural Settings: Perspectives from Global and International Education Programs," in Willis D. Hawley and Anthony W. Jackson, eds., *Toward a Common Destiny: Improving Race and Ethnic Relations in America* (San Francisco, CA: Jossey-Bass, 1995), 341–70; and Richard G. Niemi and Jane Junn, *Civic Education: What Makes Students Learn* (New Haven, CT: Yale University Press, 1998).

mandates English as the official language; and more than half of Americans don't know the number of senators." [11]

The 1990 National Assessment of Educational Progress (NAEP) *Civics Report Card*—a major test of subject knowledge for fourth, eighth, and twelfth grade students—revealed that "students have only a superficial knowledge of civics and lack depth of understanding." For example, only 38 percent of eighth graders knew that Congress makes laws; and nearly half of high-school seniors did not recognize typical examples of the federal system of checks and balances.

The 1998 national surveys and *Civics Report Card* divided scores on knowledge and proficiency into four groups: below basic, basic, proficient, and advanced. [12] At each of the three grade levels tested (fourth, eighth, and twelfth), 'basic' was defined as having "partial mastery and skills that are fundamental to proficient work at each grade," while 'proficient' was defined as representing "solid academic performance." So how many students at each grade level were 'proficient' or, even better, 'advanced'? Not many. In fourth grade, only 25 percent scored as proficient or advanced, which means, of course, that 75 percent did not reach proficiency. In eighth grade the figure was 24 percent for proficiency or advanced competence, and in twelfth grade the figure was 30 percent for the two categories. These results do not report disparities by race and ethnicity that are, if anything, even more troubling.

Lest this be seen as an issue affecting only public schools with their mixed record of academic performance, the results of a survey conducted at America's most elite colleges is likewise instructive. The American Council of Trustees and Alumni, a group that supports liberal arts education, recently posed a series of high-school level multiple-choice questions to a randomly selected group of graduating seniors at Harvard, Princeton, and Brown. [13] The results were dismal: among the United States' best students, 71 percent did not know the purpose of the Emancipation Proclamation, and 78 percent were not able to identify the author of the phrase "of the people, by the people, for the people." Seventy percent could not link President Lyndon Johnson with the passage of the historic

[11] Cited in Margaret Stimman Branson, "The Role of Civic Education," a report issued as part of the *National Standards for Civics and Government* (Calabasas, CA: Center for Civic Education, 1998), available on-line at http://www.civiced.org/articles_role.html [accessed May 6, 2003].

[12] National Center for Education Statistics, National Assessment of Educational Progress, *1998 Civics Report Card for the Nation* (Washington, DC: U.S. Department of Education, 1999), 40; available on-line at http://nces.ed.gov/nationsreportcard/civics/ [accessed May 6, 2003].

[13] Jerry L. Martin and Ann D. Neal, *Losing America's Memory: Historical Illiteracy in the 21st Century* (Washington, DC: American Council of Trustees and Alumni, 2000). See also Scott Veale, "Word for Word/Pop Quiz; History 101: Snoop Doggy Roosevelt," *New York Times*, July 2, 2000, late edition–final, sec. 4, p. 7, col. 1.

1965 Voting Rights Act. Yet, 90 percent could correctly identify rap singer Snoop Doggy Dog.

Some ask whether it is legitimate to hold immigrants to a standard unmet by citizens, as if any ignorance among the latter is good reason to allow the same among the former. Yet, the question does contain a point. The implications of these data are troubling for Americans and immigrants alike.

Americans do not have and are not acquiring the levels of basic information and proficiencies that are essential to living in and supporting a democratic republican form of government. These deficiencies apparently extend from America's most average students to its "best and brightest." Accordingly, these findings raise serious questions about whether American children will have the tools needed to shoulder the responsibilities of living in and helping to guide the United States through dangerous and difficult times. These deficiencies certainly do not give much comfort to those who believe that it is no difficult matter to be sufficiently versed in the history, politics, and policies of two or more cultures.

III. American National Identity

To this point, I have used the term 'national identity' as if there were some shared understanding of the term and, of course, there is not. Social psychologists who use the term tend to equate it with 'patriotism', and 'patriotism' with what can only be called 'aggressive nationalism'. Essentially, this entails agreement with survey items that reflect a tendency to see the world in an "us" versus "them" way and a willingness to take whatever steps are necessary to see that "us" comes out ahead. Needless to say, love of country does not necessarily require a citizen to be quick to war, or to support one's country regardless of what it does. What 'patriotism' does actually mean is a matter to which I will turn further below.

Others, being both outside of psychology and unfamiliar with it, fare no better. Eytan Meyers defines what he terms a "national identity approach" to immigration policy as focusing on several factors:

> The unique history of each country, its conceptions of citizenship and nationality, as well as debates over national identity and social conflicts within it, shape its immigration policies. . . . Much of this literature can be characterized as historical sociology or political sociology, and it builds upon social and psychological theories, and concepts such as national identity, nation building, prejudice, alienation and social closure.[14]

---

[14] Eytan Meyers, "Theories of Immigration Policy: A Comparative Analysis," *International Migration Review* 34, no. 4 (2000): 1245–82.

If this sounds like a hodgepodge of different terms with little theoretical specification, Meyers is perhaps to be excused. After all, he is not a psychologist and even the father of the term 'identity', Erik Erikson, was extremely vague about its meaning.[15]

The idea that the character or psychology of a people is related to its capacity for particular kinds of politics has a long history. How, exactly, to understand this link has had its share of false starts. National character studies, which were popular in the 1940s and 1950s, tried to find antecedents of political institutions and cultural practices in very early childhood experiences. The swaddling of Russian children, it was said, made them vulnerable to a lack of individual initiative.

Along similar lines, the authoritarian German family had made German citizens susceptible to a strong father figure. Members of the early culture-and-personality school often wrote as if personality were culture writ large, and they viewed the former through the powerful but scarcely refined lens of early psychoanalytic theory. Those uncomfortable with a view of internal psychology as little more than a barely contained caldron of urges set for life in instinctual stone had many legitimate questions to ask.

In 1963, Gabriel Almond and Sidney Verba, in their classic study, *The Civic Culture*, approached national psychology and its relationship to political practice in a different way.[16] Using survey research in five countries—some democratic, others developing—they tried to uncover the psychological correlates of successful civic culture. They found that citizens who were active, informed, and had the expectation of impact were more often to be found in those countries that had developed effective civic cultures. Whichever came first, the democratic culture or the psychology related to it, it was clear that there was a relationship between the capacity for, and the exercise of, democratic practice and a particular psychology necessary to sustain it.

The question of what are the sources of civic integration and national attachment is, of course, related to the question of what public psychologies are consistent with democratic practice. Yet, it is also a very separable question, and a critical one, whether the United States has sufficient

---

[15] In one place, Erikson defines "ego identity" as "that which consists of role images." Shortly thereafter, he defines "self-identity" as what "emerges from experiences in which temporarily confused selves are successfully reintegrated into an ensemble of roles which also secure social recognition." Erik H. Erikson, *Identity: Youth and Crisis* (New York: W. W. Norton, 1968), 211. Elsewhere, he defines "self-identity" as "the more or less actually obtained, but forever to be revised, sense of the self within social reality." Erik H. Erikson, *Identity and the Life Cycle* (New York: Norton, 1980).

If this sounds somewhat vague, it is. Erikson himself recognized its ambiguity: "I have tried out the term identity . . . in many different connotations. . . . Identity in its vaguest sense suggests . . . much of what has been called the self by a variety of workers. . . ."

[16] Gabriel A. Almond and Sidney Verba, *The Civic Culture: Political Attitudes and Democracy in Five Nations* (Princeton, NJ: Princeton University Press, 1963).

sources of cohesion and attachment among its diverse population to sustain the level of national integration that is necessary for democracy to prosper.

Americans do live in a country where there is intricate and increasing interconnectedness, but far less relatedness. Robert Putnam is right, Americans are less connected. They are, in his words, "bowling alone." [17]

The primary response to this issue has been institutional. The consensus has been that Americans need to revitalize their civic networks. Thus, the U.S. has seen White House Conferences on "Character Building for a Democratic Civil Society," a National Commission on Civic Renewal, and many thousands of other initiatives designed to mend the frayed fabric of American civic culture.

There is much to say about these important efforts, but here I want to point out that they proceed on the idea that public psychology will follow civic institutions; that is, if you improve the civic infrastructure, then you will increase individuals' sense of connectedness and presumably support for America's democratic institutions. This may well be the case, but the likelihood of accomplishing such change during America's "Second Civil War" is a matter I have not seen analyzed.

At any rate, I would like to approach the matter from a more directly psychological perspective and ask the following questions: What is the basis of a person's attachment to his or her country? And, once we arrive at an answer, what are the implications of this understanding for the very large number of immigrants who have chosen to make the United States their home?

A. The creed

Some theorists of immigration and American identity believe that they already have the answer to both of the above questions. It is 'the creed'. In the view of theorists from both the Left (Michael Walzer) and the Right (Samuel Huntington), the national creed is all that Americans need to be united.[18] Cultural aphorisms such as "Democracy is the best form of government" or "Everyone should have the right of free speech" garner almost uniform approval in public opinion surveys. And since everybody agrees, it is tempting to say that we have found the holy grail of political cohesion, but we have not.

The agreement is illusory. One is reminded here of the classic study that found that almost every American supported free speech, until the first

[17] Putnam, *Bowling Alone*.

[18] Michael Walzer, *What It Means to Be an American* (New York: Marsilio, 1996). Samuel P. Huntington, *American Politics: The Promise of Disharmony* (Cambridge, MA: Belknap Press, 1981).

time he or she was asked about a specific application of the principle that was controversial. Of course, consensual agreement by itself is no necessary reflection of desirable democratic process.[19]

No, neither the creed nor the willingness to profess it will rescue us from our difficulties for several reasons. First, it is too abstract. People can agree with many things in the abstract, but American politics takes place in the contentious, increasingly ferocious, here and now of real problems and policy debates.

Second, the creed is almost entirely cognitive. It is in the realm of the mind, not the emotions. Yes, one can have positive attachments to abstract aphorisms, but they are not the bonding glue of national attachment. One does not die for the aphorism "Democracy is the best form of government." One dies, if so inclined, for a particular manifestation of democracy.

Third, an emphasis on the creed almost completely neglects the importance of psychological characteristics that can and do unite Americans as a people. The creed suggests that Americans are bonded together because they share support at the stratospheric level of what amount to cultural clichés. Yet, there is another level at which Americans share something very fundamental that helps bind them together: their psychologies.

B. American psychology

I am not suggesting that there is some modal American character of the type that anthropologists tried to ascribe to Russians, Germans, and others. (Recall my discussion above of the "early culture-and-personality school.") What I do want to suggest, however, is that from the earliest days of America, the country has flourished because of the particular motivations of its immigrants, and they and their offspring have been influenced, in turn, by institutions and practices that call forth and reinforce these very same motivations.

I have dealt at greater length elsewhere with the evidence to support this view,[20] but here I shall briefly lay it out. America does have a national psychology, but it is not to be found solely in early childrearing practices. Nor does it consist of a limited set of traits that everyone shares. And, it

[19] Alan Wolfe's in-depth study of Americans and their approach to moral conflict found a new ethic that can be summed up by what has become almost an eleventh commandment: "Thou shall not judge." He attributes it to an emphasis on pragmatism rather than values in making tough personal decisions, a reluctance to second-guess the tough choices of other people, and ambivalence or confusion as the "default" moral position. See Alan Wolfe, *One Nation, After All: What Middle-Class Americans Really Think about God, Country, Family, Racism, Welfare, Immigration, Homosexuality, Work, the Right, the Left, and Each Other* (New York: Penguin Books, 1998).

[20] Stanley A. Renshon, "American Identity and the Dilemmas of Cultural Diversity," in Stanley A. Renshon and John Duckitt, eds., *Political Psychology: Cultural and Crosscultural Foundations* (London: Macmillan, 2000), 285–310.

is not to be found in any so-called essential national characteristics to which every American must adhere.

American national psychology is built on the motivational foundation of those who first immigrated to the United States. They were looking for a new and better life, one in which their skills could be put into the service of their ambitions. Others came looking for the freedom to express their religious views and the opportunity to build a society consistent with them.

Freedom and opportunity came together in a particular way in the religious colonies, but in quite another way in those colonies dominated by immigrants searching for economic advancement. In neither sort was freedom or opportunity an isolated, absolute value. In the case of colonists seeking religious freedom, it was embedded in a community context, and in the case of those seeking economic opportunity, it coexisted with a strong belief in public social and political equality.

The common denominator among all immigrants was first of all ambition and, secondly, courage. Those who came to the United States gave up familiar surroundings, which was no small matter, and in doing so, took large risks. No written report or rumor could adequately prepare new immigrants for what they faced. Those who were able to pursue and fulfill their ambitions for a better life had to be able to persevere through hard times and circumstances—of which there were many.

The physical realities of frontier conditions required a psychology of courage, independence, and self-reliance. Seizing opportunity required talent and hard work. America was rich in promise, but only for those willing and able to survive, persist, and thrive in difficult circumstances.

Those who prospered had to adapt. The past could no longer operate as a ready crutch. Each new challenge demanded its own solution. Thus, the early Americans were forced by necessity to honor the present more than the past and to solve problems innovatively rather than apply timeless principles. In short, forward-looking thinking became a necessity as well as an outlook.

Often having nothing more to rely on than their own ingenuity, and dealing with novel circumstances, Americans became pragmatists: they focused on what worked. America was not at first a country of revolutionary innovations, but in many ways pragmatism did prove ultimately to be revolutionary. At any rate, it was successful, and repeated success led to a sense of can-do optimism.

Some who undertook this new life hoped that they would succeed. Others were sure that they would. However, beneath both sets of feelings was a conviction that their efforts would count, and their success—if it came—would be a matter of hard work and luck (or providence), but not of luck alone. In short, these people had an expectation of personal effectiveness, which, when combined with hope or faith, gave them confidence and an optimistic outlook.

Therefore, we can say that Americans—at least those who had the most chance to be successful—shared a variety of characteristics. They were ambitious risk takers, with the courage of their aspirations. They were willing to endure enormous hardships, not once or twice, but repeatedly. The life they left behind, as bad as it was, must have looked good on occasion, but they persevered for the chance to realize their ambitions. "If at first you don't succeed, try, try again" became an aphorism for the generations.

The early Americans also needed resilience. America is often called the land of second chances, and for good reason. The opportunity for re-invention accompanied the risks of failure in a free, capitalist society. You could try, try again, but you first needed to be able to pick yourself up off the floor to do so.

Success in the United States was substantially oriented to the future and the present, rather than the past. Big ambitions were, of necessity, coupled with a pragmatic bent. What counted was what worked.

Above all, people were the authors of their own salvation, both in religious and secular terms. Individual effort, not fate, became the key to success. "God helps he who helps himself" became another aphorism for the ages.

My point here is not that every American exhibits high levels of each of these psychological elements. David Miller quotes David Hume as remarking that the vulgar think that everyone who belongs to a nation displays its distinctive traits, whereas "men of sense" allow for exceptions. Miller suggests thinking of national traits in terms of Wittgenstein's metaphor of a thread whose strength does not reside in a single strand running through the length of a garment, but rather in the overlapping of many fibers.[21]

What I am suggesting is that the United States was built on the particular combination of psychological elements that I have just described. Further, these elements have defined America's national psychology for the past two-hundred-plus years of its existence.

These elements of American national psychology have constituted the psychological center of gravity for American national culture. They have provided individuals with the psychological keys with which to unlock the riches of opportunity and to fulfill their responsibilities as free citizens. By providing opportunity, America has fostered ambition. By encouraging freedom, America has placed a premium on being prepared to make use of it.

Subsequent generations of Americans did not acquire these psychological capacities in a vacuum. Institutions were geared to develop and support them. The United States was not a feudal society, so one's station in life could advance or decline. As a result, families prepared their chil-

---

[21] David Miller, *On Nationality* (Oxford: Clarendon Press, 1995), 26–27.

dren for success, however that might be defined. Since a central part of success was seen to be hard work and its associated characteristics (the expectation of accomplishment through effort, setting and meeting goals, balancing responsibilities and pleasure), families had an incentive to instill the virtues and necessities that undergird success: diligence, seriousness of purpose, perseverance, and resilience.

The work of the family as a psychological preparatory institution was supplemented and reinforced by other American institutions—most notable the school and the workplace. Schools taught subjects, but in doing so reinforced the development of the habits of success already encouraged by the family. Material had to be mastered, tests passed, and focus developed. The national habit of acquiring ever more sophisticated skills and knowledge for the eventual rewards that they were assumed to bring grew over time—from minimal schooling early in America's history to today's nearly universal expectation of at least a high school diploma, and typically more.

All of these were considered preparatory for "making it," and one did so in the world of work and opportunity. Here, too, the psychological lessons that began in childhood and continued through school played a large role. Ambition, assumption of prudent risks, the development of habits associated with hard work, and the ability to sustain oneself through the vicissitudes of capitalist life all helped to foster and reaffirm the peculiarly American psychology.

These interlocking and related mechanisms of American national psychology are painted here in broad strokes. Moreover, the point obviously is not that every American acquired and developed these characteristics to a substantial degree. What does seem clear is that the basic cultural foundations of American society—freedom and capitalist opportunity— provided the psychological setting within which Americans lived and prospered. There is, then, a necessary relationship between America's national culture and the psychological characteristics that foster success within it.

Does this mean that national integration of immigrants ought to take place primarily at this basic psychological level? Not wholly, but it does play a role. Americans applaud immigrants who show ambition, who try to achieve work-related excellence, who are anxious to move toward self-sufficiency, and who remain pragmatic and optimistic about themselves and their new circumstances. Americans can appreciate the new immigrants' struggles to maintain community as they pursue their ambitions. Americans can appreciate their strivings toward achievement and self-reliance. And Americans can appreciate immigrants' desire for political, economic, and social equality. Americans do so understanding that, from a democratic perspective, no person is inherently better than any other. Yet, Americans also recognize that the United States allows economic, political, and social disparities that come from differences in skills, ability, and desire, as well as from the (hopefully) transitional circumstances of finding and building a new life.

Every country rewards the psychology that it favors, and America is no different in this respect. This is why many generations of American immigrants have managed to build successful personal and community lives.

We have examined two important factors: creed and psychology. Are these sufficient to develop the sense of attachment and integration that is so necessary to democratic functioning in an increasingly diverse country? No. There is one more absolutely essential element that helps to unite and bond both the creed and American psychology: patriotism.

C. Patriotism

Patriotism is the missing link in discussions of American national identity and integration. It is the missing link in discussions of civic integration. It is the glue that bonds together American psychology with support of the American creed. And, it is the emotional amalgam that makes real diversity possible.

Patriotic feelings cannot be legislated. However, they can certainly be encouraged, and they can most certainly be retarded by indifference to how well new citizens become integrated into, and attached to, American society.

Most discussions of patriotism portray it as a simple or a simplistic and aggressive love of country, but there are many definitions of patriotism. While people clearly hold strong views about patriotism, there is little in the way of sustained theory.

We know very little about patriotism and its emotional sibling, loyalty. Duty, honor, and country are stirring ideals, carried out, often at high cost, by small groups of dedicated Americans. However, these ideals are not the sustained coin of the larger society (post–September 11th being a marked departure). Even the words 'loyalty' and 'patriotism' set off more arguments than quests for knowledge.

I realize that words have power, and this is why I refer to 'national attachments' rather than 'loyalty'. Yet, I have come to believe that, regardless of which term is used, the phenomenon to which it refers is more than a simple love of country or a thoughtless, aggressive defense of it. This essay is not the setting in which to spell out such a theory, but I think that it is reasonable to suggest that patriotism is much more complicated than either its supporters or its critics allow.

I see American patriotism as including a warmth and affection for, a commitment to, a responsibility toward, a pride in, and support of the United States—its institutions, its way of life and aspirations, and its people. Love may be a summary term that covers all these things, but I think that each of these elements is discrete.

It would take some time to spell out the bonding implications for immigrants that come with these various forms or elements of attachment. A warmth and affection for one's country, for example, is a primary form of attachment and can obviously help individuals to weather the vicissitudes of immigrant (or even established) life in the United States. Some of these elements may be present in incipient form even before an immigrant arrives on U.S. soil. Others may take time to develop. But all of them are affected in some way by the pull of dual citizenship and dual loyalty.

IV. Dual Citizens: What's Different?

Advocates of dual citizenship can point, with some justification, to the fact that there have always been persons with multiple national attachments among the American populace. Yet, there are profound differences between earlier periods of mass immigration and now. Consider the hyphenated Irish-American or Jewish-American identity. Does the former, for example, mean that such a person is an *Irish*-American, an Irish-*American*, an *Irish-American*, or an *American* of Irish descent? Each of these possible permutations reflects a psychological identification with, and arrangement of, some of the basic building blocks that form one's identity.

It seems very unlikely that, either in the past or in the present for that matter, most Irish-Americans and Jewish-Americans would see their "home country" identifications as either equal to, or more important than, their American identity. Moreover, if any of their fellows from the "old country" were to suggest that they should more strongly identify with it, most would likely respond clearly, straightforwardly, and without much self-doubt: no. They might be interested in some aspects of their "home countries," but most, if not all, would say that they were Americans first and primarily.

This is less and less the case today. Consider a hypothetical scenario in which Irish-American and Jewish-American equivalents for 'black' or 'Chicano' ('Hispanic') were available. Let us call them 'white' and 'European'. In fact, these terms, while available, have never been embraced by Irish-Americans and Jewish-Americans. To embrace them would effectively decouple their personal identities from their preferred identification with America.

Can anyone seriously argue that such a "decoupling" of identity would be chosen by Irish-Americans and Jewish-Americans, as sociologist Rubén Rumbaut found was the case in second-generation Americans of Mexican descent? He found that almost half of respondents from this group selected a racial or pan-ethnic identity, and that another eight percent would select an identity exclusively allied with their parents' national origin.[22]

---

[22] Rubén Rumbaut, "Assimilation and Its Discontents: Between Rhetoric and Reality," *International Migration Review* 31, no. 4 (1997): 923–60.

Would a random sample of second-generation Irish-Americans or Jewish-Americans find almost fifty percent of them selecting a self-identification that did not include an American element? I think not.

The claims of states on their dual citizens has led to conflict in the past, and it is surely true that we are not likely to go to war with Great Britain over the kidnapping of our and their dual citizens, as was the case in 1812. Yet, while international military conflicts that engage or test the loyalties of dual citizens in the United States cannot be ruled out, the real problem is not war but cohesion.

Do dual loyalties equal conflicted loyalties? Loyalty is a complex concept and an even more complex emotion. Psychologically, loyalty is basically an attachment to, a sense of identification with, and feelings toward a person, place, or thing. These can run from the shallow to the profound, from the episodic to the immutable, and from the singular to the diverse.

Primary nationality, the one that we are born into, begins to take root very early, indeed before a child is born. In most cases, the history and practices that bring together a particular couple are themselves influenced by the cultural expectations and understandings that the individuals acquired while growing up in their country and culture. How they prepare for their child and how they relate to him are also conditioned by the same factors. Of course, the parents speak to the child in their own language, which is soon to be his, and, as he grows, they serve as guides through and interpreters of the cultural landscape that he must learn and traverse. Being embedded in, and attached to, one's country of origin begins early.

A very large number of studies of children, dating back many decades, document that children begin to incorporate the symbols of their nationality and country very early, and they are deeply resistant to change. Why is this significant? It is significant because loyalty to a nation and feelings of attachment to it begin at a primal age and become increasingly consolidated as a child develops. Why are people willing to die for their country? Why do great national accomplishments bring pride? Why do the symbols of a country—such as its flag or constitution—carry such great emotional weight and political power?

The early formation of national attachment explains why a reporter for *The New York Times*, covering the attitudes of African immigrants to the United States, could write," Many African immigrants say that whether they stay here for two or 20 years, Africa is, and always will be, home."[23] It explains why the Funeraria Latina, a large mortuary service provider, transports 80 percent of its bodies out of the United States. It also explains why Alejandro Ruiz, who left Mexico and began work on landscaping crews around Denver, became a U.S. citizen, and raised ten children, forty

[23] Amy Waldman, "Killing Heightens the Unease Felt by Africans in New York," *New York Times*, February 14, 1999, late edition–final, sec. 1, p. 1. col. 4.

grandchildren, and three great-grandchildren in the United States, can still say he wants to be buried at "home," meaning Mexico.[24]

Or, consider the reactions of some Mexican immigrants who were interviewed about whether they would apply for U.S. citizenship in light of California's Proposition 187. (Among other things, and before a federal judge overturned major portions of the law as unconstitutional, Proposition 187 excluded illegal aliens from public schools and public social services, including nonemergency health care. Immigrants seeking such taxpayer-funded services were required either to "obtain legal status or leave the United States.") Some of the answers given by Mexican nationals regarding whether they would become U.S. citizens included the following: "Never, I was born in Mexico, raised in Mexico, and I want to die in Mexico ..."; "[G]iving up my Mexican citizenship is like giving up a child of mine ..."; and "It's as though I'm betraying my country, my people, and my culture...."[25]

In one of the few systematic, in-depth studies of the identifications of Muslim immigrants with their country of origin and with the United States, Kambiz GhaneaBassiri, an Iranian doctoral student at Harvard University, found that Muslim immigrants are extremely ambivalent about the United States. The study found that "a significant number of Muslims, particularly immigrant Muslims, do not have strong ties or loyalty to the United States." Indeed, GhaneaBassiri's questionnaire showed that more than 50 percent of his sample of immigrant Muslims in Los Angeles and almost a third of Americans who had converted to Islam felt more allegiance to a foreign country than to the United States.[26]

V. Conclusion

The basic question raised by the findings discussed in the previous section has little to do with disloyalty and much to do with conflicted loyalties. At the center of what should be a vigorous debate is the most profound question: Should the United States, as a matter of policy, condone or encourage multiple loyalties, or should the nation's energies be focused on ensuring that new arrivals and citizens alike are encouraged to take steps that truly connect them with the United States?

Becoming an American is not simply a matter of agreeing that democracy is the best form of government. It is a commitment to a psychology and the way of life that flows from it. Moreover, it ultimately entails an appreciation of, a commitment to, and, yes, even a love for all that the United States stands for and provides.

[24] Bruce Finley, "Hearts Torn between Old, New Worlds," *Denver Post*, August 23, 1998.

[25] Alfredo Corchado and Kendall Anderson, "Mexicans' Interest in Citizenship Up; Proposition 187 Prompts Increase," *Dallas Morning News*, December 1, 1994, 27A.

[26] Kambiz GhaneaBassiri, *Competing Visions of Islam in the United States: A Study of Los Angeles* (Westport, CT: Greenwood Press, 1997).

It is easy to view America instrumentally. It is a place of enormous personal freedom and great economic opportunities. A 2001 study by the Council on American-Islamic Relations found that eighty-two percent of respondents agreed with the following statement: America is a technologically advanced nation that we can learn from. Yet, only thirty-five percent agreed with this statement: America is an example of freedom that we can learn from.[27]

America has always recognized that many immigrants arrive seeking treasures that are in such short supply in so many of the countries from which they emigrate. The fear that self-interest will come at the expense of developing genuine appreciation for and emotional connection to the U.S. has, I think, always been the subtext of attempts to ensure that new arrivals "become American."

America reached its present state of political, economic, and social development by providing extraordinary personal freedom and abundant economic opportunity. In doing so, America leveraged personal ambitions as a tool to transform individuals' social and economic circumstances. In the process, it helped them develop and reinforce the psychological elements that are necessary not only for personal success but also for the civic prudence required of citizens in a democracy. An emphasis on consistency, hard work, delay of immediate gratification, prudence, pragmatism, and optimism are among these psychological elements.

This has been the historical trade-off of American receptivity to immigration: America takes the chance that it can leverage immigrants' self-interest and transform it into authentic commitment. Immigrants agree in coming to the United States to reorient themselves toward their new lives and away from their old ones. This involves some basic proficiencies, such as learning to be at home with English and understanding the institutions and practices that define American culture and life. In the process, and as immigrants become more successfully integrated, they are better able to reflect on the ways in which their search for freedom and opportunity fits in with the history, with all of its vicissitudes, that has shaped the idea and promise of America.

It is only at this point of deeper reflection that the transformation from self-interest to genuine emotional connection can be made. Thus oriented toward their new home, immigrants can become part of the fabric of American cultural and political life. Leaving a life behind, even a life that one wanted to leave, is, of course, difficult. Yet, generations of earlier immigrants thought the sacrifice worthwhile.

Dual citizenship and its associated bifurcation of attention and commitment change this traditional and successful recipe for integration.

[27] Ihsan Bagby, Paul M. Perl, and Bryan T. Froehle, *The Mosque in America: A National Portrait* (Washington, DC: Council on American-Islamic Relations, 2001). Available on-line at http://www.cair-net.org/mosquereport [accessed July 10, 2003].

Immigrants increasingly come from countries that encourage dual citizenship. These nations' purposes in doing so are primarily self-interested. It may be to ensure a continuing flow of financially critical remittances from emigrants working in the United States. Or, it may be to organize their nationals to further their "home country's" policy preferences, such as amnesty for those nationals who entered the United States illegally or the support of bilingual policies that help to maintain and facilitate ties to the "home country." Whatever the specific purposes, sending countries are increasingly mobilizing to retain their emigrants' emotional attachment and to deepen their commitment to the "home country." Modern technology and travel facilitate this quest.

These developments set the stage for conflicts of interest among new immigrants from different countries (many of whom retain deep attachments to their nations of origin), and between new immigrants and their more established countrymen (many of whom have become U.S. citizens). Given the geographical distribution of new immigrants, it is possible that whole states and certainly some localities will be comprised of a substantial portion of dual citizens with active and deep connections to their countries of origin. Will these immigrants be willing or able to set aside these connections in favor of their community's interest or America's national interest? Whether this is possible as a matter of psychology or politics remains to be seen.

To a democracy—especially one facing issues of the acceptance of its basic institutions and cultural premises—the costs of allowing large numbers of immigrants to retain dual citizenship, and thus multiple loyalties, are likely to be substantial. Immigrants' increasing capacity to utilize technology to maintain these ties, coupled with pressure on them from their "home countries" to do so, means that the costs of dual citizenship will only escalate in the future. Moreover, in a time characterized by serious concerns regarding the decline of social capital and its implications for American civic life and the dangers of catastrophic terrorism, the split attachments of large numbers of dual citizens ought to be a source of deep concern.

No country, and certainly no democracy, can afford to have large numbers of citizens with shallow national and civic attachments. No country facing divisive domestic issues arising out of its increasing diversity, as America does, benefits from large-scale immigration of people with multiple loyalties and attachments. No country, striving to reconnect its citizens to a coherent civic identity and culture, can afford to encourage its citizens to look elsewhere for their most basic national attachments.

Political Science, the Graduate Center, the City University of New York

POLICY IMPLICATIONS OF ZERO DISCOUNTING:
AN EXPLORATION IN POLITICS AND MORALITY*

By Tyler Cowen

I. Introduction

What are our political obligations to future generations? How does morality suggest that we weight current interests against future interests? Do politics or markets place greater weight upon interests in the very distant future? How should we discount future costs and benefits?

A 'discount rate', by definition, tells us how to compare future benefits to current benefits (or costs) in a consequentialist calculus. A zero discount rate means that the future counts for as much as the present. Insofar as the discount rate is high, we are counting future costs and benefits for less.

Elsewhere, I have argued that we should consider using a zero rate of intergenerational discount for well-being and sometimes for dollars as well.[1] We should not weigh the interests of future people less, simply because they come in the future. Here I seek to extend these arguments. I consider in detail what a zero discount rate would mean for policy-making, and for ethics more generally.

Economists, who tend to be market-oriented (at least relative to philosophers), usually resist the idea of zero discounting. They see market prices as prima facie indicators of the value of resources.[2] Market rates of interest are typically positive and nonzero in both nominal and real (i.e., inflation-adjusted) terms. Economists therefore usually favor some positive rate of time-discount, based on these market interest rates, perhaps adjusted for risk or other complicating factors. Furthermore, a zero discount rate would appear to lend too much weight to the very distant future. Many economists fear that a zero discount rate would involve the sacrifice of too much current consumption for benefits in the very distant future. The current sociology of the debate places positive discounting as

---

* I thank Bryan Caplan, Christian Gollier, Robin Hanson, Ellen Frankel Paul, and fellow contributors to this volume for their useful comments on an earlier draft of this essay.

[1] See Tyler Cowen and Derek Parfit, "Against the Social Discount Rate," in *Philosophy, Politics, and Society*, 6th ser., Peter Laslett and James Fishkin, eds. (New Haven, CT: Yale University Press, 1992), 144–61; and Tyler Cowen, "Consequentialism Implies a Zero Rate of Intergenerational Discount," in *Philosophy, Politics, and Society*, Laslett and Fishkin, eds., 162–68.

[2] See Robert C. Lind et al., *Discounting for Time and Risk in Energy Policy* (Washington, DC: Resources for the Future, 1982); and the essays in Paul R. Portney and John P. Weyant, eds., *Discounting and Intergenerational Equity* (Washington, DC: Resources for the Future, 1999).

121

a "conservative" or "right-wing" view, or certainly no further left than the mainstream.[3]

My informal polling over the years suggests that many advocates of greater state spending—especially noneconomists—like the idea of a lower discount rate. These individuals typically would like the United States government to spend more money on education, infrastructure, and the environment. These individuals have not always worked through the technical, economic, and philosophical issues, but they see a lower discount rate as providing support for all of these policies. They believe that we are not caring enough about the future. Therefore, zero discounting serves as a "left-wing" view in most cases.[4]

I argue that the current sociology of views on this issue does not match the reality. A zero rate of discount is likely to lend the most support to policies that favor a market economy, economic growth, and technological innovation. Indeed, some arguments for a market economy may *require* a zero or very low rate of discount. Positive rates of discount usually imply that we should grant considerable importance to the alleviation of immediate suffering. Market liberalizations, whatever virtues they may have in the long run, often *increase* immediate suffering. Furthermore, market economies tend to invest their surpluses in long-term growth rather than redistribute them to the suffering poor. Market economies and market reforms therefore look better, the greater the weight we place on the relatively distant future.

A zero rate of discount also boosts the more general case for a free society. A free society is better today than a corrupt and totalitarian alternative. But one hundred years from now, the difference in human welfare will prove far more pronounced. If we apply a positive rate of discount, then this future difference is not a big deal. If we apply a zero rate of discount, then the case for a free society becomes that much stronger.

Finally, a zero discount rate will have significant repercussions for ethical reasoning. In Section IV, I argue that zero discounting would help the prospects of utilitarianism, provide a new argument for rule-utilitarianism, and increase the weight of consequentialist factors, relative to deontology, in plausible versions of pluralism.

These arguments do not, themselves, either favor or damage the case for a zero rate of discount. We should not first look for the conclusions we want and then work backwards toward the assumptions. Nonetheless, a process of reflective equilibrium requires that we consider the implica-

---

[3] Wilfred Beckerman presents one statement of a market-oriented view, critical of zero discounting, in Wilfred Beckerman, *Through Green-Colored Glasses: Environmentalism Reconsidered* (Washington, DC: Cato Institute, 1996).

[4] See, for instance, Robert Solow, "The Economics of Resources or the Resources of Economics," *American Economic Review* 64, no. 2, Papers and Proceedings of the Eighty-sixth Annual Meeting of the American Economic Association (1974): 1–14.

tions of our beliefs. Toward this end, my investigation will illustrate how a zero rate of discount would accord, or not accord, with our other moral and practical intuitions. This investigation will improve our understanding of what is at stake in the discount rate debates. I hope to stimulate interest in these debates, shake up individuals on each side of the political spectrum, point out an unrecognized robustness of consequentialism, and improve our understanding of which policy recommendations are likely to fit together.

Throughout this essay, I couch the analysis in terms of utilitarianism. In particular, I consider the wealth-maximizing ordinal utilitarianism that one finds in economics, as well as interpersonal cardinal utilitarianism. I do not adhere to these views as our best moral theories, all things considered. Nevertheless, I adopt them as a working tool for two reasons. First, I am concerned with rebutting some common presumptions of economics, and thus I adopt this framework for heuristic reasons. Second, and more importantly, most plausible moral theories have a strong consequentialist element and must somehow compare present well-being to future well-being. Ordinal and cardinal utilitarianism are the only moral doctrines that offer a formal and generally accepted framework for such comparisons. I therefore use this framework simply because nothing better is available for the consequentialist part of our broader moral theory. Still, the results of this essay ultimately must be embedded in a deeper and more fully fleshed out pluralistic framework, where utilitarian results are but one factor in a broader assessment. My entire analysis of policy is subject to this important qualification.[5]

In addition, I do not address as a separate issue how we might discount present versus future manifestations of other values, such as equality, justice, or community. Utility and wealth are the easiest values to study in this manner, and thus I start with them, but without denying the importance of a broader study for other values as well.

This essay proceeds as follows: Section II provides a brief look at (but not a complete resolution of) the debate on intergenerational discounting. Section III asks how a zero rate of discount would change our evaluation of various policies. I start with the general question of economic growth and then consider specific policies governing savings, welfare programs, and government versus market provision of goods and services. Section IV asks how a zero discount rate would influence current debates over utilitarianism. Section V offers some concluding remarks.

---

[5] My current research seeks to argue that a broader pluralistic theory will likely track many of the utilitarian recommendations in these cases. Both pluralistic and utilitarian theories will be led to endorse policies that strengthen and extend the prospects of our civilization. See Tyler Cowen, "Civilization Renewed," manuscript in progress (George Mason University, 2003). That longer manuscript will also consider how we might "discount" our deontological obligations through time. In my contribution to this volume, however, I offer only some general remarks on pluralism, at the end of Section IV.

The survey in Section II uses some technical economic language, but the remainder of the essay, including my central arguments, remains intelligible to the general reader. So, I would urge readers to skip over any difficult passages in Section II rather than getting bogged down in them. The import of those arguments will, in any case, become clear in subsequent sections.

II. ARGUING FOR A ZERO OR LOWER DISCOUNT RATE

The arguments for a zero discount rate typically focus on the concept of well-being. Derek Parfit, for instance, has argued that there is no compelling moral reason for attaching a positive rate of intergenerational discount to benefits and costs in the distant future.[6] A given cost or benefit, once it arrives in the future, is no less real than a cost or benefit today. Parfit and I have written: "Imagine finding out that you, having just reached your twenty-first birthday, must soon die of cancer because one evening Cleopatra wanted an extra helping of dessert."[7] Or consider the comparison prospectively. Under any universally applied positive-discount rate, no matter how low, one life today can be worth more than one million lives in the future, or the survival of the entire human race, if we use a long enough time-differential for the appropriate comparison.[8]

The following table shows some comparisons between present and future benefits, using various positive rates of intergenerational discount:

TABLE 1. *Estimated number of future benefits equal to one present benefit based on different discount rates*

Years in The Future	1%	3%	5%	10%
30	1.3	2.4	4.3	17.4
50	1.6	4.3	11.4	117.3
100	2.7	19.2	131.5	13,780.6
500	144.7	2,621,877.2	39,323,261,827.0	4.96×10^2

How would a zero rate of discount on well-being translate into a discount rate for dollars? Clearly a dollar today, *if* we invest it to yield $1.05

---

[6] Derek Parfit, *Reasons and Persons* (New York: Oxford University Press, 1986).

[7] Cowen and Parfit, "Against the Social Discount Rate," 145.

[8] The following discussion in the text does not consider risk. There is unanimous agreement on discounting for risk: if a future event may not come to pass, then we should count it for less.

next year, is worth more than a dollar next year. This follows from the 'dominance principle', which states that more of a good thing is preferred to less. But this argument does not show that a dollar's worth of *consumed resources*, this year, is worth more than a dollar's worth of consumed resources next year. To address this comparison, we must consider the relative marginal utilities of consumption in each period, not the marginal product of capital or the rate of return on savings.

Economist John Broome articulates the strongest case for positive discounting. He argues for discounting dollar benefits, though not necessarily for discounting well-being. Economies typically grow wealthier over time. So a dollar today is worth more, at the margin, than a dollar in the future, for the same reasons that a rich Tyler values a dollar less than does a poor Tyler. This judgment does not require interpersonal comparisons of utility, but, rather, requires only that we can transfer dollars back and forth in time by borrowing and lending. In economic jargon, the positive interest rate equalizes marginal rates of substitution over time, or in other words, it expresses the value of a future dollar relative to a current dollar.[9]

The Broome argument does justify positive discounting of dollars for small policy changes, at least if we are willing to accept an economic framework more generally. But the argument does not necessarily justify using the observed market rate of discount when we consider significant changes in wealth. As with all cost-benefit methods, the argument takes the overall distribution of wealth as given and examines a small change in allocations, that is, small in value relative to the wealth of the individuals in question. But when wealth effects are large for the individuals involved, market prices no longer measure marginal rates of substitution for the two relevant outcomes. In other words, the market rate of interest measures the rate at which people are willing to trade off marginal dollars across time, but it does not measure the rate at which they are willing to trade off larger sums of money (i.e., infra-marginal dollars). Similarly, the market interest rate does not measure the value of a life today versus the value of a life tomorrow.

A simple example will clarify the point for those who are unfamiliar with economic jargon. A man wandering lost in a desert probably has a higher marginal value of water than I do, sitting in my suburban Virginia home. But this does not give us any information about how to forecast the relative values of "I lose all my water" against "He loses all his water." Either he or I would die without water, and the value of his life may be greater than, less than, or equal to mine. The original difference in mar-

[9] John Broome, "Discounting the Future," *Philosophy & Public Affairs* 23, no. 2 (1994): 128–56. See also Kenneth J. Arrow, William R. Cline, Karo-Goran Maeler, et al., "Intertemporal Equity, Discounting, and Economic Efficiency," in James P. Bruce, Hoesung Lee, and Erik F. Haites, eds., *Climate Change 1995: Economic and Social Dimensions of Climate Change* (Cambridge: Cambridge University Press, 1996), chap. 4; and Thomas C. Schelling, "Intergenerational Discounting," *Energy Policy* 23, nos. 4/5 (1995): 395–401.

ginal values for water does not measure or forecast, even imperfectly, the comparative value of our two lives. The two concepts are entirely distinct. In similar fashion, the market rate of interest measures the value of small changes across time, but not large ones (i.e., infra-marginal changes). The difference between marginal and infra-marginal effects is recognized in the theory of cost-benefit analysis, but it is commonly neglected when intergenerational discount rates are discussed or applied.[10]

Many intergenerational policies—including those regarding the environment, health, and genetic engineering—involve significant changes in wealth for many of the individuals involved. Such policies constitute large rather than small changes. For the purposes of cost-benefit analysis, a change can be large in the relevant sense even if it is small relative to total national output. Cost-benefit analysis refers to individual valuations, and the measured changes must be small for each affected individual if market prices are to yield an accurate cost-benefit measure.[11]

Finally, when considering large policy changes, it should be noted that not everyone in the future will be richer than everyone in the present. The large policy changes, if enacted, might make some people in the future very poor. Man-made environmental catastrophe is a simple example here. So the characterization of the future as full of richer people, even if true in general, does not necessarily hold for the individuals in question. To the extent that the relevant future individuals are poorer than current individuals, this suggests negative discounting of dollars, not positive discounting.

The debate on intergenerational discounting is stuck at these points. Positive discounting of dollars, using the risk-adjusted market rate of interest, is appropriate for "small" policies. It is not necessarily appropriate for large policies that affect the marginal utility of money. In these cases we do not know the correct rate of discount for dollars. Some philosophical arguments, such as those I discussed above, suggest zero discounting for well-being, but this does not determine a discount rate for dollars. If we match dollars to welfare, one-to-one, the zero-discounting

[10] On small versus large changes, see the survey of Jean Drèze and Nicholas Stern, "The Theory of Cost-Benefit Analysis," in *Handbook of Public Economics*, vol. 2, ed. Alan J. Auerbach and Martin Feldstein (Amsterdam: North-Holland, 1987), 909–89. We might try to save the positive discounting argument by invoking transitivity. This claim would run as follows: if we are willing to discount dollars at a positive rate, then we must discount lives at the same rate. At the margin we can always invest dollars to save lives. Differential discount rates for dollars and lives thus suggest an unexploited opportunity to improve social welfare. This argument, however, begs the question. It suggests that we should invest more dollars to save future lives. It does not show that a life today is worth more than a life tomorrow, taking the extent of investment as given.

[11] The requirement that we examine "small changes to wealth" is extremely restrictive in the intergenerational context, given the compound nature of discounting. The relevant cost or benefit must be small, not only in present value terms, but also when it arrives in the future. If we compare a small benefit today to a temporally distant benefit of equivalent present value, the future benefit, when it arrives, will not be small for those who experience it. The future benefit, when it arrives, will involve significant changes in the marginal utility of money, again vitiating the arguments for positive discounting.

argument would apply to dollars as well, but we cannot make this cardinal judgment very easily. We are thus left with the following:

1. For small changes in wealth, discount dollars by the (risk-adjusted) market rate of interest.
2. For changes in well-being, use a discount rate of zero.
3. For large changes in wealth, try to figure out how well-being maps into dollars. This may imply a positive, negative, or zero rate of discount.

As a practical matter, we usually do not have a very good idea of how well-being maps into dollars. For instance, we do not know the identities of future generations, much less their utility functions. At the same time, we must devise some simple and workable rule for judging large policies that affect the distant future.

I wish to consider the rule of a zero discount rate—as applied across dollars—in this context. We do know that such a zero rate cannot be correct for small decisions at the margin, for the reasons given in Broome's argument. Provided that capital is productive, an extra dollar today will be worth more than an extra dollar in the future. Nonetheless, a zero discount rate remains a possible option for large-scale changes, especially if they involve significant changes in wealth and span many generations. For these questions we have no answer that proves superior to the zero rate concept.

Rather than pursue the debate further at a philosophical level, I wish to see what policy implications would follow from a very low discount rate of this nature, be it zero or something very close to zero. We must, however, keep in mind that this zero rate is for large projects and changes only.

III. What Policies Would Follow?

Zero discounting would shape our views of numerous economic policies. The first policy recommendation would be to approach the maximization of the sustainable rate of long-run economic growth.[12]

The importance of a high rate of economic growth increases, the further into the future we look. If a country grows today at two percent, as opposed to growing at one percent, the difference in welfare is relatively small. Over time, however, the difference becomes very large. For instance, had America grown one percentage point less per year between

---

[12] Note that we should not strictly maximize the rate of economic growth. At the maximum, there will always exist some small increase in current consumption that will lower growth yet improve welfare, given Broome's argument. Nonetheless, in a long-run context we should come close to growth maximization. The following discussion in the text is therefore approximate rather than exact.

1870 and 1990, the America of 1990 would be no richer than the Mexico of 1990.[13] At a growth rate of five percent per annum, it takes slightly more than eighty years for a country to move from a per capita income of five hundred dollars to a per capita income of twenty-five thousand dollars, defining both in terms of constant real dollars. At a growth rate of one percent, such an improvement takes 393 years.

Note that maximizing the long-run rate of growth refers to gross domestic product (GDP) as properly understood, and not necessarily as currently measured. 'True GDP', if I may use this term, includes leisure time, household production, and environmental amenities, which are not always measured correctly in current GDP statistics. Current GDP statistics have a bias toward what can be measured, rather than what contributes to human welfare. For this reason, "maximizing the rate of growth" does not mean that everyone should work the maximum number of hours in a day. A twenty-hour workday might maximize measured GDP, but certainly would not maximize sustainable true GDP, once we take into account the value of leisure.

Economists do not always agree on which policies will maximize the growth rate. Almost all economists agree, however, that a stable market order, private property, and the rule of law are conducive to economic growth, at least for measured GDP. Statistical studies of economic growth find that market-oriented policies are generally conducive to growth.[14] Infrastructure spending and investment in education are the government policies that do the most to promote growth. Noninfrastructure spending, high and volatile inflation, and regulatory interventions all damage growth, at least on average. The statistical methods employed in these studies are geared more toward showing correlation than proving causality. Nonetheless, economic theory and a wide variety of case studies provide more general support for these postulated empirical effects. Economic models stress favorable market institutions, effective provision of public goods, infrastructure, high levels of savings, and technological innovation as critical factors behind growth.[15]

Considering true GDP, rather than measured GDP, may lead us to revise some of the recommendations for maximizing growth. In particu-

[13] Tyler Cowen, "Does the Welfare State Help the Poor?" *Social Philosophy & Policy* 19, no. 1 (2002): 36–54.

[14] The classic study here is Robert J. Barro, "Economic Growth in a Cross Section of Countries," *Quarterly Journal of Economics* 106, no. 2 (1991): 407–43. See also Kevin B. Grier and Gordon Tullock, "An Empirical Analysis of Cross National Economic Growth 1951–1980," *Journal of Monetary Economics* 24, no. 2 (1989): 259–76; and Paul G. Mahoney, "The Common Law and Economic Growth: Hayek Might Be Right," *Journal of Legal Studies* 30 no. 1, pt. 1 (2001): 503–25.

[15] Note that maximizing the rate of economic growth is not the same as choosing the policies that yield the highest observed growth rate. Arguably, it is possible to exceed today's maximum observed growth rates. A government could introduce freer markets, greater encouragement to savings, or other policies. A zero rate of discount would provide force to each of these recommendations.

lar, current GDP statistics may understate the value of the environment. (I return to environmental questions below in this section.) That being said, growth-enhancing policies also tend to give us more leisure time, which is a real, if not fully measurable, contribution to human welfare.

Economists still disagree about other growth-related questions. It is unclear how subsidies to technology affect the rate of growth, or how fixed and floating exchange rates affect the rate of economic growth. In these regards agnosticism is called for.[16]

Note that we wish to maximize the growth rate over time, not just for a single year. Maximizing the sustainable rate of economic growth does *not* imply pursuing immediate growth at the expense of all other values. The key word here is *sustainable*. Policies that seek growth at breakneck speed are frequently unstable in both economic and political terms. Until his forced exile in 1979, Mohammed Reza Shah Pahlavi, the Shah of Iran, tried to bring his country into the modern world as rapidly as possible. Growth rates were high for a while but in the longer run could not be maintained. Since the Iranian Revolution, Iran has had, for the most part, strongly negative rates of growth. The Shah's forced modernization did not, in fact, maximize economic growth, and a more cautious set of policies likely would have been better.

More generally, maximizing the rate of sustainable growth typically implies an economically healthy present as well as a very rosy future. Current wealth and future wealth are highly correlated. So the best way for a society to be wealthy in the future, for the most part, is to be relatively wealthy and stable now. Current economic sacrifices, if they are truly impoverishing, tend to wreck political stability and destroy social capital, damaging all future generations. Well-functioning institutions are the greatest gift that we can leave to future generations. For this reason, producing wealth across generations is more akin to a positive-sum co-operative game than to a war or a fight for spoils. Therefore, we should not expect a zero rate of discount to ruin current prospects for a prosperous and livable country.

John Rawls shies away from a zero rate of discount on the grounds that it may require unacceptable sacrifices from the current generation in the form of excessive savings.[17] His concerns are not very specific, but let us look at a real-world example in more detail. Arguably a zero rate of discount may sometimes recommend behavior similar to what we saw in post–World War II Japan, where a generation worked extremely hard for the future and saved a good deal. This may be objectionable on Rawlsian grounds (since the generation that works hard is poorer than generations to come), but it is not necessarily unacceptable in utilitarian terms. The

---

[16] On technology issues, see Linda R. Cohen and Roger G. Noll, eds., *The Technology Pork Barrel* (Washington, DC: Brookings Institution, 1991).

[17] See John Rawls, *A Theory of Justice*, rev. ed. (Cambridge, MA: Harvard University Press, 1999), 252.

investment brought an extraordinary return. Furthermore, the Japanese work ethic of that time was sustainable, in part, because it was voluntary rather than coercively enforced. Since each hardworking citizen *wanted* to provide so much for the future, the investment was compatible with relatively free and thus growth-enhancing institutions. So we can look approvingly on the Japanese example, without necessarily wishing to coerce other citizenries to do the same.

To further address this concern, consider bequests. The material sacrifice of a generation is determined not by how much it saves at a given point in time, but, rather, by how much it bequeaths to the next generation, in lieu of consumption. Now, bequests are a one-time wealth transfer, which do not raise the rate of growth permanently or even in the short run. So, if a generation matures in a society with a high rate of growth, we should not look to bequests as the cause of their good fortune. Instead, the older generation has given the greater gift of growth-conducive institutions. The postwar Japanese generation did not leave enormous bequests to its children. The key gift was not based on total abstinence from consumption, but, rather, was based on wise investments, good rules of conduct, good political institutions, good values, and so on. Growth-enhancing institutions do require hard work from the people who produce them, but, again, we should not think of the investment as a pure zero-sum game across generations. Bequests do have a potential zero-sum element: Should I spend a dollar or leave it for my heirs? However, bequests are precisely not what accounts for a high rate of ongoing growth.

In sum, maximizing the sustainable rate of growth of true GDP is a plausible policy recommendation. It is usually good for the present, and it will make the future a very rosy place. Using a zero rate of discount does not give rise to any obviously unacceptable or counterintuitive conclusions in this regard. Given the nature and causes of economic success, it will not place the interests of different generations in extreme conflict. Good institutions are the most important "bequest" a generation can leave to the future. With this general background in mind, let us next consider some specific policies in detail.

A. The welfare state

Arguments continue over the proper size and scope of the welfare state. I do not wish to engage the entire debate, but a zero rate of discount would matter at the margin for how we think about the issues.

More specifically, a zero discount rate will tend to weaken the case for an extensive welfare state. To some extent, a welfare state can be justified as a long-run investment in social capital. It may preserve political stability or enable individuals to get better education, both of which involve payoffs in the long run. Nonetheless, most welfare states have expanded beyond this point. Most welfare states offer payments that create some short-run benefit, such as the immediate alleviation of poverty, at the expense of long-run economic growth and job creation. Most of the Western European polities, for instance, fit this pattern. There is little doubt that the welfare state benefits the citizenry in the current period. Recipients enjoy more security and providers get a feeling that they are helping their fellow citizens. For these reasons, extensive welfare states have proven very popular with Western European voters.

The long-run consequences of these welfare states, however, tend to be severe. Many Western European economies have had double-digit rates of unemployment for the better part of two or three decades. Rates of job creation have been correspondingly low. Western Europe also has experienced recurring bouts of very sluggish growth. While the welfare state is not the only culprit here, even left-wing European parties commonly recognize that their welfare states are a drag on long-run growth and economic performance.

The longer we look into the future, the more serious the negative effects of slower economic growth. (I have already explained the logic of compounding.) For this reason, a zero rate of discount tends to militate against extensive welfare states, at least welfare states that extend beyond the point where they build up social capital and encourage growth.

B. Savings

Savings in a modern economy typically yield a positive rate of return. The riskless rate of return, as we might find on short-term government securities, tends to run slightly over one percent in the United States. The question then arises whether the government should subsidize a higher rate of savings. If a savings decision yields more than one percent, but we evaluate the investment at a zero percent rate of discount, then arguably we are not saving enough money. Additional investment would bring a yield greater than what is required to justify the investment.

Currently the U.S. tax system discourages savings. Savings income is doubly taxed, once in the form of regular income and a second time as interest income. Capital gains face double taxation as well, albeit at lower effective real rates than savings income. The corporate income tax discourages investment through the corporate form and involves double taxation as well, given the corporate tax and the tax on dividends when distributed to individuals. Inflation often operates as a tax on savings. Using a zero rate of discount would imply that we should eliminate such penalties on savings and investment. We might apply a broader public choice perspective to the question and ask whether governments, on net, tend to encourage or discourage savings. Since most governments tend to discourage savings, there is a case for laissez faire in this realm.

We also might go further and institute a tax subsidy for savings. Individuals who save could be granted some form of tax deductibility, just as they currently receive tax deductibility for charitable donations. Japan has had such a policy for most of its post–World War II history. Similarly, we might choose to apply the subsidy on the demand side, such as having an investment tax credit, as the United States did through part of the 1980s. Using a zero discount rate will cast such policies in a more favorable light.

It does not necessarily follow, however, that an optimal subsidy will drive the real interest rate down to zero. Any subsidy, whether implicit or explicit, strains the government budget. At some point a subsidy would consume too much government revenue, or so impoverish the current real economy as to destroy social capital and thus imperil future economic growth. In sum, some subsidy to savings and investment is likely called for, though we do not know exactly how much.

More generally, we should not draw hasty conclusions from simple economic models of savings and investment.[18] Many economic models contain a small number of variables. They might have a savings rate, a discount rate, a marginal product of capital, and not much else. If we accept the simple assumptions of these models, it would follow that savings should rise until the marginal product of capital equals the discount rate, in this case, zero. This exact result, however, is not robust enough to account for more institutional detail. The real-world problem is to provide some additional stimulus to savings without endangering the government budget, social capital, political consensus, and the ability of useful political institutions to persist over time. Once viewed in this more realistic light, we can see that a zero discount rate does not imply any extreme conclusions about subsidizing savings, despite what some of the simpler models suggest.

C. The environment

We should be especially concerned about environmental problems that lower the long-run rate of growth. Many scientists, for instance, believe that the greenhouse effect will increase the number of virulent and persistent storms. These storms will come only in the long run, but a zero rate of discount means that we must pay great heed to these future consequences. More generally, many environmental problems hurt the prospects for long-run growth, especially once we include suitable measurements for environmental amenities into true GDP.

At the same time, a zero rate of discount does not give environmental policy total priority over all other concerns. An obsessive focus on preserving the environment would damage seriously the long-run rate of growth and thus would not be recommended. When we look at *particular* environmental investments, the zero discount rate often tends to favor the

---

[18] Rawls (*A Theory of Justice*, 251–53) surveys some of these models.

environment. This is one reason why economists get nervous about a zero rate of discount. When we look at overall patterns of investment, however, we are again led to favor maximizing the sustainable growth rate of true GDP, which leads to reasonable limits on environmental protection.

In some cases a zero rate of discount will militate *against* environmental concerns. Return to the greenhouse effect. Many of the costs of the greenhouse effect appear to be "one-time" in nature, such as the costs of relocating coastal and inland settlements. In long-run equilibrium, transition effects aside, it is no worse and arguably better for the world to have a warmer climate (since we spend more resources warming space than cooling it). At the same time, stopping the greenhouse effect might permanently lower the rate of economic growth. When the rate of discount is zero, maximizing the growth rate tends to take priority over avoiding one-time expenditures and one-time adjustments. Even if these one-time expenditures are large, we will back that value over time, due to the logic of investment compounding.

As a sociological matter, we typically find that market-oriented economists, and conservatives more generally, are skeptical about investing to prevent long-run environmental damage. These same individuals are likely to herald the praises of economic growth and to favor a positive discount rate. Environmentalists usually hold a different bundle of positions. They believe that the environment needs special protection for its long-term health, but they place a lower value on the long-run benefits of growth, while discounting the future much less than do conservatives and market-oriented economists.

The analysis of this essay suggests a different approach. We should worry more about environmental problems that lower the rate of true GDP growth and worry less about environmental problems that involve one-time expenditures and adjustments. Furthermore, if environmentalists invoke a zero rate of discount in their favor, they should also pay more heed to maximizing the sustainable rate of economic growth.

D. Economic "shock therapy"

Most shock therapies have taken far longer to succeed than had been expected by their advocates. When Communism fell as of 1991, it was a common belief that the former Soviet Union and its satellites would need only a few years of shock therapy before they would become normally functioning market economies. It is now early in the twenty-first century and not all of these economies have turned the corner. Some may never become healthy. Arguably the reformers have not "done enough," but what they have done has taken far longer to pay off than had been expected.

Market-oriented reforms in Chile and New Zealand also took a long time to bring prosperity. The New Zealand reforms did not start until 1984. As of the early 1990s, the economy was just emerging from continued recession. Apart from a short boom in the mid-1980s, New Zealand experienced almost a decade of serious adjustment problems, despite having done things "the right way," by most accounts. The Chilean experience is comparable. President Augusto Pinochet's reforms started in the early 1980s and, despite their radical nature, took the better part of a decade to turn the economy around.

We see many cases where shock therapy brings a decade or more of suffering and inferior economic performance. Given the costs of the previous regimes, shock therapy might still be worth it, even with a positive discount rate. Nonetheless, positive discounting places the case for shock therapy in some jeopardy. A zero discount rate makes the case for shock therapy much stronger, provided that such reforms pay off at some point in the future with a higher rate of economic growth.

E. Market vs. government provision of goods and services

A common question is whether the market or government should supply a particular good or service. Many considerations enter into play here, such as whether we are dealing with a public good, the extent of corruption in the government, the extent of trust and social capital in the private sector, and so forth. I will not attempt to address these numerous and complex issues. Instead, I will argue that, all other things being equal, a zero rate of discount tends to tilt in favor of private sector provision.

The arguments for a zero discount rate do imply some degree of market imperfection, especially for actions that affect the very distant future. Overall, however, a zero discount rate may reflect favorably on markets, relative to government. Market practice comes much closer to a zero discount rate than does governmental practice.

Markets for short-term high-quality securities in the United States generate implicit (near) riskless discount rates between one and two percent. The federal government gives several indications of using higher discount rates. At typical interest rates, governments are typically net borrowers and the private sector is typically a net lender. (Of course, governments sometimes run measured surpluses, as did the United States for a few years under President Clinton, but deficits have been far more common for many decades.) The magnitude of government borrowing is far greater when we consider the unfunded liabilities of the government, such as we find in social security and health programs. Some of these unfunded liabilities, when they come due, will be paid off with taxes, rather than by borrowing. Such unfunded liabilities suggest that the federal government is keen to make current promises, with less thought of how to pay them off in the future.

Anecdotal observation also suggests that politicians frequently behave with very high discount rates. Reelection is considered a dominant motive of politicians, if only for evolutionary reasons. (Politicians who do not pay heed to reelection do not "survive.") Electoral cycles range from two years to six years in the United States, which comes close to the world average for democracies. Washington politics is obsessed with the here and now: solving immediate problems, responding to the evening news, and tracking short-term opinion polls. It is not oriented toward the long haul. Nor do voters use especially farsighted criteria for evaluating politicians. Many voters do care that their lives are improving, or that the economy is prospering at the current moment, but they pay little attention to long-run trends or complicated long-term effects of policies. It is well known that most voters cannot name their representatives or do not understand how policies work. If things are going well now, most voters simply do not have the information to form a pessimistic prognosis for the longer horizon. Politicians, therefore, focus on the current moment to the neglect of the distant future.

The self-reported discount rates of government agencies also tend to be higher than market rates of interest. We should take this evidence with a grain of salt, however, as agencies do not always use the rates that they report. (To provide one example, the Office of Management and Budget reports a discount rate of seven percent.) It is not always clear how much these rates contain an adjustment for risk, if at all, or whether government *should* discount for risk.[19] Nonetheless, no government agency is willing to insist upon a riskless rate as low as one and a half percent, as we find used in markets.

Many market decisions reflect a higher rate of discount than we find in the market for Treasury bills. Evidence on consumer expenditures often suggests much higher implicit rates of discount. A typical study of this kind would examine, for example, whether consumers are willing to invest in energy-efficient appliances. Typically the consumer would have to pay more now, but would receive energy savings in the future. Commonly, the implicit rates of discount associated with such expenditures run in the range of twenty to thirty percent, but sometimes the rates run as high as three hundred percent. Such studies, however, do not typically present a truly risk-free expenditure. Rightly or wrongly, many consumers may be skeptical as to whether they will actually reap the energy savings. They do not always believe the claims made by suppliers. Furthermore, very high discount rates tend to cancel or disappear in an aggregate market setting. Individuals may show high discount rates in particular choice settings, but their regular market behavior differs, as measured by going rates of return.[20]

---

[19] On risk, see Kenneth J. Arrow, *Essays in the Theory of Risk-Bearing* (Amsterdam: North-Holland, 1971).

[20] See George Loewenstein and Richard H. Thaler, "Anomalies: Intertemporal Choice," *Journal of Economic Perspectives* 3, no. 4 (1989): 181–93. Venture capitalists also commonly use high hurdle rates for evaluating an investment, often in the neighborhood of twenty to thirty percent, although, again, these figures may reflect risk or agency problems within the firm and within project evaluation (perhaps managers are too eager to start new projects).

A closer look at these studies also shows that very high discount rates are context-specific. When individuals are considering a future pain or burden, they typically discount *negatively*, not positively. They would prefer that the costs arrive sooner rather than later. Arguably, anticipation of future costs involves psychological pain, so many people prefer to go to the dentist now and get it over with. Studies also find very low discount rates when the cost or benefit is large, or when the cost or benefit lies very distant in the future.[21] These are exactly the conditions that lie behind most of the policy issues we have discussed. Very high discount rates are found only for small expenditures in the very near future, precisely the circumstances where the arguments for a zero discount rate did not apply in any case.

IV. Debates on Utilitarianism and Obligation

In addition to its implications for policy, a zero discount rate may have implications for philosophical debate as well. More specifically, a zero discount rate may make utilitarian theories more plausible. Furthermore, the argument for redistribution is likely to shift. Contrary to common philosophical opinion, the case for redistribution depends more on "here and now" considerations, and less on impersonal consequentialism.

Many utilitarians believe that they are forced to take extreme positions on our obligations to the current poor. Today several billion people stand just at or below the poverty line. Millions of children die each year from malnutrition, diarrhea, malaria, AIDS, and other avoidable maladies. If maximizing aggregate utility is our goal, then it would appear that we who live in affluent societies should devote considerable resources to assisting these individuals. Our marginal dollar buys an ice cream cone, a newspaper, or pet food. We could be half as rich and our marginal dollar would still purchase a luxury rather than a necessity of life. Some consequentialists have welcomed this line of reasoning. They believe that we have strong obligations to redistribute a significant portion of world income.[22]

Critics such as Bernard Williams suggest, instead, that this example provides a strong counterexample to utilitarian reasoning. Were we true utilitarians, all of the able people of the world would become "slaves" to the misery of the very poor. The demands of the suffering are so enormous that few individuals would be able to carry out their life projects. We can imagine, for instance, that every individual would be obliged to work for charity, or to send most of his or her income to India or Haiti. A

---

[21] See Shane Frederick, George Loewenstein, and Ted O'Donoghue, "Time Discounting and Time Preference: A Critical Review," *Journal of Economic Literature* 40, no. 2 (2002): 351–401.

[22] See Peter Singer, *Practical Ethics* (Cambridge: Cambridge University Press, 1993); and Shelley Kagan, *The Limits of Morality* (Oxford: Oxford University Press, 1991).

mother might have to abandon her baby in order to send food to the babies of others, and so forth.[23]

Examining the implications of a zero rate of discount may offer a fresh perspective on this debate. A healthy, growing economy brings a very large stream of future benefits. It will take in large numbers of immigrants, elevate many people from poverty, and yield significant technological innovations. In the more distant future it may generate space colonies, artificial intelligence, or other extraordinary benefits. As long as we expect the wealthy society to survive a reasonably long time, it will produce a very large expected value in terms of utility. We can think of any pocket of self-sustaining productive investment as bringing *enormous* value over time.

A poorer society is, virtually by definition, less productive. Investing in the poorer society will save lives today but will yield a lower return in the future, relative to investing in the richer society. If we look far enough into the future, this difference in productivity, through compounding, may swamp the current higher return from giving to the poor society.

It is now easy to see how the choice of discount rate will have bearing on this debate. If we discount the future at a positive rate, the long-term benefits of investing in the wealthier society will become very small, the further we look into the future. It will be that much harder to justify investing in the wealthy society, relative to the alleviation of immediate suffering. Alternatively, a zero discount rate places greater weight on the very distant future. In this case, long-run capacities play a much greater role in determining the correct utilitarian allocation of resources.

A zero discount rate does not *prove* that selfish investment brings more aggregate utility than does massive charity. Depending on the values of the particular parameters, such as the expected lifespan of the more productive economy, it still may be the case that the utility returns to immediate charity are higher. Nonetheless, a zero discount rate implies that current suffering has a *much* smaller impact on the utilitarian calculus, relative to long-run investment in highly productive societies. It becomes more likely that a utilitarian can favor investment over massive redistribution.[24]

We can also see the circumstances under which the utilitarian *should* favor large-scale redistribution toward the very poor. It might be the case that, for whatever reason, the world was going to end in the very near

[23] See J. J. C. Smart and Bernard Williams, *Utilitarianism: For and Against* (Cambridge, MA: Cambridge University Press, 1973).

[24] It is easy to find one case where the investment always dominates. If the world will continue forever (or at least for a very long time), and the rich have a roughly constant marginal utility of money, then there is always some investment that welfare-dominates the redistribution. The logic of potential compounding kicks in here. Note that the argument requires that poor countries do not have access to the same investment opportunities as do rich ones.

future. Under these circumstances, the redistribution would stand a much greater chance of being favored in utilitarian terms.

Note also that a zero discount rate does not affect the comparison between current *consumption* (buying an ice cream cone) and current charity. The act of benevolent charity likely remains more important in utilitarian terms. We need not, however, give away so many aggregate resources that it hurts the capacity of the richer society to invest or to generate useful incentives for wealth creation. In this regard the obligations of the richer society can remain limited.

In other regards, a zero discount rate may make life more difficult for utilitarian reasoning. The epistemic critique is one of the classic objections to utilitarianism. It is very difficult to calculate the expected value of most individual actions, given the extensive chain reactions that they set off. Utilitarianism, therefore, may fail to provide useful guidance in many (most? all?) cases.

Calculating consequences becomes *much* more difficult when the rate of discount is zero. At positive rates of discount, most future consequences cease to matter much within a thirty-year horizon or so. With a zero rate of discount, welfare-relevant consequences seem to go on forever, or at least until the end of the world. What if I bend down to pick up a banana peel? If nothing else, this will likely affect the identities of all my future children, if only by changing the timing of future conceptions by a slight amount.[25] It is easy to multiply comparable difficulties, using other mechanisms.

Believers in a zero discount rate might then be plagued with a kind of extreme moral nervousness. Under this worldview, virtually every action has truly enormous consequences for our future. And our estimates of welfare consequences will have very high standard errors. We realize that any moment we might be doing something that will lead to truly terrible results, or lead to truly wonderful results.

One response to these calculation problems might be a greater reliance on rules of thumb. If the consequences of particular acts are so very difficult to calculate, then perhaps we must rely more on rules and general principles. This conclusion may well be true, but, of course, the consequences of any rule will be hard to calculate as well. Extreme moral nervousness will remain. And rule-utilitarianism will have won only a partial victory. Ironically, we find that the more necessary rules become, the less we can be sure that these rules are a good thing. We become extremely nervous about any rule we might choose. This same nervousness, of course, may explain why it is so hard to adhere to rules-based prescriptions, whether in politics or in the realm of personal life.

Finally, a zero discount rate has implications for many pluralistic moral theories. A pluralistic moral theory typically counts several values as

---

[25] See Parfit, *Reasons and Persons.*

POLICY IMPLICATIONS OF ZERO DISCOUNTING 139

values that matter. In particular, let us focus on pluralistic theories that give weight to both deontological and consequentialist considerations. A theory of this kind might embody the following: "Consequences matter, but so do rights violations. We should violate rights only if it brings some very large potential benefit or avoids some very large potential cost. Otherwise rights are sacrosanct." I believe that many people, both among philosophers and among the general citizenry, hold views of this form.

A zero discount rate will shift the balance toward consequentialist considerations, at the expense of deontology. Recall from the above discussion that even very small actions can have very large expected values, given that the future matters as much as the present. Any small but perpetual improvement, for instance, will involve a very large present value. Given the theory I expressed above, therefore, we should be willing to violate rights to bring a small but long-lasting improvement. Our longer time-horizon makes rights violations easier to justify in a pluralistic theory, at least provided that the relevant acts have long-term consequences.

This shift in emphasis arises from the very nature of deontology. Deontological considerations simply tell us "do" or "do not," but they do not weigh competing values. So a change in the discount rate will affect the weight of consequentialist considerations, but not the weight of deontological considerations. With a zero discount rate, consequentialist considerations will tend to swamp deontological ones, again provided that the relevant time-horizon is sufficiently long.[26]

V. CONCLUDING REMARKS

I have examined a number of implications of adopting a zero rate of discount. Most of all, a zero rate of discount suggests that having a (broadly) free society is more important than many people think. A zero rate of discount also directs our attention toward the importance of economic growth, a healthy long-run environment, favorable treatment for savings, and economic "shock therapy." A zero rate of discount increases our skepticism of government provision of goods and services, large welfare states, and global charitable obligations toward the very poor. It also makes consequences more important, makes utility more difficult to calculate, provides a greater rationale for rules, but plagues us with moral nervousness at the unknown and manifold implications of even our most mundane acts.

---

[26] Deontologists do not typically claim that "a rights violation tomorrow is less bad than a rights violation today." This kind of thinking in terms of trade-offs is precisely what deontology rejects. Deontology simply tells us "don't infringe rights," albeit with a potential caveat for extreme consequences.

The case for a zero rate of discount is strongest either when we consider well-being directly or when we consider policies that have very large effects on individuals' wealth. In any case, examining the discount rate issue forces us to refine our intuitions, our policy positions, and our assessment of utilitarian calculation.

Economics, George Mason University

REFLECTIONS ON ESPIONAGE

By Harvey Klehr

I. Introduction

In 1995 the United States National Security Agency (NSA), the Central Intelligence Agency (CIA), and the Federal Bureau of Investigation (FBI) made public the story of a forty-year American intelligence operation code-named Venona. Shortly after the Nazi-Soviet Pact in 1939, American military intelligence had ordered companies that were sending and receiving coded cables overseas, such as Western Union, to turn over copies to the U.S. government. Hundreds of thousands of cables were sent or received by Soviet government bodies. Beginning in 1943, spurred by rumors and concerns that Stalin might conclude a separate peace with Hitler, the U.S. Army's cryptographic section began work trying to read these Russian cables. It had very limited success until 1946, by which time the Cold War was already underway. Some twenty-nine hundred cables dealing with Russian intelligence activities from 1942 to 1946 eventually were decrypted successfully in whole or in part as a result of Soviet technical errors in constructing and using "one-time pads" that American code-breakers were able to exploit. These cables implicated more than three hundred Americans as having been involved with Soviet intelligence services during World War II, a time when the United States and the USSR were allies.[1]

The Venona documents have sparked a renewed interest in issues of espionage, although in truth there has hardly been a time in the past fifty years that espionage has not generated public fascination, not only in the United States but also in Great Britain. One of the remarkable aspects of the response to Venona has been the effort by a number of people to defend westerners who spied for the Soviet Union. The moral status of spies and spying has been debated for a long time. In the twentieth century the advent of Communism and the willingness of so many citizens of democratic countries to spy on its behalf against their own nations gave this debate added urgency. That so many writers and intellectuals continue to see justifications for espionage against their own countries after the collapse of Communism warrants a new look at the connections between morality and espionage, connections that are illuminated by a more precise and nuanced view of the moral status of the spy. Justifying

---

[1] For a complete description, see John Haynes and Harvey Klehr, *Venona: Decoding Soviet Espionage in America* (New Haven, CT: Yale University Press, 1999).

espionage directed against democracies is not easy, and the recent attempts to do so have not been successful.

Espionage is almost as ubiquitous a historical phenomenon as it is a reviled profession. Intelligence gathering and the use of spies have a long pedigree. The history of intelligence organizations has been traced back to the societies of ancient Egypt, Babylonia, Assyria, Persia, and the Hittite Empire.[2] In Homer's *Odyssey*, Odysseus disguises himself to infiltrate Troy. The ancient Greeks wrote at length about the variety of spies, distinguishing among fake deserters, merchants, neutrals, and those recruited from within an enemy's population.[3] English journalist Phillip Knightley has called spying the world's second oldest profession.[4]

While recognizing its necessity, commentators have also accepted its moral ambiguity. Spying requires deception and secrecy. Those who engage in it must violate a variety of laws and moral principles. A historian of ancient Greek espionage notes that spies who betray their fellow citizens "have always been perceived in the Western tradition as corrupt and corrupting."[5] But even those who spy for a democratic society must walk a fine moral line. Paul Seabury notes that in a democratic society practitioners of spying need to be "able to maintain their integrity while being liars and obfuscators."[6] An international law text written during the American Civil War quotes a commentator who noted:

> Spies are generally condemned to capital punishment, and not unjustly; since we have scarcely any other means of guarding against the mischief they may do us. For this reason, a man of honor, who would not expose himself to die by the hand of a common executioner, ever declines serving as a spy. He considers it beneath him, as seldom can be done without some kind of treachery.[7]

Democratic societies have always been troubled by the use of spies. It is not simply that democracies rely on public discussion and abhor secrecy. They also struggle with the moral compromises that are required by their own spying and the reprehensible characters of many spies. Popular modern spy novelist, John Le Carré, has one of his most memorable characters, Alex Leamas, angrily explain: "What do you think spies are;

[2] Francis Dvornik, *Origins of Intelligence Services: The Ancient Near East, Persia, Greece, Rome, Byzantium, the Arab Muslim Empires, the Mongol Empire, China, Muscovy* (New Brunswick, NJ: Rutgers University Press, 1974).

[3] Frank Russell, *Information Gathering in Classical Greece* (Ann Arbor: University of Michigan Press, 1999), 105.

[4] Phillip Knightley, *The Second Oldest Profession: Spies and Spying in the Twentieth Century* (London: A. Deutsch, 1986).

[5] Russell, *Information Gathering in Classical Greece*, 106.

[6] Paul Seabury in *Covert Action*, no. 4 of *Intelligence Requirements for the 1980s*, ed. Roy Godson (Washington, DC: National Strategy Information Center, 1981), 107.

[7] Henry Halleck, *International Law* (San Francisco: H. H. Bancroft & Co., 1861), 406.

priests, saints and martyrs? They're a squalid procession of vain fools, traitors too; yes; pansies, sadists and drunkards, people who play cowboys and Indians to brighten their rotten lives."[8] And yet, democracies also admire the self-sacrifice that they imagine motivates some spies. The first popular spy novel written by an American, based on American history, and set in the American countryside was James Fenimore Cooper's *The Spy*. It is an account of Harvey Birch, a member of General Washington's espionage corps who pretends to be a British agent and, pledged to secrecy, nobly suffers the "ostracism and hatred" of his neighbors to his dying day.[9]

II. The Morality of Espionage

For almost as long as there have been spies there has been debate about the morality of espionage. In the Hebrew Bible the first mention of spies suggests how dangerous a false charge of espionage can be. It comes when Joseph's brothers arrive in Egypt to buy grain. Joseph, as governor, meets them, learns who they are, and, remembering their ill treatment of him, charges them with espionage: "You are spies, you have come to see the weakness of the land."[10] Despite their repeated, frantic denials, Joseph demands that they prove their bona fides by leaving one brother hostage, returning to Canaan, and bringing their youngest surviving brother, Benjamin, back to Egypt. Joseph repeatedly tests his brothers, plants false evidence against them, and deceives them as to his motives before revealing his true identity. Significantly, the first accusation of espionage in the Bible is a false charge, made for ulterior purposes. Just as significantly, its targets are themselves not blameless but harbor a guilty secret, making them vulnerable to manipulation.

The first account of actual espionage in the Bible is likewise revealing. It is a botched operation. God tells Moses to "send men to spy out the land of Canaan." He suggests that one prominent figure from each of the twelve tribes be selected; Moses tasks them to "see what the land is, and whether the people who dwell in it are strong or weak, whether they are few or many, and whether the land that they dwell in is good or bad, and whether the cities that they dwell in are camps or strongholds, and whether the land is rich or poor, and whether there is wood in it or not. Be of good courage, and bring some of the fruit of the land."[11]

---

[8] John Le Carré, *The Spy Who Came in From the Cold* (New York: Bantam Books, 1963), 210–11.

[9] James Fenimore Cooper, *The Spy: A Tale of the Neutral Ground* (New York: Hafner Pub. Co., 1960). The quotation is from the introduction by Warren S. Walker, 6.

[10] Gen. 42:6–17. The Oxford Annotated Bible, Revised Standard Version (New York: Oxford University Press, 1962).

[11] Num. 13:1–20.

It takes this band of spies forty days to complete their mission. Upon their return they meet with Moses and Aaron and the entire Israelite population to report that the land of Canaan flows with milk and honey, but "the people who dwell in the land are strong, and the cities are fortified and very large." Despite the pleas of two of the spies that the Israelites forge ahead and conquer the land, the other ten insist that the task is hopeless, inciting the population to agitate for a return to Egypt. This first espionage mission ends in ignominious failure for the society. Commentators have argued that it was doomed from the start. Although God had already promised the land to the Israelites, their lack of faith in His word had led them to demand a group of spies to reconnoiter the territory. (In Deuteronomy 1:22, Moses reminds the Israelites that "all of you came near me and said, 'Let us send men before us, that they may explore the land for us, and bring us word again of the way by which we must go up and the cities into which we shall come.' " Angered, God told them through Moses to send out the spies "they pleased," but determined to punish the Jews.) After the debacle of their public report, God announces that the Israelites will be required to wander in the desert for forty years, one for each of the days "that you spied out the land." He further denies entry into the Promised Land to everyone over the age of twenty, with the exception of the two spies who had argued for the invasion, Caleb and Joshua, the latter of whom would actually lead that invasion years later.[12]

One intelligence analyst notes that this operation was doomed from the start. Those selected as spies were public figures; their names are provided in the Bible. Each one had significant political and military responsibilities that affected his evaluation of the information that he was gathering. The collected intelligence was openly discussed at a public meeting. Although no details are given of how they gathered their information, there is no indication that the spies spoke to anyone or did anything more than observe the inhabitants and their cities. All in all, the Israelites mounted an intelligence operation that lacked professionalism and violated a number of essential precautions. Having launched a risky venture, they paid a heavy price for its failure.[13]

Later espionage operations described in the Old Testament are far more successful. Moses sends out spies who wind up capturing Jazer.[14] More significantly, Joshua, a veteran of the earlier failure, recruits two anonymous spies, ordering them: "Go, observe the land and Jericho."[15] Arriv-

---

[12] Num. 13:21–31; and Deut. 1:22–38. Nehama Leibowitz, *Studies in Bamidbar (Numbers)*, trans. Aryeh Newman (Jerusalem: World Zionist Organization, 1980), 135–41.

[13] John M. Cardwell, "A Bible Lesson on Spying," *Studies in Intelligence* (Winter 1978), available on-line at http://www.parascope.com/ds/articles/ciaBibleStudyDoc.html [accessed in January 2003].

[14] Num. 21:32.

[15] Josh. 2.

ing in Jericho, these unnamed men befriend a harlot named Rahab who is willing to hide them when the authorities learn of their presence and try to arrest them. In return for her help and insight into the public mood, they agree to spare her and her family during the coming battle. When they return, the spies report directly and confidentially to Joshua and note to him that even though Jericho is well fortified, its inhabitants fear the Israelites because of their previous military successes and the evidence of God's miracles. Joshua then promptly launches his successful attack on the city.

Other biblical stories describe spy operations ordered by David and Absalom.[16] In none of these stories does spying upon one's enemy incur any moral taint. There is, however, a clear contrast between the ingredients of a successful and an unsuccessful espionage mission. Joshua's anonymous spies never receive any credit for their actions. Their primary source is not some notable or upstanding citizen but a prostitute who, in return for her assistance in betraying her countrymen, is promised and receives protection. There is no suggestion that the spies somehow acted ignobly by concluding a deal with someone of ill repute. Unlike Moses' spies, who slipped in and out of enemy territory without being discovered, Joshua's operatives had to flee for their lives but still succeeded. As in another verse from the Hebrew Bible that explicitly mentions espionage, the spy is someone acting on behalf of his own people: in Judges, the tribe of Dan sends "five able men" to spy on a land that they intend to conquer.[17]

There is one notable exception to this positive portrayal of spies. Although she is not called a spy, Delilah, the Philistine woman who betrays Samson, acts much like one. Approached by Philistine leaders who ask her to "see wherein his great strength lies, and by what means we may overpower him," Delilah deceives her lover in return for money. Her first three efforts to learn his secrets fail, but she finally succeeds in wresting from him the secret of his strength, cuts his hair, and delivers him to the Philistines.[18]

The New Testament offers a more negative view of spies and espionage. In contrast to the Old Testament, where most espionage is carried out by Israelites responding to God's command to conquer the Promised Land, in the New Testament spies betray Jesus Christ.[19] In the one case, the Israelites are the beneficiaries of espionage; in the other Jesus is the victim. In the Gospel of Luke, for example, the scribes and high priests, anxious to discredit Jesus and to trick him into violating the law, "watched

---

[16] 1 Sam. 26:4; and 2 Sam. 15:10.

[17] Judg. 18:2.

[18] Judg. 16.

[19] One significant exception to this negative portrayal is Rahab, the woman who had aided Joshua's spies. In Heb. 11:31 she is praised: "By faith Rahab the harlot did not perish with those who were disobedient, because she had given friendly welcome to the spies."

him, and sent spies, who pretended to be sincere, that they might take
hold of what he said, so as to deliver him up to the authority and jurisdiction of the governor." These spies ask Jesus if they should give tribute
to Caesar, to which he cannily and notably replies, "Render to Caesar the
things that are Caesar's, and to God the things that are God's."[20] Likewise offering a negative view of spies, in his Letter to the Galatians Paul
warns against "false brethren secretly brought in, who slipped in to spy
out our freedom which we have in Christ Jesus, that they might bring us
into bondage."[21] The spy here is someone pretending to be loyal or a
friend but actually serving the interests of the enemy. He is the agent
provocateur, encouraging actions designed to discredit the cause that he
ostensibly supports.

The archetype of the betrayer, the man who pretends to be a loyalist but
who is secretly working for the opposition, is, of course, Judas. One of
Christ's disciples, he is willing to betray his teacher and master for money.
Bought by the high priests for thirty pieces of silver, he identifies Jesus to
the soldiers by kissing him on the cheek. His reward proves empty, and
he hangs himself. Judas gave his name to all the spies who sell out their
friends and compatriots. Unlike Joshua and his spies, he is not a patriot
sent behind enemy lines but a disciple betraying his own people.

Historically, the spy who betrays his friends, his country, or his people
has been a mercenary. Delilah, Judas, and Benedict Arnold all were bought
with cash payments. No doubt the moral revulsion evoked by spies is
linked to the motives for pecuniary gain that has driven so many of them.
Montesquieu expresses the sentiment in *The Spirit of the Laws* (1748) when
he notes that "the trade of a spy might perhaps be tolerable were it
practiced by honest men; but the necessary infamy of the person is sufficient to make us judge of the infamy of the thing."[22]

While some have been repulsed by the sordid motives that drive many
spies, others have worried about the impact of spying on the moral health
of the regime that employs them. Immanuel Kant warns that even in
wartime, a state is "permitted to use any means of defense except those
that would make its subjects unfit to be citizens." The first restraint he
deduces from this rule is that "means of defense that are not permitted
include using its own subjects as spies; using them or even foreigners, as
assassins or poisoners . . . or using them merely to spread false reports—in
a word, using such underhanded means as would destroy the trust required to establish a lasting peace in the future."[23] Kant seems to leave

---

[20] Luke 20:20. In Matt. 22:15 it is the Pharisees who send not spies, but some of their own
disciples.

[21] Gal. 2:4.

[22] Charles de Secondat, baron de Montesquieu, *The Spirit of the Laws* (1748; reprint, trans.
Thomas Nugent, New York: Hafner Press, 1949), 202.

[23] Immanuel Kant, *The Metaphysics of Morals*, trans. Mary Gregor (Cambridge: Cambridge
University Press, 1991), 154.

open the possibility of employing foreigners as spies, provided they neither lie nor cheat nor kill, although exactly how useful they would be if
they were required to be honest about what they were up to is an open
question. Spying for Kant is a dishonorable profession that taints those
who acquiesce in its use. A life of deception taints not only the one doing
the deceiving, but also those who connive in it.

Such high-minded idealism has always had to confront the realities of
the world of nation-states. Justifications for spying have ranged from its
usefulness to rulers to its acceptance in international law. Thomas Hobbes
argues that it is "necessary to the defense of the city, first, that there be
some who may, as near as may be, search into and discover the counsels
and motions of all those who may prejudice it." For Hobbes this means
that rulers require spies: "[T]hey who bear rule, can no more know what
is necessary to be commanded for the defense of their subjects without
spies, than those spiders" who learn by the movement of their webs'
threads when danger threatens.[24]

Similarly, Machiavelli would not have felt that there was any moral
dilemma in using spies. Although he never explicitly discusses espionage, Machiavelli not only accepts but also praises a ruler who uses
whatever means are necessary to learn about the intentions and capabilities of his enemies, both foreign and domestic. (He does warn that conspiracies rarely succeed because they will usually be betrayed by some
disgruntled conspirator.) He warns the leader and would-be leader not to
assume that Christian virtues can result in a successful and well-ordered
state. It is necessary, he asserts, to understand that "he who abandons
what is done for what ought to be done, will rather learn to bring about
his own ruin than his preservation. A man who wishes to make a profession of goodness in everything must necessarily come to grief among
so many who are not good. Therefore it is necessary for a prince, who
wishes to maintain himself, to learn how not to be good."[25] If the prince
himself must be able to lie and deceive, to present himself as what he is
not, how can such stratagems be avoided by those citizens or employees
who serve his purposes?

Machiavelli makes explicit throughout his writings that deceit, subterfuge, covert operations, and even political assassination are part of the
arsenal that a ruler may have to employ. A successful ruler must "know
well how to use both the beast and the man." To understand how to act
as a beast, "he must imitate the fox and the lion, for the lion cannot
protect himself from traps, and the fox cannot defend himself from wolves.
One must therefore be a fox to recognize traps, and a lion to frighten
wolves."[26]

---

[24] Thomas Hobbes, *De Cive* (Garden City, NJ: Anchor Books, 1972), 13:7.

[25] Niccoló Machiavelli, *The Prince and the Discourses* (New York: Random House, 1950), 56.

[26] Ibid., 64. In *Discourses*, bk. 3, chap. 6, Machiavelli treats at length of conspiracies and
conspirators but these are not, strictly speaking, spies.

One animal Machiavelli never mentions, however, is the mole, that creature of the underground that does its best work in the dark. It is no accident, as Marxists are wont to say, that Karl Marx was inordinately fond of the mole and that he himself was known as "the Old Mole." Marx compared the struggles of the working class to the burrowing of the mole, laboring out of sight in capitalist society until the moment when revolution erupts. The Old Mole's doctrines provided a heady rationale for hundreds of the twentieth century's most successful moles, who were able to burrow into positions of authority in capitalist societies and work to undermine them.[27]

Espionage per se is not illegal in international law. In the seventeenth century Hugo Grotius noted the paradox that it is perfectly legal for a state to dispatch or employ spies but also perfectly legal for the target state to punish spies if it catches them: "[T]he law of nations unquestionably permits the sending out of spies ... yet if they are caught they are commonly treated with great cruelty.... If there are men who refuse to employ the aid of spies, when it is offered them, their refusal must be attributed to loftiness of mind and confidence in their own revealed resources, not to any idea of what is lawful or unlawful."[28] Virtually every country engages in espionage and understands that others do as well. It may well be illegal in every country (or at least in those with minimal standards of individual rights) to intercept private communications, but every country in the world encrypts and encodes its diplomatic and sensitive communications, recognizing that others will attempt to break into them, without protesting that some kind of violation of international law is occurring.

Although the United States has employed spies from the Revolutionary War onward, there has always been a strain in American life that has regarded spying with distaste. Part of the reason, no doubt, has been the belief that a healthy and vibrant democracy need have no fear of any enemy and has nothing to hide from one. In a similar vein, Pericles boasted that open, democratic Athens did not have to rely on subterfuge:

---

[27] Marx compared the communist revolution to a mole, paraphrasing Shakespeare's *Hamlet*, 1.5.162: "Well said, old mole!" Marx added:

> But the revolution is thoroughgoing. It is still traveling through purgatory. It does its work methodically. By December 2, 1851, it had completed half of its preparatory work; it is now completing the other half. First it perfected the parliamentary power in order to be able to overthrow it. Now that it has attained this, it perfects the executive power, reduces it to its purest expression, isolates it, sets it up against itself as the sole target, in order to concentrate all its forces of destruction against it. And when it has done this second half of its preliminary work, Europe will leap from its seat and exultantly exclaim: Well-grubbed old mole!

Karl Marx, *The Eighteenth Brumaire of Louis Bonaparte* (1851–1852; reprint, Moscow: Foreign Language Publishing House, 1983), 121.

[28] Hugo Grotius, *The Law of War and Peace* (1670), trans. Louise R. Loomis (New York: Walter J. Black, 1949), bk. III, chap. 4, p. 302.

It was "an open city and do[es] not, by periodically expelling foreigners, keep them from seeing and learning things, lest some enemy benefit from what is open to his view. We trust less to our equipment and guile than to our personal courage in action."[29]

Another factor has been the belief that espionage is a dishonorable activity that runs counter to democratic values. Because it requires secrecy, it cannot be subject to the same demand for transparency that is usually made regarding political issues. It is difficult for representative bodies to exercise control and oversight. The methods and techniques of espionage often raise disturbing questions of propriety and legality. The individuals attracted to it or indoctrinated in its culture are often perceived as dangerous to democratic values. Consequently, many Americans have regarded espionage, particularly in peacetime, as a blight on our moral standards. Shortly after he was appointed Secretary of State in 1929 Henry Stimson received a series of decrypted diplomatic telegrams from the American Black Chamber, the office run by Herbert Yardley that had been successfully breaking foreign codes since 1919. Stimson "regarded it as a low, snooping activity, a sneaking, spying, keyhole-peering kind of dirty business, a violation of the principle of mutual trust upon which he conducted both his personal affairs and his foreign policy." As he later noted: "Gentlemen do not read each others' mail." His opposition led to the dissolution of the American Black Chamber.[30] Similarly, in October 1945 President Harry Truman disbanded the Office of Strategic Services (OSS), which had been created during World War II to serve as a national intelligence agency, amid fears that it could become an "American Gestapo." Concern with "dirty tricks" perpetrated by American security agencies prompted Congress to restrict what American spies could do following the Church Committee hearings in 1975 and in the 1990s led to rules that forbade the CIA from recruiting human rights violators as sources.

This distaste for the secret world of espionage, however, has generally given way, particularly in the twentieth century, to realistic concerns about national security. As Secretary of War in the 1940s Stimson overcame his scruples to allow extensive spying. The CIA was created in 1947 and the following year received authorization to conduct covert operations. Following the terrorist attack on America on September 11, 2001, earlier restrictions on CIA recruitment of unsavory characters were lifted. Even when elected officials have tried to limit or restrict the activities of intelligence agencies, few Americans have gainsaid the need for this country to spy on enemies, adversaries, potential enemies, and, even perhaps, friends. Employing spies is regarded as part of the necessary business of

[29] Thucydides, *The Peloponnesian War*, Walter Blanco and Jennifer T. Roberts, eds. (New York: Norton, 1998), 73.

[30] David Kahn, *The Codebreakers: The Story of Secret Writing* (New York: Scribners, 1996), 360.

governing. But if the need for the government to spy is widely recognized, Americans remain ambivalent about the people so employed and what they should be allowed to do. It is one thing to seek to ascertain the capabilities of a potential enemy, another to try to recruit a foreign politician to act in a certain way, and still another to bribe or coerce or threaten someone to obtain information.[31]

III. Varieties of Spies

In discussions about morality and espionage it is useful to recall that there are different types of spies. A country may employ its own nationals or citizens to obtain information about another country, or it may seek to use citizens of that other country to obtain information. Both types of recruits may be engaging in espionage and be labeled as spies, but their activities, behavior, and characters elicit very different evaluations.

Citizens of a country who spy for it are patriots. We may not approve of the country that they serve. We may deplore the tactics that they use or the methods that they employ to gather their information, but their actions are not much different than those of soldiers engaged in a particularly difficult or dangerous mission. Unlike soldiers they do not wear uniforms, and this difference may subject them to punishments from which soldiers are exempt under international law. Like Joshua, these spies are willing to go behind enemy lines to ferret out information that the enemy wishes to conceal.

There are actually two types of patriotic spies and international law treats them rather differently. Every modern intelligence agency employs the first type: officers or employees who recruit, supervise, and give orders to agents who obtain secrets. These officers are almost always citizens of the government that employs them and are loyal to its principles. Many of these men and women serve in diplomatic positions, often as minor functionaries or bureaucrats in an embassy or consulate, while their major task is to obtain secret information about the country to which they are posted. They have diplomatic immunity from arrest and punishment by their host government. In the modern world every state understands that such "spies" are a normal part of a country's diplomatic mission. If caught in the act of obtaining information from a source, they will be declared persona non grata and expelled. Such activities, however, are part and parcel of the normal relationship among nation-states. Even spies are protected by diplomatic immunity provided that they have the correct credentials. Under international law, even if some of the American diplomatic personnel who were held hostage by Iran in the late 1970s

---

[31] See, for example, David L. Perry, " 'Repugnant Philosophy': Ethics, Espionage, and Covert Action," *Journal of Conflict Studies* 15, no. 1 (1995): 92–115, for an effort to determine the moral limitations on espionage.

were CIA officers, the Iranians were obligated not to arrest and punish them.

The second type of patriotic spy is a citizen of one country who lives under cover in another country to spy on it; these spies are at greater hazard and in a more morally ambiguous position than the first type. While spies with diplomatic immunity are perceived to be serving the interests of their government, merely disguising their espionage work, the undercover spy, or agent in place, pretends to be a normal inhabitant of the country that he is seeking to undermine. He must disguise not only his job but also his loyalties. Many of the fictional and true-life heroes of popular espionage lore fall into this category. Since international law provides that a spy captured behind enemy lines is subject to the death penalty, such espionage carried on in wartime requires considerable bravery and a willingness to take enormous risks. No American spy better symbolized this than Nathan Hale, hung by the British in 1776, a statue of whom adorns the CIA's Langley, Virginia, headquarters. Whether or not he ever uttered the famous phrase that is attributed to him, regretting he had but one life to give to his country, Hale's willingness to spy even though it was considered a dishonorable task for a gentleman and a graduate of Yale College, reflected a recognition that loyalty to one's country sometimes requires personal sacrifices.[32] James Fenimore Cooper's fictional spy, Harvey Birch, likewise linked valor and personal sacrifice as essential elements in the success of the Revolutionary War and the creation of a nation.

Americans have admired and honored spies who are willing to risk their lives to provide vital information about America's enemies. Nor are Americans alone. Every country has its mythic heroes who disguise their identities to blend in with the enemy and ferret out his secrets. Even when these spies have been adversaries, Americans have had a grudging admiration for their exploits. No nation used more "illegals" than the Soviet Union. Living under false identities in America, England, occupied France during World War II, and other nations throughout the world, such agents did not enjoy diplomatic immunity. "Illegals," however, shared with KGB and GRU officers assigned to embassy positions an allegiance to the Soviet Union.[33]

Not all "illegals" were Soviet citizens. A number of dedicated Communists had enlisted in the intelligence service of the Communist International, or Comintern, in the 1920s and shifted over to Soviet intelligence

---

[32] See, for example, William Ordway Partridge, *Nathan Hale, the Ideal Patriot: A Study of Character* (New York: Funk & Wagnalls Co., 1902).

[33] A word on nomenclature. The USSR's main foreign intelligence organization, commonly known in the West as the KGB, used a variety of names from its origins as the Cheka shortly after the Russian Revolution. For simplicity, I have used KGB throughout this essay to refer to its various incarnations. The GRU, or military intelligence, is a separate organization that often had a fierce bureaucratic rivalry with the KGB.

work late in the decade or in the 1930s. Regarding themselves as soldiers in an international army, such people were among the most effective and romanticized KGB and GRU officers. Multilingual, at home in working-class bars and corporate boardrooms, cultured and dedicated, many of them lived lives that were stranger than fiction. Their actions, activities, and fates mirror the moral ambiguities and horrors of the twentieth century.

Theodore Mally, a one-time seminarian studying for the priesthood in Hungary, was drafted into the army of the Austro-Hungarian Empire and taken prisoner in World War I. The Bolsheviks converted him to Communism in a prisoner-of-war camp. Assigned to the Cheka, the USSR's first internal security agency, he grew disillusioned with the internal repression that accompanied the collectivization drives of the 1920s, and secured a transfer to foreign intelligence. His longest assignment was to Great Britain; in 1935 he became the illegal resident for the KGB in London, where he oversaw the early espionage work of the "Cambridge spies," Kim Philby, Donald Maclean, Anthony Blunt, and Guy Burgess. In 1937, at the height of Stalin's purge of the Soviet intelligence services, Mally was recalled to Moscow. Responding to a friend who pleaded with him not to go back to certain death, he noted that "he could be killed abroad as well as in Moscow" and that "it would be better for him to meet his fate in the cellars of the Lubyanka." He was shot in 1938. Today his portrait hangs in a "History Room" honoring heroes of the Soviet intelligence service at the headquarters of the Russian intelligence service (SVR).[34]

Léopold Trepper, a Polish Jew, immigrated in the 1920s to Palestine, where he joined the Communist Party. Sent to France to work among Jewish immigrants, he later moved to Moscow for training in Comintern schools. Disillusioned by the purges of the 1930s that swallowed up hundreds of his old friends, he joined Soviet intelligence to better fight Nazism. As head of the "Red Orchestra," a huge Communist spy network, he operated under cover as a raincoat manufacturer in Paris and Brussels until he was arrested by the Gestapo. Trepper built a continent-wide circle of agents, used innocent people as fronts for his activities, betrayed a number of his agents in order to save others, pretended to cooperate with the Germans while feeding them false information, and managed to escape and remain in hiding until World War II ended. Upon returning to the Soviet Union in 1945 he was jailed as a traitor, rehabilitated after nine years, and reunited with his family. They returned to Poland, where he assumed a position within the decimated Jewish community. Appalled by the upsurge of anti-Semitism in 1967, he launched a campaign to be allowed to immigrate to Israel. For years the Communist authorities harassed him before finally allowing him to leave Poland in 1973.[35]

[34] William Duff, *A Time For Spies: Theodore Stephanovich Mally and the Era of the Great Illegals* (Nashville, TN: Vanderbilt University Press, 1999), 156.

[35] See Léopold Trepper, *The Great Game: Memoirs of the Spy Hitler Couldn't Silence* (New York: McGraw-Hill, 1977); and Gilles Perrault, *The Red Orchestra*, trans. Peter Wiles (New York: Simon & Schuster, 1969).

The Soviets used illegals like Mally and Trepper because they had the sophistication and skills to blend in with their surroundings. They, in turn, served the Soviet Union because they were convinced that its triumph would advance the cause of humanity. In the service of that cause they willingly risked their lives and sought to subvert and weaken enemies of the Soviet Union. While their unhappy fates were partially linked to suspicions that as foreigners and, in Trepper's case, as a Jew, they were inherently suspicious, under Stalin even native-born intelligence officers were frequent victims of waves of purges that swept through the intelligence agencies. Part of the admiration for their exploits, no doubt, is connected to the punishment to which they were subjected by the regime that they had so loyally served.

The Soviets used "illegals" as spies in the United States because they knew that American counterintelligence agencies carefully watched and monitored the activities of Soviet diplomatic personnel in order to detect their involvement with espionage. Although the KGB station chief in the United States during much of World War II, Vasili Zubilin, nominally a Second Secretary in the Soviet consulate in New York, was able to evade surveillance at times and meet with agents, it was a time-consuming process and not always successful. For example, one FBI bug planted in the home of an American Communist official in California in 1944 overheard Zubilin offering money in return for the use of a group of sources.[36]

The illegals, however, were unknown to the FBI. At the same time that Zubilin was being followed, Ishak Akmerhov was living under an assumed name in Baltimore, Maryland, posing as a fur merchant. Akmerhov was a Tatar and a veteran KGB officer who had served illegally in the United States in the 1930s and returned illegally in the early 1940s. He supervised a number of spies who were able to meet with him and turn over material that they had filched from the government offices in which they worked. Akmerhov sent 59 rolls of microfilm to Moscow in 1942, 211 in 1943, 600 in 1944, and 1,896 in 1945.[37] He returned to Moscow in 1946, received a decoration, and continued to work for the KGB until his retirement. Not until after he left the United States did American counterintelligence learn about his activities.

Soviet citizens arrested in the United States for spying might not enjoy diplomatic immunity, but their status was different from American spies. In 1957, for example, the FBI arrested a man known as Rudolph Abel. His real name was William Fischer. Born in Great Britain to a Russian émigré family that returned to Soviet Russia when he was a young boy, Abel was later recruited into the KGB. In 1948 he entered the United States on a false passport, and then lived quietly in New York, posing as an artist,

[36] See Haynes and Klehr, *Venona*, 230–31.
[37] Christopher Andrew and Vasili Mitrokhin, *The Sword and the Shield: The Mitrokhin Archive and the Secret History of the KGB* (New York: Basic Books, 1999), 111, 118, and 129.

while running several agents, including Ted Hall and Morris and Lona Cohen (discussed below).

Abel, who had left his wife and children in the Soviet Union, was arrested in 1957 after his assistant, a Soviet illegal with a severe drinking problem, turned himself in to U.S. authorities. At the subsequent trial, Abel's defense lawyer attempted to discredit this man, Reino Hayhanen, by noting that "he entered the United States on false papers . . . he has lived here every day only by lying about his true identity, about his background, about every facet of his everyday life . . . he was trained abroad in what his 'cover' should be here, meaning that he was trained in the art of deception. He was trained to lie. In short, assuming that what the government says is true, this man is literally a professional liar."[38] The jury found the argument unpersuasive because it described Abel as much as Hayhanen. Every illegal has to be a professional liar. After serving several years in prison, Fischer was exchanged for Francis Gary Powers, pilot of the U-2 spy plane that had been shot down over the Soviet Union in 1960. Abel earned the grudging admiration of his American captors for his professionalism, dedication, and discipline.

If the first category of spies consists of those who serve their country or adopted nation, the second is comprised of those who betray it. Beginning with Benedict Arnold, Americans have been harshly unforgiving of those citizens who have provided enemies with America's secrets or turned on their own country to serve another. Even when a spy's employer has been a country with which America is friendly, both the public and the government have reacted with fury. When Jonathan Pollard was arrested in 1985 for spying for Israel, an ally of the United States, the Justice Department sought and received one of the harshest punishments ever for peacetime espionage, despite Pollard's claim that he never intended to harm the United States.[39]

The citizen who spies for another country violates one of the most basic clauses of the democratic social contract; by his actions he threatens the ties that bind a country of individuals together. Having freely consented to become a citizen or choosing to remain one despite the option of leaving, an American is regarded as a traitor (in fact if not in law) if he or she places loyalty to another country above loyalty to America. The sense of betrayal is relevant in a way that it is not if the spy is a resident alien or other kind of noncitizen. (Only in recent years has the issue of dual citizenship and dual loyalty become a complicating factor.) While a noncitizen resident in America is expected to obey American laws, only a citizen owes loyalty to the nation.

[38] Louise Bernikow, *Abel* (New York: Trident Press, 1970), 155.

[39] Wolf Blitzer, *Territory of Lies: The Exclusive Story of Jonathan Jay Pollard, the American Who Spied on His Country for Israel and How He Was Betrayed* (New York: Harper & Row, 1989).

The disdain in which such spies are held is linked to the motives that most have for spying. Like Judas or Benedict Arnold, most are not very admirable people. In recent years, virtually every American citizen charged with and convicted of espionage has spied for base motives. Aldrich Ames, a CIA officer arrested in 1994 for spying for the Soviet Union and providing information to the KGB that led to the deaths of at least ten Soviets who were cooperating with American intelligence, was greedy. He sold to the Soviets, in return for direct payments of $2 million to support a lavish life style, the names of more than two dozen "human assets," as well as information compromising CIA officers and covert operations.[40] John Walker, Jr., who had recruited his own son, brother, and best friend to spy for the Soviet Union, likewise had no ideological ax to grind. Arrested in 1985, this retired Navy man and a one-time member of the Ku Klux Klan had supplied the Soviets with highly classified communications and encryption information over a seventeen-year span, simply for money.[41] Robert Hanssen, an FBI counterintelligence agent who received a life sentence in May 2002 for spying for the Soviet Union and then Russia, from 1985 until his arrest in February 2001, appears to have been motivated by a desire to demonstrate that he could outsmart people whom he regarded as his intellectual inferiors.[42]

It is usually human weaknesses that lead people to turn on their own countries, even when those countries have despicable regimes. For example, Reino Hayhanen, Rudolph Abel's assistant who betrayed him, was no devotee of democracy. Hayhanen had just been recalled to Moscow because his drinking was interfering with his work. He turned himself in to the American embassy in Paris rather than face demotion and punishment in Moscow. By all accounts, he was far less impressive a human being than Abel, even though the latter faithfully served an unpalatable regime.

The three hundred or so Americans exposed by the Venona decryptions were not, with possibly an exception or two, spies for such base reasons as ego, money, or avoiding disgrace. Not all of the people revealed in the decryptions, in fact, were conventional spies, stealing secrets and turning them over to another government. Some were talent spotters, identifying potential recruits for Soviet intelligence; others were couriers, ferrying information from a spy to a KGB officer; others operated safe houses where KGB officers could meet their sources; and still others performed various kinds of support work that enabled the spy rings to flourish.

---

[40] David Wise, *Nightmover: How Aldrich Ames Sold the CIA to the KGB for $4.6 Million* (New York: HarperCollins, 1995).

[41] Pete Earley, *Family of Spies: Inside the John Walker Spy Ring* (New York: Bantam Books, 1988).

[42] Elaine Shannon and Ann Blackman, *The Spy Next Door: The Extraordinary Secret Life of Robert Philip Hanssen, the Most Damaging FBI Agent in U.S. History* (Boston: Little, Brown, & Co., 2002).

Many of these people incurred expenses and were reimbursed. A few were supported full-time to enable them to work exclusively for Soviet intelligence. During this period only a tiny handful of Soviet spies, however, were bought and paid for. KGB records shown to an American historian identify one particularly remarkable mercenary spy, Congressman Samuel Dickstein, a New York Democrat, whose chief claim to fame is that he introduced the resolution that created in 1938 the first Special Committee on Un-American Activities, known as the Dies Committee. Code-named Crook, demonstrating that the KGB had a sense of humor, Dickstein hoped to use the Committee to develop information on Nazi activities in America that he could then turn over to the Soviets for money. History sometimes takes ironic turns, but few more devilish than this. The KGB aided and abetted the creation of what would become the symbol of anticommunism in America: the House Committee on Un-American Activities. Eventually concluding that Dickstein's information was not worth what they were paying him, the KGB dropped him from its roster, and he moved from the House of Representatives to a New York judgeship.[43]

IV. JUSTIFYING ESPIONAGE

Most of the Americans who spied for the Soviet Union in the 1930s and 1940s did not do so for money. A few received bonuses or expenses but virtually all of them spied because of ideological enthusiasm. They were Communists or Communist sympathizers, committed to the Soviet Union. In the Venona decryptions, the KGB's code name for American Communists was "Fellow Countrymen." And for many spies, the Soviet Union was, if not their native land, a second homeland, more deserving of loyalty than the land of their citizenship.

Three examples are representative of these ideological spies. Nathan Gregory Silvermaster, a government economist and leader of a productive spy ring that included Harry Dexter White, an assistant secretary of the U.S. Treasury, first volunteered his services to Soviet intelligence after the Nazi attack on the USSR. Upon being awarded a medal for his work, Silvermaster told his Soviet controller, Ishak Akmerhov, that "his work for us is the one good thing he has done in his life."[44] Philip Jaffe was a wealthy, pro-Communist, greeting-card manufacturer, editor of a left-wing magazine (*Amerasia*), and an aspiring Soviet spy. In 1945 an FBI wiretap overheard Jaffe explain that a real radical had to be prepared to defend the Soviet Union at all times: "I would say that the first test of a real radical is, do you trust the Soviet Union through thick and thin, regardless of what anybody says? It's the workers' government, the one

---

[43] Allan Weinstein and Alexander Vasiliev, *The Haunted Wood* (New York: Random House, 1999), 140–50.

[44] Venona 1635 KGB New York to Moscow. November 21, 1944.

shining star in the whole damned world and you got to defend that with your last drop of blood."[45] In late 1948 or early 1949, Julius Rosenberg told his brother-in-law David Greenglass, whom he had recruited for atomic espionage when the latter served at Los Alamos during World War II, that "we've got to be like soldiers. It doesn't matter if Stalin is sending his troops to be killed. What difference does it make as long as the victory is ours?"[46]

This vicarious identification with the Soviet Union had several sources. Many of the spies or their parents had been born in Russia. A visceral Russian loyalty animated them. Many were Jews who believed that the Soviet Union had abolished the anti-Semitism that had driven their families to America. Most were convinced that the USSR was building a shining new egalitarian society that would usher in the kingdom of heaven on earth. Others saw Stalin as the great bulwark against fascism and were filled with admiration for the heroism and sacrifice of the Russian people in standing up to Hitler.

Harry Gold was not a Communist, but scarred by exposure to American anti-Semitism and convinced that the USSR was embarked on a noble economic experiment, he agreed to provide industrial secrets to the KGB and then to work as a courier for Los Alamos physicist Klaus Fuchs and Army sergeant David Greenglass. Morris Cohen was a New York high-school football star who attended Mississippi A&M College. He joined the Communist Party of the United States (CPUSA) in 1935, and two years later he enlisted in the International Brigades to fight the Franco forces in Spain. Wounded in battle, he volunteered for special assignments and soon entered a select Soviet school in Barcelona to train intelligence operatives. "[T]he Soviet comrades," he later told an interviewer, "suggested that fighting against fascism could be advanced by going into [their] Service. . . . So I said to the comrades: 'Yes.' "[47]

Cohen did not reveal his espionage activities to his wife, fellow-Communist Lona Petka, until after they were married. She was initially horrified and accused him of treason, but Morris explained to her that "if I betrayed America for money, or if I had betrayed the party or my convictions, that would have been a different thing since I would have betrayed the ideas which made up my credo."[48] Lona was persuaded and herself became a courier for a Soviet spy ring that smuggled atomic secrets out of Los Alamos. The Cohens quietly dropped out of sight and left the United States as members of Julius Rosenberg's spy ring were

[45] To the Director from SAC Guy Hottel; June 14, 1945; FBI File 100–267360–531, Box 120, Folder 6, Philip Jaffe Papers, Emory University.
[46] Ronald Radosh and Joyce Milton, *The Rosenberg File: A Search for the Truth* (New York: Holt, Rinehart & Winston, 1983), 73.
[47] Joseph Albright and Marcia Kunstel, *Bombshell: The Secret Story of America's Unknown Atomic Spy Conspiracy* (New York: Times Books, 1997), 32.
[48] Ibid., 48.

being arrested in 1950. They themselves were arrested in 1961 in Great Britain, where they had been posing as rare-book dealers, using the identities of a deceased couple, Peter and Helen Kroger, while working for Soviet intelligence. In 1967, they were exchanged for a British academic falsely accused of espionage by the Soviets. This is the only known case of the USSR repatriating spies who were not Soviet citizens, although they both later received Soviet citizenship and died in Russia.

One of the Cohens' espionage contacts while they were in the United States was Theodore Hall, who offered yet another high-minded motive for committing espionage. One of the major surprises of the Venona documents was the revelation that Hall, a young, Harvard-educated physicist, had been an important Soviet spy at Los Alamos during the development of the atomic bomb. Hall had graduated from Harvard College in 1944 when he was only eighteen years old. He was immediately recruited by the Manhattan Project and dispatched to New Mexico, where he did work on the physics of implosion. Returning home on leave in October, he told his college roommate, Saville Sax, like Hall a fervent young Communist, the nature of his work. They agreed that the Soviet Union should be informed. Sax meandered around New York looking for a KGB officer and was eventually led to Sergey Kurnakov, a Russian journalist who worked for Soviet intelligence. Kurnakov met with Hall and found him to be "politically developed," but asked nonetheless why he was willing to turn over American secrets. Hall responded, according to Kurnakov's report to Moscow, that "there is no country except for the Soviet Union which could be entrusted with such a terrible thing." He worried that after the war the United States might blackmail the Soviet Union if the U.S. had a monopoly on atomic weapons.[49]

When his espionage activities were disclosed in 1995, Hall was living in retirement in Great Britain. Although the FBI had investigated and questioned Hall in the 1940s and 1950s, it had never been able to gather enough evidence to indict or to try him. As a matter of policy the government had determined never to use in court any Venona material. So, even though the government knew he had been an important Soviet atomic spy, it would not indict him unless it could develop other admissible evidence that demonstrated his guilt. No American scientist turned over more significant information about the atomic bomb than Hall. (Klaus Fuchs, who was convicted of atomic espionage by the British in 1950, was not an American, but a German-born British physicist who had worked and spied at Los Alamos. Robert Oppenheimer, director of Los Alamos during the war, has been accused of being a Soviet source. His relationship with Soviet intelligence is still not entirely clear, although recent

[49] Weinstein and Vasiliev, *The Haunted Wood*, 196.

evidence suggests that he did cooperate with the KGB. If true, this would demote Hall to the second most important American atomic spy.)[50]

After release of the Venona material exposing him, Hall was unapologetic about his actions. He explained that "during 1944 I was worried about the dangers of an American monopoly of nuclear weapons if there should be a postwar depression" because it might encourage a fascist America to launch a nuclear war. While admitting that he had been mistaken about "the nature of the Soviet state," he still believed that he had contributed to world peace by ensuring a nuclear balance of terror. "I still think that brash youth had the right end of the stick. I am no longer that person; but I am by no means ashamed of him."[51] After his death in 1999 Hall's wife, Joan, was more vehement, defending his "humanitarian act." His daughter praised his espionage and called for a new generation of scientists "who dare to come forward as he did."[52]

There is a clear difference between explaining the motives that led people to betray their country and justifying that betrayal. That Ted Hall believed the United States would become a fascist country after World War II and that the Soviet Union needed to be able to protect itself may explain why he gave the KGB vital defense information. It hardly justifies his act, as the Hall family seems to believe. In any case, the justifications for their actions offered by the spies themselves must be taken with a large dose of skepticism. By his own admission Ted Hall, who was in the Army at Los Alamos, violated his oath of allegiance, to say nothing of the fact that he lied to and deceived his coworkers, security officials, FBI interrogators, and numerous other people about his actions over the years. Documentary evidence also demonstrates that Hall's belated justification for his treachery, that he wanted to contribute to a nuclear balance of terror, is an ex post facto rationalization. His explanation to Kurnakov in 1944 suggests that he was providing atomic information to the Soviet Union because he had more faith in Stalin's Russia than he did in the United States. It was, he thought, the only country that could be trusted with such information. In addition, Hall did more than give the KGB data while the war was raging. He remained in touch with Soviet intelligence after he left Los Alamos in 1946 and helped it recruit at least two other atomic scientists over the next few years.

Despite his daughter's portrait of Hall as a courageous dissenter, he did not "come forward" to protest American policies that he opposed or thought dangerous. He never "took credit" for what he had done; he only

[50] On Oppenheimer see Jerrold and Leona Schecter, *Sacred Secrets: How Soviet Intelligence Operations Changed American History* (Washington, DC: Brassey's, 2002), 50.

[51] Albright and Kunstel, *Bombshell*, 288–89.

[52] Joan and Ruth Hall, interviewed in "Family of Spies," *Secrets, Lies, and Atomic Spies*, a NOVA television production (Boston, MA: WGBH Educational Foundation, 2002). Transcript available on-line at http://www.pbs.org/wgbh/nova/venona/fami_joanhall.html.

admitted his espionage after he was publicly exposed by Venona material released fifty years after his actions. Hall, in fact, had an opportunity to come forward and to take credit for enabling the USSR to construct an atomic bomb. Shortly before the Rosenbergs' execution, Hall, consumed by guilt, suggested to his KGB controller that he should go to the authorities. Since in sentencing them to death, the judge had blamed the Rosenbergs for giving the Russians "the secret of the atomic bomb," Hall thought that confessing his own, far more important role in atomic espionage might save them from their fate. The Russian disagreed. So did his wife to whom he had confessed his espionage activities before they were married. Faced with this moral dilemma, Ted Hall did nothing. On the day of the Rosenbergs' execution, the Halls drove past Sing Sing prison on their way to a dinner party. They were distressed.[53]

The emotional loyalty of children to their parents should also not blind us to the costs that spies impose on their families. Since 1975, the Rosenberg children have attempted to rehabilitate their parents' reputations, charging in books, articles, interviews, and documentaries that they had been framed and persecuted by a corrupt and vengeful government.[54] Even the Venona decryptions and the revelations of the Rosenbergs' one-time KGB controller, Alexander Feklisov, in his autobiography and in film interviews, about Julius's key role in espionage, have elicited only their grudging admission that Julius might have been a low-level spy.[55] What these now-adult offspring have been unable to confront is that their parents, who could have saved their lives by confessing to espionage, chose to become martyrs and consciously made their children orphans rather than admit what they had done.

In the wake of the Venona revelations other commentators have adduced a variety of additional justifications for the espionage committed by American citizens during this era. For decades, defenders of spies such as Alger Hiss, Harry Dexter White, or the Rosenbergs based their arguments on the innocence of their subjects. They were not spies but had been framed. Cold War tensions, a repressive and corrupt FBI, and a coterie of liars and perjurers had resulted in a series of miscarriages of justice. Patriotic Americans, guilty of nothing more than progressive sympathies, had been tarred and, in the case of the Rosenbergs, murdered after falsely being accused of espionage. There was, in other words, no need to justify espionage because none had taken place. But, it turns out that documentary evidence from multiple sources demon-

[53] Albright and Kunstel, *Bombshell*, 240.

[54] See, most notably, Robert and Michael Meeropol, *We Are Your Sons: The Legacy of Ethel and Julius Rosenberg* (Boston: Houghton Mifflin, 1975). The Rosenberg children were adopted and their last names were changed.

[55] Alexander Feklisov and Sergei Kostin, *The Man Behind the Rosenbergs*, trans. Catherine Dop (New York: Enigma Books, 2001); and Robert and Michael Meeropol, interviewed in "Family of Spies," *Secrets, Lies, and Atomic Spies*; transcript available on-line at http://www.pbs.org/wgbh/nova/venona/fami_meeropol.html.

strates that Hiss, the Rosenbergs, and White, among many others, did cooperate with Soviet intelligence. This evidence has led to a number of efforts to minimize, rationalize, or justify espionage.

The most famous rationale used to justify espionage comes from a remark by British novelist and essayist E. M. Forster. Anthony Blunt, eminent art historian and pillar of the British art world, when he was publicly exposed as a Soviet spy in 1979, quoted Forster's remark of 1939: "[I]f I had to choose between betraying my country and betraying my friend, I hope I should have the guts to betray my country."[56] Blunt was being rather unfair to Forster. Taken in context, Forster's remark was a condemnation of not only patriotism, but Communism as well. Immediately before making his choice between friend and country, Forster noted: "[P]ersonal relations are despised today. They are regarded as bourgeois luxuries, as products of a time of fair weather which is now past, and we are urged to get rid of them, and to dedicate ourselves to some movement or cause instead. I hate the idea of causes." And just after defending personal relationships—that bourgeois affectation—Forster defended democracy as "less hateful than other contemporary forms of government" because of its assumption that the individual is the basic unit of society.[57]

Blunt's rationale is, in any case, not very persuasive. Far more than Great Britain, which was a real country inhabited by real people with real institutions, communism was an ideal vision. A spy like Blunt did more than betray an abstraction like the state. For a cause, he also betrayed family and friends and coworkers, who believed him to be what he was not—a loyal citizen and an honest man. The number of relatives and friends he betrayed dwarfed the handful of fellow spies and Communists whom he protected in the name of loyalty.

Several historians have recently suggested that those Communists who spied out of idealism were premature citizens of a global world. Notions of patriotism that stress loyalty to a single nation are, they believe, either outmoded or inappropriate to understanding ideological espionage. Ellen Schrecker, author of several books on McCarthyism, and former editor of *Academe*, the journal of the American Association of University Professors, has conceded that American Communists spied for the Soviet Union, but asks "were these activities so awful?" She notes that "it is important to realize that as Communists these people did not subscribe to traditional forms of patriotism; they were internationalists whose political allegiances transcended national boundaries. They thought they were 'building . . . a better world for the masses,' not betraying their country."[58]

---

[56] Miranda Carter, *Anthony Blunt: His Lives* (New York: Farrar, Straus, & Giroux, 2001), 178.

[57] E. M. Forster, *Two Cheers for Democracy* (New York: Harcourt, Brace & Co., 1951), 68–69.

[58] Ellen Schrecker, *Many Are the Crimes: McCarthyism in America* (Boston: Little, Brown & Co., 1998), 178–79, 188.

Likewise, Bruce Craig, director of the National Coordinating Committee for the Promotion of History, attempting to justify Harry White's espionage, has linked it to Franklin Roosevelt's policy of friendship with the Soviet Union: "In his [White's] mind he could justify transmitting oral information to the NKVD . . . and, based on the assumption the information he was providing did not harm American interests, he was willing to give his handlers his personal opinions and observations on the future course of American politics." Peering retroactively into White's mind, Craig judges that "he probably believed that by answering questions posed by representatives of the Soviet underground he would be able to provide America's present and future friend with an insider's view of the American bureaucracy and thereby advance the goal of Soviet/American partnership." For Craig, "in the final analysis White's loyalties transcended any that he might have felt for his ancestral homeland of mother Russia or for the country of his birth."[59]

Craig ignores inconvenient facts. White did more than provide answers to innocuous questions about the bureaucracy or his personal views: one Venona cable shows White providing a KGB agent with the details of America's negotiating position at the first United Nations conference in San Francisco. He also had worked for Soviet intelligence since 1936, well before there was any "partnership" with the USSR. And while "his ancestral homeland" of Russia knew about his loyalty, or lack thereof, the United States, his country of birth, did not know about his loyalty to Communist Russia. Like Schrecker's transcendence, Craig's is asymmetrical.

The Soviet Union's American spies did not provide information to some mythical transcendent authority or some nonexistent world government but to the intelligence services of a foreign country. It is true that the United States and the Soviet Union were allies when much—but not all—of the espionage revealed by Venona took place. The USSR had suffered greatly resisting Nazism. Ted Hall argued that it therefore deserved to receive any information that would be of use to it. Robert Meeropol, son of the Rosenbergs, thinks that atomic scientists like Fuchs and Hall were simply "sharing information with their Soviet counterparts." While some people regard such activities as spying, others, like Meeropol, think of them simply as acts of "international cooperation."[60] Likewise, Victor Navasky, former editor of *The Nation*, has contended: "There were a lot of exchanges of information among people of good will, many of whom were Marxists, some of whom were Communists, some of whom were critical of US governmental policy and most of whom were patriots."[61]

---

[59] Bruce Craig, " 'Treasonable Doubt': The Harry Dexter White Case" (Ph.D. diss., American University, 1999), 581, 585–86, and 588.

[60] Robert and Michael Meeropol, "Family of Spies," *Secrets, Lies, and Atomic Spies*.

[61] Victor Navasky, "Cold War Ghosts," *The Nation*, July 16, 2001. As cited on-line at http://www.thenation.com/doc.mhtml?i=20010716&s=navasky.

Such arguments substitute the individual judgment of a single citizen for the legal authority of a democratic government. If Franklin Roosevelt had decided to share atomic information with Joseph Stalin, then it might have been a wise or a stupid policy decision, but Roosevelt was legally authorized to do so. He was answerable to the people of the United States. If Ted Hall had moral qualms about building an atomic bomb, then he was free to leave Los Alamos; at least one prominent scientist, Joseph Rothblatt, did. If Hall believed that classified scientific information should have been shared with Russian scientists, then he might have argued for such a policy. However, neither the law nor his fellow citizens authorized Hall to give sensitive information to anybody he chose, much less an intelligence officer of another country. And Hall did not ask anyone's permission. He did not choose to renounce his American citizenship after the war ended and move to the USSR to help it build an atomic bomb. Most tellingly, the information about the atomic bomb had nothing to do with helping the Soviet Union fight Germany, nor did all of the details about American diplomatic and military matters that these spies gave to the KGB. Most of the information was useful in helping undermine American interests or advance Soviet interests in the postwar world. Even if the spies believed that they were advancing the cause of Communism in the United States, their chosen means provided a direct benefit only to the Soviet Union. In fact, their spying required them to avoid participation in above-ground Communist activities for fear that FBI agents monitoring the Communist Party might stumble over espionage activities.

Another justification offered by apologists or the spies themselves for having committed espionage is that the spies actually assisted the United States. Hall hinted at this in his belated admission, maintaining that the information enabled the Soviet Union to resist American hegemony and thus benefited the cause of world peace and, ultimately, America. Historian Athan Theoharis has similarly argued: "American spies may have aimed to further Soviet interests and betray their own nation, but the effect of their actions compromised neither long-term nor immediate U.S. security interests." In fact, argues Theoharis, the theft of American secrets was actually in America's interests: "[T]he information about U.S. industrial productivity and military strength provided by the Silvermaster group—the numbers being overwhelming—might have deterred Soviet officials from pursuing an aggressive negotiating strategy."[62]

Like several other attempts to excuse espionage, this one fails to meet minimal tests of accuracy about the facts. A great deal of the information that was passed on to the USSR in the 1940s remains unknown because the Venona decryptions largely deal with tradecraft and not the actual espionage "take" that was shipped to Moscow in diplomatic pouches.

---

[62] Athan Theoharis, *Chasing Spies: How the FBI Failed in Counterintelligence but Promoted the Politics of McCarthyism in the Cold War Years* (Chicago, IL: Ivan R. Dee, 2002), 16–17.

Much of the data that was sent to the USSR by American spies enabled it to develop nuclear bombs, radar, jet engines, proximity fuses, and other high-tech weapons. Science and technology espionage saved the USSR billions of rubles over the years and enabled it to maintain military parity with the West.[63] Other information enabled the Soviet Union to know in advance American negotiating tactics at such sensitive meetings as Yalta and the United Nations conference in San Francisco. The claim that such espionage prevented World War III is far less credible than the assertion that by strengthening the Soviet Union it prolonged and worsened the Cold War.

V. Conclusion

All countries spy. Since the United States has engaged in espionage, how can its government or citizens become indignant or mount a moral high horse about Soviet espionage? Theoharis writes:

> Nor was it particularly unusual that Soviet agents operating in the United States during World War II recruited ideologically driven sources. Both U.S. and Soviet intelligence operatives paid the sources they recruited, and both also looked for recruits who for ideological reasons were willing to betray their country's secrets—whether they were committed American Communists and Communist sympathizers (for the Soviets) or disaffected Soviet Communists (for the United States).[64]

There are numerous flaws in this comparison, beginning with the inconvenient fact that neither the United States nor Britain aggressively spied on their Soviet ally during World War II. Trying to read Soviet coded cables was a passive kind of spying far less intrusive than the use of hundreds of active American agents recruited by Soviet intelligence. In fact, when key Soviet agents Kim Philby, Guy Burgess, and Donald Maclean reported to the KGB that Great Britain had suspended efforts to spy on the USSR during World War II, Stalin concluded that they must be lying and were most likely double agents. He could not believe that any capitalist government would forgo the opportunity to spy on the Soviet Union; after all, his regime had mounted an extraordinarily large espionage assault on the United States and Britain precisely when they were allies. As a result of Stalin's incredulity, for several years the KGB seri-

---

[63] Andrew and Mitrokhin, *The Sword and the Shield*, 216–20.
[64] Theoharis, *Chasing Spies*, 237–38.

ously believed that its most well-placed British spies were feeding it disinformation.[65]

Theoharis also implies that the nature of the regime for which one works is irrelevant. Is a disaffected Soviet citizen who spies for America because he believes in democracy the moral equivalent of a disaffected American citizen who spies for Russia because he thinks that America is a bourgeois dictatorship and Stalin's USSR a real democracy? Both may "legally" be put to death by the regimes that they betray, but the regimes themselves are not morally equivalent. In any kind of moral calculus, the regime that a spy serves is relevant. Spying for an ally, like the Soviet Union during World War II, is morally and legally different from spying for an enemy such as Nazi Germany. But there is also a moral difference between spying for a democracy and spying for a totalitarian regime.

Just as the regime that one serves must be taken into account in any moral calculus, so must the regime one betrays. Many of the spies exposed by Venona had taken explicit oaths of allegiance to the United States, either when they became naturalized citizens, or when they joined the armed forces or entered government service. They had agreed to security restrictions. They lived in a democratic country with laws that prohibited them from transmitting secret or sensitive information to any unauthorized person. Lauchlin Currie, a Harvard-trained economist, was a Canadian who became a naturalized American citizen in 1934, the same year that he went to work for the U.S. Treasury Department. In 1939 Whittaker Chambers, a one-time Soviet spy who exposed Alger Hiss, told a State Department official that Currie had assisted a Soviet espionage ring. Currie is identified in Venona as being an important Soviet source while serving as a presidential assistant and administrator of the Foreign Economic Administration. Currie chose to become an American citizen and chose to work for the American government. He did not turn over confidential information to other American allies but only to the Soviet Union. When he appeared before the House Committee on Un-American Activities after being named as a spy by Chambers and by Elizabeth Bentley (another defector from Soviet intelligence), Currie lied under oath. He then moved to Colombia and eventually became a citizen of that country. His allegiance to the United States may have been fleeting, but it was in force when he turned over confidential information to the KGB.[66]

All of these spies betrayed their country, but virtually none renounced his American citizenship or the privileges it provided. (Currie is one of

---

[65] Nigel West and Oleg Tsarev, *The Crown Jewels: The British Secrets at the Heart of the KGB Archives* (London: HarperCollins, 1998), 159–68.

[66] On Currie, see Haynes and Klehr, *Venona*, 145–50. Roger Sandilands, a protégé of Currie and a British academic, has denied that Currie was a spy. See Roger Sandilands, "Guilt by Association? Lauchlin Currie's Alleged Involvement with Washington Economists in Soviet Espionage," *History of Political Economy* 32, no. 3 (2000): 473–515.

the few exceptions.) When a number of these spies were subpoenaed before congressional committees, they exercised their rights under the Fifth Amendment to refuse to answer and were not punished. Most of the American citizens identified in the Venona decryptions were never prosecuted because the government could not develop additional corroborating evidence and did not want to publicly divulge the Venona project. Despite unequivocal evidence of their guilt contained in Venona decryptions, the American legal system protected them from summary arrest and conviction. Some lost government jobs or suffered public humiliation or scorn, but otherwise they escaped the legal consequences of their actions. The American legal system and its constitutional protections that they worked so zealously to subvert spared them.

To be a spy is to engage in deception and lying. Even if spying does not directly involve betrayal, it requires encouraging others to betray their country. It may lead to preying on human weakness and greed. Yet, the gentlemanly view that spying is always dishonorable is both naïve and dangerous. Whether deception and betrayal are justified cannot be determined in the abstract. Some regimes are so odious that remaining loyal to them taints an individual. Some enemies are so dangerous that their defeat transcends other reservations. Some motives that lead to betrayal are base and dishonorable, but others may be admirable. Good regimes and good motives may not, of course, always coincide. That many Americans who spied for the Soviets were idealists does not compensate for their betrayal of American secrets. German Communists who spied for the Soviet Union during World War II were in a very different situation. By the same token, Soviet citizens who betrayed their country because they believed in democracy surely merit a different evaluation than Americans who chose to spy on behalf of the Soviet Union. Perhaps E. M. Forster got it wrong when he denigrated the value of causes and insisted on remaining loyal to his friend. There are countries whose values are worth defending, even if that defense sometimes requires betraying one's friend or other unpalatable deeds. Some causes are not worth betraying either friend or country: Communism was one of these causes.

Politics and History, Emory University

MR. PINOCCHIO GOES TO WASHINGTON: LYING IN POLITICS*

By Robert Weissberg

I. Introduction

A more provocative subject than "lying in politics" is difficult to imagine. Everybody, from the proverbial "Joe Sixpack" to ivory-tower philosophers, can wax eloquently on the subject, if only because easy-to-find, shocking (and occasionally sexually "juicy") examples abound. If moral outrage were judged an essential vitamin, then condemning dishonesty undoubtedly guarantees a daily megadose. Unfortunately, at least for those who crave self-indulgent outrage, the anti-lying case is less than 100 percent compelling. It is a quagmire of the first order, if only because those who cherish frankness also usually confess to lying. Hannah Arendt once suggested that lies are a necessary and justifiable tool of the statesman's trade.[1] Formulating damnation criteria invites mind-boggling paradoxes, and strident defenders of truth-telling, with scant exception, admit that falsehoods are "sometimes" permitted for "good" reasons. And what might be these "good reasons"? Who can say for sure? Centuries of erudite scholarship on this point might be encapsulated as "Lying to me is bad, but I can consent to deceiving others for noble purposes, as artfully decided by myself."

In this essay, I offer some observations regarding lying that stress its public character—the mendacity of those who are sworn to uphold public trust. I eschew simple morality or facile homilies. The point of departure is that establishing dishonesty is astonishingly complicated, filled with linguistic and cultural vexations—let alone moral predicaments—that bedevil conclusive judgments. The quest for a mendacity-free politics may be quixotic and dangerous to democratic governance. Make no mistake, blanket lying is not to be condoned, yet to believe that "everyone knows what a lie *is*," or that it is straightforward to discern horrible falsehoods from innocuous little white fibs, is simple-minded. Yet, all is not lost—I conclude that elections can play a vital though admittedly rough-and-ready role in protecting us from mendacity.

* Needless to say, writing about lying in today's university setting is difficult given their commitment to truth. Several friends did, however, manage to assist this effort, namely, Wayne Allen, Jay Budziszewski, and Nino Languilli. I would also like to thank my Illinois colleagues for offering useful examples for this essay.

[1] Hannah Arendt, *Between Past and Future: Eight Exercises in Political Thought* (New York: Viking Press, 1968), 227.

My analysis, sadly for those seeking to restore truth, will doubtless muddy larger lakes rather than purify once-obscure ponds. After a brief case study, my conceptual dredging operation begins by focusing on several similar-looking definitions about what certifies a lie versus other forms of deceit. These formulations are, for better or worse, gold mines of escape clauses and serve as the dishonest politician's coterie of unwavering friends. Moreover, the reader will discover that truth is not universally cherished, and that for some political arrangements dishonesty may be *integral*. To counsel unrelenting truthfulness might disrupt the very fabric of civic life. Inquiry then expands to a domain seldom mentioned in philosophical accounts—the courts. Under trying conditions, judges and juries must reach unambiguous conclusions regarding both the existence of lying and its punishment. Here, as they say, the rubber meets the road in protecting society from the allegedly dangerous fibber. I conclude by touching upon the difficult issue of protecting ourselves from truly horrendous mistruths versus rooting out mendacity everywhere. As valuable as truth may be, its forced imposition may bring its own pathologies.

II. The "Lying" Cosmology

In May of 1960 an unarmed American U-2 photoreconnaissance plane was shot down deep inside the Soviet Union. High altitude reconnaissance missions had been conducted by the U.S. Central Intelligence Agency (CIA) since 1956, a fact carefully hidden from all but top U.S. officials, and the Soviets knew their intention. That the pilot—Francis Gary Powers— and the plane wreckage were in Soviet hands now, seemingly confirmed the Soviets' claim that the venture was a clandestine spying mission. Faced with a stunned American public, a flabbergasted Congress, and an awaiting Paris summit meeting between the United States and the USSR, President Eisenhower hastily announced that the U-2 was really an errant civilian weather plane, engaged in a research project over West Germany. The cockpit oxygen system had failed, he said, accidentally sending the pilot adrift deep into the Soviet Union. Was Eisenhower unequivocally lying? With a few clever twists and turns, could the president deny the truth and still not technically lie? Moreover, if Ike (as Eisenhower is also known) was, indeed, certifiably lying, was his behavior reprehensible, immoral, or otherwise reproachable?

In history's "official" record Eisenhower offered a bold-faced lie. Still, this verdict is not preordained. Much depends on the veracity of facts elsewhere, and if these specifics are untrustworthy, then Eisenhower escapes conviction. The president might have genuinely believed the cover story—Allen Dulles, the CIA director overseeing the surveillance program, was the real liar, so the trusting Eisenhower was *absolutely* speaking the truth, as he understood it. Alternatively, while the president was verbally offering his face-saving account, he could have simultaneously via winks and sheepish grins indicated to observers that the weather research account was bogus. Since his nonverbal message was intentional, charges of mendacity would derive solely from a transcript that could not convey his body language. Another possibility: Eisenhower's off-the-record conversations could have ensured that the truthful message, which contradicted the cover story, was widely conveyed, so he was simultaneously both truthful and deceitful.

Ike could also have obeyed medieval Catholic theological teachings and spoken vaguely while, unbeknownst to all but himself, he mentally qualified the cover-up to convert it into unqualified truth. That millions heard information that *might* have been misconstrued matters not; God discerns men's true thoughts, and to speak the truth to God is paramount, for He, not mere mortals, will pronounce judgment. All that was necessary was for the president to say publicly, "The U-2 was collecting scientific information" and then quietly add with nobody to overhear, "regarding Soviet rockets," and, happily, God would have deemed the president a truth-teller.

Half-truths, as distinct from half-lies, also evade the outright lie, for deceit derives only from retrospective evaluation, not from anything Eisenhower personally said at that time. It *was* true, after all, that the spying mission was civilian administered (the CIA is independent from the Pentagon and Powers was an *ex*-military pilot). It was true that the particular U-2 flight had mechanical problems (later confirmed by Powers), and the mission's purpose was (vaguely but fittingly) "research." Going one step further, the president could have sworn that the plane was not spying on Russia since (left unsaid) it was (perhaps) flying over the airspace of the Ukraine, a nominally independent republic of the USSR at that time. At worst, Ike would have been less than 100 percent candid, but not a liar.

What if the president, as counseled by some of his advisors, had remained entirely silent (or "out playing golf") and permitted Allen Dulles to shoulder the blame, totally absolving Ike? If challenged, the president could have said, "No comment," and thus been spared the onus of spreading falsehoods. Or if forced to react, Ike could have unleashed a torrent of Babel, none of which would have been factually wrong, but all of which would have said nothing precise regarding the U-2 incident. A variant might have been to mumble incoherently so that his response would have resembled a sort of Rorschach test to cover up the lie, in which listeners heard what they wanted to hear without the president confessing anything. Who knows what might happen to Ike's reputation as the historical record becomes more complete?

Ambiguity similarly attends the alleged harmfulness or immorality of Eisenhower's behavior. It is arguable that beyond short-lived embarrassment, the lie was innocuous. No constitutional oath of office or law was violated: foreign intelligence gathering is legal and mandated by statute.

Ike's account—assuming that it was a lie—certainly did not injure Soviet interests (though the surveillance certainly did), and probably provided the Soviet Union a major propaganda advantage. Members of the diplomatic corps (and probably the press, as well) were not outraged; they expect deceit, and unexpected frankness might even be judged as an alarming rejection of established etiquette. As for the American public losing respect for Eisenhower (or for the government itself), this is doubtful, at best. Surely presidents enjoy considerable slack when it comes to subterfuge for the sake of national security, and that this dishonesty was directed toward fighting an avowed enemy surely made it commendable. The exposé of the ill-fated mission might have gladdened patriots since it highlighted America's technological prowess. Members of Congress could not claim to have been misled, since they were never even informed of the "weather" flights in the first place. Nor had any American outside Ike's administration put his or her reputation on the line by defending the U-2 project as atmospheric research. Overall, the reaction seemed to be that the U.S. had been caught conducting vital surveillance, and misrepresentation, no matter how clumsy, was the most convenient way of sustaining pretenses that nobody believed.

III. What Is a 'Lie'?

The above illustration is scarcely unusual and exemplifies the nightmarish problems of disentangling truth from falsehood. Depending on definitions, and how inexact information is to be evaluated, Ike could be classified as everything from an archetypal purveyor of lies to an honest but misinformed fool, to a champion of truth as he (imperfectly) understood it. Moreover, a final judgment requires more than assembling facts, though facts are certainly essential. A verdict invariably reflects what is meant by 'lie', and this key element is by no means patently obvious. Nor was Ike's behavior unambiguously immoral. More than semantic gymnastics is involved; the disconcerting reality is that applying 'liar' to a public official can often depend on endless uncertain choices. Our parade of possible escape clauses is only the beginning.

The most useful place to plunge into this foggy topic is to acknowledge that 'lie' is an exceedingly vague term. English supplies countless synonyms that approximate 'lie'. That these routinely replace it, often for innocent textual variety, can be exasperating. Psychiatrist Charles V. Ford, in his *Lies! Lies!! Lies!!!* lists twenty-five verbs, twenty-one nouns, and five adjectives that, in varying degrees, connote falsehood.[2] This compilation is clearly partial; conspicuously omitted proxies include evasion, hoax, bias, disingenuousness, misstatement, double-talk, and

---

[2] Charles V. Ford, *Lies! Lies!! Lies!!!: The Psychology of Deceit* (Washington, DC: American Psychiatric Press, 1996), 25.

untold other synonyms available in a decent thesaurus. Society's voracious appetite for lying undoubtedly encourages creativity: Winston Churchill, for example, favored 'terminological inexactitude'. A particularly versatile dodge is to confess one's mendacity using esoteric terms: historians prefer 'dissimulations'[3] while psychiatrists favor 'confabulation' or, for the bold wordsmith, 'reduplicative paramnesia'. Would Americans be outraged if Eisenhower pleaded guilty to a prevarication? President Nixon used the term 'dissembled'.[4] Spokesmen for Nixon who were caught lying simply said that the exposed falsehoods were no longer operable, a ploy converting a lie into something as emotionally neutral as an obsolete computer system. Contemporary versions have played upon 'spin', as in 'spinning the news' or 'spin Doctor', to connote trickery without mentioning the "L" word.

This mendacity menu is hardly exhaustive. Each expression (among dozens) supplies its own special, and potentially highly useful, baggage. Imagine the following multiple-choice quiz question: Which word or phrase *best* describes President Eisenhower's behavior in accounting for the U-2 incident? Select from the following list: lying, misrepresenting, manipulating, being hypocritical, distorting, propagandizing, whitewashing, fabricating, faking, being selective with the facts, providing a trumped up story; acting disingenuously, without objectivity, and without candor; or all of the above. Choices are consequential—being deemed "not quite candid" is less provocative than being called a "naked liar," while "not objective" and "manipulative" differ in their ethical connotation. Would "operational problems" be an acceptable euphemism for "being shot down by a Soviet missile," since being hit by a missile has been known to cause mechanical malfunction? The potential vocabulary choices are most bountiful, and each can, in principle, be reasonably justified, yet language rules cannot possibly be imposed.[5]

Confusions multiply when venturing into non-English terminology. That translations may misconstrue cultural nuances compounds this fuzziness and potentially awards interpreters the power to mitigate or boost mendacity. For example, a distinctive Russian word for lying is *vranyo*, an untrue account told to those who recognize this falsity. A 'tall tale' might be a rough English equivalent. As in misleading children about Santa Claus being a real person, *vranyo* is usually not malicious since its ficti-

---

[3] This is the term of choice in Perez Zagoran, *Ways of Lying: Dissimulation, Persecution, and Conformity in Early Modern Europe* (Cambridge, MA: Harvard University Press, 1990).

[4] Cited in Paul Ekman, *Telling Lies: Clues to Deceit in the Marketplace, Politics, and Marriage* (New York: W. W. Norton & Company, 1985), 25.

[5] Combining esoteric terminology with euphemism can ingeniously disguise awkward messages. Intent might not even be noticed, save among cognoscenti. When the U-2 pilot failed to commit suicide—as was prearranged if captured—Francis Gary Powers' detractors said "He was no Nathan Hale," a historical reference that was probably lost on many Americans, and one that easily escaped the onus of counseling something immoral and illegal though required by government contract.

tious character is usually understood as such by adults. By contrast, *lozh* is an outright lie intended to deceive and is therefore reprehensible. Since Soviet officials knew the truth about the U-2 flight, Eisenhower was merely guilty of *vranyo*, not *lozh*, and thus, in the eyes of the Soviets, he was merely a nonmalicious tale-teller, not a liar.

If choice of vocabulary does not sufficiently confound matters, then the frequency of a statement, totally apart from its explicit content, might signal a lie or truthfulness. J. A. Barnes, an Australian sociologist, in his *A Pack of Lies*, cites anthropological studies of cultures in which statements shift in truth-value via repetition, even if unchanged.[6] Among Navajos an actual falsehood is not considered deceitful unless repeated for a fourth time, since it is not taken seriously the first three times around. A Navajo would therefore judge Eisenhower's story to be truthful since it was said but once. Only incessant denial, then, makes for lying. Conversely, among Iranians repetition enhances veracity. A single dinner invitation will be perceived as insincere and thus ignored; if offered a third time, however, it suddenly becomes authentic and likely to be accepted. American culture exhibits parallels: to insist on paying a restaurant bill just once is typically judged perfunctory; after the third time, however, the "let me pay, *please*" offer is decreed sincere and will likely be accepted.

Enhancing such ambiguities are the cultural contexts surrounding untruthful behavior. Consider simple marketplace haggling. In many commercial negotiations the initial price, let alone "my final offer," is well understood as fluid and, technically, insincere. The seller, by his cultural norms, is hardly misrepresenting himself to a tourist when he initially says, "The vase costs five hundred rupees, a steal!" though privately he would happily accept a third, and this latter figure is the "real" price known "to everyone" (save perhaps naïve outsiders). The buyer is expected to bargain, not to accuse the seller of predatory fraudulence. Likewise, an "honest" expression of emotion may be culturally embedded, and this could easily engender misunderstandings from foreigners. Is a Japanese person "lying" when stoically reacting to a provocation, given powerful cultural prohibitions against public emotion? Is a person "trying to pass" as upscale by displaying a ten-dollar fake Rolex watch, or is such decorative misrepresentation a "a valid subculture lifestyle" lacking any deceptive purpose? Would it make any difference if the phony Rolex were so substandard that nobody was fooled?

These cultural interpretations of "lying" easily infect politics. Speech striking an American as outrageously hyperbolic (for example, "Death to American imperialists!") might merely be "honest" where extreme embellishment is *de rigueur* and everything is automatically drastically discounted. When Muhammed Saeed al-Sahaf, the Iraqi Minister of

---

[6] J. A. Barnes, *A Pack of Lies: Toward a Sociology of Lying* (Cambridge: Cambridge University Press, 1994), 67.

Information told reporters that "Iraq will not be defeated, Iraq has now already achieved victory—apart from some technicalities," he was conceivably not lying despite an indisputable looming U.S. victory in the war between the two countries. Rather, the official sincerely believed what he said, and who knows what these "technicalities" might have been—perhaps deploying some secret weapon to snatch victory from the jaws of defeat. Brutal honesty (for example, "We are displeased with America") might not even be recognized as critical commentary where overstatement is culturally revered. Similarly, those who put mail-order college degrees on office walls are hardly shamed fibbers where counterfeit Mount Blanc pens and five-dollar Prada handbags are displayed proudly—these deceits prove "consumer savvy," not authentic social class.

Exaggeration, a close relative of lying, is also affected by cultural nuance. Cultures (and subcultures) differ in their tolerance for truth-trimming. Where absolute forthrightness is the norm, even a slight exaggeration becomes a lie. Elsewhere, however, substantial inflation is permissible without it becoming mendacious. In the first instance, a candidate for public office who promises a 5 percent spending increase for health care would be a liar if he or she really only intended a 4 percent boost. In a different cultural setting a promise of doubling outlays on health is "close enough" to the candidate's 4 percent intention to qualify as being truthful. Truly preposterous exaggeration can also shed the deception label. A candidate promising to abolish all taxes is probably not, technically, lying since this outrageous pledge is obviously a rhetorical flourish, not a realistic proposal. A more modest pledge to "cut taxes by 30 percent" might be interpreted as a lie, however, since it is plausible and therefore might be intended to deceive.

Plunging into formal explications of lying scarcely lifts the fog. The *Oxford English Dictionary* (second edition) provides a fairly straightforward denotation typically echoed elsewhere. It defines a lie as:

> An act or instance of lying; a false statement made with intent to deceive; a criminal falsehood. . . . In mod. use, the word is normally a violent expression of moral reprobation, which in polite conversation tends to be avoided, the synonyms *falsehood* and *untruth* being often substituted as relatively euphemistic.

Barnes supplies a slightly different version:

> [A] lie, for our purposes, is a statement intended to deceive a dupe about the state of the world, including the intentions and attitudes of the liar.[7]

---

[7] Ibid., 11.

Sissela Bok, a philosopher, in her widely cited *Lying*, offers a third and analogous rendering:

> I shall define as a lie any intentionally deceptive message which is *stated* [italics in original].[8]

These generic definitions explicitly stress a perpetrator's *intent*. Propagating false or misleading information does not inevitably constitute lying, and no lie occurs if the speaker believed untrue information to be correct. Hence, it will be recalled, if Eisenhower genuinely believed his cover story, then his dissimulation does not qualify as dishonesty. Given that the public record abounds with sincere inaccuracy, this explicit-intent "escape clause" is, indeed, welcome news to those who fear criticism. Without such a clause, most public officials would be rightly classified as chronic liars, and there is no telling where this deficiency might lead if society punished untruths. Yet, equally obvious, since unconditionally establishing intent is quite arduous, and may itself be effortlessly falsified, this "intent to deceive" element in standard definitions of a lie invites eternal trouble. The relevant parallel is the notoriously painstaking and time-consuming task of establishing motive in criminal cases, a luxury seldom available in politics except retrospectively. Even then, "smoking gun" evidence is rarely forthcoming. Devious leaders can usually insulate themselves from awkward facts and thus be—technically— perfect truth-tellers while spreading the most horrendous misinformation. "Just do it, and don't tell me how," is a time-honored bureaucratic ruse to escape accusations of consciously perpetrating evil.[9] President Reagan's evasiveness during the Iran-Contra scandal probably reflected this opportune fiction. While his critics disparaged him as inept, oblivious, and a careless administrator, among other shortcomings, affixing the liar label on him was nearly impossible.

An interesting addition to our cabinet of mendacious curiosities might be called the "unintentional lie." This deceit is, at least according to the perpetrator, "accidental" or otherwise a result of ineptitudes as minor as an arithmetic mistake. For example, on June 21, 1998, the U.S. Justice Department announced that, thanks to the Brady Law regulating handgun purchases, some sixty-nine thousand people had been prevented from buying guns in 1997. That day, President Clinton (a Brady Bill ad-

---

[8] Sissela Bok, *Lying: Moral Choice in Public and Private Life* (New York: Vintage Books, 1999), 13.

[9] This tactic can be more encompassing than issuing "Don't tell me" instructions: better to appoint sympathizers who are inclined to lie without any coaxing or hidden direction! Drawing these miscreants from institutions renowned for disinformation makes this tactic especially easy to use. These subordinates will lie, falsify information, or destroy records on one's behalf without needing the potentially legally awkward "Don't tell me" command. This is their "style." Countless bureaucracies can thereby be converted to one's nefarious ends with scarcely any "smoking gun" evidence of deceit.

vocate) announced that this legislation had stopped "hundreds of thousands" of evildoers from acquiring firearms. Was Clinton lying? Or was he merely stretching the truth or otherwise attempting to con the public? Answers depend on certain difficult-to-establish facts. A Clinton aide eventually (and conveniently) attributed this huge discrepancy to an "editing error."[10] Perhaps a misplaced comma plus an extra zero converted 69,000 into 690,000, or maybe the president read the prepared statement with Hillary's glasses or was blinded by floodlights. In any case, since Clinton's spokesman claimed that the president's statement was honest in intent, was he lying? Was the person who committed the alleged editorial error the true liar and was Clinton "just following orders?" What if this discrepancy had passed unnoticed and become a certified fact in public debate? A further addendum to this quandary is that the original Justice Department proclamation was also a misstatement—many denials under the Brady Law were because of minor errors in completing forms, not because of prior criminal offenses.

And, of course, no cabinet of mendacious curiosities would be complete without a reference to Clinton's "lawyer-like" deceptions in escaping from perjury over his alleged sexual escapades. Here, as an astonished public discovered, commonplace words such as 'is', 'alone', and 'sexual relations' could be twisted so that black would appear white and vice versa. To refresh our memories: Clinton denied having a "sexual relationship" with White House intern Monica Lewinsky since, in his thinking, a few periodic intimacies short of intercourse did not constitute "a sexual relationship." Although dismissing Clinton's behavior as exceptional and purely expedient is tempting (not to mention too reprehensible to be treated seriously), its legal foundation is quite intellectually prestigious. Indeed, to say that oral sex is not "sex" is the natural outgrowth of an earnest constitutional philosophy. Truth be told, the Clinton example is more a matter of salaciousness than of shaky legal pedigree.

Robert F. Nagel, a professor of law, calls this approach the "Yale Argument," as a matter of convenience since it has been associated (though hardly exclusively) with Yale Law School, from which Clinton graduated. Basically, what might be an untruth is converted into truth by shifting levels of abstraction ever upward. To take an example enshrined by some as the epitome of contemporary jurisprudence, it might be said that the Constitution's guarantee against unreasonable searches and other Fourth Amendment rights imply a fundamental "right to privacy," which, in turn, leads to a right to control one's person, which, in turn, extends constitutional protection to abortion. This creative legal reasoning, continues Nagel, "has become so basic to modern constitutional interpreta-

---

[10] Cited in Carl Hausman, *Lies We Live By: Defeating Double-Talk and Deception in Advertising, Politics, and the Media* (New York: Routledge, 2000), 45.

tion, that it is taken for granted."[11] It is through such abstract reckoning, for example, that flag burning becomes "speech" and, at least according to one Harvard law professor, the Tenth Amendment guarantees certain government services.

The Clinton equivalent, at least according to Nagel, occurred when Clinton said that he "was not alone" with Lewinsky since, by this logic, others were also in the White House (and the entire East Coast, and the planet) at the same time. Moreover, this hyperabstract world can create its own unique and, of the utmost importance, *authoritative* vocabulary (much like Soviet esoteric terminology). In this context, Clinton's tortured grand jury testimony might be likened to speaking in a foreign tongue, a specialized discourse in which, for example, oral sex is not even "sex." If ordinary citizens get confused or accuse the president of lying, this is understandable since they cannot be expected to follow discussions in this specialized idiom. That ample opportunity exists to derive this "special language" (for example, by "updating" old ideas or discovering previously unsuspected nuances) makes this strategy, needless to say, a godsend for those who embrace flexibility with the truth. This style is also especially notable for its reliance on copious "documentation" to bury the disbeliever under an avalanche of "scholarly" footnotes and citations to buttress taxonomic novelties. Sophistic verbiage may be insufficient for the novice, yet very often those who embrace this "Yale" approach manage to convince themselves that they *really are* telling the truth, though *this* truth requires enormous intellectual exertion to divine.[12]

Anthropologists investigating liar-friendly cultures have likewise observed the role of specialized terminology in dividing truth from falsehood. Michael Gilsenan found that in one Lebanese Muslim village, outside of a few incontestable subjects such as mechanical ability, lying infused all social relations.[13] The Arabic word *kizb*, usually translated as lying, was more closely associated with a playful inventiveness, a verbal quickfootedness, or even an impromptu wit rather than evil intent. Youngsters would lie to trick rivals and thus outshine the duped. Adults routinely fabricated stories to embellish their otherwise dreary adventures or to enhance social standing. For the villagers, endless lying thus resembled the leisurely kicking around of a soccer ball for sheer amusement.

---

[11] Robert F. Nagel, "Essay: Lies and Law," *Harvard Journal of Law and Public Policy* 22, no. 2 (Spring 1999): 605–17.

[12] Nagel adds that Clinton's lying is consistent with the odd urge to "improve" the world by altering language. This labeling-brings-real-change view is generally associated with the cultural Left (especially postmodernism) but it flourishes elsewhere. "Poor nations" thus become "developing nations" so as to suggest progress, regardless of evidence, or even when data suggests economic backsliding.

[13] Michael Gilsenan, "Lying, Honor, and Contradiction," in *Everyday Life in the Muslim Middle East*, ed. Donna Lee Bowen and Evelyn A. Early (Bloomington: Indiana University Press, 1993).

Nevertheless, as in all societies, mechanisms must exist to separate humdrum fantasizing from truth, if only in emergencies. Gilsenan claims that judiciously inserting phrases like "without joking" or "by your father's life" signal veracity to the culturally attuned. He offers the example of a reported shooting, an account that would normally be disbelieved except that the phrase "by your life" was appended to the tale. The listener now "knew" that, indeed, the claimed event truly occurred. Unfortunately, outsiders are unlikely to be familiar with the import of such locutions, and with the idea that their omission absolves liars from any responsibility: "She should have known I was lying since I did not say 'by your life' since this signifies truth." Similar telling phrases exist in contemporary American society: "I'm not joking around" or "I'm being serious!" signal truthfulness in situations when lying is generally expected.

The complexity of 'intent' goes beyond the travails of establishing it. As philosopher Frederick A. Siegler and others make clear, something believed to be fraudulent by the speaker may in fact turn out to be true.[14] The upshot is that while a lie was intended, a lie was not told. For example, in his 2000 presidential campaign George W. Bush said that the U.S. economy stood in danger of a recession, which many took to be a lie at the time since it seemed contrary to all available evidence and respected opinion. That such a downturn did follow Bush's victory unexpectedly absolves Bush from mendacity: he told the truth, though for reasons of campaign expediency, not because it was true. Plainly, the addition of a verification requirement regarding "what was really known" at the time makes certifying lies arduous. And who can vouch for the truth-certifier's honesty? Political rhetoric overflows with self-serving and dubious pronouncements, many of which are disbelieved by the speaker, yet an ineradicable chance remains that they might, just might, be correct. At a minimum the accused liar can always insist that verdicts are premature, and that one day "Communism *will* bury capitalism."

Siegler similarly raises the difficult but commonplace issue of people passing on deceits with absolutely no awareness of their duplicity, often in good faith or as part of a respectable job. Using Siegler's example, how do we classify the "honest" radio announcer who mechanically reads dishonest propaganda while oblivious to its veracity? Surely he deceives others and must certainly realize his job's built-in deceptive purpose. Or might the dishonest writers, not the dutiful announcer, be the dishonest ones? When government-sponsored lies are considered, this attribution of responsibility is, obviously, hardly trivial. By this reckoning almost every election campaign worker or public information officer (let alone those in the CIA, National Security Agency, etc.) becomes a liar just by showing up for work.

[14] Frederick A. Siegler, "Lying," *American Philosophical Quarterly* 3, no. 2 (April 1966): 128–36.

These (and comparable) accounts also assume that there really is something called "*the* truth," and that this precious commodity can be established to everyone's satisfaction. Of all the possible escape clauses, this is by far the most encompassing and enticing. Even the hard sciences, that bastion of truth *über alles*, will confess that beyond statements true merely by definition, uncertainty can never be entirely banished. How can one *ever* lie if truth *never* exists? From this perspective, one can only contradict what is *believed* to be true, at *that* moment, by *these* particular people. And who is so above suspicion that he can attest that his singular version of truth outshines all rivals? Even accepted scientific laws (e.g., Newtonian physics) can sooner or later fail the cosmic truth test. Philosophically, of course, this is a colossal can of worms, and even strident positivists willingly concede that scientific statements can only be falsified, never absolutely confirmed.[15]

Accepting the possibility of hard-edged truth does not end discussion—certainty *cannot* be guaranteed. One compilation intended to debunk myths passed off as rock-solid truth begins with "We believe that truth exists; that it is an absolute" and then a few sentences later intones, "Just as the horizon recedes as we approach it, and does not exist in itself, so truth may never be unveiled, reached or apprehended."[16] There are practical problems as well. Historical "facts" routinely shift as new information surfaces and previously certified facts acquire a different appearance. Witness how the U.S. Communist Party's "peaceful" activities of the 1930s and 1940s are now regarded as truly subversive, thanks to once-secret Soviet Bloc archival information that has finally surfaced and revelations from decrypted Soviet diplomatic communication from World War II. Appending "a lie" to an assertion might only mean that a statement contravenes current and imperfect information, and this might abruptly change. Today's honored truth-teller becomes tomorrow's vilified liar, maybe, so better reserve judgment or become the eternal skeptic.

This escape from the dishonesty accusation by challenging the very idea of fixed truth has been an especially valuable ruse for buttressing ideologically tinged, fictitious history. How do we classify the assertion that Socrates was black, or that Aristotle stole his knowledge from Africans, when no hard evidence supports either contention? Imposing a verdict of lying is hardly straightforward, despite the preposterous character of these claims. Leaving aside whether Afrocentric historians actually believe these claims (a fact beyond discernment), a case could be made that these claims *might* be true, or that it is the speaker's "mere opinion" that these assertions are accurate. In principle, it matters not whether the odds are .5 or .000005—a possibility is a possibility and is

---

[15] These quandaries are further developed in David Nyberg, *The Varnished Truth: Truth Telling and Deceiving in Ordinary Life* (Chicago: University of Chicago Press, 1993), chap. 3.

[16] Cited in Ronald Duncan and Miranda Weston-Smith, *Lying Truths: A Critical Scrutiny of Current Beliefs and Conventions* (Oxford: Pergamon Press, 1979), 1.

thus worth bearing in mind. Nor must one's opinion meet the standards of scientific truth: as Arendt argued, "facts" are often made into facts by the weight of assembled opinion, not indisputable reality.[17] Maybe the earth was once flat. A brief initial disclaimer that "this message consists entirely of 'possibilities' and/or 'opinion' and may not be suitable for everyone" could then serve as a license to lie.

Paul Ekman, drawing on his extensive psychiatric experience, offers a more complex understanding to address these thorny issues.[18] He begins with a generic definition of what constitutes a lie, but his medical background brings out various psychological qualifiers, making for both hard-headed realism and frustrating complexity. For one, a lie must entail free will: the liar must choose to lie and know the difference between truths and falsehoods. If the would-be perpetrator is unable to do so, lying is impossible. Several recognized medical pathologies, for example, Korsakoff's psychosis and Munchausen Syndrome, entail habitual dishonesty.[19] Individuals with multiple personalities pose a uniquely fascinating dilemma: Will the real liar please stand up? Another exasperating psychiatric disorder entails something called "affective truth," a "truth" that clearly belies reality when uttered but, nevertheless, is sincerely held as truth by the speaker. The next day, however, this "truth" may be understood as a lie. Among the less severe, commonplace psychological illnesses that entail habitual lying are borderline personality disorder and antisocial personality disorder, illnesses affecting millions of normal-appearing people. The quip that Washington could never tell a lie, Nixon could never tell the truth, and Reagan could never tell the difference humorously captures the mental gyrations symptomatic of these disorders. The message is clear if a tad devious: if certified psychopaths are elected, then we cannot accuse our leaders of lying.

One need not suffer a permanent brain dysfunction or an incurable brain disorder such as Alzheimer's to escape the responsibility of discerning truths from falsehoods. Debilitation can be entirely temporary, even limited to the very moment when a seeming falsehood is uttered. Our growing tolerance of an ever-expanding list of disabilities offers multiple enticing possibilities. Plausibly, one's thoughts could have been briefly impaired by alcoholism, drugs, stress, and mental exhaustion, plus untold but nonobvious physical illnesses such as a brain tumor or dementia, all of which weaken clear thinking. Further, perpetrators with hyperactive imaginations could be added to the list of the exculpated with the claim that, like children, they cannot distinguish "is" from "ought." The perfect defense, naturally, would be to attribute an *apparent* lie to circumstantial, mind-clouding stress, and since it is this (non-

---

[17] Arendt, *Between Past and Future*, 243.
[18] Ekman, *Telling Lies*, chap. 2.
[19] See Charles V. Ford, Bryan H. King, and Marc H. Hollender, "Lies and Liars: Psychiatric Aspects of Prevarication," *American Journal of Psychiatry* 145, no. 5 (May 1988): 554–62.

visible) physical condition, not free choice, that engenders the fib, the perpetrator is *permanently* blameless. In other words, being asked to tell the truth may energize a disability into existence, so telling the truth is medically impossible. This logic may seem bizarre, but it appears regularly in criminal defenses based on the accused being drunk, insane, or otherwise not in a normal frame of mind, even if the faulty mental state was self-induced.

Another element in assessing falsehoods is volition. Coercion plainly interferes with volition, and it comes in assorted forms, some of which may be hidden, and range from torture to sodium pentathol ("truth serum"). It is possible, then, to claim that one misspoke due to compulsion, and thus escape the onus of lying.[20] Surely Eisenhower would not be classified as a liar if Allen Dulles, the CIA director, had held a pistol to Ike's head during the news conference. What if years afterward Ike finally admitted that his wife's life had been threatened by rogue CIA agents, and he lied to save his beloved Mamie? Would he now be, decades later, off the hook? What if this "fact" were beyond confirmation? But the more realistic dilemmas concerning coercion involve less than life-threatening pressures—loss of a job, blackmail, public humiliation, and similar threats that might, in often indiscernible ways, impair free will.

Ekman adds a second critical dimension that was omitted in his generic definition of a lie: the recipient's willingness to be deceived.[21] Again, a reasonable addendum, but one that inevitably invites mischief since expectations of mendacity are routine and falsehood is occasionally preferred to truth. Nobody, for example, castigates actors or magicians for deception; spectators perfectly grasp the sham. Brilliant trickery is delightful, and unconvincing performers might be booed off the stage. Those who appreciate fiction and fantasy are likewise connoisseurs of lies, though, as in professional wrestling, the line between realism and entertainment is often disputed. Life overflows with welcomed, dimly recognized deceits: demagogues fervently promise unobtainable prosperity to the desperate; teachers award inflated grades to thankful dolts; and untold numbers of therapeutic falsehoods abound. Entire cultures embrace outrageous conspiracies for their supposed salutary value while rejecting harsh, unvarnished realities.

The ample opportunities that exist for self-delusion constitute a troublesome issue that cannot be stressed enough when attempting to verify lies. Psychologist Roy F. Baumeister details the everyday seductive incentives that propel potential liars toward self-delusion, notably, the ease of avoiding unpleasant information or the opportunity to shift blame to

---

[20] For those who appreciate oddities, in ancient Athens slaves gave legal testimony only under torture, and since one cannot lie without free will (assuming torture grievously restricts free will), such testimony was, by Ekman's definition, truthful. Chalk up another accomplishment for the ancients.

[21] Ekman, *Telling Lies*, 27–28.

others.[22] It is not uncommon to use alcohol or drugs to induce delusions of power or nerve (so-called Dutch courage). The capacity for self-delusion may well be genetically hardwired, since adroit deceivers might, conceivably, be more adept at impregnating females in contrast to those males who honestly admit their inability to protect every sexually willing woman.[23] Ford, writing as a psychiatrist, argues that self-delusion is common in certain professions (e.g., sales) and, significantly, may even be a prerequisite for vocational success.[24] It can be a powerful political weapon, too. A candidate cognizant of his private qualms about a popular program might inadvertently appear insincere when endorsing it, an accurate depiction of his ambivalent views. By contrast, a rival possesses the advantage if he or she deludes himself that the proposal is, contrary to initial reservations, truly worthy. Constant repetition may also be convincing to the point where lingering doubts vanish and one's very persona becomes irrevocably and "honestly" altered. The candidate initially unconvinced about increased educational spending *genuinely* may become an advocate after delivering countless pro-funding speeches and, perhaps, acquiring a (self-manufactured) reputation for sincerity.[25] Or, virtue-seeking officials might study method acting or undergo hypnosis to achieve the appearance of absolute honesty.

Yet, as the rationally inclined might argue, "lying to oneself" is a logical impossibility if lying requires expressing something *known* to be false.[26] Technically speaking, this type of lie (which Plato calls "the lie in the

[22] Roy F. Baumeister, "Lying to Yourself: The Enigma of Self-Deception," in *Lying and Deception in Everyday Life*, ed. Michael Lewis and Carolyn Saarni (New York: Guilford Press, 1993). A similar sympathetic analysis is offered by Marcel Eck, *Lies and Truth*, trans. Bernard Murchland (London: Macmillan, 1970). Eck's account is noteworthy since it derives from his experiences as a therapist treating lying patients, many of whom seem to lie for understandable, if not commendable, reasons.

[23] Other fascinating self-deception issues are raised in Daniel Goleman, *Vital Lies, Simple Truths: The Psychology of Self-Deception* (New York: Simon and Schuster, 1985), particularly the chapter entitled, "The Virtues of Self-Deception." A second possible self-deception survival benefit is that it may reduce anxiety and thus promote health: Why worry? Be happy. More generally, the commonplace nature of self-deception suggests an underappreciated usefulness. Karl E. Scheibe ("In Defense of Lying: On the Moral Neutrality of Misrepresentation," *Berkshire Review* 15 [1980]: 15–24) dwells at length on both the benefits of misrepresentation, including its appreciated role in Greek mythology, and the medical benefits of self-deception. A similar sympathetic depiction of lying is offered by Nyberg in his introduction to *The Varnished Truth*. He even argues that some deceit is *necessary* to social stability and mental health (2). According to this reasoning, parents who occasionally lie to their children may, in fact, be genuinely helping them, depending on the situation.

[24] Ford, *Lies! Lies!! Lies!!!*, 276–79.

[25] The possibilities beyond voluntary self-delusion abound. Ford depicts several severe mental disorders (e.g., spontaneous confabulation) that are associated with an inability to distinguish truth from falsehood. Speakers effortlessly invent new "memories," complete with bold-faced lies, without any visible, telltale embarrassment. Such individuals are particularly well suited to a public life, where traits such as a quivering voice or nervous body language hint at dishonesty. Yet, recall that mendacity associated with a severe mental disorder would not qualify as a lie, according to conventional definitions.

[26] Raphael Demos, "Lying to Oneself," *The Journal of Philosophy* 57, no. 17 (1960): 588–95.

soul") only exists as "a lie" until the precise moment when the person believes it. The key element is a *change* in beliefs, hardly an act that is intrinsically mendacious. One might lie about liking broccoli but, eventually, after sufficient self-convincing, one "genuinely" comes to savor it. Of course, those with a psychiatric bent might argue that contradictory beliefs can easily coexist; one might simultaneously love and hate the same person (or broccoli) with these feelings emerging under different conditions. Lying (or truth-telling) then becomes circumstance-dependent or, to probe deeper, a function of which belief ultimately gains ascendancy. The implications of this duality are bizarre: certifying an act of lying would be unachievable unless one were privy to the would-be perpetrator's inner sanctum, an advantage plausibly unavailable even to the speaker.

A further potentially troubling wrinkle concerns "nonverbal deceit." Technically called "metacommunications," these behaviors modify overt verbal or written statements. That is, one communicates *A* via one method, and simultaneously denies *A* another way. Though seldom addressed formally, these behaviors are inescapable and—more important—are integral to certifying lies.[27] The key question is which communication method ought to be accepted as authoritative. Obvious examples include rolling of the eyes, smirking, inadvertent stuttering, edgy body movement, avoiding eye contact, and untold other, culturally laden clues that involuntarily reveal that something is "going on" beyond manifest verbal communication. Multilevel communication can work both ways—disguising truth (e.g., being "poker-faced") or appearing forthright while being disingenuous. An example of the latter is when American television correspondents reporting from oppressive regimes shrewdly utilize subtle voice inflections to escape censorship: "This is the *official* explanation about *nonexistent* shortages!" Jurors occasionally subordinate sworn testimony to nonverbal cues, assuming that the latter reveal the "real" truth: those who "look shady" or "too nervous" are deemed not credible, and their verbal testimony is discounted. With "nonverbal deceit" the opportunities for double-dealing are immense. The cunning speaker can always claim candor based on some barely discernable gesture—a sly wink—that supposedly overrides everything else.

Modern technology affords ingenious opportunities to convert truth into falsehood and vice versa using metacommunications. The American

---

[27] Interestingly, psychologists who empirically examine nonverbal cues to achieving deception find mixed outcomes: sometimes these cues fool viewers, and sometimes they don't. Effectiveness varies by technique and by characteristics of the liar. A useful overview of this deciphering effort, including studies using trained professionals, such as customs inspectors and police officers, is presented by Bella M. DePaulo, Julie I. Stone, and G. Daniel Lassiter in "Deceiving and Detecting Deceit," in *The Self and Social Life*, ed. Barry R. Schlenker (New York: McGraw-Hill, 1985). One can only imagine what could happen if campaign professionals were to discover this literature and train their clients to become proficient liars without "leaking" falsehoods.

television news program *60 Minutes* achieved notoriety by posing disconcerting questions to interviewees and then contrasting their verbal reassurances with close-up shots of sweating brows or tightened lips, all socially understood indicators of mendacity. In an instant, ostensible denials of wrongdoing by business executives or public officials became inadvertent visual "admissions" of guilt, thanks to clever camera work. The opposite is equally possible; judicious editing may transform a speech laced with clumsy contradictions and suspicion-generating mannerisms into believable "honest truth." In both instances, the final verdict regarding truthfulness essentially resides with editors and directors since they— not the listeners—selectively include or exclude revealing nonverbal cues.

Recent research at the Massachusetts Institute of Technology using powerful computers and artificial intelligence, enables experts to put new words into persons' mouths in ways that defy detection.[28] One might become "a liar" without even knowing it. In one particular demonstration, a woman on videotape was shown speaking and singing *convincingly* in Japanese, a language unknown to her. Though presently limited to simple static "headshots," the huge commercial market (e.g., in dubbing films) makes advanced applications inevitable. As one research scientist familiar with the project warned, "It's only a matter of time before somebody can get enough good video of your face to have it do what they like." History can now not only be rewritten, but completely redone, visually and orally: old footage of Eisenhower's press conference may now "really" show Ike "telling the truth."

If the problem of metacommunications seems daunting, wrestling with outward behavior unaccompanied by words may be even more vexing. Can one lie with silence or deceive by other nonverbal means, and thus render oneself absolutely blameless regardless of intent? This well-recognized dilemma rests on the commonplace understanding of a lie as being a *statement* (presumably verbal or written) designed to deceive. Without overt voicing, the future victim can only guess at another person's intent, and as we all recognize, confusion can easily arise. Kant, *the* champion of absolute truth (see below), offers an illustration of someone who does everything to physically suggest that a vacation is imminent, for example, he packs his bags. Such behavior permits—but does not *require*—observers to conclude that he is about to depart. But, if no such trip were planned, is there deceit? No, according to Kant, since such a trip was never overtly confirmed; the observers themselves drew the erroneous conclusion, though understandably so. Surely, leaving town was not preordained nor the only possible interpretation of his actions; he might have packed the suitcases for another person or just out of nervous habit.[29]

---

[28] Gareth Cook, "At MIT, they can put words into our mouths," *Boston Globe*, May 15, 2002, Metro section.

[29] This example from Kant is offered in Roderick M. Chisholm and Thomas D. Feehan, "The Intent to Deceive," *The Journal of Philosophy* 74, no. 3 (March 1977): 143–59.

The manipulation of "honest" behavior in order to deceive while escaping the opprobrium of lying is a godsend to the devious. Entire industries service this ruse: advertising and cosmetics come readily to mind. Familiar examples from individual behavior include wearing athletic attire to display falsely one's "physical fitness" or ignoring all social invitations to demonstrate one's nonexistent workaholic commitment. Academics routinely cite unread books, "suggesting" (but not confirming) erudition. In the public sphere we find petty dictators bedecked with bogus but genuine-appearing military medals, or slothful legislators brandishing technical tomes well beyond their reading level. Since nothing overt is said about the *implied* accomplishments, nobody is—literally—lying. Imposing government buildings and grandiose monuments are classic tools to mislead. The offense here, technically, is playing on the gullibility of others who accept outward impressions as the truth, not mendacity.

IV. How Are Lies to Be Judged?

Conceptually separating truth from impostures is difficult enough, but formulating an evaluative framework that justifies or condemns lying in the public realm is even more daunting. It is not haplessness we suffer when calibrating public lies. Recall W. C. Field's quip about abstinence: Giving up drinking is easy; I've done it a thousand times. Classification schemes abound, each celebrated by its author as authoritative; it is the practical utility of such schemes when concretely applied that is debatable. Conceivably, evaluative schemes are pointless; at best they provide a decent public face on immorality or, conversely, provide a handy weapon to discredit foes. And if this pessimistic assessment is, indeed, correct, then how are we to confront "bad" lies in the public sphere when they suddenly surface? Can anything be said beyond, "That's a lie! Shame on you!" or, "Everyone does it, so no big deal"? Let us briefly consider some notable categorization efforts. My point is simply that, while schemes and admonitions galore might win intellectual beauty contests, they fail when organizing the civic household.

We commence with the "hard-liners" who (apparently) prohibit *any* lying, public mendacity included. Among the most influential of this group is Augustine (354–430 A.D.), who unmistakably insists that God forbids all lies, period. By 'lie', Augustine means a falsehood uttered to deceive, so a speaker has to believe that what he said was, indeed, false.[30]

---

[30] Again, everything rests on this difficult-to-establish 'intent'. Augustine also expressed problems with biblical accounts justifying lying for good purpose, such as that of the Hebrew midwives who lied to Pharaoh in order to spare the lives of male children. Augustine held that these and comparable actions were not "really" lies. For a more comprehensive account of how Augustine navigated these and other obstacles, see Joseph Boyle, "The Absolute Prohibition of Lying and the Origins of the Casuistry of Mental Reservations: Augustinian Arguments and Thomistic Developments," *The American Journal of Jurisprudence* 44 (1999): 43–65.

To reiterate, it is intent to deceive, not whether the proposition is factually correct, that certifies a lie. God, says Augustine, gave human beings speech to express their thoughts to each other, but to deceive intentionally would endanger the deceiver's immortal soul and, likely, lead to yet more lies and sins. Nor should one commit an evil act, even if good, such as saving a life, might come of it (and divine providence might yet prevent the evil from occurring). A parallel can be made with murder; if we admit that "some" murder is acceptable, then where does one stop?

Nevertheless, like a skilled legislator drafting a draconian law, Augustine bows to human nature and occasional necessity. For one, he admits that remaining silent can occasionally substitute for a lie without a lie being told when the purpose is to accomplish a good deed.[31] He further acknowledges that on *some* occasions, for example, shielding the innocent from persecution, one might equivocate—issuing statements that are neither literally true nor factually false or, in other instances, withholding certain information. Lying does not occur if the listener misinterprets the utterance, even if the speaker knows that his ambiguous or incomplete statement could mislead. If questioned about the whereabouts of someone fleeing persecution, one can answer, "Who knows?" all the while knowing the fugitive's exact location, and still not be classified a liar according to Augustine.

Though convenient for some purposes, ambiguity may not be sufficient for those circumstances in which lying seems attractive, if not honorable (e.g., shielding an ill person from news that might cause even more illness). Fortunately, Augustine offers a way out of this predicament while still affirming the absolute prohibition against lying. The quandary is addressed by first formulating an eightfold classification scheme for lies, resting on intention and harm, beginning with the most grievous lies (e.g., false religious teachings), and ending with the least harmful falsehoods that may, in fact, promote the good (e.g., by preventing injury). The latter lies, being lies, are still absolutely forbidden by God, and certainly cannot be encouraged or justified, but—and here is the loophole—they are pardonable sins, and thus possibly forgiven by God, depending on the repentance of the liar.[32] The Augustinian motto is never, never lie, but if you must, God *may* forgive you if the harmless lie accomplishes good without engendering harm. This formulation is clearly not a legal scheme

---

[31] Subsequent theologians took Augustine's use of silence and widened it into something approaching evasiveness. Another subterfuge of Augustine's was something called a strict mental reservation, a silent qualification not generally used by others in this context. An example would be a person who is asked about marital unfaithfulness and answers "no" while mentally adding "not today." The Pope condemned this tactic as a lie on March 2, 1679, and it remains generally understood as a lie. The use of equivocation, in contrast, is often called a "broad reservation" and, as noted, is not mendacious provided that the statement is not knowingly false. Ironically, Augustine's authority was widely used to expand such dodges despite his own hard-line position (see *Catholic Encyclopedia*, s.v. "Lying," available on-line at http://www.newadvent.org/cathen/09469a.htm. [cited January 24, 2003]).

[32] Augustine makes this point in his *Enchiridion*, chap. 22, p. 29, as cited in Bok, *Lying*, 33.

that mere mortals can adjudicate; we can only speculate about how God will ultimately classify a particular falsehood. Who knows if Eisenhower received his heavenly pardon, and who are we to anticipate God's wrath?[33]

Thomas Aquinas (c. 1225–74) embraces a similar-appearing hard-line position some eight hundred years later than Augustine, though the room to maneuver is, as a matter of practical expediency, conveniently stretched. Following Augustine, Aquinas argues that intent to deceive certifies the lie, and to lie is absolutely forbidden. His *Summa Theologiae* repeatedly pronounces lies to be mortal sins, and a mortal sin alone causes destruction and death of the soul. Is the liar, regardless of the lie, therefore eternally doomed? Not quite—as with Augustine, for Aquinas the loophole arrives via the pardonable sin. *Some* lies, notably those that are helpful without inflicting harm and those said in jest ("just kidding"), are divinely pardonable. Other deceits, particularly those that subvert the virtues of faith and religion or are intended to injure one's neighbor in name or possessions, are unforgivable. The trick, then, is to secure the favorable categorization. Nevertheless, as before, classification is ultimately beyond mortal reach: God, not judge and jury, decides the liar's fate, though the Church might offer a preliminary assessment. A savvy public official, attuned to Aquinas's teachings, could justify mendacity by intoning, "My lie—despite what you might think—is harmless, even helpful, but if I'm wrong, God will punish me in the hereafter, and for others to insist otherwise, is presumptuous."

The most unforgiving hard-liner of them all is Immanuel Kant (1724–1804). His attack on lying—defined as intentionally declaring an untruth to another—is absolute. Lying is forbidden even for the most benign reason, including saving the life of the innocent threatened by evil. The pardonable-sin loophole is gone. Not even self-defense or resistance to coercion is allowable. To tell the truth is an unconditional duty, applying in all circumstances, and even an innocent "little lie" destroys the liar's human dignity and harms mankind generally by vitiating the sources of law. Agreeing with Augustine, Kant argues that speaking falsehoods renders the liar less than human. Expediency and absolution count for nothing.

To appreciate the absoluteness of Kant's strictures, consider Kant's own "tough case" illustration—deceiving a prospective murderer in the hunt for a victim in one's own house (now a commonplace example in this ongoing debate). Should one refuse to answer the evildoer's inquiry, or tell him or her to look elsewhere? Neither, contends Kant. Telling the truth, even if it inescapably invites evil, remains one's duty, and, as a practical matter, even a well-intentioned lie may well impose unforeseen negative consequences on the liar, namely, developing the habit of lying.

---

[33] This resolution assumes, naturally, a belief in God. If there is no God, then the lie cannot be pardoned. But, since God's existence is beyond proof, resolution must wait until Judgment Day and cannot be anticipated. All in all, for those seeking a life of pardoned sin, Pascal's Wager again makes perfect sense.

Further, the intended victim may have fled the house, and the evildoer, if told the "lie" to look elsewhere, might encounter the victim on the street (an unlikely scenario if the truth be told). Perhaps, even if the pursued were still in the house and the would-be killer were told this truth, the would-be killer could be quickly apprehended within, but not easily apprehended if in pursuit elsewhere. In any case, endless hypothetical contingencies aside, by performing one's duty to be truthful, the person who is asked about the sought-after victim is absolutely blameless, regardless of consequences, including if the murderer succeeds. If a lie "for good reason" had been told, and the intended victim were still murdered, the liar would now share some of the responsibility for evil, at least according to Kant.

Dissenting from the position of the "hard-liners" are Plato (c. 429–347 B.C.) and Machiavelli (1469–1527), both of whom cut enormous slack for leaders to lie. Plato, famously, proposes the "noble lie," the fictions and comparable deceptions told to ordinary people to preserve social harmony. These lies are not self-serving, as one might offer misstatements to hide bribery or marital infidelities. The purpose of such lies *must* be the educative good of the whole, and in the *Republic* their most illustrious purpose is to provide a convincing rationale for political hierarchy and class distinctions (the familiar tale of the gods' mixing the rulers with gold, the auxiliaries with silver, and the farmers and tradesmen with lesser metals). Similarly, occasions may arise when a city's rulers fittingly mislead the people or enemies for the civic good, though here, unlike the noble lies, the deceits may eventually be confessed.

Plato is not, however, an apologist for mendacity; lies must be judged by their ultimate civic purpose. Some lies are forbidden. In Book III of the *Republic* Plato repeatedly inveighs against subversive myths, namely, Homer's tales of the gods, which might promote vices such as adultery or encourage citizens to escape their civic responsibilities by blaming others for their immoral urges. It is unwise, for example, to tell of the terrible rapes by Theseus, son of Poseidon and Perithous, son of Zeus, for these will surely mislead mere mortals. Put into modern terminology, the intemperate and rash Zeus should not be held up as a role model; only when the gods instruct wisely are these myths to be cherished.

Given the necessity of judgment, how is one to assess the value of such lies, noble or otherwise? Might the gods (or God) sit in final judgment and punish catastrophes? Are the pluses to be weighed against the minuses? Hardly. Promulgating mendacity is the domain of those who rule, and it is entirely up to them to decide, for they are wiser than those below.

Even more extreme is, of course, Machiavelli. No convoluted philosophical rationales or appeals to divine authority for deceptions are needed: experience shows lying to be an absolute necessity of statecraft, and to insist otherwise invites defeat. People, according to Machiavelli, are naturally inclined to evil, selfishness, and egoism, and to believe that one's enemies will not stoop to deceit is perilous fantasy. The purpose of politics, fundamentally, is the cunning accumulation and preservation of power in order to achieve glory; morality among leaders is immaterial, a distraction. To quote Machiavelli, "[A] prudent ruler cannot keep his word, nor should he, when such fidelity would damage him; and when the reasons that made him promise are no longer relevant."[34]

It is not that morality is totally irrelevant. The citizens' dispositions—notably loyalty, attachment to family, and frugality (among others)—can be immensely valuable in a well-organized state. (Machiavelli greatly admired the virtues of the Swiss.) It is also important that the ruler *appear* to embody such virtues as courage and decisiveness. However, statecraft as properly practiced exempts rulers from such constraints. Put bluntly, the successful prince must be a great liar and hypocrite: truthfulness should *never* be the evaluative standard.

Rounding out our brief foray into classic treatments is how Islam assesses lying. There are two instances where lying is absolutely forbidden: lying about Allah and lying against Muhammad.[35] Elsewhere, tolerance of lying seems relatively generous and depends on the peculiarities of each situation. Scholarly interpretations strongly suggest that Islam countenances falsehoods to save one's life, to effect peace or reconciliation, to persuade a woman (as in falsely promising gifts), and on the occasion of a journey. Supposedly, distinguished Muslim theologians, such as the Imam Abu Hammid Ghazali, claim that Islam permits unrelenting dishonesty (and murder, to boot) to achieve one's ends if more honorable pathways fail. Recent events, for example, the former Afghan government's claimed detachment from al Qaeda, illustrate this fondness for deception among extremist Muslims, especially when deceiving so-called infidels.

Modern attempts to supply useful demarcation lines between truth and lies have scarcely settled the matter. Quite predictably, utilitarian philosophers have devised formulas to separate "good" from "bad" lies, and their efforts have, equally predictably, fallen into obscurity. Henry Sidgwick (1838–1900) offers a familiar utilitarian case: lies (defined by intent to deceive) should be judged exclusively by their consequences.[36] A parent who tells a child that eating too much candy will certainly bring on diabetes (statistically unlikely) is justified since the likely health benefits, such as fewer cavities, far outweigh the risk of possibly discrediting the

---

[34] Niccolo Machiavelli, *The Prince*, ed. Quentin Skinner and [trans.] Russell Price (Cambridge: Cambridge University Press, 1988), 61–62.

[35] This discussion is drawn from *Comparative Index to Islam*, s.v. "Lying," accessed on-line at http://answering-islam.org/Index/L/lying.html [cited January 24, 2003]. Given the inherent conflicts in religious doctrine, this analysis may not be completely definitive, nor can I vouch for the expertise of these commentators. Still, that Islam does tolerate lying in several ordinary, day-to-day circumstances does seem clear.

[36] Henry Sidgwick, *The Methods of Ethics*, 7th ed. (1874; reprint, London: Macmillan & Co., 1907) as cited in Sissela Bok, *Lying*, 272–75.

parent or inciting future cynicism in the child. Even when someone falsifies religious doctrine—unequivocally forbidden by both Augustine and Aquinas—Sidgwick is forgiving if the misrepresentation effectively furthers communication. Although this approach distinguishes among lies by calibrating their consequences, it escapes all the practical baggage of certifying the speaker's "real" motives or uncovering unvoiced reservations, the downfall of earlier classification approaches. Nor, obviously, must we rely on an unseen or unknowable God to punish the miscreants in the afterlife.

Yet, as Bok observes, Sidgwick and like-minded utilitarians offer formulas that are alluring only in the abstract.[37] Concrete applications are far more vexing. Consequences—the key element in utilitarian assessments— are scarcely predictable, even for the simplest, cut-and-dried acts. A parade of tiny white lies about personal hygiene—"I really did brush my teeth"—might turn a child into a violent psychopath later in life, an outcome clearly beyond the predictable. What if the person who was hunted in Kant's would-be murder story were Adolph Hitler's great- great grandfather, so millions of lives could have been saved by honestly exposing the intended victim's whereabouts? Accurately foretelling consequences for public lies is doubtless impossible. Plausibly, Eisenhower's embarrassment at being caught in a lie instigated rapid development of satellite surveillance technology, and the military intelligence gained thereby sharply reduced the likelihood of a nuclear Armageddon. Or alternatively, Ike's ill-advised deceits poisoned a growing rapprochement between the United States and the USSR and disastrously extended the Cold War another three decades. Who knows for sure? Calculating such imponderables from endless hypothetical scenarios is pointless.

Even if consequences were predictable down to the fourth decimal place, this does not eliminate judgments regarding alternative outcomes. This assessment is inevitable since a single act has multiple results, and calculating the value of each outcome "package" is never objectively straightforward. In the U-2 instance, were all the consequences of honesty "better" than all the results of lying? Who is to do this addition and weighing, and according to what calculus? Answering this question is even more formidable than predicting the future. To believe that these divergent outcomes can be mechanically summed and choices made between varying packages without bitter political struggle is a daydream.

Bok also correctly notes that utilitarian evaluation abolishes the moral onus attached to lying and cheating. A falsehood, insofar as it is to be judged exclusively by impact, differs not one iota from truthfulness. The utilitarian calculus effortlessly frees the miscreant from any moral discomfort or social opprobrium. The possibilities for secret rationalizations are also apparent; what commences as a moral predicament can be quickly

---

[37] Bok, *Lying*, 49–52.

twisted into a "good deed" and, after a point, the honesty-mendacity distinction vanishes. The pernicious situation can further deteriorate as fresh lies are advanced to cover past fabrications, until extracting even the tiniest truthful tidbits is hopeless. Society itself could become unlivable: Why fret over a speaker's public dishonesty when we should be disputing alternative outcome scenarios?

A final noteworthy scheme is what might be called "contextualism," which resembles situational ethics. Advocates claim that the blanket condemnation of lying as immoral, disruptive, or reprehensible fails to appreciate that lies are *necessary* for human relationships, not a defect to be expunged wherever possible. Lying is, after all, endemic in daily existence: even the clothes we wear and our household furnishings are designed to deceive (e.g., newly constructed "eighteenth century English cottages" decorated with manufactured "antiques"). Unadorned nudity — the "naked truth" — is both undesirable and impractical, if only because clothes protect us against the elements. Moreover, banishing such fictions would undermine effective psychological functioning and deprive humans of our beloved culture, especially the arts: even photographs these days are seldom reflections of unvarnished reality. Who can be happy in a world governed exclusively by cold, hard-edged truth? It would be a lifeless world bereft of romance or beauty. As Oscar Wilde quipped, "The aim of the liar is simply to charm, to delight, to give pleasure. He is the very basis of civilized society." It is not that lies should replace truth as the gold standard; everything is a matter of practical circumstances, not unforgiving dogma.

These various classification schemes for judging lies hardly exhaust the subject, and, obviously, my overviews are only snapshots.[38] It would take scant effort to spin out even more good-lie, bad-lie systems. What is inescapable, however, is the divergence between the various schemes, and this is no small impediment for judgment-seekers. Criteria selection, alas, may be largely a matter of taste, if not momentary convenience. No one scholarly understanding trumps the others. Those appalled at Eisenhower's hasty cover-up can invoke Kant; Ike's supporters might counter with Machiavelli. Theologians can debate which of eight (or three) categories Ike's lies fall into, and whether God will ultimately grant him a pardon. Utilitarians, meanwhile, have lifetime employment teasing out the consequences of Ike's actions, and they might long savor Ike's tale for its aesthetic charm as part of society's cultural heritage.

---

[38] The ease by which personal preferences can be raised up to "noble principles" is illustrated by Nyberg (*The Varnished Truth*, 10–11), who sorts "good" from "bad" lies without any explicit moral standard. Large-scale tax evasion, dishonest appeals by televangelists, cigarette advertising, false reasoning regarding sexism and racism, sexual infidelity, and several other behaviors are reprehensible lies. However, various social graces that distort a harsh reality are forgivable lies (among others). Nyberg is apparently a (selective) Philosopher-King, willing to dispense absolution as he sees fit.

Philosophical deficiencies—that is, ambiguous terminology or contra-dictory precepts—are not the culprit here, though, to be sure, these flour-ish. Far more damaging is that few people in the "real world" find these idiosyncratic musings of intellectuals useful. In commercial language these evaluative schemes are unmarketable products. This disinterest in eval-uative schemes exists despite the public's insatiable appetite for scandal and journalists' penchant for exposing official double-dealing. Explaining this inattention is not exactly rocket science: observers are quite content with their own homemade evaluative frameworks, namely, those of mo-mentary opportunism. Why fret about pardonable sins, future net ben-efits, or comparable "Great Thoughts" when crass self-interest suffices? Why not just castigate enemies as liars while helping friends to escape the same indictment? This is the triumph of ideology, not theology, and it is doubtful whether this inclination is reversible. If this point seems dubi-ous, just count the number of Republicans who were uneasy over Clinton being charged with perjury or feminists who were outraged over his convoluted interpretation of "sexual relationship." One can only surmise that if two-thousand-plus years of cogitation have failed to supply an accepted evaluative formula, we will continue to wait.

V. Lying and the Law

A remarkable feature of the "lying literature" is its neglect of the law. Philosophers, political theorists, psychiatrists, and untold other academic professionals dwell on the most arcane distinctions to (supposedly) illu-minate mendacity, save legal proceedings. Even Bok's outwardly com-prehensive *Lying* only momentarily touches on perjury, and then without any reference to statutes. (Her concern is the lawyer-client relationship.) This indifference is stunning. A civic life in which the justice system is plagued with chronic dishonesty is unthinkable. Better to have undue campaign hyperbole or leaders unable to tell truth from falsehood. After all, only the courts can protect the rule of law and severely punish liars, so falsification in the legal system should be front and center in any account of lying.

More important, the exigencies of trials force us to confront lying *seri-ously*. We can endlessly debate the philosophical or linguistic quandaries inherent in lying, but how should a judge or jury act when asked to believe improbable tales in a murder case? Juries seldom have the luxury to wait for historical evidence regarding ultimate societal benefits. Might the judge summon a theologian to see if the accused's likely falsehood is merely a minor sin ultimately punishable by God? Or does the accused's dishonesty menace the very foundations of civic life? Clearly, regardless of how lying is treated in learned tomes, it is in the courts where lying is concretely defined and punished. If the situation is bleak here, then we are surely defenseless against mendacity.

The law addresses dishonesty in multiple places, and we should note at the outset that lying is not automatically a crime. Going from lying to conviction for lying is an immense distance. Section 1001 of Title 18 of the United States Code, for example, covers defrauding the government in business, supplying false information in employment applications, and similar dealings raising issues of truthfulness.[39] Laws on obstruction of justice, slander and libel, deceptive advertising, and securities fraud likewise touch upon lying. There was, of course, a robust debate during the Clinton years on how the constitutional term "high crimes and misdemeanors" might apply to lying in high office. Nevertheless, we shall limit inquiry to courtroom behavior.

A useful starting point is what the law calls "impeaching a witness" — attacking the witness's credibility or believability. This is not the crime of perjury, a subject that we shall examine below. "Being impeached" may not even bring any legal sanction. Establishing that a witness is not believable is the issue, and discrediting a witness may not involve unmasking an outright intent to deceive (i.e., lying), but this is beside the point. The key question concerns witness credibility regardless of motive. An absolutely honest witness may not be credible simply due to faulty memory, impaired eyesight, mental illness, or distance from the events about which testimony is given, among dozens of other honest explanations. There are other medical reasons that might be cited to diminish a witness's credibility, for example, Alzheimer's or drug abuse. Such an impaired witness may not be telling the truth, but is technically not lying.

Federal and state evidentiary guidelines plus established legal custom are often a jumble of opaque regulations and guiding judicial pronouncements. These rules even baffle lawyers who do not specialize in uncovering the whole truth and nothing but the truth. For these reasons, explications of witness impeachment can vary somewhat across legal texts. This confusion is hardly unexpected given, as I have previously depicted, the multiple meanings of a 'lie'. (This point should be recalled when my conclusion considers the implications of ridding society of mendacity.) Nevertheless, a few simple principles are apparent.[40] In general, a witness can be impeached either by intrinsic or extrinsic evidence. Intrinsic evidence derives from information that directly comes from the

---

[39] Chad B. Pimental, "False Statements," *American Criminal Law Review* 38, no. 3 (Summer 2001): 709–32.

[40] This discussion draws heavily from Steven I. Friedland, *Evidence Problems and Materials*, 2d ed. (New York: Matthew Bender and Co., 2000); and Stephen A. Saltzburg, Michael M. Martin, and Daniel J. Capra, *Federal Rules of Evidence Manual*, 8th ed., vol. 3 (Newark, NJ: LexisNexis, 2002). Only U.S. federal rules, particularly Rules 608 and 609 of the Federal Rules of Evidence, are considered here. Individual state codes are probably roughly comparable, but this cannot be assumed on many minor though potentially critical points. Differences also pertain to civil versus criminal cases. Our neglect of state-by-state rules is no small matter since criminal cases are usually tried in state courts. There are also unwritten custom and principles that hark back to the common law (compounded by the inevitable ambiguities). Finally, rules often change by both statute and judicial interpretation.

witness, for example, factual inconsistencies offered in statements. Intrinsic evidence can also be drawn by exposing contradictions to previous testimony or by showing a purported fact to be demonstrably incorrect (e.g., that the witness claimed to be watching a nonexistent TV show). A witness's commission of past criminal acts that displayed a penchant for lying (such as insurance fraud) is especially relevant here, though this tactic can be constrained (see below).

By contrast, extrinsic evidence concerns evidence offered independently by other witnesses or documents. Extrinsic evidence is most common when a witness resists impeachment attempts by evasiveness or by endlessly pleading "I can't remember." Somebody asserting no knowledge of another person might be impeached by a photograph showing the two together or by proof revealing that the two once shared a jail cell. Securing opposing testimony can also challenge recollections; for example, if a witness said he saw a fistfight, other onlookers could deny this account. Establishing bias—that the witness had previous altercations or romantic relationships with the accused—can likewise cast doubts on veracity. For largely practical reasons, courts generally prefer intrinsic evidence regarding witness credibility since assembling extrinsic evidence is difficult and time-consuming ("a trial within a trial").

While the idea of lying in court will surely draw rebuke from defenders of truth, the American legal system scarcely wages war on this mendacity. The quest for "truth" at all costs is not the only aim; extracting truth must be balanced against other values, including optimal use of time. One clue into how noncredible testimony is assessed is provided by the multiple opportunities available to an impeached witness. Escape routes abound over and above conceding defective hearing, blurred vision, or similar "honest" errors. For one, an impeached witness can be rehabilitated during court proceedings by skilled questioning. "Refreshing one's memory" is one recognized rescue tactic; a friendly lawyer steers his or her client toward accuracy by "reminding" the witness of certain other details. Interestingly, Rule 612 of the Federal Rules of Evidence allows "refreshment" via evidence not otherwise admissible in court, for example, hearsay. These "refreshment facts" need not themselves be authenticated. (Refreshment can also demonstrate incredulity, as well.) Moreover, according to Rule 613, if a witness says "I don't remember" or fails to supply past testimony, then no contradiction exists, and thus no false testimony. However, in extreme cases of contrived "forgetting" impeachment is possible with a single statement.

Rules concerning the exclusion of past criminality in impugning a witness's veracity are especially revealing. The issue here is whether statements can be challenged on the grounds that the witness is a convicted criminal, "a bad character," or a proven liar, so why believe that a leopard has changed its spots? Nevertheless, according to federal standards, prior criminal conviction cannot usually be used to impeach truthfulness if the

conviction is older than ten years or the person was released from confinement more than ten years ago (whichever is later). Nor can alleged
false testimony be challenged on these grounds if the witness was pardoned or had his sentence annulled, provided that no intervening felony
conviction occurred. Finally, a past conviction cannot be used to impeach
if that crime was similar to the currently charged crime, the crime was
inflammatory, or the witness has been impeached in other ways.

In short, these (and other) restrictions offer handy escape routes from
appearing to be a noncredible witness. Talented trial lawyers undoubtedly have countless useful ploys to sway jurors, independent of what is
permitted by the rules. Note well, these afforded protections are integral
to the American legal system, not despicable ruses to protect deceit. It is
a matter of balancing the need for truth with other valuable rights. If only
for practical reasons, such as limits on what can be investigated or how
many character witnesses can be called, attaining absolute truth from
witnesses is an unreachable goal. These complicated rules offer only minimal adequacy for truth-finding, not a mechanical instrument to unearth
unvarnished reality.

Whereas to impeach witness credibility only exposes lack of credibility,
the demonstration of perjury criminalizes deceit, although, in a few instances, an impeached witness invites court reprimand. Again, this simple idea of perjury has burgeoned into an immensely knotty legal subject,
complete with multiple statutes and endless commentaries, but the core
of perjury at the federal level is giving false testimony to a grand jury, to
a court, and (where specified by statute) during other proceedings such as
discovery or legislative hearings.[41] There is also the offense of suborna-
tion of perjury—convincing another to commit perjury. The question at
hand, then, is when does one commit perjury, and how does the federal
government treat this offense as reflected in prosecution and sentencing?

The simplest element (relatively) of perjury is that the lie must be under
oath. Federal rules are imprecise regarding this oath and, in fact, wording
can differ by jurisdiction (and provisions exist for those who refuse to
swear on a Bible or otherwise invoke religion). The oath must, however,
be statute-based and be administered by competent lawful authority. Improper oaths include those given to grand juries exceeding their appoint-
ment terms, to legislative committees operating beyond their authorized
jurisdiction, or to those without a quorum. Likewise, the court in which
the oath is given must have proper jurisdiction if the oath is to be valid.
However, having a law declared unconstitutional does not retroactively
void conviction, nor does being inappropriately charged permit escape
from perjury. The absence of counsel likewise does not invalidate a per-

---

[41] 18 U.S.C. §1621 (2001). A reasonably succinct though occasionally technical summary of
federal perjury law can be found in Angel Saad, "Perjury," *American Criminal Law Review* 34,
no. 2 (Winter 1997): 857–81.

jury conviction. Perjury can also occur in either civil or criminal cases and when testifying under a grant of immunity, unless it can be shown that this immunity was closely connected to the matter covered by the grant.

A perjury conviction requires a showing that the defendant knew that his or her testimony was false. The legal emphasis is on *willfully* offering false testimony. The burden of proof is on the government, and a slippery witness and clever defense lawyers often devise ingenious escape routes.[42] Evidence must be direct, or if that is not feasible, circumstantial proof must be compelling. If doubts arise, the bias is against the government's case. Confusion, errors of memory, mistakes, or even inconsistencies do *not* automatically prove perjury. The prosecutor's desire to elicit some testimony may, in fact, breed tolerance for imperfect recollections, and the reasonable possibility always exists that the witness misconstrued the question or read too much into it. Burgeoning immigration makes the translation problem especially vexing since non-English speakers can readily become confused or garble their answers (and, of course, this can be faked). Tolerance for honest mistakes versus calculated mendacity is particularly common in far-ranging grand jury proceedings.

Nor is perjury committed if a response is evasive, intentionally misleading, ambiguous, or arguably false, provided that it was literally true. Also, "attempted perjury" is not a crime: if a witness believes that the sun rises in the west and "lies" by saying it rises in the east, no perjury is committed. An example of escaping perjury by playing upon uncertainty occurred in a case when the defendant was asked if he had ever traveled to Florida with a "Mr. X".[43] The response was "no," and though the government had evidence that the two individuals were in Florida together, *conceivably* they did not travel there together. Proof of perjury required unambiguous evidence showing that the two had traveled together, and the government lacked such proof. No matter how strong the government's suspicion that, indeed, the two had traveled together, a perjury conviction was impermissible.[44] The Supreme Court has ruled that it is the prosecutor's responsibility to ask unambiguous questions and to insist on clear answers.[45] Precise prosecutorial questioning is oblig-

---

[42] Law journals are filled with ingenious successful defenses, but it is difficult to quantify the value of these tactics. Richard H. Underwood's "Perjury! The Charges and Defense" (*Duquesne Law Review* 36, no. 4 [Summer 1998]: 715–94) recounts a defendant's attempt to pass off a phony college transcript in order to enlist as a Navy doctor. When asked if he submitted a transcript from Ohio State University, he said, "No." The judge did *not* rule the admission perjury since the defendant knew the document to be fake, and thus not "an OSU transcript."

[43] *United States v. Wall*, 371 F. 2d 398 (6th Cir. 1967).

[44] The cultural differences problem discussed in the previous section should be recalled. Jurors may have dissimilar interpretations of words, let alone of lying. A defendant who denies that he beat his wife might be telling the truth in a culture where mere slapping around does not comprise "beating." Similarly, rules of evidence can vary culturally (e.g., the credibility of hearsay evidence may reflect the source's social standing or age).

[45] *Bronston v. United States*, 409 U.S. 352 (1973).

atory since the jury's interpretations cannot be assumed. In fact, a perjury conviction can be overturned on appeal if the appeals court rules that the question eliciting alleged perjury was "fundamentally ambiguous." If contradictory statements are given, it is the government's obligation to prove them absolutely irreconcilable (though the prosecutor has no obligation to demonstrate which one is false).

There are, of course, limits to a court's acquiescence to such linguistic game playing. In one instance a defendant trying to escape a perjury verdict claimed that his reference to a "juice loan" applied to orange juice. The judge ruled that the jury could probably surmise that this slang expression referred to a loan with excessive interest (the term "juice" derives from "they will squeeze you if you don't pay"). In another case, a defendant denied meeting a woman in a New Orleans motel and later claimed to be truthful since the motel was actually outside city limits. Nevertheless, the judge held that in the context of the questioning, the defendant surely realized that the query concerned the New Orleans metropolitan area.[46] On the whole, however, being technically correct is a sturdy defense even if this might mislead.

The issue of perjury by silence, a topic long debated by theologians and philosophers, also periodically surfaces. As legal scholar Peter Meijes Tiersma notes, silence is not the same thing as evasion by hemming or hawing or otherwise being inarticulate. Nor is it equivalent to refusing to testify or avoiding a court appearance altogether. At least one state court (California) has ruled that absolute stone silence may be grounds for perjury. In this case a prospective juror named Meza repeatedly remained silent when asked about whether he knew the defendant or whether there was anything that would hinder him from rendering an impartial verdict.[47] Eventually, however, Meza admitted to being the defendant's brother-in-law and further owned up that bad blood existed between them. Meza then went on trial for perjury. Interestingly, Meza's original California trial found that silence precluded perjury and he was therefore acquitted. The California Court of Appeal then set aside this acquittal on the grounds that nonverbal actions can substitute for verbal or written statements. Similar convictions have resulted from not filling out forms, but legal consensus scarcely exists on this "defense by silence."

An additional element of perjury is materiality—whether the falsehood actually concerns the issues of a case, not ephemera. If Alfred E. Neuman states his name *sans* middle initial, this is not perjury unless the "E" were relevant to trial proceedings. The customary standard of materiality is whether or not a statement *might* influence the trial's outcome, regardless of whether it actually does. This includes statements that enhance or

---

[46] Both of these examples are from Peter Meijes Tiersma, "The Language of Perjury: 'Literal Truth', Ambiguity, and the False Statement Requirement," *Southern California Law Review* 63, no. 2 (January 1990): 373–431.

[47] *People v. Meza*, 188 Cal. App 3d 1631; 234 Cal. Rptr. (1987).

impugn witness credibility. Materiality can be deceptively complicated; for example, lying about a seemingly trivial item could misdirect court inquiry and therefore be "material" despite its apparently petty nature. (What if the missing "E" signifies gang membership?) Again, the burden of proof regarding all of these requirements rests on the government, though judges enjoy ample discretion in deciding materiality.

These safeguards make securing a perjury conviction arduous. Sections 1621 and 1623 of Title 18 of the United States Code cover perjury, and each has its own requirements, and the government is free to elect either section in its prosecution. Both, however, offer hurdles to successful prosecution. Under Section 1621 two witnesses are required to convict, though in exceptional instances one witness plus substantial evidence may suffice. Section 1623(e) requires the difficult "proof beyond reasonable doubt" standard. Under Section 1623(a) a witness can also be indicted for perjury based on materials such as books, records, recordings, or similar items that are submitted as evidence and known to be false.

Conveniently for the accused, Section 1623 (but not 1621) permits testimony that invites perjury to be recanted or modified. This defense must be done explicitly; the old version must clearly be retracted and repudiated and in the same legal proceedings in which false testimony was initially offered. Though far from a guaranteed immunity against perjury, courts can look kindly upon such behavior, especially if the potential perjurer uses this newfound honesty to show lack of deceptive intent. Grand jury witnesses in particular might be cut greater slack since they lack counsel to protect them from leading questions that can ensnarl them in contradictions. Perhaps the best defense against a charge of perjury is to be acquitted. Though a "not guilty" verdict does not formally annul a perjury charge, it is unlikely to be pursued further by the government since the testimony was credible to the jury, a fact consistent with honest testimony.

Perjury is a serious offense under federal law, and in a criminal case perjury might cause a witness to be considered an accessory to the crime. The relevance of honest testimony is also well understood by judges who treat it with the utmost attention. Nevertheless, but hardly surprising in light of the depicted roadblocks, perjury cases are relatively rare (at least in federal court) despite anecdotal evidence that perjury is on the increase. According to some observers, despite its frequency, perjury is simply not a high priority crime in a beleaguered, often overworked system.[48] Between 1993 and 1999 the number of federal district court perjury cases averaged around 100 annually (from a high of 126 to a low of 85). During the same period, the total number of criminal cases filed was approximately 50,000 per year, so perjury is clearly a tiny drop in the

---

[48] Anecdotal evidence on the widespread incidence of unchallenged perjury is presented in Underwood, "Perjury! The Charges and Defense," 716–17.

bucket. (The perjury figures are for charges brought, not convictions.) Of the 126 cases filed in 1999, only 106 brought convictions. Though sentences can be tough, imprisonment of up to five years plus hefty fines (depending on the statute), only 80 of the 106 people convicted in 1999 served prison time, with the average sentence being 22.9 months.[49] To be sure, the vast bulk of criminal cases are tried in state courts, and the number of perjury convictions in these courts is indubitably much larger, but the message here is clear: the Federal Government is hardly waging a war on courtroom mendacity.

VI. Conclusion

My analysis began with an obvious paradox: condemnations of public mendacity are ubiquitous and yet lying abounds. My aim has not been to argue any side in this conflict or to reconcile these positions. That task is hopeless; it seems to be the human condition to castigate the liar and simultaneously to promote deceit. One might surmise, as a few observers speculate, that this duality is hardwired into our DNA. Surely no society can endure without honesty somewhere, yet deceit has proven itself an absolutely vital survival tool. No doubt, much of humanity would never be born if not for the persuasive powers of less-than-forthright seducers. If history is our guide, calls for "complete honesty" are therapeutic delusions. Any anthropologists discovering deceit-free societies have apparently kept their findings secret; accounts of the near opposite are more commonplace. Will Rogers's taunt about prohibition in Oklahoma is appropriate here: Oklahomans will always vote dry so long as they can stagger to the polls.

The biological inevitably of lying, though likely true, is immaterial to our acquiescence to dishonesty. The more practical point is that *systematically* separating liars from truth-tellers with something approaching 100 percent success is a quest doomed to failure. The account given in this essay is a catalogue of loopholes available to the chronic teller of falsehoods. The menu overflows, ranging from bona fide psychological disorders to convoluted linguistic interpretations of what 'is' is. If these fail, insist that one's lie "might" be true. Then, who can say for sure what future investigations might uncover? Attempts to devise and legally impose anti-dishonesty mechanisms, for example, polygraphs, have proven less than successful, though modern technology may eventually provide a solution (and countermeasures as well). Nor can one marshal a parade of "Great Thinkers" to condemn deceit. The battle of dueling quotations will be eternally inconclusive; virtually every view is endorsed somewhere in some dense tome. Further, add cultural variations in what com-

[49] Administrative Office of the United States Courts, *Annual Report of the Director, 1999* (Washington, DC: Administrative Office of the United States Courts), 204–6.

prises truth and falsehood: some societies seemingly *depend* on deceit. Futile court efforts to stamp out witness deceit or to punish perjury speak loudly here: it might be accomplished, but only with a near-impossible effort that could undermine cherished civil liberties. Lastly, all the king's horses and all the king's men—attorneys, investigative journalists, government regulators, and other guardians of public honesty, including worthy volunteers—have failed to put together a meaningful bulwark against the tide of dishonesty.

Given these failures, what might be the next step in purifying public discourse? Should Bill Gates establish a foundation to promote heartfelt speeches condemning dishonesty? What about instituting truth by ordeal or resurrecting Torquemada to restore public truth-telling? What about establishing an "unbiased" National Truth Commission to verify contentious statements, as a board of rabbis might verify meat as kosher? *Quis custodiet ipsos custodies*? ("Who will guard the guardians?")[50] Surely, upping the criminal penalty for lying would be pointless when the standards themselves make conviction arduous. Imagine incarcerating office seekers for outlandish predictions about Social Security. Their rock-solid defense is obvious: "Just wait and see!" Equally foolish are utopian schemes to inculcate a more truth-minded citizenry via education or early socialization. This is pure fantasy in a world where experts disagree on mundane historical fact, parents lie to children for "good reason," and easy-to-anger interest groups uphold fictions masquerading as truth. Why should we venerate George "I cannot tell a lie" Washington when he was, after all, a slaveholder? Anti-mendacity training is also likely to fail. A robust psychological literature strongly counsels against the hope that lie detection skills can be developed.[51]

The deepest problem plaguing any ameliorative effort concerns the very essence of lying: intent. The intent to deceive, not intrinsic truth or falseness, is the lie's quintessential element. This inner condition must be proven, and is, therefore, depending on the standards of proof, the mother of all loopholes. So long as this ingredient remains beyond scrutiny, or rendered irrelevant via recourse to some psychological disorder, the verdict of lying must *necessarily* be inconclusive, save in the most obvious circumstances. One might say that a statement appears to be a lie, is likely to be false, or even that it is most certainly a lie, but doubts will probably remain.

Yet, beyond a certain point, seeking entry into this inner sanctum to gain "smoking gun" proof of mendacious intent undeniably invites to-

---

[50] History buffs will recall that during the 1964 U.S. presidential election those who mistrusted Barry Goldwater's psychic competence suggested the creation of a national mental health certification committee headed by esteemed psychiatrists. This never came to pass, but even if it had, it would not guarantee our immunity from deceptive presidents who might lead the nation into war by promising easy victories and misrepresenting defeats.

[51] See, for example, Bella M. DePaulo and Robert Rosenthal, "Telling Lies," *Journal of Personality and Social Psychology* 37, no. 10 (1979): 1713–22.

talitarianism. Establishing truth is difficult enough in a courtroom where there are oaths and cross-examinations. In everyday discourse the obstacles are even greater. Recall the many failed experiments to detect lying, from use of certain drugs, to physical coercion and torture, to lie detectors. The link between vigorous campaigns to unearth truth and totalitarianism is absolutely inescapable; the invasive technology to confirm lies is the technology to destroy freedom.

Such imposed honesty would, moreover, probably be incredibly disruptive politically. Discussions on untold currently taboo topics (e.g., race) would be impossible. Heretics might flee to Amsterdam or pretend to be converts to escape death threats. Civility and decorum would also decline. So long as one's private thoughts are free, incentives to lie are irrepressible since one can always lie again and say "But I really believe it, so I'm not lying," or "According to my personal definition, black really is white." To surrender this privacy to secure a more honest civic life—an impossible act, anyhow—is a horrendous bargain, inviting a Stalinism on steroids. Better to have a world that includes some lying than to authorize a government to peek into what we really believe. It is one thing to implore greater honesty; another to compel it.

This dreary portrait scarcely counsels fatalism or some yet-to-be-invented government program. At least in the public realm, we are not at the mercy of swarms of Pinocchios and opportunistic sophists, though in private relationships they are more abundant. There is a sturdy defense against lying in the public realm, one impervious to all the concocted linguistic and philosophical excuses for mendacity. It is perfectly suited to making reasonable judgments under sometimes difficult circumstances and has little directly to do with theology, morality, or any other arduous truth-justification. Neither must two witnesses be subpoenaed nor must mendacity be proven beyond a reasonable doubt across countless cultural settings. This great instrument of punishment to combat public dishonesty is the democratic election. Provided that liars can be banished via the ballot box, regardless of their subterfuges or self-imposed delusions, civic life can be realistically honest—not perfect, but close enough for civil society. Of course this assumes that truth in politics is desired by most people, a flattering assumption, as the continued popularity of certain former leaders famous for deception suggests.

Elections resemble trials but with the advantage that punishment need not rest on any tough evidentiary requirements or arcane interpretations of abstract relationships. The very "up or out" crudeness of elections is the key to their effectiveness—"frontier six-shooter justice," if you will. It is sufficient that the voter smell an unacceptable lie; a complex trial is unnecessary. One merely votes to punish, and if the miscreant is not standing for reelection, then penalize his or her party instead. Or, conversely, if voters appreciate artful deceit, as an audience might relish a conjurer, then reelect the liar. Voters, not psychiatrists or theologians, must decide whether the trickery was "really" deceit, whether it was material, and whether punishment is deserved, among multiple other issues. Judgment by voting is, admittedly, not terribly sophisticated, but compared to alternatives, it is the most useful weapon in the public arsenal of a democracy. Perhaps it is the *only* reliable popular weapon, as Clinton's impeachment trial indicated. In short, if you don't like liars, don't put them in office. If fooled, don't reelect them. If they are not standing for reelection, retaliate against their party. Anything more invites a troubled public life, and that's the honest truth.

Political Science, University of Illinois at Urbana-Champaign

A SUBJECT OF DISTASTE; AN OBJECT OF JUDGMENT

By John Haldane

It really is of importance, not only what men do,
but also what manner of men they are that do it.
—J. S. Mill, *On Liberty*

I. The Private and Personal Lives of Public Figures

In recent years it has become increasingly common in the United States
and in the United Kingdom for newspapers and other media to expose
problematic aspects of the private lives of political (and other public)
figures; or, since the facts may already be in the public domain, to draw
wider attention to them and to make them the subject of commentary.
These "problematic aspects" may include past or continuing physical or
psychological illness, eating disorders, drug and alcohol abuse or dependence, financial difficulties, family conflict, infidelity, or certain sexual
proclivities of both the political figures themselves and of their family
members or intimates. In the United States, the most prominent cases are
probably those of President Bill Clinton in relation to a series of alleged
extramarital affairs leading up to the scandal involving White House
intern Monica Lewinsky, and of President John F. Kennedy, also in relation to marital infidelities. The latter exposure was, of course retrospective, as were revelations of similar matters concerning other presidents
and holders of high office. Up until the mid-1960s, while it was sometimes known to the press that politicians had "problems" in their private
lives, it was rare for these to be made public. Sometimes it might be
reported, or more likely hinted, that a figure had a "complex" or "difficult" personal life, and the public was left to infer whatever it might from
this (generally concluding that infidelity, alcoholism, or both, were probably at issue). The recent culture of exposure results from a combination
of factors, including changed attitudes toward public discussion of sexual
conduct, changed standards of sexual behavior, recognition of the scale of
Cold War espionage and of its practice of blackmail, a general decline in
social deference, a threat to the print media posed by the growth of
television, and the rise of satirical entertainment. All of these elements
were present in the case that marked the establishment of the culture of
exposure in the U.K.: the 'Profumo scandal' of 1963. For those unaware of
this episode, it may be sufficient to say that it involved the then-secretary
of state for war, members of the British aristocracy, a Soviet naval attaché,

and a number of "society" call girls, and that it contributed to the resignation of Prime Minister Harold Macmillan and the subsequent fall from power of the Conservative Party.[1] In the United States, the culture of exposure developed somewhat later and took shape in the period of the Watergate scandal, which damaged the American public's perception of the governing classes just as the Profumo scandal had in Britain.

The reticence in reporting and commentary characteristic of the first half of the twentieth century was largely cultural; that is, it was a matter of general discretion and of judgment as to what it was decent to say of someone, and of what information was fit matter for reception into family homes. No doubt, however, it also expressed a degree of solidarity among members of the political class, and of self-interest on the part of journalists who could not afford to lose access to sources. These considerations now apply far less extensively: the idea of restraining reportage on the ground of respect for the parties in question, or out of regard for readers' sensitivities, now seems remote and almost quaint. Memories of the Clinton scandal being securely fixed in public consciousness, I need not cite the sort of salacious details that are now commonly reported in newspapers or in other media. Suffice it to say that they presume on the part of audiences very different attitudes regarding what are tolerable, let alone welcome, subjects of public discussion. As for solidarity and mutual interest, the intensity of competition within and between the various media, which has been made all the more intense by the development of the Internet, is now such that no reporter is likely to forgo an opportunity to relay a scandal for fear of losing subsequent access to sources. Everyone talks, everyone wants to talk, and everyone wants to listen—or so it can seem.

As in the United States, so in the United Kingdom: as memorable as Clinton's problem-strewn career is the troubled life of Princess Diana, which, like the former, was charted in ever increasing detail. This coverage was the subject of some complaint, and following her tragic death there was much talk of curbing the trend to report and comment on the private lives of public figures. However, this talk was without discernible serious intent and certainly without effect. The year of the princess's death also saw the election of the New Labour government; since then, several of its leading figures have seen aspects of their lives, and those of their families and intimates, become the subject of intensive reporting and commentary. The press has carried accounts of Prime Minister Tony Blair's wife's property dealings with a "confidence man" and the public intoxication of Blair's son; of a Home Secretary's son's attempted drug dealing; of the Lord Chancellor's son's drug addiction and associated prosecution in the U.S.; and of a Foreign Secretary's extramarital affair, as well as

---

[1] For details of this and other scandals involving members of both houses of Parliament, see Matthew Parris, *Great Parliamentary Scandals: Four Centuries of Calumny, Smear, and Innuendo* (London: Robson Books, 1996).

reports of the personal peccadilloes of other lesser government officials. The press has also raised the issue of people's sexual proclivities to the point where a shadow cabinet contender for the leadership of the Conservative Party admitted to a homosexual past, and another front-bencher confirmed his settled gay identity. Assuming that members of the royal family also count as political figures in the context of a constitutional monarchy (in which one party or coalition governs at the sovereign's pleasure and another constitutes Her Majesty's loyal opposition), the list of subjects of exposure, dissemination, and commentary must include the marital difficulties of three of the queen's children, as well as the behavior of other royals.

Such are some of the facts concerning the presentation and discussion of public figures' private lives. How should one judge these facts? It is pretty clear that any reasonable answer will have to take account of circumstances, form, and content. That is to say, some methods of acquiring information about public figures violate norms of justice by being intentionally deceitful or otherwise dishonest, or by involving threats. Also, some forms of exposure or public presentation are so gross and gratuitous as to be beyond principled defense. Had, for example, explicit photographs of Ms. Lewinsky and President Clinton been taken during their intimacies, it would have been quite improper for these to be made public, for they would be shockingly offensive, and such obscenity would serve no clear public purpose not already achieved by general verbal reports of the sort of thing that took place (whatever that public purpose might have been).

Again, some matters are so far removed from a public figure's office, or from the exercise of his or her duties, that no case for revelation or publication can be made from the side of public interest (as against public prurience). It may be of relevance to know the state of the lining of the president's bowels, inasmuch as this bears upon his capacity to carry on the work of his office, but it is hard to conceive a likely circumstance in which it would be relevant to know of the size of his private parts. (That said, however, it is reported that at least one postwar occupant of the Oval Office was keen to draw attention to this aspect of himself, and it might well be a matter of public interest to know about *that* behavioral fact.)

Similarly, while some matters may be of sorts that are relevant to evaluating the conduct of public figures, revelation may still be ill advised. Even if the means of acquiring such information were not unjust and the proposed manner of presentation would not be gratuitously sensational, it may well be the case that other concerns outweigh the benefits of revelation. The interests of third parties might be such that publication would irreparably damage them. The cost of these unintended but foreseen secondary effects of otherwise legitimate exposure may simply be too high. Public humiliation is a terrible thing and it ought not to be occasioned lightly.

II. An Initial Dialectic

So much will readily be agreed, I think, even when it is accepted that there is a general liberty of public speech and a particular freedom of the press and media (whether derived from general liberty or independent of it) to report and comment upon what, in good conscience, they judge to be appropriate subject matter. But what of other cases in which the foregoing objections to revelation do not hold, or in which further considerations may defeat them? Among the most common grounds given in justification of exposing or making more widely known private problems are the following.[2]

First, that public figures are in a categorically different position from other members of society. They stand upon a stage, presenting one or other aspects of themselves to the populace or some constituency within it. Like musical or theatrical performers, or street or media evangelists, their occupancy of the public realm is not *per accidens* but *per se*, and as such their lives may legitimately be inspected and commented upon. In short, the right of privacy is implicitly relativized to a status or role, and it diminishes in scope as these features become more extensively public.

Second, that while all persons have a general interest in privacy, and perhaps, thereby have a right to keep personal information undisclosed or closely confined, this establishes a defeasible presumption of privacy, not an absolute entitlement to it. This presumption lapses when disclosure serves some relevant and pressing public interest. The state of health of the commander in chief evidently bears upon matters of public interest, as does the fact that a legislator's personal circumstances provide an immediate incentive to favor (or disfavor) relaxing prohibitions on activities in which he, his family, or his close associates are involved. Likewise, the fact that someone's reputation for honesty, reliability, and so on, is a fabrication sustained by publicists and is belied by a personal history of deceit, duplicity, and disloyalty, provides reason to disclose relevant aspects of this history in the service of disabusing the public of its illusions. (It is here allowed that this category of warrant for disclosure may not be conclusive, for other interests may prove countervailing.)

Third, it may be supposed that some general public good is realized by the disclosure of personal details where these provide entertainment or satisfaction. This justification can be developed in a variety of ways— some high, some low, some simple, some complex—but the basic idea is that people benefit from learning of the lives of others, and this benefit can only be common and extensive where the others in question are public figures.

---

[2] This initial taxonomy of justifications for public disclosure follows David Archard's discussion in David Archard, "Privacy, the Public Interest, and a Prurient Public," in Matthew Keiran, ed., *Media Ethics* (London: Routledge, 1998). Archard suggests that public gossip about the private lives of individuals may serve a valuable social purpose.

In Section IV below, I proceed to a further kind of justification that is related to all three of those given above, but that is more complex and is linked to a particular philosophy of common public and political life that would now appear to be virtually moribund, namely, traditional conservatism. In this kind of justification, four considerations are prominent. First, political morality supervenes upon a range of normative social relations that imply various mutual responsibilities. Second, there are different, reasonable expectations associated with different roles and stations. Third, the character of public agents is of legitimate interest because of their special normative relationship to others. Fourth, we learn about ourselves and develop apt responses by viewing the lives of others, and people with public roles provide salient and influential examples. In showing how these four considerations cohere as part of a single account, one needs to see how freedom and value, and individuals and society, stand in relations more or less opposite to those in which they are now commonly conceived. Thus, to help illustrate the relation between individuals and society, for example, the family might be analogized to a complex organism, the parts of which function and enjoy life through their contribution to the life of the whole. While the limits of such a comparison should be evident even to those who favor it, the point that I wish to make is that for the traditional conservative a comparison such as this makes better sense of his experience and understanding of society than do discussions of individuals and their relationships in markets, contracts, and wholly voluntary associations. Before pursuing the kind of justification linked to traditional conservatism, however, let me acknowledge three rather obvious responses to the three grounds given above for exposing or making more widely known hitherto private aspects of the lives of public figures.

First, those who find themselves the objects of public interest may do so in virtue of public offices that they have chosen to pursue, but, equally, they may not. The occupant of the Oval Office arrived there by having placed himself before the American public and having sought and won electoral approval; this is not true of Britain's Queen, nor of the immediate members of her family. However, while the resources of hereditary office may provide some protection from or compensation for the liability to probing investigation, there are likely to be no such mitigating factors available to those who find themselves unexpectedly drawn into the limelight in consequence of special circumstances or associations. The lover of someone who murders children, and who herself has been party to consensual torture at his hands, may have chosen her intimate unwisely, but she is not, on that account alone, fair game for exposure, any more than are countless others who find themselves in undesirable relationships. Even those who have sought the limelight might have done so on the implicit understanding that it was this or that aspect of themselves that was to be displayed for appreciation and criticism, and not other, "reserved" features. The sportsman who seeks employment and reward on the basis of his physical prowess does not by this fact alone render himself a legitimate target of inquiries into his marital fidelity or financial competence. The principle 'if public then fair copy' has no credibility, save to the extent that it represents an elliptical reference to some other, more feasible but limited justification.

Such a justification may be forthcoming under the heading of the second category of warrant, namely, public interest. There are documented cases where the competence of public figures has been chronically impaired due to causes that, like the impairment itself, have been kept secret from the public. Likewise, there are known cases where public figures have sought to change laws for reasons of personal interest. There are also on record cases where the reality of a public figure's life gives the lie to each and every claim to merit or virtue that he had presented in his public declarations. All such cases provide some warrant for disclosure and commentary, but for every example like these there are twenty or thirty or a hundred specious defenses along the following lines. *"The man is a drunk or has a chronic illness."* Well, we are all in some way or another and to some degree slaves to our appetites, and it is too easy to point to a single impediment or addiction, overlooking a spread of vulnerabilities or dependencies. Likewise we are all prone to sickness, to days off, and to impaired efficiency, and we may be less aware of the fact and the effects of these, and less diligent about managing and compensating for them, than is someone burdened with a significant and continuing health problem. *"She favors relaxation of the ban because her son is in violation of it."* Might not the experience of her son's situation have drawn her attention to a legislative situation that she had not previously considered, thus leading her to see its iniquity? *"He criticizes pornography but then spends time with it."* Is not the troubled sinner well placed to recognize the vice and the viciousness of his sin? May not his verdict be more valuable than that of one abandoned to temptation, or of another impervious to it? The overall point is clear, I hope: here, we are in the field of particular cases, not of a general justification.

The third would-be warrant for disclosure, publicization, or commentary—that some public good is served by entertaining or otherwise satisfying people's curiosity—is liable to shock those who take themselves to be formed of finer material. The simple fact, however, is that humankind does delight in tales of fracture and dislocation, the more so when these involve abandonment to base appetites or expose inabilities to cope. This datum is not easily explained, but only the ignorant, the ideologically blinded, or the self-deceived would deny it. The relevant rejoinder is not that it isn't so, but that its being so provides no more warrant for disclosure than does the fact of our common baseness provide justification for gratifying it.

III. Individuals and Institutional Contexts

Thus far, then, I have considered how the circumstances, form, and content of the disclosure or broader dissemination of personal information might render the exposure unjustified and reprehensible. I have also considered grounds on which the presumption of privacy or confinement might be defeated. To carry the discussion forward, I shall next describe two examples (both real), and discuss the ambivalence some decent and conscientious souls might feel in contemplation of them.

First, it happened not so long ago that someone stood for the leadership of a major political party in the U.K. who had been viewed with favor by a former leader of that party who was very widely admired within (and beyond) it. The candidate's personal life, however, at least in the past, was at odds with the values of the majority of the party and probably of the majority of its core supporters. In addition, there was reason to think that the candidate's moral opinions were likewise at odds with the party and its followers, though he was cautious about how he expressed himself and could not be quoted as publicly endorsing views considered to be anathema by those sharing the party's traditional outlook. The party being one that favored discretion and decorum but also upheld traditional personal morality, its members felt themselves in something of a bind: Would it be permissible, let alone proper, to advert to facts about the candidate's personal life in public discussion of his suitability for the leadership of the party? (The matter was never fully resolved in the minds of the faithful. Later, a senior member of that same party revealed in her memoirs that she had had an affair with a previous [married] leader, who had subsequently become Prime Minister.)

In the second, more recent example, the generally well-liked leader of another British political party was the subject of an extended interview on the BBC's principal television news and current affairs program. The purpose of the interview was to review the progress of the party since the general election and to assess the interviewee's leadership. In the course of the program, the interviewer, who is known for his generally combative style, surprised his guest and viewers by commenting that when he and his researchers were preparing for the interview, they were advised that the leader might well be drunk, this being purportedly his common condition. Having announced this, the interviewer then asked the leader how much he was liable to drink in the course of an evening, and whether he thought that he drank too much. In reply, the guest managed about as well as any human being might in such unexpected circumstances, and in the following days there was much commentary to and fro on the matter.

The leader survived the controversy, but no one can doubt that he suffered, whether in public repute or in personal embarrassment. Setting aside questions on the accuracy of the report of his drinking, and on whether, if true, the drinking impaired his fitness for office, broader issues arise about the manner of this disclosure and its relation to the character and quality of British public culture. (One MP from the governing New Labour Party complained in Parliament that the questioning was "highly personal and irrelevant to political debate." In response, the Leader of the House of Commons acknowledged that "[many MPs were] taken aback and distressed at the degree of personal questioning." The original interviewer was then moved to offer the following, less than fulsome apology: "I am sorry if any offence has been caused. Maybe there was one question too many on drink." Some will think that one question was one too many.)

Here, it is important to be aware that the BBC is a national public broadcasting service, free of commercial advertising and funded out of a compulsory U.K. license fee payable subsequent to the purchase of a television. The BBC was established and is regulated under a series of royal charters dating from 1922; its governors are appointed by the Crown to ensure that, among other things, it "maintains the high standards and values expected of the BBC as the nation's broadcaster." The formal opening declaration of the current charter serves as a reminder of the constitutional context within which the BBC is located: it begins, "Elizabeth the Second by the Grace of God of the United Kingdom of Great Britain and Northern Ireland and of Our other Realms and Territories Queen, Head of the Commonwealth, Defender of the Faith," and later continues

> in view of the widespread interest which is taken by Our Peoples in broadcasting services and of the great value of such services as means of disseminating information, education and entertainment, We believe it to be in the interests of Our Peoples in Our United Kingdom and elsewhere within the Commonwealth that there should be an independent corporation which should continue to provide broadcasting services.

The historic and continuing main home of the BBC is Broadcasting House in London. In the marble entrance hall stands an untranslated Latin inscription:

> *Templum hoc artium et musarum Anno Domini mcmxxxi rectore Johanni Reith primi dedicant gubernatores precantes ut messem bonam bona proferat sementis ut immunda omnia et inimica paci expellantur ut quaecunque pulchra sunt et sincera quaecunque binae famae ad haec avrem inclinans populaus virtutis et sapientiae semitam insistat* (This temple of the arts

and muses is dedicated [to Almighty God] by the first governors in
the year of Our Lord 1931, John Reith being the Director General, and
they pray that good seed sown may bring forth good harvest [and]
that all things foul or hostile to peace may be banished hence, and
that the people inclining their ear to whatsoever things that are lovely
and honest [and] whatsoever things are of good report may tread the
path of virtue and of wisdom).[3]

It is very likely that a far greater percentage of the early generations of
BBC studio and management staff would have been able to construe all
or part of the meaning of this inscription than could their counterparts in
Broadcasting House today. More importantly, it is very probable that
whether or not they could read the Latin original, those earlier generations would have recognized, if only in general terms, the New Testament
origins of the metaphor and of the message, drawn respectively from
Christ's parable of the sower (Matt. 13) and from Paul's instruction to the
Philippians. "[B]rethren, whatsoever things are honest, whatsoever things
are pure, whatsoever things are lovely, whatsoever things are of good
report; if there be any virtue, and if there be any praise, think on these
things" (Phil. 4:8).[4] Finally, it is highly likely that most of the early BBC
staff members agreed with the message, and that they embraced and
implemented its ideals. From the outset, and under Lord Reith's strong
direction, the BBC cultivated a high-minded public service ethos, which
saw broadcasting as contributing to the common good of the nation by
enlightening and improving the minds and morals of its listeners.[5] In this
connection the BBC was involved with the Adult Education Movement
and began the practice of broadcasting a daily Christian religious service.
Certainly the type of ennobling programming that the BBC was long
associated with conformed to the ideal of the common good.

Current BBC output indicates how far the corporation and the culture
have come from Lord Reith's lofty conception of public broadcasting.
Even those in the BBC who certainly would not share his Calvinist pu-
ritanism and opposition to unalloyed entertainment are increasingly given
to worrying about whether the corporation retains any significant public
service vocation. All of this noted, however, the example of the party
leader challenged over his drinking, like the preceding example of the
would-be leader with a "problematic" personal past, is a case where a
figure who is already in the political sphere seeks further popular support
and in this context is subjected to public inspection. Is it unreasonable

[3] My translation, deploying the language of the King James version of the biblical phrases.
[4] I follow again the language of the King James version.
[5] For an account of the aims and values of the BBC as Reith himself conceived them, see
John C. W. Reith, *Broadcast over Britain* (London: Hodder & Stoughton, 1924). For a more
impartial and rounded account, see Asa Briggs, *The BBC: The First Fifty Years* (Oxford:
Oxford University Press, 1985).

that in such circumstances the issue of sexual ethics should be introduced or the matter of intemperance raised?

IV. Contexts, Ideas, and Values

Anyone who studies the history of philosophy, or of ideas more generally, from a period when people held presuppositions very different from his own—say, the period of classical antiquity, or of the patristics, or of the high Middle Ages—is likely at some point to be struck by the inadequacy of his own contemporaries' understanding of the past. He may come to regard their flawed understanding as due, in no small part and perhaps overwhelmingly, to their failure to understand the premises commonly deployed by thinkers of that other time. These premises may, but need not have been entertained as self-evident. On the contrary, they may have been regarded as hard-won insights. Some examples of the latter are the idea that nature is teleologically ordered and, hence, is implicitly normative; the idea that existence is analogical, such that individuals, families, principalities, and cultures all *really* exist, be it in a different way in each case; and the idea that knowledge may be acquired by co-naturality as well as by empirical discovery or theoretical inference. These ideas are not always expressed, let alone articulated, in contexts in which they are relied upon, hence the liability of later thinkers, missing what may have been essential, to dismiss the ideas of earlier times as inadequate to the problems that still confront us, or even as inadequate *tout court*.

This reflection was brought to mind when I was thinking about the serious difficulties that now confront moral and political conservatives of a certain type or family of types. In Britain and America, the second half of the twentieth century saw a long war between Right and Left in which, by the 1980s, the Left was defeated. The victory was in the field of political economy, but so convincing was it that conservatives could easily have thought that it was only a matter of time before other ground would be retaken. Those who did think so were wrong. What became apparent as the smoke cleared and the generals gathered their troops, was that the forces of the Right were massed in two camps, standing at quite some distance from one another: in one camp stood economic/social liberals, in the other social conservatives. Alternatively, if both are to be termed 'conservatives' (because of their common suspicion of generalized claims of social justice and their wish to conserve older modes of material acquisition, use, and retention in the face of radical redistributivists), then we should follow the American practice and distinguish them as 'economic' and 'traditional' conservatives, respectively.[6]

---

[6] For a taxonomy and description of the different styles of contemporary conservatism in the United States, see Charles W. Dunn and J. David Woodward, *The Conservative Tradition in America* (Lanham, MD: Rowman & Littlefield, 1996).

The fact and the extent of their differences were to some degree obscured by their history of shared opposition to domestic state socialism, and by their structural relationship within political parties (in Britain the Conservative Party and in the U.S. the Republican Party). These parties were committed to protecting "traditional ways of life" from the threat posed by international Communism. Once this threat receded, however, it became clear that the Right was divided between those who thought that the defeat of the Left should bring a restoration of the social forms that had been celebrated in popular imagery, literature, and broadcasting during and after World War II, and those who thought that liberty, not virtue, was the business of politics. Many in the latter group had little interest in the social modes of the past. Examples of this division include attitudes toward sexual and family issues, reproduction, abortion, euthanasia, drug control, arts funding, public support and censorship of broadcasting and publications, separation of church and state, public support for religious schools and other faith-based services, and so on. While the division is twofold—first, concerning the issues themselves, and second, concerning the proper role of government in relation to them—it is the prevailing views on the issues that most concerns traditional conservatives.

The general drift in political discourse in the English-speaking world has moved through four phases. The first phase consisted of judging that government (be it state and local, or national) had a responsibility to promote personal rectitude. In the second, people thought that while something might be morally right, it was not the business of government to promote or inhibit individual virtue (other than that pertaining to regard for the rights of others and for the rule of law). The third phase was one of uncertainty in which people were unsure about what might be right in this or that regard. Hence, they concluded that these were matters for individual conscience and not public policy. In the fourth phase, people reasoned that there simply were no moral-cum-political issues of the sort hitherto supposed, or that if there were such issues, then they would fall within the realm of individual autonomy and personal choice; hence, they would fall either outside the scope of law or within it as matters to be protected as liberty rights. (Any attempt to identify phases in this drift of political thought and culture is liable to be imprecise, given that the four phases described above have not always been made explicit and they remain in contest. Nonetheless, lines can be traced, both socially and intellectually, as, for example, in the history of the American Right, with the four phases exemplified by the writings of Alexander Hamilton [1757–1804], Andrew Jackson [1767–1845], H. L Mencken [1880–1956], and Murray Rothbard [1926–95], respectively.)[7]

---

[7] For an account of these developments, see again Dunn and Woodward, *The Conservative Tradition in America*, and the classic presentation of a form of Burkean conservatism by Russell Kirk, *The Conservative Mind* (London: Faber & Faber, 1954). See also Bruce Frohnen, *Virtue and the Promise of Conservatism: The Legacy of Burke and Tocqueville* (Lawrence: University Press of Kansas, 1993).

So, by stages, personal virtues once nourished and tended to by the state have been left to flower or fade by themselves, and vices that the state once sought to suppress and even to uproot have been tolerated and supported to the extent of being allowed public expression and validation. Obvious examples lie in the areas of sexual activity, personal relationships, and reproduction.

Evidently, from the perspective of traditional conservatives, this is an unhappy and unexpected movement away from their vision of society and understanding of politics. Ironically, they may even find that when it comes to particular policy issues, they now share common ground with some on the old Left. This should not be surprising to anyone familiar with the history of Christian Socialism in Britain[8] and in some European countries (and even in one narrow strand in the United States represented, for example, by Dorothy Day and Peter Maurin, the founders in 1933 of the Catholic Worker Movement). Christian Socialism is of older vintage than the more familiar form of anticapitalist socialism, which held that traditional social values were instruments of oppression fashioned and deployed by the forces of capital. In contrast, Christian Socialism took these values to reflect genuine human goods of common life, and its demand for political change was directed at the fact that economic and social circumstances made it impossible for the mass of men and women to realize these traditional values. To put it oversimply, the only changes that Christian Socialists wanted were ones that would make it possible for the many to flourish as did the few, allowing the many to enjoy the benefits of a traditional home, a traditional education, and a traditional lifestyle. Not for these people the politics of cultural revolution, the hermeneutics of suspicion, the praxis of subversion, the rhetoric of redefinition, and so on through the litany of cultural theory devotees.

Thus a new kind of opposition has emerged within the conservative fold, primarily over social values. By contrast, disputes between traditional conservatives and economic/social liberals over political economy seem largely instrumental. Traditional conservatives have no objection to the idea that the resources and power of political society may be used to uphold traditional moral values, and that some redistribution of wealth and some provision of public services might be legitimate means, though

---

[8] The Christian Socialist movement, which unlike Marxist socialism believed in private property and was opposed to revolution, originated in the middle of the nineteenth century and drew its inspiration from a surprising variety of sources, including the Chartist movement, the cooperative communitarianism of Robert Owen, and the counter-Enlightenment romanticism of Thomas Carlyle and Samuel Coleridge. The founding figures of British Christian Socialism are Frederick D. Maurice and Charles Kingsley, who with others authored a series of pamphlets under the general title *Tracts on Christian Socialism*. Members of the movement later founded and led the Independent Labour Party (formed in 1893), from which Labour and New Labour derive. The Society of Christian Socialists was formed in the United States in 1889. Given some knowledge of this history, it is perhaps more intelligible that traditional conservatives may find points of agreement with this strand of socialism. It also serves to explain why figures such as G. K. Chesterton and other distributivists are claimed by both the Left and the Right.

they are likely to enter a series of reservations. First, that just as property is the bulwark of responsible liberty, so the family is the primary locus of moral formation and of the goods of common life. Second, that initiatives implemented and administered by permanent bureaucracies should be viewed with some suspicion, in part because bureaucrats tend to favor uniform policies without regard to particularities of time and place, in part because they tend to become removed from the moral realities of everyday life, and in part because bureaucratic power tends to corrupt in the measure to which it is possessed. Such considerations also lie behind the traditional conservative's opposition to "professional politicians," an opposition often misrepresented by critics as a self-serving defense by those who wish to reserve ample time for making money—which is not to say, of course, that the critics' charge is never justified.

Even so, the problem for traditional conservatives is not the state *per se*, but the existence of false and harmful conceptions of it. One such conception was that associated with Communism, but that was a problem of the past. The problem of the present and of the foreseeable future is that the state is now widely conceived in terms that are no less damaging to human virtues and values as traditional conservatives understand them. These include various forms of contractualism, such as the rights-based, egalitarian liberalism of Ronald Dworkin, and to a lesser but still significant degree the political liberalism of John Rawls, as well as the market liberalism associated with certain kinds of individualism. In addition, the effort to counter such conceptions of the state is made more daunting by the recognition that among those who advocate them are former allies in the war against Communism abroad and state socialism at home.

The division of the Right that I have adumbrated may also be cast in terms of 'conservatives' versus 'neoliberals', a distinction that has been a commonplace of American political commentary for the past twenty years, if not longer. More recently, this distinction has become prominent in British commentary, as the Conservative Party has tried to determine its broad orientation in the post-Thatcher era and in the wake of two devastating general election defeats. To understand the challenge facing the Conservative Party, one needs to appreciate the extent to which the traditional scheme of opposition between Britain's parties is no longer applicable or even intelligible. The rightward move toward the political center that began under Tony Blair's predecessor as leader of the Labour opposition has been carried further by Blair, to the point where New Labour ceased to use the term 'socialism'. More significantly, it ceased to formulate policies on the basis of egalitarianism or of a conception of the state as an administrative device for redistributing material benefits in accord with universal rights. At the same time, New Labour repositioned itself as the party willing to tackle crime at home and oppose tyranny abroad. These changes removed the party from the main line of right-wing criticism and left Conservatives in a state of enduring uncertainty as they tried to work out what they stood for, beyond opposition to socialism.

In nineteenth-century Britain, industrialization brought men and women from the countryside into towns and cities, changing the modes of their labor and introducing them first to new kinds of property (factories, machinery, manufactured goods, and shops) and then to a new concept of property. This new concept was not the familiar idea of the personal ownership of visible, tangible things, but the ownership of stocks and shares. These changes in the circumstances of the population resulted in a new kind of insecurity, not resulting directly from the vicissitudes of nature (as had been their situation on the land), but arising from financial speculation and short-term capital investment. By the end of the century, conservatives and socialists alike agreed that the gathering of the populace into centers of seasonless manufacture had changed the environment of politics by giving rise to general national problems calling for collectivized solutions. It was this belief that resulted in such social legislation as the creation of national insurance, the establishment of labor exchanges, and the introduction of old-age pensions. Moreover, it was this collaboration that gave meaning and warrant to the claim of Sir William Harcourt, made during the passage through Parliament of the 1894 budget, that "We are all socialists now."[9]

Consensus on the idea of collectivized solutions to national needs continued up to the period of "the Thatcher revolution," which began in 1979 with the election to power of the Conservative Party and continued until Margaret Thatcher's resignation as leader in 1990. What went somewhat unnoticed, at least by traditional conservatives, was the fact that in the years following World War II a second social transformation had supervened upon the material base established by nineteenth-century industrialization, urbanization, and the later shifts from heavy manufacture to light industry, to assembly work, to retailing, and then to service industries. This postwar transformation involved the contraction of the family through declining birth rates and relocation for housing and employment opportunities. The transformation also entailed changing conceptions of production, further removing goods from traditional notions of labor. A relatively affluent urban populace, freed from the material necessity of mutual dependence within the family and neighborhood, and increasingly detached from and unfamiliar with the historic narratives of God, of ordered nature, of paternal governance, and of nation and family as nonvoluntary forms of association, gave rise to the need for a new style of politics, no longer responsive to persons as members of collectivities but to individuals directly. This resulted in a raft of liberalizing social legislation in the areas of personal relations, sexual practice, conception, leisure, and culture. So far as political consciousness is concerned, it is in respect to such matters as these, and the conditions from which they

[9] Harcourt was Professor of International Law at Cambridge (appointed in 1869), Solicitor-General (appointed in 1873), Home Secretary (1880–85), and then Chancellor of the Exchequer (1886, 1892–95) in William E. Gladstone's last two administrations.

arose, that someone might recall Harcourt's words and say "We are all liberals now."

But if this really is the state of affairs, and if it endures, then traditional conservatism has no future—at least at the level of the state. Someone of an earlier age, of the generation, say, of those who established the BBC as a public corporation and composed its inscription, when confronted with the issue of how to deal with a public figure whose personal life was problematic, might well have returned for guidance to Matthew's gospel. There he or she would have read the following:

> Moreover, if your brother sins against you, go and tell him his fault between you and him alone. If he hears you, you have gained your brother. But if he will not hear, take with you one or two more, that by the mouth of two or three witnesses every word may be established. But if he refuses even to hear the church, let him be to you like a pagan and a tax collector. (Matt. 18:15–20)

This is the principal site in the New Testament for the idea of what later came to be termed 'fraternal correction': the charitable criticism by one community member of the behavior of another. Following Augustine's *Treatise Concerning the Correction of the Donatists*, and Aquinas's discussion in *Summa Theologiae* (IIa, IIae, q.33, a.1), Catholic moral theologians traditionally distinguished 'fraternal' from 'judicial correction' (the latter being the responsibility of a duly constituted authority to those within its jurisdiction), and distinguished both from 'paternal correction', which is the prerogative (and duty) of a superior with regard to those in his charge. In addition, Catholic theologians developed (in the style familiar to secular philosophers from their study of ecclesiastical just war theory) a set of conditions specifying the circumstances under which the obligation to offer fraternal correction becomes grave. The two sets of conditions listed below, which have no single source but are a gloss based on my consideration of various casuistical discussions, refer respectively to (*A*) private and (*B*) public correction. In the case of the former, the reproof is to be addressed directly to the wrongdoer; the latter arises where the former is for some reason infeasible or proves ineffective, or where the common good is directly threatened.

(*A*) *Private Fraternal Correction*
1. The matter at issue is itself grave.
2. There is little prospect of self-amendment.
3. There is no one else in a position to offer the correction.
4. There is a likelihood that the correction will bear fruit.
5. There is no prospect of harm arising from making the correction (such harm being unmerited or disproportionate to the good of correction).

(B) Public Fraternal Correction
1. The matter at issue is itself public.
2. The matter bears on the standing of a third party or on the common good of the whole community.
3. A public correction is required in order to prevent scandal.
4. The wrongdoer has relinquished or forfeited the right not to be subject to detraction.

There is much that might be said about these and other aspects of the notion of fraternal correction; in this context, however, I am not concerned with the details but with the general idea. Of course, its original circumstance is that of a community of like-minded believers, and this might be thought to exclude its application outside such a context. I can, though, see no reason to think that its religious origin occasions such a general restriction. Nevertheless, I do believe that this notion of fraternal correction needs to be applied to our era with some caution, for the reasons that I mentioned above when speaking of ideas drawn from a period when people held presuppositions very different from our own. For presupposed by this notion of fraternal correction are interpersonal relations akin to those of a family rather than of a voluntary association. Likewise, there are presumptions of objectivity in moral judgment, of morality's application to human beings as such, and of moral knowledge being naturally available to all. There are also presumptions of the continuity of moral action through the unifying structure of a person's character, and of a relationship between the 'personal' and the 'social', which is different from that of the 'private' and the 'public' as these terms are now conceived in liberal theories.

Someone might balk at this last claim, recalling a passage in the writings of Mill, who is, after all, nothing if not a liberal. Having insisted in *On Liberty* that "the only purpose for which power can be rightfully exercised over any member of a civilized community, against his will, is to prevent harm to others,"[10] Mill later goes on to say:

> There is a degree of folly, and a degree of what may be called (though the phrase is not unobjectionable) lowness or deprivation of taste, which though it cannot justify doing harm to the person who manifests it, renders him necessarily and properly a subject of distaste, or, in extreme cases, even of contempt: a person could not have the opposite qualities in due strength without entertaining these feelings. Though doing no wrong to anyone, a person may so act as to compel us to judge him, and feel to him, as a fool or as a being of an inferior order; and since this judgement and feeling are a fact which

[10] John Stuart Mill, *On Liberty* (1859), ed. Gertrude Himmelfarb (London: Penguin Books, 1974), chap. 1, para. 4, p. 68.

he would prefer to avoid, it is doing him a service to warn him of it beforehand, as of any other disagreeable consequence to which he exposes himself. It would be well, indeed, if this good office were much more freely rendered than the common notions of politeness at present permit, and if one person could honestly point out to another that he thinks him in fault, without being considered unmannerly or presuming. We have a right, also, in various ways, to act upon our unfavourable opinion of anyone, not in the oppression of his individuality, but in the exercise of ours. We are not bound, for example, to seek his society; we have a right to avoid it (though not to parade the avoidance), for we have a right to choose the society most acceptable to us. We have a right, and it may be our duty, to caution others against him, if we think his example or conversation likely to have a pernicious effect on those with whom he associates. We may give others a preference over him in optional good offices, except those which tend to his improvement.[11]

This comes in a section of chapter 4 entitled "Of the Limits to the Authority of Society over the Individual," and I do not doubt that there are those who will judge that, in this passage, Mill himself far exceeds those limits. Some may say that this is a passing aberration and not evidence of the inadequacy of a criterion of public policy limited to the prevention of harm. What then might they make of another apparent lapse, as when in the following chapter of the same work Mill contends that "there are many acts which, being directly injurious only to the agents themselves, ought not to be legally interdicted, but which, if done publicly, are a violation of good manners, and, coming thus within the category of offences against others, may rightly be prohibited"?[12] Here the point concerns prohibition rather than correction, but if the greater interference with liberty is held to be permitted, then it is hard to see how the lesser should not be. I leave it to others, however, to worry as to whether the sorts of policies that Mill appears not only to countenance but also to recommend sit ill with contemporary liberalism. To the extent that they may be felt to do so, this should remind us of the proximity of Mill's thought to that of older "perfectionist" ideas reaching back to Aristotle, and the natural law theories associated with traditional conservatism. These ideas provide a distinctive basis on which to address the examples of public disclosure that I gave earlier, but they also entail presuppositions of a communitarian and teleological sort that may now be felt to be widely rejected, if not falsified. If this should be so, then what is the Aristotelian, or the Augustinian, or the Thomist, or the Burkean to do?

[11] Ibid., chap. 4, para. 5, pp. 143–44.
[12] Ibid., chap. 5, para. 7, p. 168.

Earlier in this section, I opposed traditional conservatism to neoliberalism, but perhaps there is an emerging basis for re-alliance. Each has strong reservations about the modern state: the latter because of doubts about the very idea of political community; the former because, while they fully believe in community, they also believe that the modern state does not and probably cannot realize it. In this situation, advocates of these two camps of the conservative movement might do well to set aside their differences and collaborate in the effort to devolve political power downward. If this devolution were to occur, then certain questions about the extent and separability of the public and the private, which currently exercise us greatly, would seem less pressing, because for one or another reason they would indeed be so. Welcome harbingers of devolution are the United Kingdom's trend toward decision-making at national and regional assemblies (and in the case of Scotland, at a national lawmaking parliament), as well as the move in the United States to emphasize the fact that state governments, and not the federal government, are governments of general jurisdiction. What may be said of the role of quasi-political institutions, such as the BBC and the monarchy in Great Britain and the Public Broadcasting Service in the United States, is less clear, but needs more serious philosophical reflection than it has received hitherto.

V. CONCLUSION

I have not been concerned to provide a general answer to the question of when it is right to advert to problematic aspects of the private life of a public figure, or to draw wider attention to the person's misdeeds and to make them the subject of commentary. Evidently, cases have to be considered in relation to general principles and values, as well as in regard to their circumstances, form, and content. It is easy enough to observe that some methods of acquiring information are unjust, that some styles of exposure are beyond principled defense, that some matters are so remote from a public figure's office as to fail any reasonable test of public interest, and that the anticipated consequences of exposure may be so grave that what would otherwise constitute legitimate revelation should be avoided or at least postponed until relevant circumstances have changed.

Important as these considerations are, however, they are supplementary to general issues concerning presumptions of privacy, entitlements to free speech and commentary, and responsibilities of correction and caution. It is unsurprising that the issues of privacy, on the one hand, and of public commentary, on the other, have been subjects of considerable interest to liberal social and political philosophers, since both sets of issues seem to flow from the idea of liberty, especially the liberty of individuals. Within this framework, the matters to be resolved are how best to conceive of the relevant freedoms and how to relate them one to another so as to avoid, limit, or arbitrate conflicts among them.

There are, though, further matters to be considered arising from the interests of the community and the responsibilities of social membership. In essence, these are neither liberties nor rights (though they may entail both); rather, they belong within the sphere of personal and social values. What is at issue is the good of individuals and of societies. Mill wrote of how degrees of folly and lowness render persons "necessarily and properly" subjects of distaste, and of how corresponding actions, "though doing no wrong to anyone," compel us to judge the agent. As the rest of the passage and the context of the work make clear, however, Mill is not concerned simply with warrants for private judgments and discretionary policies. He also has in mind our responsibilities to such persons as fellow citizens and to others whom they might influence, perhaps especially through their occupancy of public offices.

In deliberating about when and how to exercise these responsibilities, one should begin to see the merit of the criteria that I set out above under the headings of private and public fraternal correction: grave matter, the standing of others, the common good, the avoidance of scandal, and so on. How strongly one feels the draw of these, and how far one is disposed to see public and private correction as interconnected and nondetachable, provide measures of the extent to which one's conception of social life is akin to that of the traditional conservative. Of course, conservatism may not be the only political outlook that can accommodate the idea of mutual responsibilities set within a framework of common life and the common good, but traditional conservatism can lay claim to have been the tacit philosophy of the communities that constituted most of Europe and America until quite recently. To the extent that many people still regard this conception of social life as having genuine appeal, traditional conservatism remains a viable alternative to both liberalism and neoliberalism as a basis on which to found a social and political morality. That said, I return to my earlier observation that traditional conservatism cannot serve as a political philosophy for the modern state. Whether this tells against traditional conservatism or against the modern state is a matter for history, not philosophy, to judge.

Moral Philosophy, University of St. Andrews

AGAINST CIVIC SCHOOLING*

By James Bernard Murphy

I. Introduction: What Is Civic Education?

A fierce debate about civic education in American public schools has erupted in response to the terrorist attacks of September 11, 2001. Many liberals and conservatives, though they disagree strongly about which civic virtues to teach, share the assumption that such education is an appropriate responsibility for public schools. They are wrong. Civic education aimed at civic virtue is at best ineffective; worse, it is often subversive of the moral purpose of schooling. Moreover, the attempt to impose these partisan conceptions of civic virtue on America's students violates the civic trust that underpins vibrant public schools.

Here is how the recent debate has unfolded and what we might learn from it. In response to demands from teachers about how to deal with the messy emotional, racial, religious, and political issues occasioned by the September 11 attack and its aftermath, the National Education Association (NEA) offers a Web site titled "Remember September 11." The site is full of materials about how to counsel distressed students; how to place September 11 in some kind of historical, cultural, and international context; and what moral lessons might be drawn from the attack.[1] These moral lessons range from "Remembering the Uniformed Heroes at the World Trade Center" to "Tolerance in Times of Trial." Similarly, the National Council for Social Studies (NCSS) offers lesson plans for "9/11" on its Web site[2]: these materials range from "The Bill of Rights" to "My Name is Osama," the story of an Iraqi-American boy taunted by his peers because of his name and Muslim customs. Although the materials offered by these organizations vary widely, their pervasive theme is well articulated by the president of the NCSS: "[W]e need to reinforce the ideals of tolerance, equity, and social justice against a backlash of antidemocratic sentiments and hostile divisions."

* For comments on an earlier draft of this essay, I am indebted to Mark Stein, Lucas Swaine, Shelley Burtt, Stanley Fish, Mary Beth Klee, Ellen Frankel Paul, and the other contributors to this volume. I also wish to thank my indefatigable research assistants and copyeditors, Karen Liot and Emily Mintz. I began this inquiry in response to questions about the relation of academic to moral excellence from the late Patty Farnsworth, to whom I dedicate this essay.
    [1] Available on-line at http://neahin.org/programs/schoolsafety/september11/materials/hshome.htm [accessed April 30, 2003].
    [2] Available on-line at http://www.socialstudies.org/resources/moments [accessed April 30, 2003].

The generally liberal civics lessons offered by the NEA and the NCSS were quickly attacked by conservatives for promoting an unprincipled tolerance, for focusing too much on America's flaws, and for failing to impart a proper knowledge and love of American institutions and ideals. A group of distinguished conservative educators and commentators pub-lished a set of their own civics lessons emphasizing love of the United States and its ideals, the heroism of the rescuers of September 11, and the need for better knowledge of American history and institutions.[3] These sharply divergent views of proper civics lessons led a reporter for the *New York Times* to note that the anniversary of September 11 threatened to bring back the "culture wars" into U.S. classrooms.[4] Even leading polit-ical pundits could not resist entering the civic education fray. Thomas Friedman offered his mildly liberal "9/11 Lesson Plan," in which he championed American democratic government while admitting that the United States is not perfect and that its conduct abroad causes dismay even among its friends.[5] William J. Bennett offered a more conservative lesson by insisting that "American students should be taught what makes this nation great. . . . Even with its faults, America remains the best nation on earth. . . ."[6]

The strident polemics we frequently find in these civics lessons might well lead one to think that liberals and conservatives can find no common ground. Broadly, one might say that liberal responses to "9/11" empha-size the need to resist jingoism and to consider why hatred of America might be in some ways justified, while conservative responses emphasize the nation's virtues and the need for resolve to defend them in times of danger. According to conservatives, liberal civics lessons amount to little more than preaching unprincipled toleration even of the intolerable; ac-cording to liberals, conservative civics lessons amount to little more than preaching unprincipled jingoism and triumphalism. Still, despite these profound differences about the content of civic education, both liberal and conservative advocates insist that civic education in American schools must reach beyond mere civic knowledge and civic skills to shape stu-dents' deepest civic values, attitudes, and motivations. In other words, liberals and conservatives agree that civic education must aim at impart-ing proper civic virtues, though they obviously disagree stridently about which virtues to impart.

[3] See Chester E. Finn, Jr., et al., *September 11: What Our Children Need to Know* (Washington, DC: Thomas B. Fordham Foundation, 2002): available on-line at http://www.edexcellence.net/Sept11/September 11.pdf [accessed April 30, 2003].
[4] See Kate Zernike, "Lesson Plans for Sept. 11 Offer a Study in Discord," *New York Times*, August 31, 2002, late edition–final, sec. A, p. 1, col. 3.
[5] Thomas L. Friedman, "9/11 Lesson Plan," *New York Times*, September 4, 2002 (editorial), sec. A, p. 21, col. 5.
[6] William J. Bennett, "A Time For Clarity," *Wall Street Journal*, September 10, 2002 (edito-rial). I comment on these debates in James Bernard Murphy, "Good Students and Good Citizens," *New York Times*, September 15, 2002 (editorial), sec. 4, p. 15, col. 2.

Among contemporary political theorists, the debate over civic education closely parallels, albeit at a lower "temperature," the polemics over
the civics lessons of September 11. Conservatives, such as Lorraine Pangle
and Thomas Pangle, defend the views of those American founders who
argued that the vast majority of Americans do not need to acquire the
virtues of political participation, just the virtue of vigilant judgment of
their elected officials.[7] By sharp contrast, Benjamin Barber, a liberal, insists that all citizens ought to be educated in the civic virtues necessary for
competent political participation.[8] And where the Pangles emphasize the
virtues of patriotism, zeal for public service, and vigilance, Amy Gutmann, a liberal, emphasizes toleration and mutual respect.[9] Even among
liberals there is very little agreement about which civic virtues to teach in
schools. Some liberal theorists insist that the political virtues of toleration,
civility, and a respect for democratic procedure rest upon the acquisition
of the moral virtues of individuality, respect for moral diversity, and
autonomy.[10] In their view, liberal democratic politics depends upon morally liberal citizens. Other liberal theorists insist, by contrast, that liberal
political virtues, such as political tolerance and respect for the rule of law
and democratic procedures, do not depend upon liberal moral virtues
such as respect for moral diversity or autonomy. One might be, for example, a very good citizen of a liberal democracy without being morally
liberal.[11]

What do these debates about civic education in schools teach us?
Despite the vociferous disagreements about the proper content of civic

---

[7] According to the founders: "[T]he civic virtues to be fostered in the vast majority of
Americans as national and also as state citizens are not so much virtues enabling partici-
pation in rule as they are virtues enabling vigilant judgment of the few representatives who
are to participate in rule." See Lorraine Smith Pangle and Thomas L. Pangle, "What the
American Founders Have to Teach Us about Schooling for Democratic Citizenship," in
Lorraine M. McDonnell, P. Michael Timpane, and Roger Benjamin, eds., *Rediscovering the
Democratic Purposes of Education* (Lawrence: University of Kansas Press, 2000), 26–27.

[8] "Citizens are women and men educated for excellence—by which term I mean the
knowledge and competence to govern in common their own lives. The democratic faith is
rooted in the belief that all humans are capable of such excellence. . . ." Benjamin R. Barber,
An Aristocracy of Everyone (New York: Oxford University Press, 1992), 5.

[9] "Should schools go beyond teaching the most basic virtue of toleration and also teach
mutual respect?" Amy Gutmann, "Why Should Schools Care about Civic Education?" in
Rediscovering the Democratic Purposes of Education, 81.

[10] "It is probably impossible to teach children the skills and virtues of democratic citizenship in a diverse society without at the same time teaching them many of the virtues and
skills of individuality or autonomy." Amy Gutmann, "Civic Education and Social Diversity," *Ethics* 105, no. 3 (1995): 563.

[11] For example, John Tomasi argues that politically liberal civic virtues ought to be compatible with liberal and nonliberal ways of life, not only with "some philosophical ideal of
moral autonomy (such as that inspired by the work of Mill or Kant), but also with those that
come from more embedded, traditionalist ways of understanding reasons for action and
attitude (the 'reasonable Romantics,' or citizens of faith)." See Tomasi, "Civic Education and
Ethical Subservience: From *Mozert* to *Santa Fe* and Beyond," in Stephen Macedo and Yael
Tamir, eds., *Moral and Political Education, NOMOS XLIII* [hereafter *Nomos*] (New York: New
York University Press, 2002), 207–8.

education, both liberals and conservatives share two fundamental assumptions. First, they agree that civic virtue is the proper aim of civic education.[12] Although virtually all advocates of civic education use the language of civic virtues, none of them defines what he or she means by 'virtue' or how civic virtue differs from civic knowledge or civic skill.[13] I will therefore define 'civic knowledge' as an understanding of true facts and concepts about civic affairs, such as the history, structure, and functions of government, the nature of democratic politics, and the ideals of citizenship. 'Civic skills' are the trained capacities for deploying civic knowledge in the pursuit of civic goals, such as voting, protesting, petitioning, canvassing, and debating. 'Civic virtues' integrate civic knowledge and civic skills with proper civic motivations, such as respect for the democratic process, love for the nation, and a conscientious concern for the common good. I follow philosopher Linda Zagzebski in defining virtues as success terms: on this view, a person does not have a civic virtue unless he or she has both the proper motivation and the knowledge and skills to be effective in civic engagements.[14] Being effective in civic engagements certainly does not mean that one is always or even often successful: political activity is unavoidably hostage to unpredictable contingency. But no one can claim to have civic virtue who lacks the knowledge and skills to cogently debate and take a stand on public affairs, to elicit the cooperation and support of fellow citizens, and to perform one's chosen or required public duties. In short, on my account, civic skills presuppose civic knowledge just as civic virtue presupposes civic skills.

Civic education ought to aim at civic virtue and not merely at civic knowledge and skills because without a virtuous motivation, knowledge and skills lack moral worth. After all, civic knowledge and skills are routinely put into the service of all manner of immoral political conduct, ranging from the deliberate subordination of the common good to self-interest, including the use of deception, manipulation, and coercion, all the way to a traitorous betrayal of the nation to its enemies. So civic

[12] According to the Pangles, however, "[i]t is a mark of the grave difficulties into which our democracy has fallen that the very idea of civic virtue has passed out of currency. . . ." See "What the American Founders Have to Teach Us about Schooling for Democratic Citizenship," 21. In reality, as we have seen, the language of civic virtue is ubiquitous in debates about civic education.

[13] In "The Role of Civic Education," a report issued as part of the *National Standards for Civics and Government* (Calabasas, CA: Center for Civic Education, 1998), Margaret Stimman Branson distinguishes three essential components of civic education as civic knowledge, civic skills, and civic dispositions, without attempting to theorize about the relations among them. See http://www.civiced.org/articles_role.html [accessed April 30, 2003].

[14] "A virtue, then, can be defined as a deep and enduring acquired excellence of a person, involving a characteristic motivation to produce a certain desired end and reliable success in bringing about that end." Linda Trinkaus Zagzebski, *Virtues of the Mind: An Inquiry into the Nature of Virtue and the Ethical Foundations of Knowledge* (Cambridge: Cambridge University Press, 1996), 137.

education must not aim only to increase civic knowledge and civic skills; civic education must ultimately aim to promote civic virtue. Voting, debating, petitioning, legislating, and administering can be instruments of evil and injustice if they are badly motivated. Proper civic motives need not be selfless or pure, but they cannot be wholly based upon greed or hatred. As it happens, there is good empirical evidence that civic knowledge tends to foster civic virtue: as citizens learn more about political institutions and principles, their political engagements become not only more rationally coherent but also more public-spirited.[15]

Most liberals and conservatives, therefore, properly share the first assumption, without telling us why, that civic education ought to aim at civic virtue. They also share a second assumption, namely, that civic education aimed at civic virtue is a primary responsibility of public schools. Because of the nearly universal confusion of education with schooling, reflected in the pervasive use of the word 'education' to mean only schooling, most advocates of civic education never even betray awareness that civic education need not mean civic schooling. Although most civic education has always taken place outside of school, advocates of civic education almost never consider the comparative advantages of schools and other agencies of civic education. Yet all of the best empirical evidence tells us that schools are relatively weak instruments of civic education, especially of civic education aimed at civic virtue. Clear and sound thinking about civic education is impossible until we first learn to distinguish civic education from civic schooling and to theorize about the relations between them.

Citing evidence from the best empirical studies (discussed below), I will argue that schools can play a small though significant role in teaching civic knowledge and that schools can indirectly foster civic skills by encouraging extracurricular participation in student government and other voluntary organizations. These studies, however, also suggest that schools are wholly inept instruments for attempting to impart the proper motivations essential to genuine civic virtue. Moreover, I will argue on both empirical and normative grounds that the very attempt to impart civic motivations, such as moral tolerance or patriotism, undermines the essential moral purpose of schooling, which is to foster the love and skilled pursuit of knowledge. History, social studies, literature, and the sciences are bowdlerized, sanitized, and falsified when educators seek to use them as vehicles of civic uplift. As we shall see, the proper aim of schools to foster a love of genuine knowledge is always and everywhere subverted when they attempt to foster civic virtue. However, because civic knowl-

---

[15] See William A. Galston "Civic Knowledge, Civic Education, and Civic Engagement: A Summary of Recent Research," in *Constructing Civic Virtue: A Symposium on the State of American Citizenship* (Syracuse, NY: Campbell Public Affairs Institute, Maxwell School of Citizenship and Public Affairs, 2003), 35–59. Galston's brief for civic knowledge fails to consider, however, the inadequacy of civic knowledge and the dangers of its misuse.

edge often fosters civic virtue, schools can properly play an indirect role in promoting civic virtue simply by better imparting civic knowledge.

Given the nearly universal consensus across the political spectrum that public schools ought to promote civic virtue, arguing that they should not seems almost perverse. Furthermore, public schooling in the United States is itself a product of the passion for civic education. Universal public schools for the purpose of republican civic education were first proposed by French philosophers and economists, such as Jean-Jacques Rousseau and Baron Turgot, in the middle of the eighteenth century. Because John Baptist de LaSalle (1651–1719), founder of the Brothers of the Christian Schools, had already established a widespread network of local Catholic schools in France, some French *philosophes* advocated publicly funded schools to counteract the moral and political influence of the Catholic Church. These French schemes for republican civic education in universal public schools were first realized, however, not in France but in the Netherlands in the first decade of the nineteenth century. But in the 1830s and 1840s, François Guizot and Victor Cousin, both French liberals and successive ministers of public instruction, established a system of public schools for liberal and republican civic education. The French *philosophes* had a decisive influence on Thomas Jefferson during the 1780s, just as the later French liberals would deeply influence Horace Mann in the 1830s.[16]

From its inception in America in the 1790s, "[p]ublic education was to be republican civic education." [17] Although there is much to admire about this commitment to universal schooling, the dark side of civic education in public schools was evident from the beginning—not just in its strident anti-Catholicism, but also in its narrow conception of who deserved to be educated. Jefferson and his followers took the civic mission of public schools so seriously that they denied schooling to noncitizens, such as women, blacks, and Native Americans.[18] And because the fundamental premise of civic education was that civic virtue was compatible only with Protestant religion, Mann later clothed his republican civic education in the garb of nondenominational Protestantism.[19]

[16] For the origins of public schooling in Europe and America, see Charles Leslie Glenn, Jr., *The Myth of the Common School* (Amherst: University of Massachusetts Press, 1988), 15–62; for the origins in France, see Christian Nique, *Comment l'Ecole devint une affaire d'État: 1815–1840* (Paris: Nathan, 1990).

[17] Rogers M. Smith, *Civic Ideals: Conflicting Visions of Citizenship in U.S. History* (New Haven, CT: Yale University Press, 1997), 217.

[18] Lawrence Cremin says of Jefferson: "Granted his abiding concern with the education of the people, he defined the people in political terms—as free white males." See Lawrence A. Cremin, *American Education: The National Experience 1783–1876* (New York: Harper & Row, 1980), 114. Smith says of the Jeffersonians: "Education came to be so identified with preparation for citizenship that noncitizens were often denied it." See his *Civic Ideals*, 189.

[19] As Cremin says: "In essence, Mann accepted the propositions of the republican style of educational thought and recast them in the forms of nineteenth-century nondenominational Protestantism." Cremin, *American Education*, 136–137.

To understand the broad appeal of civic education in the schools today, we must look at the fate of these earlier forms of civic education. Although an ecumenical and nondenominational Protestantism appeared to be an appropriate religious and moral basis for common schools in the America of the early nineteenth century, the arrival of large numbers of Catholics and Jews beginning in the 1840s called into question this assumption.[20] Most educators have long agreed that sectarian religious education, even of the ecumenical Protestant variety, violates the civic trust that underpins public support for common schools. How can Catholics and Jews, for example, be expected to financially support common schools that teach a nondenominational Protestantism? Today, debates about moral education in schools are following much the same pattern as did earlier debates about religious education. Liberal and conservative moralists argue that their brand of moral education is uniquely ecumenical, and, hence, appropriate for common schools. Liberal moralists ask: Who can be opposed to students learning to become morally autonomous? Conservative moralists ask: Who can be opposed to students learning to become honest, courageous, temperate, and just?[21] But one person's moral ecumenism is another person's moral sectarianism: liberals are suspicious of conservative moralism, just as conservatives are suspicious of liberal moralism. Thus, proposals for moral education in public schools have become yet another front of the broader culture wars, and many educators are coming to the conclusion that both liberal and conservative moralism violate the civic trust that underpins common schools. Each of us sends his or her own children to common schools with the expectation that none of us gets to impose his or her own sectarian religious or moral values at school.[22]

Yet without any civic, religious, or moral education, public schools seem to lack a compelling moral purpose. Surely schools must aim higher than merely providing the information and skills associated with 'the 3 Rs', that is, reading, writing, and arithmetic? Herein lies the special appeal of civic education today. In civic education, many educators believe that they have found the one truly ecumenical kind of moral education. Since America's common schools are publicly funded and governed by means of democratic political processes, how can anyone object to civic education in such schools? Why would democratic citizens pay for com-

---

[20] As Diane Ravitch rightly observes: "Mann's nonsectarianism, we now recognize, was nondenominational Protestantism." See her "Education and Democracy," in Diane Ravitch and Joseph P. Viteritti, eds., *Making Good Citizens: Education and Civil Society* (New Haven, CT: Yale University Press, 2001), 18.

[21] Liberal moral education is usually neo-Kantian and emphasizes critical reflection and autonomous choice; conservative moral education is usually neo-Aristotelian and emphasizes character formation and virtue.

[22] See the critique of liberal and conservative moralism in Amy Gutmann's *Democratic Education*, rev. ed. (Princeton, NJ: Princeton University Press, 1999), 56–64.

mon schools if these schools did not train future democratic citizens?[23] Since every American citizen has an interest in promoting civic virtue in the next generation of citizens, who could legitimately object to civic education in public schools? In civic education we seem to have found a way to cut the Gordian knot of sectarian religious and moral controversy and to provide a kind of moral education that respects the deep pluralism of American society. Indeed, as we shall see, several leading contemporary political theorists argue that civic education ought to be not just one proper aim of public schooling but the primary aim.

Unfortunately, civic education aimed at civic virtue turns out to be no more truly ecumenical than was nondenominational Protestantism. Political theorists can agree no better than educators and pundits on the proper civic virtues: some insist that democratic citizens must be taught to think critically about the values of their own families and respective faiths, while others insist that even unexamined religious and moral commitments are perfectly compatible with good democratic citizenship.[24] Some theorists insist that democratic citizens must have sincere respect for those who have different moral and religious views; others insist that considerable intolerance and disrespect (within the bounds of law and civility) are fully compatible with civic virtue. These debates among political theorists presaged the public debates over the civic lessons of September 11.

In practice, then, as well as in theory, we simply cannot agree about the appropriate civic virtues. In the face of such deep and seemingly intractable divisions, holding the education of our children hostage to culture wars over civic virtue seems imprudent at best. By contrast, there is a much higher degree of agreement about what kinds of civic knowledge and civic skills are appropriate for democratic citizens. But even if we could all agree about the appropriate civic virtues, schools would remain the wrong place for such education for two reasons: first, because schools are ineffective instruments for imparting civic virtue; and second, because the attempt to impart civic virtue subverts the inherent moral purpose of schools, which is to lead students to love genuine knowledge.

II. Civic Education or Civic Schooling?

When Mark Twain bragged that he never let school interfere with his education, he was admirably clear about the difference between the two. Unfortunately, writers about civic education are rarely so clear. Philoso-

[23] Gutmann, for example, wonders "why so much taxpayer money should go to schooling that gives up on the central aims of civic education." See her "Civic Education and Social Diversity," 572–73.

[24] Gutmann, for example, insists upon teaching critical reflection, while William Galston does not.

phers differ on how widely we ought to understand the concept of education, though all agree that any concept of education must be of a wider range than the concept of schooling. Some philosophers define 'education' in very broad terms as the whole ensemble of influences that shape the formation of a human person beyond what is given by natural capacity and mere maturation; in this sense, education takes in all of the formal and informal aspects of the fostering, nurturing, cultivating, and rearing of a person.[25] Social scientists employ this broad concept of education when they speak of 'enculturation' or 'socialization'. Other philosophers restrict the meaning of 'education' to deliberate or intentional efforts to teach or to learn, thereby omitting the whole realm of tacit learning.[26] For my purposes of contrasting education with schooling, either view of education is acceptable, since all plausible understandings of education take in a vastly wider range of agencies than schools. And by 'schooling', I mean institutions that aim to inculcate general knowledge and skills rather than merely technical training for a particular occupation.

Unfortunately, in addition to these wider senses, the word 'education' is often used to refer merely to schooling, as when we speak of the "expense of education." As philosopher John Passmore observes, " 'education' does create troublesome ambiguities."[27] As we shall see, writers on education display not just verbal but also deep conceptual confusion about the relation of schools to education. Part of this confusion is driven by rhetorical inflation: education is an elevated way to speak about mere schooling. However, this use of the concept of education to refer to mere schooling, by confusing the whole for the part, makes clear thinking about schooling nearly impossible. If we vest discussions of schooling with all of the intellectual, moral, and spiritual weight of human education, then rational assessment of schools becomes untenable. We might accept the endorsement of all manner of intellectual, moral, and spiritual aims in education until we discover that the endorser meant not 'education' but 'schooling'. And to reject civic education seems suspiciously epicurean or even unpatriotic until we make clear that we reject only civic schooling. In the broad sense of education, all politics, indeed, all human endeavors take their truest measure in relation to their contribution to human education, but schooling is only one of many modalities of edu-

[25] John Dewey takes this comprehensive view of education in his *Democracy and Education: An Introduction to the Philosophy of Education* (1916; reprint, New York: Free Press, 1944), 10–22, as does John Passmore in his *The Philosophy of Teaching* (Cambridge, MA: Harvard University Press, 1980), 21–22.

[26] John Wilson argues that an intention to educate is necessary to the concept of education in his *Preface to the Philosophy of Education* (London: Routledge, 1979), 20–22. Cremin defines 'education' as "the deliberate, systematic, and sustained effort to transmit, evoke, or acquire knowledge, attitudes, values, skills, or sensibilities, as well as any outcomes of that effort"; see Lawrence A. Cremin, *Public Education* (New York: Basic Books, 1976), 27.

[27] Passmore, *The Philosophy of Teaching*, 21.

cation. I think that our tacit confusion of education with schooling helps to explain the passion and bitterness of the politics of schooling: we think and act as though all of education were at stake!

Advocates of 'civic education' usually mean by this expression only 'civic schooling'.[28] By implying that civic education is civic schooling, arguments for civic education in schools acquire great rhetorical force. Who could be against civic education? As advocates of civic education frequently point out, since the civic virtues are not innate, they must be learned. And from this true premise such advocates then falsely conclude that civic virtues must be taught in school. For example, political theorist William Galston writes: "In most times and places the necessity and appropriateness of civic education has been accepted without question. It has been taken for granted that young human beings must be shaped into citizens and that public institutions have both the right and the responsibility to take the lead."[29] If 'civic education' here refers broadly to the range of agencies by which citizens are formed, then Galston is obviously right: every polity must see to the broad political education of future citizens. Conversely, if 'civic education' refers to 'civic schooling', then Galston is clearly wrong, since many polities have educated citizens without recourse to schools.

Unfortunately, Galston goes on to make clear that by civic education, he means only civic schooling: "In the United States today, however, civic education has become intensely controversial."[30] Of course, it is only civic schooling that has occasioned controversy, not civic education. That Galston confuses education with schooling is also evident from his statement above that civic education is for "young human beings." The classical view is that although schooling is mainly for the young, moral and civic education is mainly for adults. So contemporary advocates are right in asserting that civic education is traditional, but wrong to imply, as they usually do, that civic education has always meant civic schooling.[31] Galston's impoverished view of civic education is also evident in his quotation from a recent manifesto from the American Federation of Teachers (AFT): "Democracy's survival depends upon our transmitting to each new generation the political vision that unites us as Americans. . . . Such

[28] A striking exception to this rule is the work of Nancy L. Rosenblum, who frequently takes to task other political theorists for failing to consider the importance of nonscholastic civic education: "There are good reasons to take some of the burden of democratic education off schooling and to acknowledge a division of educational labor." Nancy Rosenblum, "Pluralism and Democratic Education: Stopping Short by Stopping with Schools," in *Nomos*, 164.

[29] William Galston, "Civic Education in the Liberal State," in Nancy L. Rosenblum, ed., *Liberalism and the Moral Life* (Cambridge, MA: Harvard University Press, 1989), 89–101. As we shall see, this chapter is not about education but about schooling.

[30] Ibid., 89.

[31] As Galston does when he speaks of civic education (meaning schooling) in "most times and places."

values are neither revealed truths nor natural habits. There is no evidence that we are born with them." Unfortunately, from these true premises the manifesto jumps rashly to the conclusion that it is the schools' responsibility to transmit these values.[32] Curiously, in other contexts, Galston is well aware of the educative role of other institutions in American society. He points out that the U.S. Army might well do a better job of teaching racial harmony than American schools do.[33]

Although most advocates of civic education simply conflate education with schooling,[34] some do attempt to distinguish education from schooling. Philosopher Eamonn Callan distinguishes "between common education and common schooling on the one hand, and separate education and separate schooling on the other." He says that common education "prescribes a range of educational outcomes—virtues, abilities, different kinds of knowledge—as desirable for all members of the society. . . ."[35] Here we might think that there are many possible agencies for creating a common education in a society, from mandatory public service, to public media, to the public legal culture, to the Boy and Girl Scouts, etc. But Callan seems to have an entirely scholastic understanding of 'common education'. He rightly observes that a common education might be achieved by different kinds of schools: common schools can provide a common education, but so might properly regulated separate and private schools. If our conception of common education is a minimalist one, he says, then it will be easy to implement in separate schools, but if our conception of common education is demanding, then it will be harder to implement in separate schools.[36] On Callan's view, common education may be achieved through many kinds of schools, but it remains a wholly scholastic enter-

---

[32] "Are the ideas and institutions—and above all the worth—of democracy adequately conveyed in American schools?" See *Education for Democracy: A Statement of Principles* (Washington, DC: Education for Democracy Project, 1987), 8–9.

[33] William Galston, "Individual Experience and Social Policy: Thinking Practically about Overcoming Racial and Ethnic Prejudice," in *Nomos*, 429.

[34] As Tomasi says: "Most debates about liberal civic education proceed from the assumption that civic education concerns fitting children for the role they are to play as *public* persons." In other words, these debates proceed on the assumption that civic education means teaching civic values and virtues to children in school; the controversy is about which values and virtues to teach. Tomasi makes it clear that he shares this assumption: "What would it mean, in a diverse society, to educate people about the meaning of their political autonomy?" This is a great question, but his answer relies only on the school: "Political liberal civic education must take as its task not only the preparation of students for liberal *politics* but also their preparation for *life*. . . ." See Tomasi, "Civic Education and Ethical Subservience" in *Nomos*, 196, 198, 206. Political theorist and public schoolteacher Meira Levinson even argues that autonomy can only be learned at school—leading Rob Reich to observe that, by this logic, "prior to the advent of institutional schools, no one was autonomous." See Rob Reich, "Testing the Boundaries of Parental Authority Over Education: The Case of Homeschooling," in *Nomos*, 298–99.

[35] Eamonn Callan, *Creating Citizens: Political Education and Liberal Democracy* (Oxford: Clarendon Press, 1997), 163.

[36] Ibid., 169–71.

prise.[37] "What we need," he argues, "are common schools worthy of the ends of common education."[38] By reducing common education to a scholastic education, however, Callan undermines the force of his arguments for its necessity: "The necessity of a common education for all follows from the need to secure a sufficiently coherent and decent political culture and the prerequisites of a stable social order."[39] Even if some kind of common education is needed in a democracy, there is no reason to think that democracy requires a common scholastic education.

The most important recent argument for civic education in schools is Gutmann's *Democratic Education*. She certainly distinguishes the school from other agencies of education. "A democratic theory of education focuses on what might be called 'conscious social reproduction'—the ways in which citizens are or should be empowered to influence the education that in turn shapes the political values, attitudes, and modes of behavior of future citizens." A democratic theory of education, she says, "focuses on practices of deliberate instruction by individuals and on the educational influences of institutions designed at least partly for educational purposes."[40] Yet even assuming that a democratic theory of education should focus only on deliberate modes of education, Gutmann focuses almost exclusively on the school.[41] Indeed, she admits that "it is hard to resist the temptation to focus entirely on schooling, since it is our most deliberate form of human instruction. . . ."[42] Among the agencies of deliberate instruction, why is school the "most deliberate"? There are many sources of deliberate instruction apart from a school: ministers have a curriculum, as do wardens, parents, doctors, journalists, advertisers, coaches, and Boy Scout leaders. Perhaps Gutmann means that deliberate instruction is more prominent at school than among these other sources of education? In any event, she offers no argument or evidence that schools are more significant or effective as agents of "conscious social reproduction" than any other deliberate educator.[43]

Why must a theory of democratic education focus only on deliberate instruction? After all, many political theorists, from Aristotle to Toc-

---

[37] Ibid., 166. Callan asks advocates of separate schools to "show how a satisfactory common education can be given to children who do not attend common schools."

[38] Ibid., 220.

[39] Ibid., 166. Callan goes on to say ". . . once we reject the crazy idea that a common education can be completely repudiated . . ."

[40] Gutmann, *Democratic Education*, 14.

[41] She does briefly discuss libraries, cultural institutions, and literacy programs. And in one place she lists these agents of deliberate education: "libraries, bookstores, museums, newspapers, movies, radio, television, and other cultural institutions" (ibid., 234). Her list is interesting for what it omits, such as churches, prisons, corporations, civic associations, the Boy Scouts, etc.

[42] Ibid., 15.

[43] "We can appreciate the centrality of schooling to democratic education and still recognize that there is much more to democratic education than schooling" (ibid., 16). Whence this centrality?

queville, believed that civic education, including, and perhaps especially, democratic civic education, was mainly the by-product of growing up and participating in a democratic polity. Perhaps democratic civic virtue is a matter not of deliberate instruction, but of "habits of the heart" acquired indirectly, yet profoundly, from activities in churches, voluntary associations, and juries.[44] But Gutmann explicitly sets aside the question of how democratic schooling relates to the larger processes of democratic socialization. Unfortunately, her characterization of the field of political socialization is very misleading. First, she says that studies of political socialization "tend to focus on what might be called 'unconscious social reproduction'." In fact, many of these studies seek precisely to compare the causal significance of both unconscious and conscious agencies of education;[45] in addition, there is a branch of political socialization studies dedicated to the examination of civic education in schools.[46] Second, Gutmann says that studies of political socialization are merely descriptive: "their aim is to explain the processes by which societies perpetuate themselves." By contrast, she says, the aim of a democratic theory of education is normative, that is, "to understand how members of democratic society should participate in consciously shaping its future." When education becomes assimilated into political socialization, "it is easy to lose sight of the distinctive virtue of democratic society, that it authorizes citizens to influence how their society reproduces itself."[47]

[44] For Tocqueville's view that democratic education is a matter of laws and mores (*moeurs*), see *Democracy in America*, trans. Harvey C. Mansfield and Delba Winthrop (Chicago, IL: University of Chicago Press, 2000), 1:2, 9, 265. "Political associations can therefore be considered great schools, free of charge, where all citizens come to learn the general theory of associations." Ibid., 2:2, 7, 497.

[45] For a smattering of an immense literature comparing schooling with other modes of political socialization, see Gabriel A. Almond and Sidney Verba, *The Civic Culture: Political Attitudes and Democracy in Five Nations* (Princeton, NJ: Princeton University Press, 1963), 304, 355, 381, 387; Fred I. Greenstein, *Children and Politics* (New Haven, CT: Yale University Press, 1969), 4, 166; M. Kent Jennings and Richard G. Niemi, *The Political Character of Adolescence: The Influence of Families and Schools* (Princeton, NJ: Princeton University Press, 1974), 181–227; M. Kent Jennings and Richard G. Niemi, *Generations and Politics: A Panel Study of Young Adults and Their Parents* (Princeton, NJ: Princeton University Press, 1981), 230, 231, 269, 270; John L. Sullivan, James Piereson, and George E. Marcus, *Political Tolerance and American Democracy* (Chicago, IL: University of Chicago Press, 1982), 115–17, 251; Herbert McClosky and Alida Brill, *Dimensions of Tolerance: What Americans Believe about Civil Liberties* (New York: Russell Sage Foundation, 1983), 371, 420; Sidney Verba, Kay Lehman Schlozman, and Henry E. Brady, *Voice and Equality: Civic Voluntarism in American Politics* (Cambridge, MA: Harvard University Press, 1995), 416–60; and Robert D. Putnam, *Bowling Alone: The Collapse and Revival of American Community* (New York: Simon & Schuster, 2000), 302–407.

[46] For a smattering of this large literature, see Kenneth P. Langton and M. Kent Jennings, "Political Socialization and the High School Civics Curriculum in the United States," *American Political Science Review* 62, no. 3 (1968): 852–67; Paul Allen Beck and M. Kent Jennings, "Pathways to Participation," *American Political Science Review* 76, no. 1 (1982): 94–108; and Richard G. Niemi and Jane Junn, *Civic Education: What Makes Students Learn* (New Haven, CT: Yale University Press, 1998).

[47] Gutmann, *Democratic Education*, 15.

Gutmann's attempts to justify her focus on schools by setting aside the literature of political socialization fail. To begin with, the best studies of political socialization do not merely seek to describe the mechanisms by which society reproduces itself, but are designed precisely to answer normative questions in democratic theory, such as: What kinds of educational experiences lead citizens to various civic values, virtues, and activities? Moreover, anyone who consciously seeks to influence social reproduction should probably want to understand the mechanisms by which society reproduces itself. And even if democratic education turns out to be mainly the by-product of other kinds of social and political activity—even if citizens are formed mainly by informal modes of association—how does it follow that democratic citizens cannot deliberate about how to shape, influence, and encourage these indirect modes of civic education? Why cannot democratic citizens deliberate to shape, consciously though indirectly, the unconscious modes of civic education? Democratic deliberation can aim for full transparency, directness, and self-awareness even while conceding that democratic education proceeds mainly through obscure, oblique, and tacit agencies.

Finally, Gutmann offers no argument or evidence that the democratic education that takes place in schools, or could take place in schools, stems from direct, deliberate instruction rather than from indirect, tacit, and informal modes of student association. Indeed, although she claims that schooling "is our most deliberate form of human instruction," she argues that schools can and should teach moral values by means of their "hidden curriculum."[48] Yet, to the extent that schools teach civic virtues tacitly, they are not instruments of "conscious social reproduction"; and if schools are, in part, instruments of unconscious social reproduction, then how does Gutmann justify her neglect of all other instruments of unconscious social reproduction? In short, her distinction between conscious and unconscious modes of education does not serve to distinguish schools from other modes of socialization. Perhaps all institutions and associations engage in both kinds of education? Stephen Macedo follows Gutmann into this untenable conundrum when he celebrates the "hidden curriculum" of civic education in public schools and then attempts to argue that "public schools have an important moral advantage with respect to civic education: they pursue our deepest civic purposes *openly* and allow people to argue about these purposes in local as well as national democratic venues."[49] So public schools pursue civic education openly through their

---

[48] "Schools develop moral character at the same time as they try to teach basic cognitive skills, by insisting that students sit in their seats (next to students of different races and religions). . . ." Gutmann, *Democratic Education*, 53.

[49] Macedo even suggests that civic education in public schools is mainly tacit: "It is not simply, or perhaps even principally, the substantive curriculum of these schools that is crucial. Common schools have a 'hidden curriculum'. . . ." Yet he later warns: "The vice of a too-heavy reliance on indirect modes of civic education is that we might be led to exploit false consciousness." See Stephen Macedo, *Diversity and Distrust: Civic Education in a Multicultural Society* (Cambridge, MA: Harvard University Press, 2000), 232 and 279.

hidden curriculum! As we shall see from a number of empirical studies, the effect of schools on civic virtue is mainly tacit and indirect. So the focus on schools in these accounts of democratic education lacks any theoretical foundation.

Before we begin to understand the proper role of civic education in schools, we must first think more clearly about the relation of scholastic to other kinds of education. If we understand education to refer broadly to all kinds of learning experiences, then it becomes clear that little of our learning takes place in school, but instead takes place at home, among peers, on the job, at the library, and in places of worship, as well as under the influence of the media. Even if we understand education to refer more narrowly to deliberate instruction, then we still can see that a school-teacher is only one of many teachers in our lives: clearly our parents are teachers, as are our ministers, coaches, librarians, and doctors. Our friends also often act as teachers, as do journalists, advertisers, employers, judges, and scoutmasters. So most of our learning does not occur in school, and most of our teachers are not schoolteachers.

Lawrence Cremin describes the relation between the school and other agencies of deliberate instruction as an "ecology of education."[50] A school can relate in a general way to other agencies of education by confirming them, complementing them, or counteracting them. Which of these relations makes sense will depend, in part, upon the nature of the subject matter. Schools have a virtual monopoly on some kinds of knowledge, for example, chemistry, Latin, and calculus; schools generally avoid other kinds of knowledge, say, of obscure religious doctrines or job-specific information. But many kinds of knowledge are shared between schools and other educational sources, from English and history to sex education and, of course, civics. Since most of what we learn about politics we learn from our families, friends, the media, and voluntary organizations, school-teachers and administrators ought to decide whether what they teach about politics should confirm, complement, or counteract what students are learning or will learn from their other educators. Unfortunately, advocates of civic education almost never ask, let alone attempt to answer, this question.

We will need to think creatively about other modes of civic education because of what empirical research tells us about the effectiveness of schools. Since public schools have a long and pervasive history of engaging in civic education, political scientists over the past five decades have attempted to answer basic questions, such as: Where do citizens acquire their civic knowledge, skills, and virtues? What role do schools play in this acquisition? And, in particular, what role do high school civics courses play?

It is always risky to ground normative claims in empirical research: empirical beliefs generally change more quickly than do normative com-

---

[50] Cremin, *Public Education*, 27–53.

mitments. Our empirical findings (like our normative commitments) are always fallible, especially as they shape our beliefs about politics and society. And even though the best empirical studies of politics are framed in ways that attempt to answer normative questions about politics, these studies rarely answer our precise normative questions. The best normative arguments about civic education rely on subtle and sophisticated concepts of civic knowledge, motivation, reasoning, dispositions, skills, and virtues; but the empirical studies of civic education are usually framed in much cruder terms, such as knowledge and values. As we shall see, many studies that seem to present conflicting findings about the role of schools in civic education can be shown to converge once we distinguish civic knowledge from civic skills and from civic virtue. Moreover, when empirical studies do not converge, it is always risky to attempt to adjudicate disputes among scholars who rely on divergent studies. But, when there is a consistency of empirical findings and a substantial consensus among researchers, then normative theorists ought to take note. Research about political socialization has achieved a substantial convergence of findings and a substantial professional consensus about the relative importance of schooling and other factors in civic education. Let us cautiously consider what these studies might teach us about the proper role of the school in civic education.

Many students of political socialization follow Tocqueville in arguing that the most important schools of democracy are not schools at all but voluntary and civic associations. Studies focusing on the acquisition of civic competence or civic skills have found, not surprisingly, that these skills are mainly acquired not by children in schools but by adults in churches, unions, civic organizations, and workplaces. Gabriel Almond's and Sidney Verba's classic 1963 study, *The Civic Culture*, examined the formation of civic knowledge, skills, and attitudes in five nations. These researchers found that schools had some effect on civic skills, but not a strong effect compared to the salience of workplace experiences.[51] Almond and Verba confirmed Adam Smith's view that ordinary employment is the most powerful educative force in the lives of most people: "Of crucial significance here are the opportunities to participate in decisions at one's place of work."[52] The effect of schools on civic competence was

---

[51] In each nation those who report that they are consulted about decisions on their job are more likely than others to score high on the scale of subjective political competence.... Unlike many of the relationships between family and school participation and political competence, the relationships between competence on the job and subjective political competence remain strong even within matched educational groups.... Whether job participation leads to democratic political orientations, or vice versa, is difficult to tell; but the evidence is strong that these two develop closely together and mutually support each other.
Almond and Verba, *The Civic Culture*, 365–66; cf. 355.
[52] Ibid., 363.

mainly indirect: schools link students to all kinds of other associations.[53] Later, in 1980, Almond said about *The Civic Culture* that it "was one of the earliest studies to stress the importance of adult political socialization and experiences and to demonstrate the relative weakness of childhood socialization."[54]

Nothing is more characteristic of the modern confusion of education and schooling than the assumption that education is for children. In a major, more recent study (1995), Verba, Schlozman, and Brady found that the institutions most responsible for fostering civic skills and political participation were jobs, voluntary associations, and churches. They also found that American high schools provide civic education "not by teaching about democracy but by providing hands-on training for future participation."[55] Similarly, Robert Putnam's famous book, *Bowling Alone* (2000), endorses the findings of Verba, Schlozman, and Brady that we acquire our democratic virtues in our voluntary associations. Putnam argues that "voluntary associations may serve not only as forums for deliberation, but also as occasions for learning civic virtues, such as active participation in public life." He says that schools could do a better job imparting civic knowledge in the classroom and indirectly fostering civic skills by encouraging participation in service learning programs and extracurricular activities. He never suggests that schools themselves could become nurseries of civic virtue.[56]

Other researchers focus less on civic skills and more on civic knowledge and civic attitudes. Among these researchers, there is a widespread and long-standing consensus that an individual's civic knowledge and civic attitudes are best predicted by his or her years of schooling. For example, M. Kent Jennings and Richard Niemi survey a huge body of literature about the role of education in political socialization. They report a broad consensus that interest in politics, the possession of political skills, political participation, and support for the liberal democratic creed, all increase with years of schooling.[57] Does this suggest that schools are effectively teaching civic virtue? Actually, there is no agreement about how to explain the simple correlation between educational attainment and civic virtue. Since years of schooling correlates strongly with parental intelligence, education, and socioeconomic status, as well as with a stu-

[53] "Not only does the more highly educated individual learn politically relevant skills within the school, but he also is more likely to enter into other nonpolitical relationships that have the effect of further heightening his political competence." Ibid., 304.

[54] Gabriel A. Almond and Sidney Verba, eds., *The Civic Culture Revisited: An Analytic Study* (Boston: Little, Brown, 1980), 29.

[55] "That activity in school government or school clubs is such a strong predictor of later political activity fits nicely with our emphasis on the role of civic skills as a resource for politics. . . . Indeed, the fact that actual participatory experiences appear to be the most important school effect is a significant finding for understanding civic education." Verba, Schlozman, and Brady, *Voice and Equality*, 376 and 425.

[56] Putnam, *Bowling Alone*, 339–40 and 405.

[57] Jennings and Niemi, *Generations and Politics*, 230.

dent's own intelligence and subsequent socioeconomic status and occupation, it is very difficult to tease out the independent role of schooling.
Perhaps some other factor (or factors), such as parental education or the
student's own intelligence, causes both high educational attainment and
civic virtue?

Some researchers believe that schooling shapes political attitudes by
socializing students into a distinctive scholastic culture; this process of
socialization is thought to be primarily informal and extracurricular. Others believe that schools do not so much socialize students into a common
scholastic culture as allocate students to quite different socioeconomic
milieus: "Schools confer success on some and failure on others over and
above any socialization outcomes." [58] Jennings and Niemi believe that
schools both socialize students into a common culture *and* allocate students into quite different socioeconomic ranks; however, they report that
their data more strongly support the allocation theory.[59] To the extent that
schools merely allocate students into various social classes, they simply
reproduce the socioeconomic hierarchy of the wider society. In this sense,
the main effect of schooling on political conduct is to sort students into
various social classes, each with its own distinctive political culture.

More recently, Norman H. Nie, Jane Junn, and Kenneth Stehlik-Barry
propose two mechanisms by which schooling fosters levels of civic virtue:
the first is by sorting citizens into social and political ranks, each with its
own level of civic knowledge and virtue; the second is by enhancing the
cognitive sophistication of students.[60] Nie and his colleagues found that
students with more formal education were likely to be more politically
tolerant, not because of anything taught in school, but simply because of
their greater verbal proficiency.[61] These findings confirm many earlier
studies of the relation of educational attainment to political toleration,
that is, the willingness to accord civil liberties to those with whom one
disagrees. Samuel Stouffer pioneered this research in the 1950s. He argued that college graduates were more tolerant than others simply as a
by-product of their greater cognitive sophistication.[62] Philip E. Jacob then

[58] Ibid., 231.

[59] "While schools are in one sense supposed to perform a leveling function, they are also
expected to make distinctions, and to encourage and facilitate varying interests, skills, and
predispositions. Our results speak very much to the latter expectation. Educational institutions may indeed accomplish a leveling, but it is abundantly clear that when students leave
secondary school they have become politically stratified in many respects and that this
stratification by no means diminishes over time." Ibid., 270.

[60] "There are two theoretically and empirically distinct mechanisms linking education to
democratic citizenship. The first runs through the cognitive outcomes of education; the
other, through the impact of education on the positional life circumstances of individuals."
Norman H. Nie, Jane Junn, and Kenneth Stehlik-Barry, *Education and Democratic Citizenship
in America* (Chicago, IL: University of Chicago Press, 1996), 39.

[61] "Verbal proficiency was found to be the only significant intervening variable linking
education to democratic enlightenment." Ibid., 161.

[62] "Although many other studies have confirmed the relationship between education and
political tolerance, few authors have added anything of consequence to the cognitive explanation Stouffer proposed." Sullivan et al., *Political Tolerance and American Democracy*, 117.

investigated what it might be about college that could foster greater political tolerance: the curriculum did not seem to matter, except that students who focused on the liberal arts were better informed about politics and more active; the quality of teaching had almost no effect on the attitudes of students; and, perhaps most surprising, the style of pedagogy, that is, whether classes involved student participation or not, did not matter.[63] Other studies of the effects of college on political values also find that college increases political tolerance; these studies attribute this effect to the sheer increase in knowledge and cognitive sophistication among college graduates.[64] In a newer study, Nie and D. Sunshine Hillygus confirm the importance of sheer verbal proficiency in fostering political engagement, political knowledge, and public spiritedness. In their view, the only aspect of the curriculum that matters is the number of social science courses taken; these authors claim that these courses also contribute to greater civic participation.[65] Many researchers warn against attributing too much weight to schooling in shaping political attitudes: "Education is very weakly related to tolerance, when the relationship is controlled for other variables." [66] Jacob's finding that the liberal arts foster political involvement, combined with the consensus that the sheer amount of political knowledge and understanding fosters political tolerance, strongly suggests that the main role that school can play in fostering civic virtue is to enhance the general knowledge of students.

If schooling itself were effective in fostering civic virtue, then we should expect Americans today to exhibit a much higher degree of civic virtue than Americans of the mid-twentieth century. After all, Americans today have much more formal schooling than they did fifty years ago, let alone a century or two ago. Clearly, schooling cannot be the royal road to civic virtue, since virtually all measures of political and civic engagement in

---

[63] " 'Student-centered' techniques of teaching and stress on discussion in contrast to lecture or recitation have been strongly advocated as effective means of engaging the student's personal participation in the learning process, and encouraging him to reach valid judgments on his own on important issues. Studies of the comparative effectiveness of such methods do *not* generally support such a conviction." Philip E. Jacob, *Changing Values in College: An Exploratory Study of the Impact of College Teaching* (New York: Harper & Row, 1957), 8.

[64] See Clyde Z. Nunn, Harry J. Crockett, Jr., and J. Allen Williams, Jr., *Tolerance for Nonconformity* (San Francisco, CA: Jossey-Bass, 1978), 65 and 75; and Sullivan et al., *Political Tolerance and American Democracy*, 115 and 117. See also McClosky and Brill, *Dimensions of Tolerance*, 371: "The more one knows and understands about public affairs (as measured by our scales of political information and sophistication), the higher the probability that one will respond favorably to the various libertarian rights. . . ."

[65] "An individual's verbal skills before college entrance have two distinct effects on future civic and political activity: not only does verbal aptitude have a direct path to participation and engagement, but it also maintains an indirect path by leading students to major in the social sciences, where they are further stimulated to become politically active and engaged citizens." Norman H. Nie and D. Sunshine Hillygus, "Education and Democratic Citizenship," in Ravitch and Vitteritti, eds., *Making Good Citizens*, 50. But Nie and Hillygus were not able to determine whether taking more social science courses caused greater political engagement in students or merely reflected it.

[66] Sullivan et al., *Political Tolerance and American Democracy*, 251.

the United States show a steep decline over the past half-century.[67] Americans' vastly greater attainments of schooling have not even made them more knowledgeable about politics, let alone more inclined to vote or volunteer: citizens today know no more about politics than they did a half-century ago.[68] These paradoxes strongly suggest that the role of schooling in fostering civic knowledge and civic virtue must be quite indirect.

Most states in the United States require public schools to teach civics courses. Since advocates of civic education in public schools strongly support such courses, we might ask: What role do civics courses play in fostering desirable political knowledge, attitudes, and conduct? After a series of studies in the early 1960s, Kenneth Langton and M. Kent Jennings published in 1968 a very influential article concerned with the effects of high school civics courses on a range of political knowledge, attitudes, values, and interests.[69] They found that the high school civics curriculum had very little effect on any aspect of political knowledge or values: "Our findings certainly do not support the thinking of those who look to the civics curriculum in American high schools as even a minor source of political socialization." It is important to note, however, that they found a greater effect of civics courses on political knowledge than on political values or attitudes.[70] In 1974, Langton and Jennings, now with the addition of Niemi, revised and enlarged their earlier article. They now found that the educational level of parents and the amount of political discourse at home had a much greater impact on the measured knowledge and values of individuals than did high school courses; where high school civics courses had any effect, it was only on those students who were just finishing those courses.[71] A subsequent study by Paul

[67] Richard Brody (1978): "Over the past quarter-century, the proportion of the population continuing on to post-secondary education has doubled. In light of this development and the manifest relationship between education and participation, the steady decline in turnout since the 1960s is all the more remarkable." Cited in Nie et al., *Education and Democratic Citizenship in America*, 99.

[68] "Why, given dramatically increasing educational opportunities, higher average levels of educational attainment, and the strong relation between education and political knowledge at the individual level, have aggregate political knowledge levels remained relatively stable over the past half-century?" Michael X. Delli Carpini and Scott Keeter, *What Americans Know about Politics and Why It Matters* (New Haven, CT: Yale University Press, 1996), 199.

[69] Langton and Jennings, "Political Socialization and the High School Civics Curriculum in the United States," 852–67. They examined the effects of these courses on political knowledge, political interest, spectator interest in politics, political discourse, political efficacy, political cynicism, civic tolerance, and participative orientation.

[70] For the whole sample, civics courses had the strongest relationship on political knowledge. For black students, civics courses had a significant effect on political knowledge: "The civics curriculum is an important source of political knowledge for Negroes. . . ." Ibid., 865, 858, and 860.

[71] M. Kent Jennings, Kenneth P. Langton, and Richard G. Niemi, "Effects of the High School Civics Curriculum" in Jennings and Niemi, *The Political Character of Adolescence*, 191. "[I]n the very short run the curriculum exerts what little effect it has on those under current exposure" (192).

Allen Beck and Jennings (1982) reconfirmed the impotence of civics courses but found that participation in extracurricular activities, both in high school and beyond, fostered later political participation by young adults.[72]

These and other studies created a lasting professional consensus that the scholastic curriculum in general has some effects on the civic knowledge, but little or no effect on the civic values, of students and that civics courses in particular have essentially no effect on political attitudes or values.[73] Richard Niemi and Jane Junn challenged this consensus in their major 1998 study, *Civic Education: What Makes Students Learn*. Niemi and Junn analyzed data that enabled them to study the effects of different kinds of civics courses on students' political knowledge and attitudes. They hypothesized that certain kinds of teaching methods might significantly add or subtract from learning about politics.[74] They found that, although the civics curriculum had much less effect on political knowledge and values than did the home environment, civics courses did matter. In particular, civics courses that were taken quite recently, had a large variety of topics studied, and included discussion of current events, fostered significantly greater political knowledge.[75] As with earlier studies, Niemi and Junn found that although the curriculum had some effect on political knowledge, it had virtually no effect on political attitudes.[76]

It is too soon to tell if this study by Niemi and Junn will alter the existing consensus that civics courses do not matter; some reviews suggest that the current consensus is likely to prevail.[77] At a deeper level, though, this study largely confirms the conventional wisdom: Niemi and Junn surmise that one key reason that they found civics courses more significant than did Langton and Jennings is simply because the earlier study focused mainly on the effects of civics courses on attitudes, while their own analysis focused mainly on the effects on civic knowledge. In

---

[72] Beck and Jennings, "Pathways to Participation," 101–2. "[T]hose who engage in extracurricular activities are more likely to become politically active later on. . . ." (105).

[73] "It is fair to say that insofar as there is consensus on anything in political science, and insofar as political scientists are at all concerned about formal education and its role in political socialization, there has been a consensus that a formal civics curriculum or its equivalent is all but irrelevant to citizens' knowledge of or engagement with politics. . . ." Elizabeth Frazer, "Review of Niemi and Junn *Civic Education*," in *Government and Opposition* 35 (2000): 122. See the discussion of the scholarly consensus in Niemi and Junn, *Civic Education*, 13–20. They comment: "[T]he presumption that academic knowledge is gained entirely or even primarily in the classroom may be a truism for some subjects but not for civics" (61).

[74] Niemi and Junn, *Civic Education*, 81.

[75] Ibid., 123–24.

[76] Ibid., 140.

[77] See Jay P. Greene, "Review of *Civic Education*," *Social Science Quarterly* 81, no. 2 (2000): 696–97. Greene performed a reanalysis of the Niemi and Junn data set and found that the variable of how recently the civics course was taken collapsed into whether a student is enrolled in a civics class at the time that the civics test is taken: "If knowledge fades so rapidly that the only benefit of a civics class occurs while one is in it, then schools may not be able to do much to improve civics knowledge in the longer run." Greene found defects in other independent variables as well.

short, all of these studies confirm a more qualified consensus that civics courses might have some role in fostering civic knowledge but essentially no role in fostering civic attitudes or virtues.[78] The differential impact of schooling on knowledge and values is strongly confirmed by the two largest studies of the long-term impact of schooling: Herbert Hyman and Charles Wright's classic studies of the enduring effects of schooling on knowledge and on values concluded that schooling has a much larger effect on knowledge than on values.[79]

Ironically, political theorists have come to eagerly embrace education for civic virtue in the schools just at the moment when political scientists have reached agreement that civic education in schools has little effect on political knowledge and less effect on political attitudes.[80] Of course, the descriptive findings of social scientists, while relevant to the normative debates about civic education, are not conclusive. If one favors education for civic virtue in schools, then one is likely to regret that such education is ineffective; conversely, if one rejects education for civic virtue in schools on normative grounds, then one might be pleased to discover that it does not work. Gutmann cites the scholarly consensus about civics courses but then correctly observes: "Empirical studies measure the results of civics and history courses as they are, not as they might be."[81] No one can doubt that civics and history courses could be much better than they usually are; and perhaps these better courses might be more effective.[82] In the end, however, Gutmann concedes that political socialization at home is always likely to be much more formative than anything at school: "This conclusion is compatible with the claim that history and civics courses can and should teach democratic virtue, so long as we understand democratic virtue to include the willingness and ability of citizens to reason collectively and critically about politics."[83] Usually we assume that one

---

[78] "As expected, the overall explanatory power of the model for both political attitudes is relatively small compared with the model predicting overall political knowledge." Niemi and Junn, *Civic Education*, 140.

[79] See Herbert H. Hyman and Charles R. Wright, *Education's Lasting Influence on Values* (Chicago, IL: University of Chicago Press, 1979), 65.

[80] Not only do civics courses not have much effect but neither do history or social studies courses. See Jennings, Langton, and Niemi, "Effects of the High School Civics Curriculum," 191; and M. Kent Jennings, Lee H. Ehman, and Richard G. Niemi, "Social Studies Teachers and their Pupils," 226-27; both chapters in Jennings and Niemi, *The Political Character of Adolescence*.

[81] Gutmann, *Democratic Education*, 106.

[82] A group of political scientists and educators designed a new civics curriculum to teach tolerance and have experimentally tested its effects on students; they claim that this new curriculum causes students (on average) to express more tolerant attitudes. For the curriculum, see Patricia Avery et al., *Tolerance for Diversity of Beliefs: A Secondary Curriculum Unit* (Boulder, CO: Social Science Education Consortium, 1993). For the studies claiming that this curriculum made students more tolerant, see Patricia Avery et al., "Exploring Political Tolerance with Adolescents," *Theory and Research in Social Education* 20, no. 4 (1992): 386-420; and Karen Bird et al., "Not Just Lip-Synching Anymore: Education and Tolerance Revisited," *Review of Education, Pedagogy, and Cultural Studies* 16, nos. 3-4 (1994): 373-86.

[83] Gutmann, *Democratic Education*, 107.

ought to do something only if one can do it. While there is some evidence that schools can effectively teach political knowledge, there is virtually no evidence that schools can effectively teach political virtue, that is, a disposition to want to become a good citizen by, for example, reasoning collectively. Here we have the perfect triumph of hope over experience.

We ought not be surprised by the evidence that civic virtue is not acquired by children in school. After all, our contemporary political scientists have merely ratified the wisdom of the greatest political philosophers, ancient and modern, who insisted that civic virtue is acquired only by adults from active participation in public affairs. Plato's guardians, for example, must wait until they are thirty-five years old to begin their fifteen years of civic education, which takes place not in school but in direct participation in governmental affairs.[84] Aristotle is also clear that "a youth is not a suitable student of political science" because, although the intellectual virtues can be taught, the moral virtues result from habit.[85] For Aristotle, civic education is the responsibility of the legislator, not the teacher: the legislator uses law to educate citizens by ensuring that they acquire the right habits as they grow up.[86] Once citizens have grown up with the right civic virtues, then, as mature citizens, they might benefit from Aristotle's teaching about politics. Tocqueville beautifully captures the ancient view that schools foster academic knowledge just as politics fosters civic virtue: "The institutions of a township are to freedom what primary schools are to science; they put it within the reach of the people; they make them taste its peaceful employ and habituate them to making use of it."[87] For Tocqueville, then, schools must be dedicated to imparting knowledge; civic virtue, by contrast, will be learned in town meetings, in churches, and on juries. What we find, then, in Plato, Aristotle, and Tocqueville are very sophisticated analyses of the various agencies of civic education and a conception of civic education that does not rely on the institution of the school.[88]

Both classic political philosophers and contemporary political scientists seem to agree, then, that deliberate instruction aimed at inculcating civic knowledge and virtue is strikingly ineffective. Some knowledge of the history, structure, and functions of government and of the nature of politics might well be taught in civics courses, but not proper civic attitudes, such as a desire to contribute to the common good, a respect for democratic values, a love of country, or toleration of opposing views. Yet ad-

---

[84] Plato, *Republic*, trans. Robin Waterfield (Oxford: Oxford University Press, 1993), 540A.

[85] Aristotle, *Nicomachean Ethics*, in *Complete Works of Aristotle*, ed. Jonathan Barnes (Princeton, NJ: Princeton University Press, 1984), 1095a3 and 1103a15.

[86] Ibid., 1103b4, 1103b21, 1180a32.

[87] Tocqueville, *Democracy in America*, I:1, 5, 57.

[88] True, Aristotle does recommend public or common schooling over private schooling (*Politics*, 1337a3; *Nicomachean Ethics*, 1180a14), but there is no evidence that he thinks these schools should aim at civic education; in fact, he prefers a liberal education for leisure over a civic education (*Politics*, 1338a21–32).

vocates of civic education in schools insist that it must aim not only at civic knowledge but also at civic virtue. Naturally, advocates of civic education are free to insist that although existing methods of teaching civic virtue in schools are ineffective, some new and better kind of civics courses might work. At the same time, those of us who object to the whole endeavor of using public schools as instruments of partisan civic indoctrination may take some comfort in its near total failure.

III. CIVIC VIRTUE OR INTELLECTUAL VIRTUE?

Curiously, leading contemporary advocates of civic education in schools admit that it is ineffective.[89] What drives the passion for civic and other kinds of moral education is not the conviction that they are effective, but the conviction that without civic and moral education, schooling lacks any compelling moral purpose. It is no accident, then, that advocates of civic education in public schools all share the fundamental assumption that purely academic education consists only in the acquisition of skills and information and thus lacks an inherent moral dimension. If academic education merely involves the acquisition of amoral information and skills—if it is merely about 'the 3 Rs'—then we might as well ask: Why should any society make a fundamental and expensive public commitment to common schools?

The view that education seeks to put an amoral intellect in the service of a moral heart is powerfully expressed by Immanuel Kant. Education by means of teaching and instruction, says Kant, aims solely at the acquisition of skillfulness, and 'skillfulness' he defines as a capacity for achieving any possible end.[90] Of course, it would be deeply immoral simply to arm students with powerful weapons and give them no guidance for their use, so Kant insists upon a supplemental education in 'moralization' (*Moralisirung*): "Man must not simply be skillful for any possible end, unless he also develops a character so that he chooses only purely good ends."[91] Because Kant defines academic instruction as the acquisition of amoral skills, no amount of academic learning will contribute to moral goodness: "A man can be physically and even mentally quite cultivated but still, with poor moral cultivation, be an evil creature."[92] Thus, by describing academic education in the amoral terms of the acquisition of skills, rather than in the moral terms of conscientiousness in the pursuit

---

[89] See, for example, Gutmann, *Democratic Education*, 106–7; and Macedo, *Democracy and Distrust*, 235.

[90] Kant, *On Pedagogy (Pädagogik)* 9:449. Cf. *Groundwork for the Metaphysics of Morals (Grundlegung)* 4:423; and *The Metaphysics of Morals (Metaphysik der Sitten)* 6:392, 444–45. All Kant citations are by volume and page number from the standard Prussian Academy edition of *Kants gesammelte Schriften* (Berlin: Georg Reimer, later Walter de Gruyter & Co., 1902–). All translations of Kant are mine.

[91] "*Der Mensch soll nicht bloss au allerlei Zwecken geschickt sein, sondern auch die Gesinnung bekommen, dass er nur lauter gute Zwecke erwähle.*" *On Pedagogy (Pädagogik)* 9:450.

[92] Ibid., 9:469–70.

of truth, Kant has created a moral vacuum in academic education and generated the need for compensatory moral education. In contemporary debates about academic schooling, progressive educators emphasize the learning of certain skills, such as critical thinking skills, while traditionalist educators emphasize the mastery of certain kinds of information; but all of our contemporary pedagogues follow Kant by describing the aims of academic education in the amoral terms of information and skills.

In the current debates over civic education in schools, both advocates and critics universally frame the debate as "between people who insist that the community should be able to teach democratic values and others who insist that the community should have no more authority than is necessary to teach intellectual skills."[93] Framed in this way, a rich conception of civic virtues looks much more attractive than an impoverished conception of academic skills. Once we make a moral vacuum of academic education, how can anyone object to the need for a compensatory moral or civic education? Gutmann consistently contrasts her morally rich conception of democratic education to the morally impoverished conception of purely academic education called 'civic minimalism'. Gutmann, like the advocates of 'civic minimalism', always defines this purely academic education in the most amoral of terms: "literacy and numeracy," "the 3R's," or "basic skills."[94] If citizens expect civic education in addition to mere academics, "then they are authorized to impose some values on schools."[95] In short, academic education does not involve "values." Gutmann's conception of a proper civic education includes not only academics but also moral values: "It would need to include teaching literacy and numeracy at a high level. It would also need to include teaching—not indoctrinating—civic values such as toleration, nondiscrimination, and respect for individual rights and legitimate laws."[96]

Gutmann argues that academic knowledge helps children to live a good life in the "nonmoral" sense,[97] and, she says, the skills that we acquire from a nonmoral education can contribute to the moral education of citizens.[98] She labels as "amoralism" the view that schools should stick to only teaching academics: "An apparent attraction of this solution is

[93] See Christopher Eisgruber, "How Do Liberal Democracies Teach Values?" in *Nomos*, 74.

[94] "Mandating civic minimalism would entail *constitutionally prohibiting* citizens from requiring any more of schools than teaching the 3 R's, or some other clearly specified minimum." Gutmann, "Civic Minimalism, Cosmopolitanism, and Patriotism: Where Does Democratic Education Stand in Relation to Each?" in *Nomos*, 35.

[95] Ibid., 34.

[96] Ibid., 37. "In addition to a high level of numeracy and literacy, [it would also need to include] teaching civic values such as racial nondiscrimination and religious toleration . . ." (42).

[97] It helps children "learn how to live a good life in a nonmoral sense by teaching them knowledge and appreciation of (among other things) literature, science, history, and sports." See Gutmann, *Democratic Education*, 51.

[98] "The logical skills taught by science and mathematics, the interpretive skills taught by literature, the understanding of different ways of life taught by both history and literature, and even the sportsmanship taught by physical education can contribute to the moral education of citizens." Ibid., 51.

that schools would thereby rid themselves of all the political controversies now surrounding moral education and get on with the task of teaching the 'basics'—cognitive skills and factual knowledge."[99] Yet, she insists that amoralism is impossible in practice, because schools teach moral virtues and values informally through the "hidden curriculum" or ethos of the school. This is true, but we still have to decide whether to try to orient the ethos of the school toward intellectual or civic virtues. Macedo also describes academic schooling as equipping students with amoral weapons for any possible end: "Children must at the very least be provided with the intellectual tools necessary to understand the world around them, formulate their own convictions, and make their own way in life."[100]

Callan worries that if common schools eschew all moral and civic aims, then they will sink to the "lowest common denominator" of society's understanding of what children can learn. Such morally vapid common schools will be, he says, "unacceptable to the adherents of separate education and uninspiring to those of us who once looked to the common school with strong social hopes."[101] Purely academic education is only a "lowest common denominator," "unacceptable" to some, and "uninspiring" to others if we assume, with Kant, that it is intrinsically amoral. Given this prevailing conception of academic education, Callan rightly alerts us to a dilemma for the common school: if we reject controversial moral and civic aims in common schools, then we must defend an "uninspiring," not to mention amoral, education; but if we embrace a rich conception of moral or civic education, then our schools become inspiring to some and unacceptable to others. A minimalist academic education undermines the ideal of the school, while a maximalist moral education undermines the ideal of the *common* school.

Gutmann and others offer civic education as precisely the way of escaping this dilemma: they rightly argue that amoral academic minimalism fails to honor the moral ideal of schooling just as maximalist liberal or conservative moralism fails to honor the ideal of the common school. Therefore, to fill the moral vacuum of amoral academic education, Gutmann and others champion civic education not just as one aim of common schools, but as the primary aim.[102] Similarly, Macedo asserts that "the core purpose of public schooling is to promote civic ideals."[103] And Callan says that because schooling has such a large place in children's

---

[99] Ibid., 53.

[100] Macedo, *Diversity and Distrust*, 238. Macedo sees academics as a moral vacuum, but not public schools: "At their best, public schools exemplify a spirit of mutual respect, reciprocity, and mutual curiosity about cultural differences" (123).

[101] Callan, *Creating Citizens*, 170.

[102] "[W]e can conclude that 'political education'—the cultivation of the virtues, knowledge, and skills necessary for political participation—has moral primacy over the other purposes of public education in a democratic society." Gutmann, *Democratic Education*, 287; cf. 127 and 290.

[103] Macedo, *Diversity and Distrust*, 122.

lives, "the evolution of the roles and ideals that the institution offers to children as their schooling progresses should be designed with an eye to whatever pattern of moral development issues in the virtue of the citizen."[104] We can now better appreciate why advocates of civic education in schools care so little about the effectiveness of schools as instruments of civic education: public schools need a compelling moral purpose and civic education is a compelling moral purpose. Gutmann goes so far as to argue that without civic education, public schooling does not merit public support.[105]

If academic education intrinsically lacked a compelling moral purpose, then I would agree that our students need a compensatory moral education—and an education in the civic virtues might well be the most apt kind in a pluralistic democracy. But, as every good teacher knows, mere information and skills cannot be the aim of academic education because apart from a virtuous orientation toward truth, information and skills are mere resources and tools that can be put into the service of sophistry, manipulation, and domination. Only when the acquisition of information and skills is combined with a proper desire for true knowledge do we begin to acquire 'intellectual virtue', which may be defined as the conscientious pursuit of truth.[106] Every virtue theorist has his or her own catalogue of virtues, but what matters more than the particulars on the list is the relation among them. My developmental hierarchy of intellectual virtues begins with the virtues of intellectual carefulness such as single-mindedness, thoroughness, accuracy, and perseverance. Having acquired these virtues in elementary school, students must then learn how to resist temptations to false beliefs by acquiring the virtues of intellectual humility, intellectual courage, and intellectual impartiality. Finally, adults ought to strive for coherence in what they know and for coherence between their knowledge and their other pursuits by acquiring the virtues of intellectual integrity and ultimately wisdom. John Dewey thought that the aim of academic pedagogy was the inculcation of certain traits in students, among them open-mindedness, single-mindedness, sincerity, breadth of outlook, thoroughness, and responsibility. Dewey insisted that these academic or intellectual virtues "are moral traits."[107]

Once we grant that academic education is itself a limited kind of moral education, then the question we face is not whether to pursue moral education in schools: academic schooling is intrinsically a kind of

---

[104] Callan, *Creating Citizens*, 176.

[105] She wonders "why so much taxpayer money should go to schooling that gives up on the central aims of civic education. If schooling ceases to become a compelling public good, then it should be privately rather than publicly funded, at least for everyone but parents who cannot afford to educate their children." Gutmann, "Civic Education and Social Diversity," 572–73.

[106] See Zagzebski, *Virtues of the Mind*, 175–77.

[107] Dewey, *Democracy and Education*, 356–57; cf. 173–79.

moral education. The questions we face are, rather, What kind of moral education is appropriate to the institution of the school? Schools seem apt instruments for some but not all kinds of moral education. And is civic education compatible with the intrinsic moral aim of academic schooling, namely, the conscientious pursuit of true knowledge? As we shall see, civic education, both in theory and in practice, subverts the intrinsic moral purpose of academic schooling.

What happens to academic education in the context of schools committed to civic education? Whether we look to the history of civic education or to the ideas of civic educators, the answer is quite certain: the academic pursuit of knowledge will be corrupted through a subordination of truth-seeking to some civic agenda. The history of civic education in the United States is a cautionary tale, indeed. Many advocates of civic education rightly invoke the prestige of Jefferson, who was a leading pioneer and prophet of using common schools for republican civic education.[108] What these advocates fail to notice, however, is how Jefferson's commitment to civic education corrupted his own intellectual integrity. Jefferson's initial vision of his proposed University of Virginia reflected his lifelong commitment to the freedom of the human mind from every tyranny erected over it: "This institution," he wrote, "will be based on the illimitable freedom of the human mind. For here we are not afraid to follow the truth wherever it may lead, nor to tolerate any error so long as reason is left free to combat it."[109] But as a civic educator, Jefferson could not bear the thought of future students at his university being exposed to and corrupted by politically incorrect ideas. Thus, in order to protect them from the seductive Toryism of David Hume, Jefferson spent two decades promoting the publication of a censored, plagiarized, and falsified but politically correct edition of Hume's *History of England*.[110] When he could find no partners in this intellectual crime, he then enlisted James Madison's support as a fellow member of the Board of Overseers of the nascent University of Virginia to draft regulations aimed at suppressing political heresy and promoting political orthodoxy. Jefferson and Madi-

---

[108] See, for one example, Pangle and Pangle, "What the American Founders Have to Teach Us about Schooling for Democratic Citizenship," 21–46.

[109] Jefferson, quoted in Leonard W. Levy, *Jefferson and Civil Liberties: The Darker Side* (Cambridge, MA: Harvard University Press, 1963), 157. Levy comments about this noble aspiration: "Six years later and only a few months before his death, he viewed the law school as the place from which the path of future generations would be lit by the vestal flame of political partisanship rather than by truth or unfettered inquiry."

[110] On Jefferson's decades-long promotion of John Baxter's plagiarized, falsified, and republicanized edition of Hume, see Dumas Malone, *Jefferson and His Time*, vol. 6, *The Sage of Monticello* (Boston, MA: Little, Brown, 1981), 205–7. Arthur Bestor, "Thomas Jefferson and the Freedom of Books," in Bestor et al., *Three Presidents and Their Books* (Urbana, IL: University of Illinois Press, 1955), 1–44: "It is embarrassing, to say the least, to find Jefferson recommending such a sorry combination of plagiarism, expurgation, and clandestine emendation" (18). For Baxter's text, see John Baxter, *A New and Impartial History of England* (London: H. D. Symonds, 1796–1801); Baxter never mentions his reliance on Hume.

son succeeded in passing a resolution to "provide that none [of the principles of government] shall be inculcated which are incompatible with those on which the Constitutions of this state, and of the U.S. were genuinely based, in the common opinion. . . ." This resolution goes on to specify the texts that must be taught in the school of politics (Locke, Sidney, *The Federalist Papers*, and U.S. and Virginia constitutional documents).[111] Moreover, Jefferson came to agree with Madison's argument that "the most effectual safeguard against heretical intrusions into the School of politics, will be an able [and] orthodox Professor. . . ."[112] To this end, Jefferson and later Madison worked to ensure that only those professors who espoused a strict constructionist interpretation of the U.S. Constitution and the doctrine of states' rights would be appointed to the school of politics.[113] Because of his passion for civic education in republican virtue, Jefferson abandoned his commitment to intellectual freedom in favor of partisan indoctrination at his own beloved University of Virginia. That such a champion of intellectual freedom who swore undying enmity to every tyranny over the mind of man should himself attempt to whitewash, censor, and suppress what he called "heresy" powerfully illustrates the poisonous consequences of using schools as instruments of civic education.

Jefferson has truly been the poisoned wellspring of American civic education in schools ever since. Some historians have systematically analyzed the civic values taught in public school civics, literature, history, and social studies courses. It should be no surprise that in order to teach civic values, American textbook writers in every epoch have systematically sanitized, distorted, and falsified history, literature, and social studies in order to inculcate every manner of religious, cultural, and class bigotry—including racism, nationalism, Anglo-Saxon superiority, American imperialism, Social Darwinism, anti-Catholicism, and anti-intellectualism.[114] An early text from 1796 warns of the danger posed by the importation of French ideas and persons: "Let America beware of infidelity, which is the most dangerous enemy that she has to contend with at present. . . ." The author goes on to teach schoolchildren that Native Americans lack all science, culture, and religion; that they are averse to labor and foresight; and that "the beavers ex-

---

[111] See "Minutes of the Board of Visitors of the University of Virginia, March 4, 1825," in Bestor, "Thomas Jefferson and Freedom of Books," 43–44. Among the mandatory texts were the Virginia Resolutions of 1798–1800, which uphold the states'-rights, strict-constructionist interpretation of the Constitution, according to Bestor (27).

[112] See letter of Madison to Jefferson, February 8, 1825, in Bestor, "Thomas Jefferson and the Freedom of Books," 41–42.

[113] See the letters of Jefferson and of Madison in Bestor, "Thomas Jefferson and Freedom of Books," 39–44.

[114] Among many histories of American civic education, see Smith, *Civic Ideals*; Bessie Louise Pierce, *Civic Attitudes in American School Textbooks* (Chicago, IL: University of Chicago Press, 1930); and Ruth Miller Elson, *Guardians of Tradition: American Schoolbooks of the Nineteenth Century* (Lincoln: University of Nebraska Press, 1964).

ceed the Indians, ten-fold, in the construction of their homes and public works. . . ."[115] Later, in the wake of large-scale Irish immigration
during the 1840s and 1850s, school texts begin a massive campaign of
slander and calumny against Roman Catholicism. Textbooks not only
describe Catholicism as an anti-Christian form of paganism and idola-
try, they even blame the Church for the fall of the Roman Empire. One
speller asks: "Is papacy at variance with paganism?" A historian says
that no theme in school texts before 1870 is more universal than anti-
Catholicism; according to these texts, Catholicism has no place in the
American past or future.[116] In the period after 1870, religious bigotry
gives way to racial bigotry and all non-Anglo-Saxon peoples are described as permanently and immutably inferior due to their intellectual, moral, and physical degeneracy. Beginning in 1917, during World
War I, many states began to pass laws forbidding any instruction in
public schools that might be disloyal to the United States, including
the teaching of the German language; at the same time, many states
also passed laws requiring all public schoolteachers to be American
citizens and to swear an oath that they would teach patriotism.[117]

This subordination of knowledge to civic uplift is not merely a relic of
the past: in many states, Creationism is taught in place of biology and
geology because of the perceived moral dangers of Darwinism. And many
states continue to require American history to be falsified in order to
promote patriotism. The Texas Education Code provides that "textbooks
should promote democracy, patriotism, and the free enterprise system";
this provision is still employed to sanitize the teaching of history in
Texas.[118] In 2002 the New York Board of Regents was found to have
falsified, on moral grounds, most of the literary texts used in its exams;
here classic literature was bowdlerized in the interests of political cor-
rectness.[119] Some systematic examinations of current social studies and
history textbooks find extensive evidence of how American history is
distorted, twisted, and falsified in order to emphasize the previously
neglected contributions as well as the victimization of women and minorities.[120] Although Anglo-Saxon triumphalism now frequently gives
way to multicultural victimization, nothing has changed in the American
passion for subordinating truth-seeking to moral and civic uplift.

---

[115] Elhanan Winchester, *A Plain Political Catechism Intended for the Use of Schools in the United States of America* (Greenfield, MA: Dickman, 1796), questions 60 and 65.

[116] See Elson, *Guardians of Tradition*, 47–48, 53.

[117] See Pierce, *Civic Attitudes in American School Textbooks*, 229–39.

[118] See Alexander Stille, "Textbook Publishers Learn: Avoid Messing with Texas," *New York Times*, June 29, 2002, late edition, sec. A, p. 1, col. 1.

[119] See N. R. Kleinfield, "The Elderly Man and the Sea? Test Sanitizes Literary Texts," *New York Times*, June 2, 2002, late edition, sec. 1, p. 1, col. 1.

[120] See Gilbert T. Sewall, "History Textbooks at the New Century," A Report of the Amer-ican Textbook Council (New York, 2000); and Paul C. Vitz, *Censorship: Evidence of Bias in our Children's Textbooks* (Ann Arbor, MI: Servant Books, 1986).

No one should be surprised that American schoolbooks, like any form of human knowledge, should often prove mistaken and misguided. But textbooks do not go astray merely because their authors are fallible human beings sincerely seeking true knowledge; rather, texts go astray because their authors deliberately subordinate the pursuit of knowledge to an agenda of civic education. American textbooks are often explicitly anti-intellectual: they repeatedly emphasize that moral and civic virtue is far more important than mere knowledge.[121] What again and again proves fatal to the pursuit of knowledge is the conviction that civic virtue is more important than truth.

Civic education aimed at civic virtue in schools usually involves various kinds of duplicity on the part of educators: teachers pretend to teach American history, but actually merely use historical examples to covertly attempt to impart one or another civic virtue. This subordination of knowledge to civic uplift often proceeds through the presentation of genuine facts, but facts selected by an ulterior motive of inducing patriotism or cosmopolitanism. Just as nothing can be more misleading than a photograph, so nothing can be more fictitious than a biased selection of "facts" in the presentation of history or social studies. In response to the traditionally rosy and uplifting versions of American greatness designed to instill patriotism, we now find dark and brutal narratives of American imperialism and racism designed to covertly instill multicultural tolerance. Both the traditional and the radical narratives of American history might be equally factual just as they are equally false. Of course, any presentation of American history will be selective and, hence, in some ways biased or misleading, but the effort to present American history truthfully (using the consensus of historians as a proxy for truth) will surely fail if our motive is to use that history to inculcate one or another civic virtue.

Both conservative and progressive civic educators routinely subordinate the quest for truth to a preferred agenda for civic uplift. As we shall see, some civic educators frankly espouse the falsification of history or the weakening of academic standards in pursuit of civic virtue. Yet so deepseated is the urge to falsify American history that even when civic educators claim to reject "brainwashing" or "indoctrination," they proceed to advocate precisely that.[122]

---

[121] See Elson, *Guardians of Tradition*, 226.

[122] For example, educator William Damon argues that our schools ought to use American history to teach students to love their country: "Now I am aware that when I write this, I risk being accused of trying to indoctrinate children by brainwashing them with a whitewashed picture of America. But whitewashing is not at all what I have in mind. For one thing, it is a necessary part of character education to teach about the mistakes that have been made and the problems that persist." Of course, to describe the evils in American history, such as slavery, lynching, and the killing of the natives, as "mistakes" is the very definition of "whitewashing." See Damon, "To Not Fade Away: Restoring Civil Identity Among the Young," in Ravitch and Viteritti, eds., *Making Good Citizens*, 139.

Advocates of civic education devote virtually all of their analysis to the question of what values ought to be taught or ought to be permitted to be taught in schools. It is almost always taken for granted that knowledge should be subordinated to moral and civic uplift, so the only questions are: What values ought to be inculcated? And who should decide? Some argue that a common democratic culture requires a common democratic education in all schools, while others argue that our pluralist democratic culture requires a wide diversity of moral and civic education in schools. In legal theorist Michael McConnell's pluralist vision, every school, public or private, ought to have the right to corrupt the pursuit of knowledge in the service of its preferred ideology.[123] Apparently we must choose either to subordinate knowledge to an official orthodoxy or to permit the subordination of knowledge to all manner of unofficial orthodoxies. Just as those who see no intrinsic value to art discuss it purely in terms of its moral upshot, so those who see no intrinsic value to the pursuit of knowledge always discuss it purely in terms of its moral upshot.[124]

We might distinguish two very different ways in which the virtues of truth-seeking might be subordinated to, and corrupted by, civic schooling. The first concerns the 'curriculum', that is, the content of what is taught, and the second concerns the 'pedagogy', that is, the methods employed to convey the curriculum. Galston is refreshingly frank about the danger that civic education poses to the truth-seeking virtues of the academic curriculum. He distinguishes a philosophical education oriented toward truth-seeking and rational inquiry from a civic education oriented toward producing good citizens. He rightly observes about the purposes of civic education: "It is unlikely, to say the least, that the truth will be fully consistent with this purpose."[125] But Galston is a champion of civic education, so he bites the bullet and defends the imperative to falsify history: "For example, rigorous historical research will almost certainly vindicate complex 'revisionist' accounts of key figures in American history. Civic education, however, requires a more noble, moralizing history: a pantheon of heros, who confer legitimacy on central institutions and constitute worthy objects of emulation."[126]

Certainly young children are incapable of understanding complex accounts of American history, not because such accounts are "revisionist," but simply because they are complex. Children of any age, however, are

---

[123] "Conservative celebratory history is permissible; so is left-progressive critical history; and if Mormons want to teach that American history is the working out of the providential hand of God, that is permissible too." Michael McConnell, "Education Disestablishment," in *Nomos*, 102–3.

[124] McConnell, for example, like all the other advocates of civic education, describes academic education in purely amoral terms: "It may be necessary for all citizens to be literate and numerate . . . [and] to have a rudimentary understanding of United States history and civics. . . ." McConnell, "Education Disestablishment," 102.

[125] Galston, "Civic Education in the Liberal State," 90.

[126] Ibid., 91.

capable of understanding that their nation, like their family, is both lov-able and far from perfect. To suppose that children need to be taught in school to love their country is equivalent to supposing that children need to be taught in school to love their mothers. No advocate of patriotic education in schools has ever furnished any evidence suggesting that American students do not love their country. Galston's particular argu-ments here are very weak, indeed; few other major advocates of civic schooling have expressly embraced his open subordination of the truth.[127] But Galston rightly sees that there is an inevitable tension between edu-cating for citizenship and educating for knowledge, even in a liberal democratic society.

Galston's moralizing history pretends to teach actual history while covertly attempting to inculcate civic virtues; other parts of the curricu-lum are also misused, perhaps more subtly, to covertly teach civic virtues. Yet Callan admits, in his understated way, that when teachers try to be moral educators, "[t]here are certainly risks that the intellectual authority of the teacher will be abused."[128] The case of *Mozert v. Hawkins County Board of Education* reveals the widespread abuse of the intellectual author-ity of the teacher in many contemporary public schools.[129] In this case, Robert Mozert, a Christian fundamentalist, objected to a reading series required by his local public school that included stories about a Catholic New Mexican Indian settlement, a boy who likes to cook, Anne Frank's unorthodox religious opinions, etc. This court case has provoked endless controversy about what values ought to be taught in schools and about who should have the authority to decide. To my mind, what is troubling about this case is that these stories were part of a curriculum in English, yet they were selected not because of their beauty, renown, or even the felicity of their English style, but for the civic purpose of promoting tolerance by favorably illustrating a diversity of lifestyles.[130] Soviet edu-cation followed the same model: "Before the Revolution, Russia had 1,000 tractors; now thanks to comrade Stalin we have 250,000 tractors. How many more tractors do we have under developed socialism?"

---

[127] Galston is right that citizens embrace their civic commitments primarily through non-rational attachments but wrong to think that they need moralizing history lessons at school in order to become attached to their country. Indeed, it is precisely because the school can rely on these primary nonscholastic civic bonds that the school is free to encourage the pursuit of genuine knowledge. So Galston here again reveals his confusion of civic educa-tion with civic schooling. For a quite different critique of Galston, see Will Kymlicka, "Ed-ucation for Citizenship," in J. Mark Halstead and Terence H. McLaughlin, eds., *Education in Morality* (London: Routledge, 1999), 96–97.

[128] Callan, *Creating Citizens*, 216.

[129] *Mozert v. Hawkins County Board of Education*, 827 F.2d 1058 (6th Cir. 1987). I will not attempt to discuss the many moral, religious, and legal issues raised by this case nor rehearse the many arguments that it has generated.

[130] Gutmann describes *Mozert*: "The parents' objections were directed at an English cur-riculum that, by state mandate, was supposed to serve the purpose of civic education, not just education in the skills of reading and writing." See Gutmann, "Civics Education and Social Diversity," 571–72.

The hijacking of academic aims for a covert moral and civic agenda is more troubling than the questions of the merit of the values being taught and who should have the authority to select textbooks. According to Macedo, what might be objectionable is a covert civic agenda heavily biased in favor of only one ethical way of life; he insists that civic education promote respect for a variety of ways of life.[131] The issue is deeper than one of balance: the issue is whether deliberately attempting to inculcate moral or civic values under the guise of teaching English or any other field of knowledge constitutes an abuse of the proper intellectual authority of teachers.[132] American teachers do not claim to be exemplars of civic virtue; they are neither certified nor hired on that basis. Their authority, such as it is, rests solely on their passion for, and command of, a body of knowledge and of the techniques for communicating it to students. Teachers ought to be exemplars of intellectual virtue; whether they are exemplars of other kinds of moral and civic virtues is not essential to their authority as teachers. To place their limited but real moral authority in the service of promoting nonacademic virtues is an abuse of that authority.

Just as the academic curriculum can be wrongly subordinated to an agenda of civic education, so can academic pedagogy. Indeed, much of what is known as 'progressive' educational pedagogy—that is, teaching that attempts to respond to the spontaneous curiosity of the student, often in hands-on, collaborative projects—has long been advocated on moral and civic grounds as much as on academic grounds. Dewey, in particular, championed many progressive pedagogical innovations because he thought that they turned classrooms into laboratories of democracy. Progressive pedagogues have always insisted that their methods are egalitarian, democratic, tolerant, and caring, and that they foster autonomy in the child. Indeed, some contemporary advocates of civic education argue that democratic civic education might be pursued best not by direct manipulation of the curriculum, but through the indirect means of progressive pedagogical methods.[133]

Political theorist Joe Coleman points out that it is "no accident" that progressive pedagogical techniques "have a distinctly civic dimension";

[131] "While it would be unreasonable to insist on perfect 'balance' in school readers or other parts of the curriculum, political liberals can sympathize with objectors to a reading program so heavily biased toward a particular comprehensive view that it appears designed to advance that view and denigrate alternatives." Stephen Macedo, "Liberal Civic Education and Religious Fundamentalism: The Case of God v. John Rawls?" *Ethics* 105, no. 3 (1995): 487.

[132] Nor is the issue whether such attempts at indoctrination are effective or not. Our empirical evidence suggests that such efforts to inculcate attitudes are not usually effective, perhaps for reasons discussed by Eisgruber in his "How Do Liberal Democracies Teach Values?" 62–65. The issue is the rectitude of the intention to indoctrinate.

[133] "[W]hat if (civic) education also occurs through the ways in which children are taught and interact within the public school?" Joe Coleman, "Civic Pedagogies and Liberal-Democratic Curricula," *Ethics* 108, no. 4 (1998): 752.

after all, he suggests, they were designed largely for that reason.[134] Instead of raising the fundamental moral question of whether it is appropriate to deploy pedagogical techniques for civic ends, Coleman proceeds directly to recommending the use of progressive pedagogy to inculcate liberal civic education on the grounds that using the curriculum to do so is too "heavy-handed." [135] So a deft and subtle mode of indoctrination is superior to a crude and blunt one? Coleman argues that progressive pedagogy has also been advocated on purely academic grounds, so progressive educators need not harbor a desire to indoctrinate: "Intentionally or not, then, student-centered learning is a civic pedagogy." [136] It would indeed be a wonderful world if the most academically effective pedagogy just happened also to be the ideal kind of civic education. But how likely is that? As Coleman knows, the progressive pedagogies that he champions on civic grounds have been subjected to decades of withering attack on academic grounds by educators and psychologists.[137] We cannot hope to adjudicate that dispute here, but Coleman should tell us how to set priorities if our academic and civic aims conflict. Gutmann, by contrast, is quite clear about how to set priorities. She says that the moral primacy of political education means precisely that school pedagogy may rightly be designed to promote democratic values and virtues even at the cost of purely academic achievement.[138]

In practice, then, and in theory, we have compelling evidence that civic education represents a permanent and fundamental threat both to the academic curriculum and to academic pedagogy: the quest for civic virtue will forever attempt, and often succeed, to trump the pursuit of knowledge. How seriously we take this subordination of academic to moral education will depend upon our understanding of the values and virtues intrinsic to an academic education. I cannot attempt here to develop a full normative theory of the aims and methods of academic education. However, I can offer some reasons and evidence for my assertions that intellectual virtue is the proper aim of schooling, that intellectual virtue is a kind of moral virtue, and that, therefore, the cultivation of intellectual virtue is the kind of moral education appropriate to the institution of the school.

---

[134] Ibid., 754.

[135] Ibid., 755.

[136] Ibid.

[137] The best summary of the academic case against progressivism is E. D. Hirsch, Jr., *The Schools We Need and Why We Don't Have Them* (New York: Doubleday, 1996), which Coleman references but does not discuss.

[138] In addition to providing moral arguments against 'tracking' (segregating by academic ability), sexist education, racial segregation, and (narrowly) vocational education, even where these might be academically warranted, democratic education "also supports a presumption in favor of more participatory over more disciplinary methods of teaching. Participatory methods are often the best means of achieving the disciplinary purposes of primary schooling. But even when student participation threatens to produce some degree of disorder within schools, it may be defended on democratic grounds for cultivating political skills and social commitments." Gutmann, *Democratic Education*, 287.

Ever since Kant, academic education has been pervasively defined in amoral terms as the acquisition of information and skills that might be put to use for good or bad ends. Indeed, the obvious way to object to my claim that academic education is a kind of moral education is to point out that the information and skills acquired in school are just as easily put to use in the service of sophistry as in the service of truth-seeking. But this view of academic education in terms of mere information and skills misdescribes the actual point of scholastic education, which is to acquire information and skills in the context of a love for genuine knowledge, that is, a love for what Zagzebski calls "cognitive contact with reality."[139] In other words, good math, history, science, and English teachers do not attempt to arm students with morally neutral resources and weapons and then hope for the best. Good teachers attempt to fuse the growing acquisition of information and skills to a growing desire for genuine knowledge. In other words, proper academic education does not seek merely to provide the means for whatever ends might be chosen by the student; proper academic education encompasses both the means and the end. Dewey saw this clearly: "The knowledge of dynamite of a safecracker may be identical in verbal form with that of a chemist; in fact, it is different, for it is knit into connection with different aims and habits, and thus has a different import."[140]

A scholastic education is the acquisition of information and skills in the context of acquiring a love for truth and knowledge; a scholastic miseducation is the acquisition of information and skills in the context of learning to subordinate truth-seeking to the desire for things such as power, wealth, or fame. Indeed, if academic education were merely a matter of information and skills, then we might well wonder why we need teachers at all. Computers are quite effective at conveying information and coaching skills; thus, given how we normally describe academic education, it is not surprising that computers are increasingly replacing human teachers. The indispensable role of the human teacher is motivational: our relations to our teachers, which often rest on deep currents of affection and a desire for emulation, foster and inspire our love for learning and for the joys of a life devoted to learning. The deep affective energies between student and teacher properly serve to bond the acquisition of information and skills to a genuine love for knowledge.

We often contrast the academic education of the mind to the moral education of the heart. Indeed, Aristotle famously distinguishes intellectual virtues as perfections of the rational part of the soul from moral virtues as perfections of the nonrational part of the soul.[141] However, if academic education involves not only intellectual skills but also the right

---

[139] "I define knowledge as cognitive contact with reality arising from what I call 'acts of intellectual virtue'." Zagzebski, *Virtues of the Mind*, xv.

[140] Dewey, *Democracy and Education*, 356.

[141] Aristotle, *Nicomachean Ethics*, 1103a5.

motivation, then the scholastic virtues are not merely intellectual, but also involve feeling, passion, and love. The pursuit of truth involves just as much passion as any other love. Just as any morally virtuous person is emotionally attracted to what is good, so any intellectually virtuous person is emotionally attracted to what is true. So the contrast between an education of the intellect and an education of the sentiments is untenable since the virtues of teaching and learning require both the mind and the heart. Indeed, the very language of 'intellectual' virtues or virtues of the 'mind' is deeply misleading; the virtues of truth-seeking are as passionate as any other kind of moral virtue.

In short, our relation to our intellectual virtues is just as deep as our relation to our other moral virtues. At the same time, however, our relation to any one of our virtues is fundamentally different from our relation to our capacities and skills. Capacities and skills, like any resource or tool, are things we can use or misuse; we recognize a kind of "distance" between our selves and our resources or skills. Virtues, whether intellectual or other kinds, are aspects of persons or traits of character; virtues cannot be misused because they cannot be used at all. This is why the maxim "honesty is the best policy" is so paradoxical, for policies are things we deliberately deploy while honesty is usually thought of as an aspect of a person. An honest person cannot deploy honesty any more than he or she can deploy dishonesty. Academic education properly aims to shape who we are as persons—namely, as persons who care about the truth—and not merely to enhance our capacities and skills.

The first stage of my developmental hierarchy of intellectual virtues consists of the virtues of carefulness, such as single-mindedness, thoroughness, accuracy, and perseverance. These seem, at first, more like capacities or skills than like virtues; after all, why cannot a sophist or any other bad person make use of single-mindedness, thoroughness, accuracy, and perseverance? Here Passmore usefully distinguishes the skill of carefulness from the virtues of carefulness: a sophist can certainly acquire the skill of carefulness, but a good student learns to care about being careful: he learns to love single-mindedness, thoroughness, precision, and perseverance because these traits are inseparable from truth-seeking.[142] The higher-order virtues of intellectual courage, intellectual impartiality, and intellectual honesty are more obviously traits of character rather than mere capacities or skills. Whereas (ideally) teachers tend to focus on the virtues of carefulness in primary school, teachers in high school and college attempt to inculcate intellectual courage, impartiality, and honesty by requiring students to consider several points of view on a question, to stand up for their own judgments, to be willing to consider new and

---

[142] Passmore describes a good teacher: "He hoped to develop in his pupils not only the capacity for proceeding carefully, but a caring about, passion for, accurate statement, careful reading, sound arguments." Passmore, *The Philosophy of Teaching*, 188.

unfamiliar ideas, and to admit the limits of their own knowledge and the fallibility of their own judgments.

Finally, in our practices of praising and blaming persons, we certainly treat intellectual traits as if they were moral traits. Just as we praise people for being morally honest, courageous, and conscientious, so we praise people for being intellectually honest, courageous, and conscientious. Here, perhaps, our practices of blame are more revealing than our practices of praise, because we often praise people for admirable non-moral qualities, such as their beauty, talent, and strength; yet by praising them we do not assume that they exercise voluntary control over these qualities. By contrast, we tend to blame people only for qualities over which they do exercise at least indirect voluntary control. It seems wrong to blame people for being ugly, frail, or untalented.

We blame people for qualities that we hold them responsible for, and we hold them responsible for qualities that they have voluntary power to avoid; such qualities are moral qualities. Our practices of blame show that we expect people to be conscientious in the pursuit of truth, just as we expect them to be conscientious in the pursuit of their moral duties. Do we blame people for the quality of their beliefs? Indeed, we have a rich vocabulary for blaming people for what we take to be their unjustified and irrational beliefs. We call them (in Zagzebski's list) narrow-minded, careless, intellectually cowardly, rash, imperceptive, prejudiced, rigid, or obtuse. I would add superstitious, gullible, dogmatic, and fanatical.[143]

Of course, to say that an education in the intellectual virtues is a kind of moral education is not to say that it is a complete moral education. One can easily possess all the virtues of truth-seeking and still morally fail in many other ways through intemperance, injustice, and many other vices. As Thomas Hobbes was the first to concede about himself, intellectual courage is quite compatible with physical cowardice. Neither good teachers nor good students need be moral paragons. Does this mean that the intellectual virtues might be misused by morally bad people? Does conscientiousness in truth-seeking make a bad person even more dangerous? As we noted above, intellectual virtues cannot be misused because, being aspects of persons, they cannot be used at all. Nor is it plausible to suppose that moral evil might be aided and abetted by truth-seeking; indeed, since moral evil almost always involves false belief, conscientiousness in truth-seeking is likely to mitigate moral evil. So we must avoid claiming either that the intellectual virtues are the whole of moral virtue or that they are not even a part of moral virtue.

Even if we were to agree that an academic education is itself a kind of moral education, we still might wonder why the school is the best instrument for this kind of moral education. Aristotle says that virtues of thought can be taught, while moral virtues can only be learned from

---

[143] For Zagzebski's list, see *Virtues of the Mind*, 20.

experience and habit.[144] On his account, many virtues of thought presuppose moral virtues and, hence, moral experience and habituation. His moral virtues require the guidance of the intellectual virtue of practical wisdom—thus the necessity of teaching. Still, Aristotle seems right to observe that teaching plays a greater and more fundamental role in the acquisition of the intellectual virtues than of the other moral virtues. No one doubts that schools are apt instruments for promoting the acquisition of information and intellectual skills, but what about the motivational dimension of intellectual virtues? Are schools apt instruments for teaching the love of knowledge and a desire for truth? Here we must distinguish the child's natural desire for knowledge in general from his or her acquired desire for a particular body of knowledge. A student's love for a particular branch of knowledge, cannot, like any deep motivation, be directly taught, but, as they say, it can be caught; to the extent that schools are a setting for students to be exposed to and "infected" by the love of knowledge, then schools are apt instruments for intellectual virtue. As Passmore rightly asks: "And where else, if not a school, is the child to acquire the intellectual loves?"[145]

What evidence do we have that schools are the proper instruments for academic education? We noted above that empirical studies of civic education found that schools do have some small effect on civic knowledge even if virtually no effect on civic attitudes or virtues. There are no empirical studies, to my knowledge, of the effectiveness of schools in inculcating the intellectual virtues. However, the most influential study of the effects of scholastic attainment on the knowledge of adults may be suggestive of the important role of schools not only in inculcating a body of information but also in fostering a disposition to the lifelong acquisition of knowledge. In *The Enduring Effects of Education*, Herbert Hyman, Charles Wright, and John Reed surveyed the knowledge of adults many decades after they had completed their schooling. These authors found not only that every year of schooling contributed positively to the knowledge base of adults, but also that every year of schooling contributed positively to the propensity of adults to continue learning by reading newspapers, magazines, books, and seeking out opportunities for adult education. By including in their survey knowledge of current events, these researchers were able to establish that those adults who had the most schooling were also keeping abreast of current events most effectively. So we have some evidence that schools do effectively foster a lifelong love for learning.[146]

Once we see that the conscientious pursuit of knowledge is the inherent moral purpose of schooling, we will not be surprised by the absence of any agreement about which civic virtues we ought to teach in schools.

---

[144] Aristotle, *Nicomachean Ethics*, 1103a14.

[145] Passmore, *The Philosophy of Teaching*, 197.

[146] Herbert H. Hyman, Charles R. Wright, and John Shelton Reed, *The Enduring Effects of Education* (Chicago, IL: University of Chicago Press, 1975), 80–93.

Since none of the civic virtues is intrinsically related to the inherent moral purpose of schooling, there is no academically principled way to decide which civic virtues ought to be taught in schools. I quite strongly value a commitment to human rights, the rule of law, public service, and a love of America, but I do not see what these noble virtues have to do with pursuing knowledge of physics, French, English, chemistry, history, and math. No catalogue of civic virtues can be shown to be a prerequisite of academic excellence, a part of academic excellence, or the product of academic excellence. The simple truth of the matter is that one can be a paragon of academic virtue and a lousy citizen. Many great scholars, scientists, and educators have notoriously lacked the civic virtues by being resident aliens, cosmopolitans, or epicureans. Trying to decide which civic virtues to teach in schools is like trying to decide which sports or which crafts to teach: since none of these is intrinsically related to academic education, there are no academic grounds for deciding these matters.

Why is civic education in schools so ineffective? We saw that civics courses may well have some modest effect upon civic knowledge but essentially none on civic attitudes or motivations. Let us consider some reasons offered. Some educators argue that civics courses are inherently irrelevant to the academic curriculum. Because civic education, like driver or consumer education, lacks an intrinsic relation to the academic curriculum, it quickly becomes regarded by teachers and students as purely ancillary and irrelevant. The purely ancillary nature of civics courses may help to explain why they prove to be so ineffective. To overcome this irrelevance, many advocates insist that civic education become incorporated into the core academic curriculum, so that English, history, and social studies courses impart lessons in civic virtue. But here we become impaled upon the fundamental dilemma of civic education: if we teach civic virtue in a way that respects the integrity of the academic curriculum, then civics becomes merely ancillary and irrelevant; contrarily, if, to overcome this irrelevance, we attempt to incorporate civic education into the academic subjects, then we inevitably subvert the inherent moral aim of these subjects by subordinating the pursuit of truth to civic uplift.

Indeed, there may be something paradoxical and self-defeating about the whole project of teaching civic virtue in schools. Niemi and Junn speculate that civic education might be ineffective largely because it is so whitewashed. In the attempt to make civics promote patriotism, American civics courses, they observe, present a "Pollyannaish view of politics that is fostered by the avoidance of reference to partisan politics and other differences of opinion. . . ." So instead of a nasty contest between interest groups, we get "how a bill becomes law"—a presentation of civics cleansed of all politics as well as of all possible interest. Niemi and Junn also decry the Whiggish distortions of American history, in which the "problems"of the past (such as racism and oppression) are invariably "solved" in the present. Niemi and Junn worry that these attempts to inculcate civic trust might not just be ineffective, but might actually backfire by creating greater political cynicism.[147] The authors of a new civics curriculum designed to foster great tolerance for the diversity of beliefs claim that it has made many students more tolerant even though it also made some students dramatically more intolerant.[148] These perverse effects call into question the whole project of attempting to manipulate students' attitudes. Similarly, political theorist Christopher Eisgruber observes of the attempt to inculcate values through an academic course: "How would students react to such a course? My suspicion is that any student old enough to understand such a course would also be old enough to recognize it as propaganda—and to resent it for that reason."[149] Students are often adept at detecting when knowledge is treated merely as a vehicle for carrying moral attitudes; these students then rightly suspect the credibility of such knowledge. If teachers express such contempt for the value of the knowledge they teach, why should students value learning?

It is, in many ways, reassuring that civic education aimed directly at civic virtues is ineffective. But it would be deeply unfortunate if, as many argue, the attempt to inculcate civic virtues serves to undermine the teaching of civic knowledge. Instead of constantly subordinating knowledge to moral uplift, we ought to have more confidence in the sheer moral value of knowledge. As we have seen, the cognitive sophistication cultivated in schools by itself strongly contributes to political tolerance, that is, the willingness to extend civil liberties to those with whom we strongly disagree.[150] A leading team of political scientists offers this hypothesis: "If we are correct that the number of years of formal schooling acts to increase tolerance regardless of the manifest and subtle political content of that education, then educational attainment should act to increase tolerance even in regimes with contrary messages." These political scientists found strong evidence that years of schooling increased political tolerance even in Hungary under the Communists. Ironically, intolerant regimes foster toleration simply by schooling their citizens—even when (or especially when?) this schooling is designed to foster political intolerance.[151] In the United States, specifically political knowledge has been shown to promote political tolerance, active participation in politics, more

[147] "Instead of a balanced approach, the emphasis in teaching about gender and race appears to be exclusively on the 'good things'—the abolition of slavery, the end of legal segregation, the enfranchisement of women, the fall of many barriers to women's participation. . . ." Niemi and Junn, *Civic Education*, 150–51.

[148] See Bird et al., "Not Just Lip-Synching Anymore: Education and Tolerance Revisited," 374.

[149] Eisgruber, "How Do Liberal Democracies Teach Values?" 77.

[150] "[I]t is the cognitive outcomes of education, rather than the positional outcomes, that are responsible for the connection between education and tolerance." Nie et al., *Education and Democratic Citizenship in America*, 72.

[151] "[T]he communist regimes in Eastern Europe, with their emphasis for the last half-century on modernization through education, unintentionally created new generations of citizens who were prone to work for the toppling of the very regimes that saw to their education." Ibid., 184.

coherent political opinions, and a more rational relation between participation and one's political goals.[152] So we ought to be confident that we
are contributing significantly to civic virtue merely by attempting to impart to our students genuine knowledge and, in particular, civic knowledge. In light of the ineffective and often counterproductive nature of
civic education aimed directly at civic virtue, we have many reasons to
believe that schools are better advised simply to stick to their essential
task of pursuing genuine knowledge. No doubt this scholastic kind of
civic education is seriously deficient, but we must remember that most of
what we learn in life is not learned in school, and most of our teachers are
not schoolteachers.

What is the relation of schooling to civic education more broadly? This
is a very large question that would take us far beyond the scope of this
essay, but I will briefly consider, by way of a partial answer, the relation
of the intellectual virtues to the civic virtues. A good citizen ought to
possess the intellectual virtues because they will help him or her to resist
false beliefs. Bad politicians frequently tempt us to believe things that are
false by appealing to our national pride, our greed, our resentments, or
our fears for the future. 'Intellectual virtue' means acquiring precisely
those dispositions that lead us to resist these temptations to false beliefs.
A good citizen need not care only about the truth of his or her political
beliefs, nor must a good citizen, as a partisan, advocate the whole truth.
However, a good citizen must care about whether the views that he or she
advocates are true. So intellectual virtue might be necessary for good
citizens, but it is hardly sufficient. An intellectual paragon might well be
a lousy citizen: no amount of conscientiousness in the pursuit of truth
constitutes or even reliably leads to a zeal for public service or to the
courage to defend one's nation. Indeed, as Plato famously observes, those
who most sincerely love genuine knowledge are often the most repelled
by the inevitable simplifications and distortions of political ideology and
rhetoric. It is very difficult to reconcile a passion for knowledge with the
political imperatives to advocate partial truths, to hide the truth at times,
and to appeal to nonrational passions. None of this, I believe, amounts to
a fundamental incompatibility between intellectual and civic virtue, but it
does suggest some real tensions and moral challenges. So a scholastic
education is only a partial civic education, and the intellectual virtues are
only a part of the civic virtues.

IV. CONCLUSION: CIVICS OR CIVILITY?

Putnam's aforementioned and influential study of the decline of American civic and political participation, *Bowling Alone*, has fueled the grow-

---

[152] See Delli Carpini and Keeter, *What Americans Know about Politics and Why It Matters*,
219.

ing consternation about the waning of civic virtue in the American polity. In the face of such widespread and passionate moral concern about the decline in civic virtue, we do well to ask: Just how important is civic virtue to American democracy? How widespread must civic virtue be? Although the framers of the U.S. Constitution strongly affirmed the importance of civic virtue, they nonetheless counted upon the careful division of powers and the rule of law to compensate for a likely shortfall of virtue. The Constitution was famously described as an "engine that would go of its own," that is, it would equilibrate power, secure liberty, and govern effectively without relying upon the civic virtue of the republic's participants. Nonetheless, we cannot rely upon constitutions and laws alone to protect our democratic ideals. Does anyone follow Kant in supposing that institutional design alone can make democracy safe for a race of devils? It seems more likely that raw self-interest, lust for power, and indifference will ultimately undermine any legal or institutional arrangement. Still, it is easy to exaggerate the importance of widespread civic virtue in a large, complex, and commercial republic such as the United States.

Those who express most concern about the decline in civic virtue tend to forget that the U.S. polity is not simply a republic of citizens but also a liberal society of persons. America's deepest traditions of liberty have always affirmed each person's fundamental right not to aspire to civic virtue. Of course, every resident of the United States, whether a citizen or not, is obliged to obey the law and respect the legal rights of every other resident. Nevertheless, America does not require all citizens, let alone resident aliens, to commit themselves to work conscientiously for the good of the nation by serving in the armed forces or even by merely voting. Indeed, the American polity prides itself on its respect for whole communities of persons whose religious commitment to pacifism prevents them from being good citizens in the classic sense of being willing to fight for their nation. How many Americans would want to live in a pure democratic republic in which military service, voting, and other public service were mandatory for all? So, yes, Americans want some civic virtue but not too much, and Americans want many people to have civic virtue but certainly not everyone.

Even those who, like Putnam, are most concerned about the recent decline in civic virtue do not look to the school as either the source of or the remedy for America's civic ills. What role can schools properly play in fostering more civic virtue? Although civic virtue includes more than mere knowledge, clearly knowledge about the structure, functions, and ideals of government are essential for civic virtue. Civic knowledge is a perfectly appropriate aim for institutions of learning. Who could object to public schools teaching about public institutions? The bitter controversies over civic education and the dangers of indoctrination arise not from teaching civic knowledge but from attempting to instill certain civic attitudes, whether multicultural toleration or patriotism.

The history of civic education in schools is as old as public schooling itself and this history is a cautionary tale. The attempt to use public schools for the purpose of sectarian civic education has always led to a bitter politics of religious and moral recrimination, a deep fraying of civic trust, and a wholesale abandonment of common schools by Roman Catholics and others. Nondenominational Protestant civic education in the nineteenth century provoked many Catholics, Lutherans, and some Jews to take on the enormous burden of parochial education. With the current erosion of public confidence in common schools, the rise of private and home schooling, and the push for vouchers, the future of public education in the United States is increasingly uncertain. Much of the current dismay with public schools stems from their perceived academic failings, but many parents send their children to private schools because they believe that public schools attempt to indoctrinate their children with either liberal or conservative civic virtues. Wherever schools become battlegrounds for partisan moral and religious agendas, the whole ideal of common schooling loses public support.

Public schools in a pluralistic society have a special moral duty to forbear from all nonacademic kinds of moral education. This is because the project whereby citizens agree to educate their children together in publicly funded schools depends upon a high degree of civic trust. Each of us, with our own comprehensive moral and religious outlook, surrenders our children to a common school on the assumption that none of us is permitted to deliberately impose his or her own conception of moral or civic virtue on the rest. We all must acknowledge the temptation to want the common school to reinforce the moral and civic aims that we pursue at home, but civic trust equally depends upon our principled forbearance from advocating that the common school do so. For, as we have repeatedly learned throughout U.S. history, once public schools adopt any particular conception of moral or civic education beyond the moral education inherent to academic study, not only is the moral integrity of schooling likely to be compromised as the curriculum and pedagogy are manipulated in an attempt to indoctrinate students, but this loss of integrity also will fray the civic trust necessary for vibrant common schools.

Admittedly, it requires truly heroic forbearance to refrain from taking advantage of the naïveté of small children who are a captive audience for all manner of idealistic moral and civic uplift, to refrain from deploying the intellectual authority of the teacher in favor of a noble moral or civic aim, and to refrain from manipulating academic curricula and pedagogy for moral and civic ends. Of course, every advocate of some particular version of moral or civic education in our common schools will claim that, although all other proposals are obviously sectarian, his or her proposal is uniquely universalistic and merits the support of the entire community. However, as I have here argued, the deepest objections to moral and civic education in schools are unrelated to the question of how widely accepted or not a moral agenda might be or even how widely accepted a moral agenda ought to be. Indeed, civic moral education has always posed a uniquely powerful threat to schooling precisely because its aims are so widely and often rightly shared. The deepest objections to moral and civic education stem from their incompatibility with the conscientious pursuit of truth, which is the necessary aim of all academic schooling; for public schools, there is the additional and very important concern about undermining civic trust.

Purely academic moral education in the intellectual virtues poses the least risks for the corruption of schooling and the greatest potential for fostering the civic trust necessary for vibrant common schools. Ironically, civic trust around common schooling will be fostered best by renouncing civic education in schools. No one can plausibly claim that the attempt of schools to convey accepted bodies of knowledge to students along with the disposition and skills to seek truth reflects an uncivil intention to indoctrinate.[153] Indeed, what we mean when we accuse public schools of "indoctrinating" students is that schools have abused their proper intellectual authority by deliberately imposing some moral agenda under the guise of academic study and have thereby violated the civic trust that parents have placed in them. To the extent that the content of the curriculum and the methods of instruction are consistent with international standards of academic scholarship and pedagogy, parents have no plausible grounds for thinking that their trust in the common school has been violated.

Even if the effects of schooling are not politically neutral, even if, as we have reason to believe, the cognitive sophistication and genuine knowledge acquired in school tend to lead students to greater political tolerance, these foreseen but unintended spillover effects of schooling do not violate the proper expectations of parents or citizens. Insofar as schools intentionally aim at the virtues of truth-seeking, they have not violated our civic trust—even if the effect of this schooling is neither morally nor politically neutral. However, to demand civics lessons that offer inherently partisan conceptions of civic virtue violates the civic trust upon which vibrant common schools depend. These civics lessons would truly lack all civility.

Government, Darthmouth College

---

[153] "Certainly no one applies the word 'indoctrinate' when the schools try to teach most facts and *accepted* bodies of knowledge. That is regarded not as any unwarranted 'imposition' but as a duty." Hyman and Wright, *Education's Lasting Influence on Values*, 66.

POLITICAL MORALITY AS CONVENTION

By Norman Barry

I. Introduction

A remarkable feature of contemporary political discourse is the dominance of morality. One legacy of logical positivism (which was dominant from the mid-1930s until the end of the 1960s) and analytical (or linguistic) philosophy was the reluctance of political theorists during the twentieth century to engage in substantive argument about appropriate social ends or individual rights and values. Philosophers were content to describe the linguistic framework within which related political proposals were discussed without offering any proposals themselves. It was felt that the philosopher was not especially qualified to give political advice or make any recommendations. The technical political theorist was properly confined to the *second* level of inquiry, that is, explanation of the meaning of concepts, not the *first* level, which was concerned with questions of how we ought to live, or issues of public policy. Economists and sociologists might have the technical skills appropriate for inquiries into public policy, but as to the big questions—such as the ends and purposes of man and society—almost anybody could make pronouncements. The important point was that *reason* was incapable of adjudicating between rival versions of the good life.[1]

This emotivism, or subjectivism, in ethics, which decreed that carefully considered statements about freedom and justice were, linguistically, no more valuable than advertising slogans, was carried over into politics and jurisprudence.[2] In jurisprudence, for example, all of the claims of natural lawyers to ground the criteria of proper law in a set of universally true moral principles were replaced by explications of the notion of sovereignty or by complex descriptions of validating processes in ongoing systems of positive law. Under legal positivism, morality is sharply separated from law, so that questions about the values that *proper* law ought to serve or what is *proper* law are thought to be irrelevant or unanswer-

---

[1] See A. J. Ayer, *Language, Truth, and Logic* (1936; reprint, New York: Dover, 1952); and Charles L. Stevenson, *Ethics and Language* (New Haven, CT: Yale University Press, 1944). Even R. M. Hare, who argued that ethical statements had a logic, conceded that their ultimate foundations were beyond rational demonstration: See R. M. Hare, *Freedom and Reason* (Oxford: Clarendon Press, 1963).

[2] See Norman Barry, *An Introduction to Modern Political Theory*, 4th ed. (London: Palgrave Macmillan, 2000).

able, and certainly distinguished from objective, logical inquiries into law's meaning and status.[3]

During the heyday of logical positivism and linguistic philosophy, the public debate about politics was dominated by Marxism and by various forms of collectivism. Both of these political movements led to the expansion of the state. There was also a burgeoning libertarian movement that produced persuasive arguments from mainly, but not exclusively, economics specifically addressed to the adverse effects on liberty that this statism would have. Philosophers took little part in these debates, preferring to concentrate on narrow technical issues about the meaning of concepts and the logical coherence of statements about political values. While it is true that most political philosophers went along with the statist tendencies of the time, they would sharply differentiate their approval from their purely philosophical work. The exception was Karl Popper (1902–94), whose critique of Marxism was partially derived from philosophy. It is certainly true that jurisprudence had little or no influence on public debate, except in the narrow area where law and morality might interact. H. L. A. Hart (1907–92), the leading legal positivist, was very much involved in the debate in Britain in the 1960s and 1970s about homosexuality and prostitution, but he did not regard these issues as questions of legal philosophy.[4]

All this has changed since the publication of John Rawls's *A Theory of Justice* (1971).[5] Now, political theory, even of the analytical kind, is dominated by substantive programs, of varying degrees of generality. Marxism might have been discredited theoretically and practically, but the Left has replaced it with communitarianism or revived the role of the state with expanded notions of liberal "rights." The libertarian Right has been equally fecund in its, in effect, antipolitical recommendations. Gone is that modesty and reticence that were once features of political philosophy whenever normative questions were raised. We are now faced with a welter of conflicting and ultimately irreconcilable moral ideals. The questions discussed are no less intractable now, but under the dominance of linguistic philosophy they were regarded as (logically) meaningless. However, they are now thought to be well worth asking, and the replies have produced quite different methodological approaches. Ethical disputes, perhaps unlike those in economics and the other empirical social sciences, are much less amenable to definitive resolution, but the subjective and ideological features of these disputes, against which the positivists so effectively railed, have diminished and now the normative arguments are more sophisticated. Normative talk is not thought to be merely a matter of personal opinion. In addition to the revival of rights talk, there has

---

[3] H. L. A. Hart, *The Concept of Law* (Oxford: Clarendon Press, 1961).

[4] See H. L. A. Hart, *Law, Liberty, and Morality* (London: Oxford University Press, 1963).

[5] John Rawls, *A Theory of Justice* (Cambridge, MA: Harvard University Press, 1971).

been a resuscitation of contractarianism and of aggregative ethical criteria. The range of morality has expanded too. Until recently there was a paucity of moral argument among professional philosophers, but we now have a veritable plethora of ethical claims covering almost the whole of public life. Thus, we have medical ethics, business ethics, professional ethics, a revived natural law (or at least a moralized legalism), and many other "ethics." Where once unanalyzed notions of conventional right and wrong governed public and professional decision-making, we now have a variety of moralities, under the aegis of which these traditional notions are challenged and extra duties are imposed on the practitioners of, for example, business and law. Most important, these moralities aim at a kind of universalism, even if it is restricted to a particular country. In other words, statements about appropriate values are thought to be applicable, and are turned into law, for a whole community, thus eliminating the variety and possibility of dissent that would be permitted if decentralized decision-making flourished. A variety of different decisions among component states was once a feature of genuine federal systems of government. But in America, a controversial decision about abortion was imposed on the whole country by a judicial decision, precisely because it was felt to be authorized by morality.

A similar thing has happened to welfare in most Western liberal democracies. A particularly expansive view of morality has authorized a much greater expansion of state provision than would conceivably have happened if political authorities had followed simple convention. Furthermore, in this area in particular, the emphasis on morality led to ignoring certain frailties in the human condition. Important here is 'moral hazard': this occurs when the attempt to do good encourages people to become dependent on public welfare. As the authors of the *British Poor Law Report* (1834) put it: "Every penny bestowed that tends to render the condition of the poor more eligible than that of the independent laborer is a bounty on indolence and vice."[6] It was the aim of the Poor Law reformers to discourage people from becoming eligible for poor relief. One important result of their efforts was the substitution of relief within the workhouse for "outdoor" relief, which was a cash payment requiring no reciprocal duty.

Skepticism about morality, however, goes back a long way in the history of political thought, but we do not have to refer all the way back to the Sophists or to Machiavelli to demonstrate its intellectual potency. The anarchist-utilitarian William Godwin (1756–1836) once said: "Actions in the highest degree injurious to the public . . . have often proceeded from motives uncommonly conscientious. The most determined political as-

---

[6] See S. G. Checkland and E. O. A. Checkland, eds., *The Poor Law Report of 1834* (Harmondsworth: Penguin, 1974), 36. For a summary of the arguments, see Norman Barry, *Welfare*, 2d ed. (Buckingham: Open University Press, 1999).

sassins ... seem to have been penetrated with anxiety for the eternal welfare of mankind."[7] We are all familiar with the misery caused by people acting from good intentions, but persuasive doubts about the efficacy of morality emerge from economics. There has always been, and still is, a serious questioning of the consistency between individualistic striving in the marketplace and our highest moral endeavors. Is not the efficiency of the private enterprise/market system bought at some cost to ethics? Does not the lure of profit distract us from our social duties? Is not the anonymity of the capitalist system a reason to eschew even the basic moral duties, for example, of promise-keeping while allowing us to evade prohibitions against deceit and unfair dealing? Such complaints against the morality of capitalism have been, at least since the 1980s, more effective restraints on its vitality than Marxism ever was. In fact, Marx had nothing but contempt for moral criticisms of the market that ignored economics and the "laws" of history.

It was Bernard Mandeville (1670–1733), in his notorious *The Fable of the Bees* (1705),[8] who clearly suggested the incompatibility of the market and morality through his paradox of "private vice and public virtue." As he poetically described the market: "Each part was full of vice/But the whole mass an earthly paradise."[9] Envy, selfishness, pride, and conceit were to be valued because they provided the spur for man's achievements, and greed the motivation for productive activity. "Contentment," a psychological state of affairs much admired by his contemporary moralists, was despised by Mandeville precisely because it led to sloth and inactivity. Of course, in *The Fable of the Bees*, when the bees were moralized, they became fractious and unproductive.

Still, Mandeville must not be misunderstood: he was not advocating a generalized contempt for rules of behavior or a rejection of conventional standards. He was simply alluding to a distinction between the morality of his day, which was particularly puritanical, and the necessary rules of conduct recognized by all societies. These rules are not necessarily puritanical. He made a distinction, therefore, between the harmful and the useful "vices,"[10] and it was the latter that he was encouraging.

Of course, as Adam Smith (1727–90) was eager to point out, Mandeville made far too stark a distinction between vice and virtue and presented the latter in an extremely rigorous light. Mandeville could easily show, then, that the demands of morality were against human nature, that they were impossible to meet, and that those who recommended them were being hypocritical. Thus, Smith's ethics of the

---

[7] Quoted in Robert E. Goodin, *Motivating Political Morality* (Oxford: Blackwell, 1992), 160–61.

[8] Bernard Mandeville, *The Fable of the Bees* (1705; reprint, Oxford: Oxford University Press, 1924).

[9] Mandeville, *The Fable of the Bees*, 24.

[10] Ibid., 10.

market—encompassing the rules of justice, respect for property, and the virtue of prudence—were genuine moral values that traders relied on for their transactions to be completed. But he did little more than sanitize Mandeville, and when it came to describing how the market operated, Smith used Mandeville's language: "It is not from the benevolence of the butcher, brewer and baker that we get our dinner, but from their regard to their own interest. We address ourselves not to their humanity but to their self-love."[11] Still, some critics have said that ultimately Smith cleansed the market too effectively and admitted into his thought certain 'republican' (the eighteenth-century term for what we would today call 'communitarian') notions, which drained individualism of some of its vitality.[12]

In fact, the greatest achievement of Smith and the other Scottish economists and political theorists of the eighteenth century was to replace the idea of virtue by the value of *liberty*. More importantly, they redefined liberty so that it no longer resembled the classical notion of political *status*, best exemplified by active engagement by citizens in the political process. Instead, liberty was thoroughly individualistic and linked to commercial freedom. The common good was not the result of positive and deliberate action for the community, but the unintentional outcome of individual striving. Self-interest was not necessarily antisocial once we recognized the benign effects of Smith's "invisible hand." It is worth stressing, here, the final part of Smith's famous statement of the value of spontaneous processes: "I have never known much good done by those *who affected to trade for the public good.*"[13]

Still, in Smith the program was incomplete. There was no satisfactory explanation of the rationale of the ethics of the market, that is, how it was that self-interested individuals could coordinate their actions. Nor was there a complete explanation of morality in conventionalist terms. And there was no proper explanation of the link between human nature and morality. Of course, Smith's earlier work, *The Theory of Moral Sentiments* (1759), described an ethics that was clearly derived from a theory of human nature, and although there was no incompatibility between this and his economics, there was a different emphasis. There had to be, then, a theory of ethics that retained the rationality of ethical conduct without licensing the moralist to engage in that rationalistic social experimentation which was to become the bane, and often the ruin, of the twentieth century. It is not at all clear that contemporary moralists are aware of this

---

[11] Adam Smith, *An Inquiry into the Nature and Causes of the Wealth of Nations*, R. H. Campbell and A. S. Skinner, eds. (1776; reprint, Oxford: Clarendon Press, 1976), 27.

[12] See Donald Winch, *Adam Smith's Politics: An Essay in Historiographic Revisionism* (Cambridge: Cambridge University Press, 1978); and Istvan Hont and Michael Ignatieff, eds., *Wealth and Virtue: The Shaping of Political Economy in the Scottish Enlightenment* (Cambridge: Cambridge University Press, 1983).

[13] Smith, *The Wealth of Nations*, 456. My emphasis added.

vital distinction. However, before Smith, the utilitarianism of David Hume (1711–76)[14] had provided answers to these questions, and it is to his work that contemporary apologists for the morality of capitalism should look for solace.

II. HUME AND INDIRECT UTILITARIANISM

It is well known that Hume did not believe that ethics could be founded upon reason. He had little time for the natural law and the philosophical foundations of liberalism supplied by John Locke (1632–1704). His skepticism about abstract values derived partly from epistemological reasons, which were reproduced in the twentieth century by the logical positivists, and partly from practical reasons. Epistemologically, reason was limited to two roles: the manipulation of analytic truths and the evaluation of empirical data. The demonstration of ethical truth was, therefore, impossible since it fell outside these two criteria. Hence Hume was able to say, "'Tis not contrary to reason to prefer the destruction of the whole world to the scratching of my finger."[15] Yet this skepticism about the foundations of ethics did not turn Hume into a subjectivist or an emotivist. Ethics could not be given an *ultimate* rational foundation, but rival claims could be evaluated by a modest reason and a proper understanding of human nature. As he said on many occasions, he wanted to use reason to "whittle down the claims of reason." At the more directly political level, Hume was concerned to show that "enthusiasts," or, as we might say, ideologues, had a defective understanding of the mainsprings of human action. A particular target were the contractarians who had mistakenly thought that the Whig Government in England, established in 1688, had a rationale in social contract theory.[16] The Whigs had created a form of government that Hume might have been thought to admire. This might be so, but he had no time for its philosophical foundations. Indeed, Hume even had some respect for absolute monarchies that preserved liberty. The expediency of government was a function of experience, not heady moral philosophy.

Connected with his skepticism about rational demonstrations of forms of government was Hume's insistence on the more or less unchanging features of the human condition. The rationalist philosophers assumed that human nature could be molded to fit circumstances and that this malleability licensed writers to recommend almost any political organization or political morality. But Hume wrote: "[A]s it is impossible to

[14] Although Hume's and Smith's ethics look similar, they had a different intellectual foundation.

[15] David Hume, *A Treatise of Human Nature*, ed. L. A. Selby-Bigge, rev. P. H. Nidditch (1739–40; reprint, Oxford: Clarendon Press, 1978), bk. 2, pt. 3, sec. 3, p. 416.

[16] See David Hume, "Of the Original Contract," in *Essays Moral, Political, and Literary*, ed. Eugene F. Miller (1777; reprint; Indianapolis, IN: LibertyClassics, 1985). 465–87.

change or correct anything material in our nature, the utmost we can do is to change our circumstances and situation and render the observance of the laws of justice our nearest interest and their violation the most remote."[17] He put it even more decisively when he said, "All plans of government which suppose great reformation in the manners of mankind are plainly imaginary."[18] Against Hume's realistic view of human nature, we have seen counterposed Rousseau's claim that a change in self will accompany a change in circumstance, that is, that the signing of a democratic social contract will result in almost automatic promotion of the public good (or "General Will"). Marx's argument that the abolition of the market, private property, and the division of labor will remove all causes of dissent among people and presage unending classless harmony was similarly utopian.

For Hume, an accurate description of human nature must underlie any recommendation of social change. Thus, he was not a blind follower of tradition, as Edmund Burke might have been, but a theorist who believed that reform must be founded on correct analysis. What he wanted to do was to describe, and prescribe, those institutional arrangements that are best suited to advance social cooperation.[19] He was a believer in the market, strictly limited government, and the rule of law, but these are not a product of reason. Rather, they are the product of spontaneous evolution. Thus, Hume argued for a proper *science* of ethics, which would encompass a description of how moral judgments are made and whether they comport with a correct account of human nature. Arising out of these considerations, modest suggestions for improvement might be made.

Hume's assumptions about human nature were more expansive than those of either Hobbes or Mandeville. There are some Hobbesian elements in Hume, but Hobbes could not see that social cooperation could emerge from naturally self-interested people: it had to be imposed by the sovereign. For Hobbes, people are in constant fear of each other and do not play "repeat games." For him, there is only one round of the "prisoner's dilemma," as we moderns call it, and this induces us to obey whomsoever can guarantee our security. While in no way denying the self-interested features of man, which were insisted on by both Hobbes and Mandeville, Hume's addition of the feature of *sympathy* enabled him to show how rules can develop that enhance social cooperation;[20] they emerge spontaneously and are not the product of an absolute sovereign (as in Hobbes). With assumptions that were not vastly dissimilar to those of Hobbes and Mandeville, Hume was able to show how man can, in

---

[17] Hume, *A Treatise of Human Nature*, bk. 3, pt. 2, sec. 3, p. 537.

[18] Hume, "The Idea of a Perfect Commonwealth," in *Essays Moral, Political, and Literary*, 514.

[19] For an excellent modern theory of ethics as a form of social cooperation, see Leland B. Yeager, *Ethics as Social Science* (Cheltenham: Edward Elgar, 2001).

[20] Hume, *A Treatise of Human Nature*, bk. 3, pt. 3, sec. 1, pp. 586–91.

effect, be self-governing and his social relationships predictable. If we did not have a minimal sympathy for others, then we could not trust one another to follow rules that are for our mutual advantage. In the Hobbesian model, individuals are assumed to meet only once, in situations of dire emergency, and "trust" will not have been developed. In such circumstances, individuals will assume that their fellows will always act in egoistic ways even when self-interest would require cooperation.

Nevertheless, the partiality of our affections determines the grounding of Hume's ethics. The genius of his innovation was to show that self-interest could be advanced by a scheme of social cooperation. Thus, (the artificial) rules of justice and property derive from *"the selfishness and confin'd generosity of men, along with the scanty provision nature has made for his wants."* [21] Hume's three rules of property—the stability of possessions, the transfer of ownership by consent (and not by force or fraud), and the performance of promises or contract[22]—were shown to emerge naturally from human interaction. The important point is that these rules are not specifically designed by anyone, but they develop through repeated plays of the "social game." Unlike Hobbes, who saw the social game as a once-and-for-all experience, with no repetition, Hume envisaged it as an ongoing process in which people can shun noncooperators. Most important is Hume's account of the development of 'reciprocity', a crucial feature of market society if people are to cooperate without central direction or control. He imagined two neighboring farmers, who might have no liking or affection for each other, but who quickly learn the advantages of a scarcely conscious collaboration:

> Your corn is ripe today; mine will be so tomorrow. 'Tis profitable for us both, that I should labor with you today, and that you should aid me tomorrow. I have no kindness for you, and know you have as little for me. . . . Hence I learn to do a service to another, without bearing any real kindness, because I foresee that he will return my service. . . .[23]

Notice here that no change in human nature is proposed. People are as selfish as they always were, but they have discovered a new way of advancing their self-interest. In Mandeville's amoral, unsophisticated world, people would miss opportunities for advancement. In the way that Mandeville described them, people are too myopic to see the advantages of reciprocity.

Another feature of the human condition that Hume noticed was the universal tendency of people to value present consumption, be it for

[21] Ibid., bk. 3, pt. 2, sec. 2, p. 495.
[22] Ibid., bk. 3, pt. 2, secs. 4 and 5, pp. 501–25.
[23] Ibid., bk. 3, pt. 2, sec. 5, pp. 520–21.

goods, services, or social rules and practices, over future benefits. In the language of modern economics, people have too high 'time preferences'; they sacrifice the future for the present, and they need to develop some rules for lowering their time preferences. A thief or cheat may get temporary satisfaction from the breach of a rule, but in the long run everybody, including the cheat, will suffer from the decline in security that occurs. Admitting that private remedies are ineffectual, Hume observed that we embrace with pleasure rules, and magistrates to enforce them, as devices "by which I may impose a restraint on myself, and guard against this weakness."[24]

Hume also developed an early theory of public goods,[25] and this once again illustrates how his normative arguments stemmed directly from his account of human nature. The predilection that we have for our own interest may be so powerful that it leads us to misunderstand what this interest is. Furthermore, our relationships with others may be insufficiently close to guarantee voluntary cooperation in the supply of things that we all value. Given, then, the possibility of what we now call "free riding," Hume was prepared to countenance coercive, communal action to meet with demonstrable, collective needs.

It is accurate and enlightening to describe, as Hume did, the self-generating normative rules that govern property, the enforcement of justice and of contracts, and legitimate collective action as 'conventions'. They belong properly to *artificial*, rather than natural, morality. The latter represents the kind of conduct that is appropriate to close marital and family relationships. But because of the exigencies of the human condition, we require public execution of some common rules that have to be artificially constructed. Much of our social life, however, especially in its economic aspects, is orderly and predictable because these artificial conventions require little or no public enforcement.

It is better to use the word 'conventions' rather than 'morality' to describe Hume's normative principles, for the same reason that he railed against rationalism. In his view, rationalism simply led to exuberance, enthusiasm, and the delusion that the human mind could devise institutional arrangements in defiance of indubitably true facts about the human condition. In a similar vein, modern ideas of morality have produced doctrines about, for example, law, welfare, and social justice, in ignorance of well-established theories of human coordination and the limits of collective action. At the very least, such doctrines have paid less cognizance of the truth and relevance of these well-established theories than is necessary for reasonable reform suggestions. But it should be borne in mind that when I speak of Hume's theory of conventions, I do not mean *mere*

[24] Ibid., bk. 3, pt. 2, sec. 7, pp. 536–37.
[25] Ibid., 538. Hume's example is the draining of a meadow. Each farmer has an incentive to avoid paying his share of the cost of draining, but each grasps the mutual benefit of cooperation, otherwise it would not be done.

conventions. Although they are not natural and irresistible, like the weather, they cannot be discarded at will without very serious consequences for society. Indeed, Hume, on at least one occasion,[26] was prepared to countenance calling his principles of justice 'natural laws', so compelling did he think they were. He would have done so more openly had he not so effectively demolished the basis of traditional natural law thinking.

Hume was undoubtedly a utilitarian:

> [T]hat the circumstance of utility ... is constantly appealed to in all moral decisions concerning the merit and demerit of actions: that it is the sole source of that high regard paid to justice, fidelity, honor, allegiance and chastity; that it is inseparable from all other social virtues ... it is the foundation of the chief part of morals, which has a reference to mankind and our fellow creatures.[27]

But he was not a hedonist, for the pleasure that we experience from the relief of the suffering of others is as significant as that which we get from our own happiness. While the motivation to act morally toward people whom we know little about is undoubtedly weak compared to our virtuous action toward family and friends, Hume insisted that "[n]o man is absolutely indifferent to the happiness and misery of others."[28] Indeed, if people acted from entirely selfish motivations it is unlikely that they would be able to internalize the rules and conventions that are essential for an orderly, predictable, and flourishing society.

It is important to stress, however, what type of utilitarian Hume was, for it is this special conception as much as anything else that makes him modern. He was an *indirect* or *rule*-utilitarian who believed that the general good is generated by following established rules, of which we might not be consciously aware. This obligatoriness is essential even if greater immediate utility could be produced by the breach of a rule. He often said that the following of a rule of justice might be against the public interest, but that regular obedience to its rigor always advances utility. The more or less inflexible nature of conventions is the key to their evolutionary success. Hume would argue that to license anybody, least of all government, to abandon conventions, whose usefulness is validated by experience, would be as disruptive of social order and long-run utility as would be the rigid enforcement of supposedly rational, deontological principles irrespective of consequences. And Hume was certainly no deontological ethicist.

In the same way, Hume cannot be identified as an *aggregative* utilitarian. He was not interested in a "sum of utilities" allegedly derived from

---

[26] Ibid., bk. 2, pt. 2, sec. 1, p. 484.

[27] David Hume, *An Enquiry Concerning the Principles of Morals* (1751; reprint, Chicago, IL: Open Court, 1930), sec. 5, p. 66.

[28] Ibid., sec. 5, p. 53.

individuals' utilities, as Bentham later proposed.[29] Least of all would Hume have sanctioned the use of an individual's well-being to advance some artificially and rationalistically constructed aggregate. Indeed, it is by rejecting the aggregation argument that utilitarians can make their doctrine consistent with the oft-quoted claim that ethics should allow for the "separateness of persons": individual values and purposes should not be conflated into a single utility function appropriate for a whole community. By taking account of consequences only as they apply to individuals, indirect utilitarianism has a defense against this charge.

III. Hume in Modern Dress

The same complaint against morality that Hume addressed to rationalism can be detected in modern skeptical writers. Just as he castigated natural law and the social contract theory, today's game theorists press for an analysis of coordination via the development of conventions with little or no reference to controversial and infinitely contestable metaphysics and morality. It is really an attempt to make the theory of the market serviceable, outside the range of normal goods and services, to explain the production of socially desirable rules and practices. Phenomena of this sort, hitherto, were thought to be impervious to such reasoning. Socialists today do not deny that the exchange process coordinates economic activity much better than does the state, but they still maintain that this coercive institution, the state, is required for the design of the rules of the game, for their enforcement, and for the provision of a wide range of other public goods. Individuals cannot do these things for themselves, so the state and the political philosopher step in. The fact that both will almost always do more than what is required has encouraged modern skeptics to take up from where Hume left off, that is, to provide a coherent explanation for voluntary collective action. As we shall see, all that the skeptics have added to Hume's original analysis is considerable sophistication and some elementary evolutionary theory (which was already implicit in his doctrine).

Modern analysis proceeds from proposed solutions to the prisoner's dilemma in game theory.[30] In this game two suspects, Smith and Jones, are questioned separately by the district attorney about a robbery that they have committed. If both suspects remain silent they will face a less serious charge, carrying a short prison sentence of three years; if both confess to the offense they will get ten years each. If one, for example, Smith, confesses and implicates Jones (who remains silent) in the offense,

[29] Jeremy Bentham, *An Introduction to the Principles of Morals and Legislation* (1789; reprint, with an intro. by Laurence J. Lafleur, New York: Hafner, 1948).

[30] Anatol Rapaport, "The Prisoner's Dilemma," in John Eatwell, Murray Milgate, and Peter Newman, eds., *The New Palgrave: A Dictionary of Economics* (London: Palgrave Macmillan, 1987), 973–76.

Smith will get off lightly (one year) but Jones will receive a sentence of twelve years. The best cooperative outcome—that is, the outcome that involves the minimum combined prison sentences (a total of six years)—would require both prisoners to remain silent. However, since they cannot trust one another, rationality dictates that they confess, each hoping to implicate the other in order to get a reduced sentence. The interrogator has so arranged the "payoffs" that whatever strategy is selected by Jones it is better for Smith to confess, and vice versa. Confession is the "dominant" strategy for both.

This imaginary example has analogues in the real world, where the egoistic pursuit of rational self-interest leads to undesirable outcomes for the egoists themselves. A familiar example is the supply of internal and external defense: I would rather not pay for it, so I rely on others, who eventually refuse to pay for it, so nobody is protected. Other examples include the difficulty in controlling pollution in the absence of a legal system that permits efficient redress to harmed individuals and the preservation of endangered species when each individual has a rational incentive to exploit a niggardly nature (the "tragedy of the commons"). A more concrete example occurred in the United Kingdom during the 1970s. In industrial relations there were regular social contracts between government and trade unions to control inflation. (I leave aside the mistaken economics of such strategies.) These arrangements always failed because very soon at least one union would break the contract, leading to mass defection. It was the regular recurrence of such problems that gave government and political philosophers the legitimate excuse, according to orthodox social theory, to impose collective solutions to coordination problems.

Of course, the differences between such problems and the classic prisoner's dilemma are that, normally, the social game is repeated and, equally important, the players can communicate with one another. The classic prisoner's dilemma is a theory that can explain much social behavior. However, the iterated prisoner's dilemma provides individualist theorists with a solution that does not require collectivist action by the state. These theorists also maintain that decentralized individuals can develop Humean conventions by which their activities are coordinated and defectors from agreements punished. Produced collectively, these conventions have a rationale in people's choices and not in a ukase of government or the political philosopher.

There are many demonstrations of how people might overcome the prisoner's dilemma and coordinate their activity by voluntary methods, but I have chosen for my argument the demonstration by Robert Sugden in his *The Economics of Rights, Co-Operation, and Welfare*.[31] I have done so largely

---

[31] Robert Sugden, *The Economics of Rights, Co-Operation, and Welfare* (Oxford: Blackwell, 1986).

because he presents a specifically Humean theory, with as much skepticism about morality and natural law as Hume himself had. Reason cannot determine objective morality, but we can use our rational faculties to understand how societies will develop conventions to solve coordination problems. These conventions include traffic rules, the assignment of property titles in circumstances of potential conflict, the provision of welfare through "mutual aid," and even the production of some public goods.

Crucial to the argument is the idea that a convention is self-enforcing: over a period of time people see that following it maximizes their utilities, and this realization will secure their support. Since a particular convention is a product not of reason but of experience (and our approval of it a function of the imagination), it is not the only and necessary solution to a coordination problem. It simply survives the evolutionary process, and although adherence to it produces a kind of equilibrium, this need not be "a state of affairs that anyone would choose; it is simply the unintended outcome of the choices of many individuals, each of whom is seeking to satisfy his wants."[32] In this approach, Sugden subverts a whole tradition of welfare economics and moral philosophy (including Rawlsianism) that seeks a *unique* solution to any aggregative problem.

Conventions emerge through the repeated playing of games. For example, the traffic rule in the United Kingdom "give way to the right at crossroads" develops when drivers see some *asymmetry* in the game they are playing, that is, when they conceive of themselves as playing different roles. If the game were symmetrical, drivers would simply slow down. This would produce an equilibrium but it would be very inefficient. The search for asymmetries in repeated games can be extended throughout almost the whole of social activity, including areas of potential conflict such as the original assignment of property titles. A convention will be successful to the extent that it appeals almost immediately to the imagination, hence the "finders keepers" rule[33] and some version of the Lockean principle of first acquisition to govern legitimate property holdings. One can easily imagine the golden rule (do unto others as you would have them do unto you) emerging in this way. A rule's survival prospects will depend on its clarity; the more ambiguous a rule is, the weaker are its survival prospects. Natural selection is crucial here, and Sugden claims that "the relationship between conventions . . . is rather like that between seedlings in a crowded plot of ground: whichever is the first to show vigorous growth can stifle the others."[34] Of course, there will always be some ambiguity, and I will show in the next section how the influence of morality on law has clouded a once useful clarity.

As Sugden argues, in extended games, where there is a low probability of the game ending, the tit-for-tat strategy, which punishes defectors from

---

[32] Ibid., 22.
[33] Actually developed by Israel M. Kirzner, *Discovery, Capitalism, and Distributive Justice* (Oxford: Blackwell, 1989).
[34] Sugden, *The Economics of Rights, Co-Operation, and Welfare*, 43.

a rule, has great survival prospects.[35] In an argument borrowed from Hume, he shows how reciprocity can emerge. A brave reciprocator is prepared to initiate cooperation but is always willing to retaliate against defectors. A sucker's strategy of "turning the other cheek" would be fatal because it would allow cheats to prosper. As long as brave reciprocators meet enough cautious players, mutual cooperation can get going. Indeed, regular defectors and cheats will be bred out; they will soon run out of people to exploit. Reciprocity then emerges as the dominant strategy. Even some public goods could be provided in this way. As long as enough people get the benefit of a public good, it will be supplied. People can even provide welfare to each other; today's benefactor may be tomorrow's recipient. All of this is possible, even in the face of free riders, if the providers are held together by reciprocity.

However, a serious problem is that large numbers make a difference. If the group gets too big, then free riding is much more likely and monitoring costs accordingly higher, whereas in smaller, more intimate societies, people can be held to their moral obligations by informal pressures. This presents something of a problem for classical liberal social and moral theorists. In the ideal version of a classical liberal model of society, more or less anonymous people coordinate their activities by abstract rules (Friedrich A. Hayek's "extended order"[36]), and this is thought to be the great achievement of market civilization over a primitive, "face-to-face" society. It might be that, for efficiency reasons, in the case of large numbers, the survival of some features of more primitive orders might be appropriate. But another solution, which I will suggest below, might be to decentralize the supply of public goods, that is, to transform the monopoly state into a loosely linked collection of "clubs."

IV. Law, Constitutionalism, and Morality

Throughout the twentieth century, even in nontotalitarian regimes, the tendency was not to adapt political arrangements to the spontaneously developing rules that I adumbrated above, but to devise a rationalistic set of principles of universal application that could be used as criteria to evaluate morally any preexisting practices. Constitutions were not used as constraints on central authority, within which decentralized legislative bodies competed with each other in the supply of laws and policies. Rather, constitutions were used as *licenses* for government to act in what it considered to be the public interest. Undoubtedly this process was hastened by the rise of majority-rule democracy, which has proved to be a very weak constraint on the exercise of political power. Today it is a

[35] Ibid. See also Robert Axelrod, *The Evolution of Cooperation* (New York: Basic Books, 1984), for an extended analysis of the tit-for-tat strategy.

[36] See Friedrich A. Hayek, *The Fatal Conceit: The Errors of Socialism*, ed. W. W. Bartley (London: Routledge, 1988), 16–21.

very unimaginative political party that cannot find a moral philosophy to validate whatever program it might adopt for purely electoral purposes.

The worst feature of the moralism that drives contemporary politics is that once a decision is justified on abstract moral grounds it becomes *compulsory* for a whole nation. 'Federalism', a political arrangement that is supposed to encourage competitive jurisdictions in which various conventions and practices may flourish with no one predominating, scarcely exists in the Western world.[37] Thus it is that the U.S. Supreme Court has constitutionalized many things, especially civil liberties and related matters, that were once the responsibility of the states. The developing "constitution" of the European Union is proceeding in the same direction, though at a much faster pace.[38] Of course, in any liberal society there has to be a basic set of rules that forms the background against which jurisdictional competition takes place, but the tendency of modern moralism is to widen the scope of these rules so that every individual and every community is compelled to accept them. This enforced uniformity eradicates many rival conventions.

The most obvious feature of this triumph of moralism is the almost complete elimination of constitutional protection for economic liberties. In the historical development of classical liberalism, property and contract were regarded, legally and morally, as important as free speech and liberty of religion. Of course, a constitution is a kind of convention that protects individuals from the possibly malign consequences of pursuing short-term goals: it lowers people's time preferences. This is why the rules for constitutional change are much stricter than they are for the passage of ordinary legislation. But the rise of moralism has systematically attenuated this constitutional rigor.

It is in the theory of law that moralism has been most effective, and its impact has been greatest in the United States. This is largely because the country has a written constitution that is loosely worded in parts, and this allows for morality, which is often highly controversial, to creep into interpretations by the Supreme Court. This phenomenon happens less often in the United Kingdom, which has no written document and whose courts have much less power of judicial review. However, the common-law system, which permits a certain judicial creativity in the interpretation of hard cases, itself is now beginning to reflect moralism, albeit in a small way.

Jurisprudence has always been riven by the classic dispute between natural and positive law.[39] Briefly, natural lawyers do not merely criticize positive law on moral grounds; rather, they say that the very *meaning* of

---

[37] Switzerland might be the one exception. There, expenditure by the federal government is still less than that of the cantons.

[38] See Norman Barry, "A Classical Liberal's Conception of Political Liberty: America and Europe Compared," *The European Journal* 9, no. 3 (2001): 13–17.

[39] See Mark Tebbit, *Philosophy of Law: An Introduction* (London: Routledge, 2000), chap. 4.

law turns on its content or moral quality. Proper law is supposed to reflect universally true moral statements: in theory, a judge would not have to apply legal propositions that breached these standards. Natural law propositions have to be broad in order to accommodate the wide variety of laws in the world, many of which could be said to be consistent with natural law. Positive lawyers have good reasons for making the meaning of law turn entirely on the objective features of its validation: a valid law can have any content,[40] but this content still can be evaluated by external moral principles. With the exception of Lon Fuller (1902–78),[41] traditional natural lawyers are rare in the modern era, but *pragmatic* lawyers[42] have good reasons to reject at least one of the sparse implications of pure positivism: that judicial activity consists of reading off the statutes and the cases and applying them to new problems in a mechanical manner. This is a most unrealistic description of judicial activity, and it can be rejected without abandoning other important features of positivism. These days, morality enters law not through an understanding of supposedly true universal moral principles, but by interpreting hard cases through a more modest ethic. To maintain a foothold on legality, these interpretations are claimed to be consistent with community practice and with a rationalist understanding of traditional principles.

It might be thought that some version of natural law, or at least a notion of law that absorbs much from ethics, would be appropriate for an understanding of social order in terms of conventions. But I think that this is mistaken and that conventionalism fits better with at least a version of legal positivism. I say this for two reasons. First, the influence of morality on law has produced great uncertainty, indeed controversy, when the courts have been asked to produce uniform and compulsory verdicts on issues that divide people. Since there is no one decisive answer in some cases, the judiciary is ceasing to be a neutral arbiter. Second, the critique of positivism has tended to understand all positive law systems as types of 'command', in which the orders of some authoritative body, such as a parliament, are the *sole* source of law. But not all positive law is command, and a proper understanding of legality in nonmoral terms would concentrate on *rules*, especially those rules that authorize people to commit certain acts (marry and leave wills, for example) and allow legislative bodies to do certain things (pass laws and make regulations). They are called 'power-conferring rules' in order to distinguish them from 'duty-imposing rules', such as the criminal law; only the latter are clearly understood as features of the command model. It is my contention that a

---

[40] Ibid., chap. 3.

[41] Lon L. Fuller, *The Morality of Law*, rev. ed. (New Haven, CT: Yale University Press, 1969).

[42] Richard Posner presents a normative theory of law based on economic reasoning, and although it is not positive law, it has emphatically nothing to do with morality. See Richard A. Posner, *The Problematics of Moral and Legal Theory* (Cambridge, MA: Harvard University Press, 1999).

proper understanding of social order in terms of conventions is more explicable in positive law language than it is in terms of law as morality. An additional but crucial point is that the 'theory of competitive jurisdictions', in which a variety of conventions can flourish, is more efficaciously described in the language of positive law.

A brief account of the classic debate in jurisprudence between the positivist legal philosopher, H. L. A. Hart (1907–92) and the legal moralist, Ronald Dworkin, provides the perfect venue for the issues that I want to discuss. Dworkin is not an orthodox natural lawyer, but he is a fierce critic of positivism and a firm believer in the view that correct legal decisions reflect notions of morality. He also writes in the context of ongoing legal systems characterized by significant judicial creativity: an intellectual environment that might be thought highly appropriate for the development of a theory of conventions. It is the case, however, that Hart has provided the most sophisticated critique of the command theory of law. Furthermore, it is clear that a perusal of Hart's writings outside the field of formal jurisprudence reveals his political views to be rather close to American liberalism, a doctrine of which Dworkin, ironically, is perhaps the most prominent exponent. But Hart never confuses these political views with his theory of law. And it is the latter that provides the intellectual framework for a conventionalist theory of society, not the overt moralism of Dworkin.

Hart understands law as a system of rules, and validation consists in tracing back a purported legal proposition to its ultimate authorization by a 'rule of recognition'.[43] Thus, even under a sovereignty system, the claim of a parliament's utterances to be lawful rests upon a rule of that system. The sovereignty of Parliament in the United Kingdom derives from the courts' acceptance, dating from the eighteenth century, that they would enforce its law against any other purported claim, for example, a claim from the common law or from an international treaty. In the United States, the rule of recognition lies not just with the formal Constitution but with Supreme Court interpretations of its meaning. Thus Hart's rule of recognition, by replacing the sovereign of the command theory, can encompass a much wider range of legal phenomena. In fact, all ongoing legal systems can be analyzed by the rule of recognition model. It is a strictly positivist theory, for the appeal to the rule of recognition to establish claims to lawfulness does not depend in any way on the moral qualities that a claim may, or may not, have. In hard cases, where the meaning of rules may be in doubt, judges exercise considerable discretion. But they are not "discovering" law when they so act, for however plausible their decisions are, they are not strictly law until they have been embodied in the system and recognized in future litigation. The judiciary

---

[43] H. L. A. Hart, *The Concept of Law*, 2d ed. (1961; reprint, Oxford: Clarendon Press, 1994), 87–107.

would be advised in difficult cases to make its innovative legal rulings consistent with contemporary ethics and practice, but this recommendation has no strict legal status. Of course, it is always open to a legislature to change a ruling, again by the authority of the rule of recognition. As a legal positivist, Hart thinks that the separation between law and morality is essential for clarity and predictability in a legal order.

It is this positivism that is Dworkin's target.[44] He makes an important distinction between rules and *principles*, but principles are not features of an abstract natural law, rather, they are located in the moral tradition of a community and are actually part of the law. Whereas rules apply at all times and are readily observable in statute or common law, principles need not be; they also may conflict and judges might have to "weigh" their significance. Principles have their most important role in hard cases where there is considerable doubt about what the law is. In effect, in a theory that bears an uncanny resemblance to Hayek's jurisprudence,[45] judges "discover" the law. Of course, Dworkin's and Hayek's theory of law is most appropriate for common-law systems in which judges are constantly searching for 'nonarticulated rules', Hayek's expression for nonformalized principles. Indeed, the charge that common-law processes involve an element of retroactivity, since no one can know what the law actually is until a judge has decided, is in principle avoidable in a Dworkinian or Hayekian approach. The law was always there; it simply had not been articulated or brought to light. Thus, for Dworkin, judges are always creative or activist, though he might deny this: "So any judge's opinion is itself a piece of legal philosophy, even when the philosophy is hidden and the visible argument is dominated by citation and lists of facts." [46] Dworkin, here, means moral philosophy because he insists that ethical standards are part of the law. Allied to this position is his argument that every legal problem has one, unique answer. This is why judicial decisions can be universalized.

In Dworkin's early work there is a certain plausibility in this view. He cites a nineteenth-century New York case, *Riggs v. Palmer*,[47] in which someone who had murdered his grandfather was denied his inheritance, even though there was nothing in the formal rules that would have precluded him. However, in the face of an obvious moral iniquity, the judges invoked the principle that "No man should profit from his own wrongs." This principle need not always apply. Someone who jumped bail and invested his own money in the stock market would not be denied any

---

[44] Ronald Dworkin, *Taking Rights Seriously* (London: Duckworth, 1977).

[45] Friedrich A. Hayek, *Rules and Order* (London: Routledge & Kegan Paul, 1973). That Hayek and Dworkin should have opposite social philosophies is a reason for doubting the efficacy of their common jurisprudence. See Norman Barry, "Dworkin's Unbounded Legalism," *Ideas on Liberty* 52, no. 11 (2002): 35–38.

[46] Ronald Dworkin, *Law's Empire* (London: Fontana, 1986), 90.

[47] *Riggs v. Palmer*, 115 N.Y. 506; 22 N.E. 188 (1889).

profits that might accrue. Again, the principle of 'adverse possession' allows people to keep, under certain conditions, that to which they were not formally entitled.

However, the argument is also used quite erroneously to justify the incorporation of highly contestable principles into American law, especially. Dworkin is a rights theorist and argues that rights always "trump" utility in hard cases. Correct answers are found by the discovery of appropriate rights. This position again derives from a superficially plausible distinction that Dworkin makes between principles and policy.[48] Judges are concerned with the protection of principles, and policy is a matter for legislatures, though even here, in a constitutional order that embodies rights, their discretion is strictly curtailed. The principle that is highly contestable is equality: "Legal argument must proceed on the basis that the best way to make sense of the law must be to read it so that it represents the state's striving to treat people as equals."[49] Thus the vague and ambiguous "right to equal concern and respect" becomes the linchpin of Dworkin's legal philosophy. Of course, it has some validation in the U.S. Constitution: the Fourteenth Amendment guarantees the equal protection of the laws and forbids the states to deny fundamental constitutional rights to persons without due process, but Dworkin uses it to justify a whole range of social innovations that are highly controversial. White males who might feel that their right to equal concern and respect has been deeply compromised by affirmative action programs that benefit women and ethnic minorities cannot expect much philosophical assistance from Dworkin.[50]

It is hardly likely that Dworkin's principles would count as Sugdenian conventions. For one thing, a convention must be prominent and survive a process of natural selection if it is to secure adherence. Dworkin's principles are guaranteed to sustain, indeed promote, controversy and contestability, but he also deliberately eschews a constitutional convention that might do something to assuage the heated debates that are generated by "rights" arguments: jurisdictional competition. In the model described by Sugden, it is quite plausible to imagine a convention emerging that prescribes that the institution closest to the people should generate appropriate rules, at least rules that would be less likely to generate internal tension. Indeed, the Tenth Amendment of the U.S. Constitution,[51] by reserving to the states or to the people, all matters not *specifically* delegated to the federal government, originally guaranteed this, but the gradual de-

---

[48] Dworkin, *Taking Rights Seriously*, 22–28.
[49] Dworkin, *Law's Empire*, 263.
[50] Barry, "Dworkin's Unbounded Legalism," 36–37.
[51] There is evidence that the authors of the Tenth Amendment to the U.S. Constitution were influenced by Hume's political writings. See Douglass Adair, "That Politics May Be Reduced to a Science: David Hume, James Madison, and the Tenth *Federalist*," in *Hume: A Re-Evaluation*, Donald W. Livingston and James T. King, eds. (New York: Fordham University Press, 1976), 404–17.

mise of this legal convention, largely because of Supreme Court activism, has deprived the states of the opportunity of offering competing practices. The rise of a deontological rights mentality has produced rules that apply to everybody, with a much reduced possibility of exit. A clear example is *Roe v. Wade*,[52] under which all fifty states were compelled to follow an entirely judge-made law. The case made abortion a constitutional right; prior to that it depended on particular states. A small number of states did allow the practice. Of course, the controversy over abortion itself is morally insoluble, but the invocation of an absolute rights mentality has made it worse. Both sides of the debate invoke implicitly Dworkinian rights: pro-abortion activists cite the "woman's right to choose," while their opponents talk of the rights of the fetus. Who is right? The disagreement existed before 1973, but it was not until *Roe v. Wade* that the debate descended into physical violence on both sides. The one institutional arrangement that might have averted this discontent—competitive jurisdictions—is dismissed as "checkerboard law"[53] by Dworkin.

Furthermore, Dworkin is selective about the rights that he wants to protect. They do not include economic rights. It might be thought that the (short-lived) constitutional right to contract, which was created in the *Allgeyer v. Louisiana* decision of 1897[54] might have survived: it has exactly the same constitutional rationale as *Roe v. Wade* (both depend on a substantive interpretation of the due process clause of the Fourteenth Amendment). But the right to contract is now rarely mentioned. In fact, there never was an unlimited right to contract and a number of state restrictions were upheld by the Court even after *Lochner v. New York* (1905), the most famous case in this line. Why does Dworkin admire *Roe* so much but has so little time for *Lochner*?[55] It is much more likely that people would generate the convention of economic liberty—in this case, freedom of contract—than the right to abortion, since the latter involves deeply felt questions about life and death. Under a constitutional convention guaranteeing federalism, abortion would likely be available somewhere. It is also true, of course, that by the same argument some states might want to restrict severely the right to abortion. But it is unlikely to be abolished everywhere and jurisdictional competition is almost certain to preserve it somewhere. However, the convention of *economic* rights, by whatever method they emerge, has been made less sustainable by the Court's decision in a 1938 case, *United States v. Carolene Products*,[56] and its famous footnote 4, in which a distinction was suggested between civil and eco-

---

[52] For Dworkin's defense of *Roe v. Wade*, 410 U.S. 113 (1973), see *Law's Empire*, chap. 6.

[53] Dworkin, *Law's Empire*, 178–84.

[54] *Allgeyer v. Louisiana*, 165 U.S. 578 (1897). See Bernard H. Siegan, *Economic Liberties and the Constitution* (Chicago: University of Chicago Press, 1980), 111.

[55] 198 U.S. 45 (1905). See Dworkin, *Law's Empire*, 398.

[56] *United States v. Carolene Products Co.*, 304 U.S. 144 (1938). See Siegan, *Economic Liberties and the Constitution*, 185–88.

nomic liberties. Although economic liberties were not denied, the Court speculated in footnote 4 that legislation adversely affecting civil liberties might be subject to a more stringent, less deferential standard of review than legislation affecting economic liberties. The democratic process was thought to be an adequate guarantor of economic liberties, but a less reliable protector of civil liberties. Since *Carolene Products* the Court, indeed, has been less solicitous of economic liberty and has virtually abandoned economic substantive due process. Still, contract, tort, and property ownership remained constitutionally protected, and there has recently been a revival in the Supreme Court's protection of the rights of property.[57] Under Dworkinian law, just as under *Carolene Products*, legislatures are more or less unrestrained in economic matters.

It should be noted that I do not maintain that Hart's positivism would *necessarily* lead to a legal environment favorable to the emergence and protection of economic conventions. After all, a legislature, acting perfectly legitimately by positivist standards, could implement socialism overnight. However, by making a firm distinction between law and morality, Hart's model prevents courts from constructing rights and turning them into "positive" law without any legislative action whatsoever. Also, Hart's avowed utilitarianism is a further bulwark against the claims of absolutist and invincible rights. What is decisive in Hart's dispute with Dworkin is the fact that Hart makes a distinction between law and morality for *moral* reasons. In other words, if we fuse law and morality, then we are disabled from giving the former necessary critical appraisal (and in his nontechnical work Hart was a persistent critic of positive law in the United Kingdom). If law is a part of morality then it is protected from scrutiny. In an implicit criticism of American rationalistic liberalism, Hart says that "it is folly to believe that where the meaning of law is in doubt, morality always has a clear answer." [58] In a pluralist society it is an illusion to think that deep differences can be adjudicated by law.

Neither do I mean to suggest that there is no place for a properly formulated rights doctrine in a utilitarian conception of law. All I wish to maintain is that rights should not constitute the ultimate foundation of law. Rights are, in a sense, "argument stoppers," [59] and their invocation defeats all rival claims, especially those deriving from utility. There are good rhetorical reasons why proponents of state welfare argue for symmetry between ordinary civil rights and welfare rights, both to be satisfied by the state. But they are not symmetrical. This difference is not established by the claim that civil rights are more or less costless while expenditure on welfare seems to rise almost exponentially in democratic

---

[57] See Bernard H. Siegan, *Property and Freedom: The Constitution, the Courts, and Land-Use Regulation* (New Brunswick: Transaction, 1997); and Norman Barry, "Constitutional Protection of Economic Liberty," *Ideas on Liberty* 50, no. 11 (2000): 26–30.

[58] Hart, *The Concept of Law*, 204.

[59] Barry, *An Introduction to Modern Political Theory*, 243.

societies. After all, the protection of civil liberties does require some expenditure (except for genuine anarchists) on police, courts, etc.

The real difference between the two concepts of rights relates to personal conduct. All welfare rights theorists say that welfare recipients should have made some effort to avoid the possibly penurious situation in which they find themselves. As philosopher Alan Gewirth says, the agent "cannot rationally demand of other persons that they help him to have basic well-being unless his own efforts to have it are unavailing." [60] Yet we would not say that a person sacrificed his right not to be accosted, or worse, because he foolishly walked into an area known to be plagued by muggers. It is easy to imagine how rights would be protected in a utilitarian society; they are essential instruments for social cooperation and would emerge by convention rather than by philosophical reasoning. This also explains their persuasiveness. A modest utilitarianism demonstrates that they would be protected but not inviolable. This is no better illustrated than in the world of economics and commerce, where the traditional business enterprise of capitalist society has been the constant target of moralists. Because the object of commerce is obviously worldly, it has never been thought to exhibit more than the crudest of utilitarian rationales. However, as I shall show below, this ethical modesty is the real virtue of business enterprise. It far exceeds the ersatz grandeur of "business ethics."

V. BUSINESS AND MORALITY

Presumably few today believe in Marxist predictions, or prophecies, about the ultimate downfall of capitalism or imagine that a socialist planned economy can compete with the market in the production of wanted goods and services. But criticism of capitalism has not abated; only now the attention is focused on its ethical failings. There has been in recent years a systematic attempt to moralize market capitalism: to hold it up to very high standards of ethical appraisal, to scrutinize it critically, and to make recommendations for its improvement. Where once capitalism had to be licensed by the economist it now requires the imprimatur of the moralist. As with other attempts to moralize social relationships, what is known as business ethics imposes 'supererogatory duties', that is, those that exceed normal ethical obligations, on business agents. The morality here is specifically anti-utilitarian.

Business has been particularly troublesome for classical liberals because ever since Mandeville there has been the persistent claim that economic success depends not only on the absence of supererogatory morality,

---

[60] Alan Gewirth, "Private Philanthropy and Positive Rights," in *Beneficence, Philanthropy, and the Public Good*, ed. Ellen Frankel Paul, Fred Miller, and Jeffrey Paul (Oxford: Blackwell, 1987), 68.

but also on the suspension of familiar and uncontroversial ethical duties. As I shall show, it is only by an understanding of morality as the following of conventions that this difficulty can be resolved. Of especial critical concern are the stockholder-owned corporation and the individualism that drive the Anglo-American market. Even some nominally pro-capitalist writers compare it unfavorably with the apparently more communitarian and less "greed-driven" market systems of, for example, Germany and Japan, and they would be willing to sacrifice some efficiency to achieve these much-vaunted moral aims. It is never clear how much efficiency, nor what should determine the connection between efficiency and morality.

It is easy to see how the corporation emerged spontaneously from the free actions of individuals transacting under legal conventions, especially contract. Individuals pool their assets and create an artificial, legal "person," the corporation. They hire other persons to manage their assets and subject these individuals to strict, *fiduciary* duties: the managers must always act in the best interests of the owners, that is, the stockholders. All of the features of the modern corporation, including limited liability, were originally created spontaneously. As historian Robert Hessen writes: "At every stage of its growth the corporation is a voluntary association based exclusively on contract."[61] Adam Smith had very serious doubts about the efficiency, not the morality, of the joint-stock company.[62] He thought that the managers would not act in the interests of the owners and favored owner-managed enterprises. However, he did not anticipate the development of methods for dealing with rent-seeking managers;[63] the most important of these methods is the takeover threat. But as we shall see shortly, the problem remains serious for modern corporate capitalism.

The moralists have always maintained that the properties of the corporation do not emerge spontaneously but are a gift of the state and positive law.[64] Corporations should not be constrained only by fiduciary duties, and they must earn their "privileges" by acting for people other than stockholders. Corporate status is a kind of license, or contract, between business and society, which has to be paid for: hence the "social responsibility of business" thesis. But it is not a feature of economic conventions that business should be responsible to society or to the community. These are far too vague and ambiguous entities for the attribution of genuine obligations.

Of course, business personnel are bound by strict conventions to respect property and to honor contract and related obligations, but the

---

[61] Robert Hessen, *In Defense of the Corporation* (Stanford, CA: Hoover Institution Press, 1979), 43. See also Norman Barry, *Business Ethics* (London: Macmillan, 1998), 43.

[62] Smith, *The Wealth of Nations*, 720–58.

[63] 'Rent-seeking' is the activity by some of capturing extra market value created by others. Those who argue for economic protection, and many government employees, are rent-seekers.

[64] See Thomas Donaldson, *Corporations and Morality* (Englewood Cliffs, NJ: Prentice Hall, 1982).

moralists have endeavored to put the supererogatory duties in the same category as the compulsory ones. These moral duties properly belong to individuals in their private capacities and ought not to be imposed on employees who already have fiduciary obligations, determined by contract, to their employers. It is the latter's money that will be used for the employees' achievements. Thus, modern business ethics creates an immediate conflict of interest for company employees. This conflict is complicated by the predominant feature of the corporation: the separation between ownership and control.[65] The normally passive stockholder has little rational incentive to exert his ownership rights. His only sanction against management is to sell his stock to a corporate raider. And this is why the moralists condemn takeovers and why Germany and Japan are so popular; takeovers are not a significant feature of corporate life in these countries.

An increasingly popular demand of business moralists is to supplement the stockholder within the decision-making structure of the corporation with the notion of 'stakeholder'. For the moralists, the owner is only one of a selection of interested parties who may share decision rights. Of course, this completely undermines ownership and thence any determinate authority structure in the firm. It is true that management in firms replaces the market;[66] persons do not freely contract within the company, and they have to obey orders. They are, of course, free, in capitalist society, to leave the organization, but while they remain in it they have to submit to authority. It is perhaps this minor moral problem that the moralists have in mind when they recommend the democratization of the firm via the idea of stakeholders. But stakeholders are not limited to employees. The list typically includes suppliers, members of the community in which the firm is situated, and any group that can claim some interest in the firm's activities.

The idea of the stakeholder, however, makes no practical or logical sense, for a stakeholder-driven firm will not speak with one voice. Instead, it will have a great variety of ends and purposes, disparate values, and no determinate authority structure. The purely logical conundrum relates to Arrow's general possibility theorem and problems that are bound to occur whenever there are at least three alternative decisions with at least three decision-makers.[67] No consistent decision will emerge after successive rounds of voting and one will have to be imposed by a "dictator." This does not matter in the conventional firm, for it can be assumed that the stockholders will normally speak with one voice and with one purpose—to maximize stockholder value. Some stakeholder moral-

---

[65] Adolph A. Berle and Gardiner C. Means, *The Modern Corporation and Private Property* (1932; reprint, rev. ed., New York: Harcourt, Brace and World, 1967).

[66] See Ronald Coase, "The Nature of the Firm," *Economica* 4, no. 16 (1937): 386–405.

[67] See Norman Barry, "The Stakeholder Concept of Corporate Control Is Illogical and Impractical," *The Independent Review* 6, no. 4 (2002): 541–54.

ists seem to be dimly aware of this problem. In a specifically Kantian analysis, William Evan and R. Edward Freeman recommend that a "meta-physical director" should be appointed to the board to adjudicate impartially between rival groups of stakeholders.[68] But nobody is impartial. The metaphysical director will be a rent-seeker who will divert income to himself (by prolonging disputes between stakeholders) up to the point at which the viability of the firm is threatened.

This is not to say that all is well with the business community, least of all that its standards are beyond reproach. It is too early to make detailed comments on the business scandals, especially those involving Enron and WorldCom, that occurred in 2001 and 2002, but it is clear that they relate to the oldest problem in business conduct: How do we ensure that agents (managers and other employees) work in the interests of the principals (the owners)? In the much maligned 1980s this was guaranteed by the takeover mechanism.[69] Predators noticed that agents were not acting in the interests of owners. In contrast, the takeovers of the 1960s and 1970s had not been designed to enhance shareholder value, but rather the wealth and power of managers, who behaved like bureaucrats in a government department. The predators of the 1980s simply broke up the unwieldy conglomerates that had been created by irresponsible managers and re-turned money, in the form of higher dividends and higher share prices, to stockholders. This offended the lofty ideals of the moralists, but was quite consistent with the conventions of capitalism.

This was not so of the scandals of the early twenty-first century, for then (like now) stockholders were again victims of exploitative managers. Every business convention was broken, by means including dishonest accounting, fixing of share prices, and the deception of employees about the value of the companies. The motive for these breaches was genuine greed as opposed to the notion of "greed" used by today's moralists, who use it to denigrate anybody who does well or whose earnings exceed favored criteria of social justice. It is also noticeable that the perpetrators of the recent egregious scandals had very high profiles within the char-itable community.[70] Concededly, there is a problem in leaving business to be regulated entirely by convention for, although the market system is self-correcting, it is likely that there will be injured parties before its therapeutic effects operate. The problem is exacerbated by the fact of large numbers and the relative *anonymity* of business enterprise. These two facts make it more difficult for conventions, voluntarily accepted, to achieve

[68] William M. Evan and R. Edward Freeman, "A Stakeholder Theory of the Modern Corporation: Kantian Capitalism," in Tom L. Beauchamp and Norman E. Bowie, eds., *Ethical Theory and Business*, 4th ed. (Englewood Cliffs, NJ: Prentice Hall, 1993), 82.

[69] Barry, *Business Ethics*, chap. 6.

[70] Norman Barry, "What Capitalism Needs Is a New Gordon Gekko," *The Business*, Sep-tember 15, 2002. See also Norman Barry, "The Right Morality for Capitalism," *Ideas on Liberty* 52, no. 12 (2002): 33–37.

the prominence that is required for their efficacy. But even here, regular criminal law (itself derived from convention) is likely to be a more effective remedy than an ambitious morality.

VI. Conclusion

The demise of positivism has produced new, and fiercely competing, moralities for the appraisal of particular public policies and generated new metaphysical rationalizations to ratify more general ethical outlooks. But it has been the aim of this essay to show that not all varieties of positivism produced an arid subjectivism or amoral relativism. Indeed, as we have seen, the historical founder of logical positivism, David Hume, was far from being a relativist, but was the creator of a complex normative doctrine of human conduct, which involved the demonstration that certain rules and practices have an almost *universal* appeal. They might be, in a purely logical sense, no more than superstitions, but if certain rules and practices are grounded in utility, they are highly serviceable. Thus, to replace the heady ideals of contemporary "morality" by the more realistic demands of convention is not to endorse any kind of ethical arbitrariness or subjectivism.

In fact, a much greater uncertainty about standards and practices comes about through the attempt to appraise them by high moral principles. The contemporary obsession with "morality" in the law has generated great dissent and confusion not only about the meaning of law, but also about the range of legal rules and their applicability to social affairs. When once much of human interaction was regulated by informal rules and practices, it is now a matter of formal legal control, either by statute or by creative decisions of common-law judges. The arbitrary assumption by early legal positivists that the only genuine law had to be a product of command not only made it difficult to explain regimes that are governed by constitutions and are, therefore, subject to significant judicial review, it also made it difficult to appreciate the potency of accepted conventions. The U.S. Constitution has historically illustrated the creativity of a system of law not solely derived from command. However, the current dominance of substantive ethics has led to the replacement of more or less informal mechanisms of social control by a much more extensive and invasive constitutionalized morality. The social disturbances generated by abortion, antidiscrimination, and other civil rights decisions show just how divisive this moralization can be.

Business has been subjected to the same moral appraisal as law, but here the critique would have been more effective had it focused on breaches of established conventions rather than the creation of supererogatory duties and novel notions of "stakeholders." In fact, capitalist enterprises have not been remiss in fulfilling supererogatory duties; on the contrary, corporate charitable activity (with or without direct stockholder approval) has been a remarkable feature of corporate capitalism. Instead of their misdirected critiques, moralists should have focused on cases of managers who breached the conventional duty of acting in the interests of owners.

The obvious solution to this breach of duty is the activation of the business convention that stockholders should be more active and reassert their legal powers of ownership. Here, however, stockholders face another problem, one frequently analyzed in the social sciences: rational ignorance and passivity in the context of large numbers. The difference that any one person's actions might make is so small that it is not in his interest to act. His only sanction is to sell his shares to a corporate raider. However, activists, especially in the United Kingdom, are often not interested in maximizing stockholder value but in pressing for a moral cause. The stockholder activists of this type are actually anticapitalist. In the long run, capitalism will spontaneously develop solutions to these problems, but the solutions will not come from business ethics. Only a reexamination, and a reassertion, of conventions will lead to progress in genuine business morality.

Social and Political Theory, University of Buckingham

AUTONOMY AND EMPATHY

By Michael Slote

I. Introduction

When Carol Gilligan, Nel Noddings, and other ethicists of caring draw the contrast between supposedly masculine and supposedly feminine moral thinking, they put such things as justice, autonomy, and rights together under the first rubric and such things as caring, responsibility for others, and connection together under the second.[1] This division naturally leaves caring ethicists with the issue of how to deal with topics such as justice, autonomy, and rights, but it also leaves defenders of more traditional moral theories (now dubbed "masculine") with the problem of how to treat (if at all) the sorts of issues that ethicists of caring raise.

One response, among caring ethicists and others, has been to acknowledge the two types of moral thinking (however imperfectly correlated with sex or gender) while claiming that each is one-sided and needs to be complemented or supplemented with the other if we are to achieve an adequate understanding of morality, of the full range of moral phenomena. This says, in effect, that previous "masculine" moral philosophies have skimped on (the importance of) the sorts of affective bonds on which caring ethics focuses. This response also suggests that caring and human connection need to be situated within just social institutions whose character is not determined by caring, but, rather, by the less personal and more general principles and concepts of traditional moral/political philosophy and its descendants.

However, some caring ethicists have proceeded more boldly. For example, in a preface added to *In a Different Voice* in 1993, Gilligan suggests that an ethics of caring grounded in an ideal of connection with, rather than separateness from, others might completely displace traditional masculine approaches and give us a total picture of what can be validly said about the ethical. But what does this then mean about the supposedly masculine concepts or topics of justice, autonomy, and rights? Are we simply to discard such concepts, or is the idea, rather, that we can make sense of them in (not necessarily reductive) terms of caring and cognate notions? Gilligan's preface does not really say. But some caring ethicists

---

[1] For their classic discussions of caring and the contrast between masculine and feminine approaches to morality, see Carol Gilligan, *In a Different Voice: Psychological Theory and Women's Development* (1982; reprint, with new preface, Cambridge: Harvard University Press, 1993); and Nel Noddings, *Caring: A Feminine Approach to Ethics and Moral Education* (Berkeley: University of California Press, 1984).

have recently written in ways that seem to favor the latter option. I have in mind here work by Sara Ruddick, a recent book by Nel Noddings, and also an earlier article of my own that was subsequently incorporated into a book.[2] All of these writings treat issues of the public or political realm that are familiarly regarded as questions of justice as answerable or addressable in terms of notions such as caring. A tradition seems to be developing in which justice is said to be best understood in terms of these notions.

The supposedly masculine idea or ideal of autonomy has so far had a somewhat different history. The feminist reaction to traditional treatments of the notion has most notably consisted in emphasizing the relational character of autonomy and its underpinnings. According to such thinking, personal autonomy is not something we automatically have or are given, but, rather, develops in relation to other people: to use Annette Baier's felicitous phrase, we are all basically "second persons."[3] But this way of understanding autonomy, while tying it to and letting it exemplify the supposedly feminine notion of connection with others, does not tell us how or even whether autonomy conceived in this new fashion can be accommodated within an overall morality of caring. My purpose in this essay, however, will be precisely to indicate how I think autonomy and respect for autonomy can be understood in terms of caring. What I shall say agrees with the recent feminist idea that autonomy has to be understood relationally and in terms of connection with other people, but the relationality and connection will be more closely tied to the ethics of caring than anything (I believe) that has been said about autonomy in the recent feminist literature. However, in order to make all of this seem plausible, we shall have to see why the ethics of caring needs to incorporate another notion—empathy—more systematically or thoroughly than it has previously been asked to do.

II. Caring and Empathy

Over the past half-century there has been a tremendous revival of interest in virtue ethics. Most of that interest has been directed toward Aristotle, though there also has been a good deal of discussion of Plato's views and of ancient Stoicism. However, the ethics of caring is also widely seen as a form of virtue ethics, and my own most recent work as a virtue ethicist has been largely devoted to showing why such an ethics is plau-

[2] See Sara Ruddick, *Maternal Thinking: Toward a Politics of Peace* (Boston, MA: Beacon Press, 1989); Nel Noddings, *Starting at Home: Caring and Social Policy* (Berkeley: University of California Press, 2002); and Michael Slote, "The Justice of Caring," *Social Philosophy and Policy* 15, no. 1 (1998): 171–95, which was incorporated with some changes into chap. 4 of my *Morals from Motives* (New York: Oxford University Press, 2001).

[3] See Annette Baier, "Cartesian Persons" in Annette Baier, *Postures of the Mind: Essays on Mind and Morals* (Minneapolis: University of Minnesota Press, 1985), 84ff.; and the essays in Catriona Mackenzie and Natalie Stoljar, eds., *Relational Autonomy: Feminist Perspectives on Autonomy, Agency, and the Social Self* (New York: Oxford University Press, 2000).

sible and promising both as a form of virtue ethics and as a general, systematic approach to morality. My book *Morals from Motives* (henceforth *MfM*) sought to show that a morality of caring can encompass not only our relations with people we know but also our moral obligations to people we do not know, to human beings generally. (These moral obligations include issues of social justice.) I also argued against grounding a morality of caring in the desirability of caring relationships, as Noddings suggests, and in favor of the fundamental moral goodness of properly contoured and sufficiently deep caring motivation. But regardless of how a virtue ethics of caring is ultimately grounded, it sees the moral rightness and wrongness of actions as depending on whether they express or reflect caring motivation (i.e., a caring attitude) or whether they express or reflect a deficiency of caring (or some motive or attitude, like malice or misanthropy, that is actually *opposed* to caring).

Such an approach faces many challenges. But for the moment I want to focus on a particular one of those challenges. In *MfM*, I argued that certain sorts of caring are inherently admirable and that various relevant moral judgments are, therefore, intuitively plausible. I claimed, for example, that it is morally better if one cares more about one's friends and family than about strangers or people whom one does not know personally, and I relied on the intuitive force of such a claim in arguing against act-utilitarianism and act-consequentialism more generally. Obviously, all work in normative ethics requires some kind of reliance on intuition(s), and I believe that the intuitions that undergird a (or my own) virtue ethics of caring are plausible enough to support and sustain such an approach. But the use of intuitions comes at a price: for what one accepts on an intuitive basis is to that extent not explained, and although we know that we need to rely on unexplained intuition(s) somewhere or ultimately, it is philosophically satisfying to be able to explain any given intuition. This fact has led me to think that my own and others' previous work in caring ethics can be usefully supplemented or enriched by a further conceptual/moral emphasis.

In *MfM* I did not consider the morality of our relations with animals or fetuses, but an ethics of caring could easily say that we have, for example, a greater obligation to help (born) fellow humans than to help animals or fetuses. Such a comparative judgment has the kind of intuitive force that one might rely on in an ethics of caring (though I assume that the intuition about born humans and fetuses will operate more weakly or will be undercut altogether in someone with a strong religious conviction that the fetus has an immortal soul). Some years ago, however, and after *MfM* had been written, I was led in a different direction as a result of having my attention called to an article by Catholic thinker and judge John Noonan, in which abortion is criticized not for failing to respect the rights of the fetus, but for showing a lack of empathy for the fetus.[4] Now the

---

[4] See John T. Noonan, Jr., "Responding to Persons: Methods of Moral Argument in Debate over Abortion," *Theology Digest* (1973): 291–307.

concept of 'empathy' is different from that of 'caring', because 'empathy' involves seeing or feeling things from the standpoint of another, and it is not obvious a priori that someone who cares altruistically about the well-being of another will automatically be susceptible to the point of view of that other. But, recognizing this conceptual distinction between empathy and caring, I was absolutely galvanized by hearing about Noonan's article, because (for one thing) it immediately occurred to me that the notion or phenomenon of empathy is a double-edged sword, and reading the article did nothing to disturb this conclusion. If we believe that empathy has moral force or relevance, then since it is, in fact, much easier for us to empathize with born humans, even neonates, than with a fetus, we can argue that it is, for this reason, morally worse to neglect or hurt a born human than to do the same to a fetus or embryo. And this conclusion might end up giving more sustenance to the pro-choice position than to the pro-life view of abortion.

Moreover, it almost as immediately occurred to me that a virtue ethics of caring, rather than relying on our intuitions about our stronger obligations to born humans than to embryos, fetuses, or animals, could explain these intuitions, these differential obligations, by incorporating the idea of empathy. Instead of claiming that actions are right or wrong depending on whether they exhibit or reflect what intuition tells us is properly contoured and sufficiently deep caring, one can say that actions are morally right or wrong (or better or worse) depending on whether, or on the extent to which, they exhibit or reflect normally or fully empathic caring motivation. It would then (at least other things being equal) be morally worse to prefer a fetus or embryo to a born human being, because such a preference runs contrary to the flow of fully developed human empathy or to caring motivation that is shaped by such empathy. And similar points, arguably, could be made about our moral relations with lower animals.[5]

So, a caring ethics that brings in empathy can normatively explain what would otherwise be accepted on an intuitive basis. Once I realized this, I soon saw that the notion of empathy can also serve useful explanatory purposes in other areas of morality. As I mentioned above, we intuitively think that we have stronger moral obligations of caring toward those who are near and dear to us than to people with whom we are unacquainted and who may live in distant parts of the world. We are also inclined to think that it is morally worse not to save a child who is drowning in a fountain right in front of us than to allow some unknown, distant child to

---

[5] Noddings (*Caring*) relies heavily on a concept of "engrossment" that is closely related to (in fact, I think it constitutes one form of) empathy, but when it comes to explaining why we have stronger moral obligations to fellow humans, she relies on facts about the (non)reciprocity of the relevant caring relationships. This allows some further explanation beyond what the idea of caring alone is capable of. However, I believe that it is best to explain our differential obligations vis-à-vis animals and fellow humans in terms of the notion of empathy because of the remarkable explanatory power (as I can here only partly indicate) of the concept of empathy *in other areas of normative ethics.*

starve to death by not making a contribution, say, to Oxfam, a hunger-relief organization.

In "Famine, Affluence, and Morality," however, Peter Singer famously disagrees.[6] He holds that it makes no sense to suppose that sheer distance can make a difference to our moral obligations, and he argues that our obligations to distant people who need our help are just as strong as to a child who is drowning or starving right in front of us. But the concept of empathy can help explain and, I believe, justify the moral partialism of a caring morality, and of ordinary moral thinking, with regard to cases like those Singer mentions. A failure to help someone who is in trouble or in need right in front of us, and whose trouble or need we see, runs contrary to developed human empathy in a way that a failure to give to Oxfam does not. This has something to do with the difference that seeing or perceiving makes in eliciting or arousing empathic reactions.

This difference is something that Hume in *A Treatise of Human Nature* (1739) was well aware of, though he uses the term 'sympathy' (the word 'empathy' did not emerge until the twentieth century).[7] Moreover, Hume holds that differences in what naturally or normally arouses sympathy affect the strength of our moral obligations and what virtue calls for. What I want to argue, following Hume, is that, *pace* Singer, our lesser obligation to people whose suffering we do not immediately experience can be explained in terms of fully developed human empathy. There are, in fact, recent psychological studies of empathy that bear out what Hume already understood in the eighteenth century. Martin Hoffman's book *Empathy and Moral Development* usefully summarizes and reflects upon numerous psychological studies of the development of empathy and its role in creating or sustaining caring/concern for others. One thing that both Hoffman and authors of the previous studies emphasize is the difference that perceptual immediacy makes to the strength of empathic responses.[8] Like Hume, Hoffman and the work that he cites also point up the difference that familial or friendly relationships make to how strongly empathy is aroused. I, like Hume, want to appeal to the notion of empathy/sympathy to explain and justify our moral partiality toward friends and family. (Hoffman is more cautious than Hume about this and other normative moral issues.) Note that such partiality does not entail that it is appropriate to have no empathy or concern for strangers and people whom one has never met.

At the most general level, then, I believe that a virtue ethics of caring (of the sort that I defended in *MfM*) should be reconfigured as a virtue ethics of *empathic* caring. This enables such an ethics to explain a wider

---

[6] Peter Singer, "Famine, Affluence, and Morality," *Philosophy & Public Affairs* 1, no. 4 (1972): 229–43.

[7] David Hume, *A Treatise of Human Nature*, ed. L. A. Selby-Bigge (1739; reprint, Oxford: Clarendon Press, 1958), 316ff., 574ff.

[8] Martin L. Hoffman, *Empathy and Moral Development: Implications for Caring and Justice* (New York: Cambridge University Press, 2000).

range of moral distinctions. Most significantly, the addition or reconfig-
uration also allows us to reach a deeper understanding of deontology—
which holds, roughly, the view that it is in various crucial cases wrong to
do what will benefit people the most overall—than would otherwise be
possible. Caring is naturally regarded as encompassing or falling within
the morality of beneficence, but deontology is commonsensically regarded as restricting beneficence (and self-interest), that is, as limiting
what we can do on behalf of others (or ourselves). Our obligations to help
others can readily be seen as arising from appropriate and/or cultivated
human feelings or sentiments, but it is not easy to see how deontological
restrictions on such helping can arise from feelings. This is why deontology seems to call for some sort of rational grounding. Since an ethics of
empathic caring bases morality in feelings rather than reason, it is difficult to see how such an ethics could possibly accommodate and explain
our deontological intuitions. (Hume does not attempt a full defense of
deontology in the core sense given above.)

Of course, it is always possible for an ethics of caring to repudiate
deontology, as the sentimentalist Francis Hutcheson (1694–1746) in effect
did and as utilitarianism always has done;[9] but our deontological intuitions are rather strongly ingrained in us, and it is very difficult for most
of us to accept a theory that explains them away or treats them as derivative and limited. However, an ethics of empathic caring might have a
chance to defend deontology on a purely sentimentalist basis, if we could
show that empathy is actually sensitive to (that is, differentially aroused
by) crucial deontological distinctions as exemplified in situations of individual moral choice. This is something that I believe can be shown, and
I have elsewhere attempted to do just that.[10] But there is no space here to
discuss this further.[11] If the reader will accept my promissory note on the
issue of deontology and some of the other issues raised above, then I
would like now to show how a systematically sentimentalist virtue ethics

[9] Francis Hutcheson, *An Inquiry into the Original of Our Ideas of Beauty and Virtue*, Treatise
2: *Concerning Moral Good and Evil*, sec. 2, pt. 1 (1725), in *Complete Works of Francis Hutcheson*,
vol. 1 (Hildesheim: Olms, 1969–71). For a contemporary discussion of utilitarianism with
historical references, see J. J. C. Smart and Bernard Williams, *Utilitarianism: For and Against*
(Cambridge: Cambridge University Press, 1973).
[10] I sketch such an argument in an essay entitled "Sentimentalist Virtue and Moral Judgment: Outline of a Project," in *Metaphilosophy* 34, no. 1 (2003): 131–43. I give a fuller treatment in my work-in-progress, *Moral Sentimentalism*, chaps. 3 and 4.
[11] One might at this point also wonder whether a reliance on empathy would lead us to
make *too many* moral distinctions. For example, if people of one race or gender are more
empathically sensitive to those of the same race or gender, then the distinctions in our
attitudes and behavior that empathy explains, at least some of them, may be morally
invidious, and this would represent a serious problem for any attempt to explain morality
systematically in terms of empathic caring. I offer a response to such worries in the work
referred to above in note 10. However, the solidarity that is shared by an oppressed group
can lead to intragroup preferences that seem far from morally invidious, and an appeal to
empathy can help us both to account for this and to explain why similar solidarity among
the group of oppressors is not morally justified. (On this point see *Moral Sentimentalism*,
chaps. 2 and 5.)

of empathic caring can make sense of the value and importance of respecting individual autonomy.

III. Empathy and Respect

The ideal of respect is usually associated with Kantian and rationalist conceptions of the individual and her worth and duties. By contrast, caring and concern for (the welfare of) individuals are part and parcel of classical utilitarian and sentimentalist approaches to ethics. It is commonly thought that this latter type of approach, while focusing on individuals, makes no room for the idea of universal human moral dignity or worth (in one sense of the latter term) that must always be respected. Thus, in *Taking Rights Seriously*, Ronald Dworkin argues that justice requires the state to treat all of its citizens with equal concern and respect. The presupposition here, of course, is that (welfare-oriented) concern does not entail (Kantian) respect.[12]

However, a sentimentalist ethics that puts *empathic* concern or caring at the center of the moral life can give its own account of what respect involves. Respect is an important moral notion, and Kantians and other rationalists certainly offer articulate conceptions of what it involves. But my point here is and will be that sentimentalist virtue ethics also can offer a conception of respect, and I believe that its conception is actually less metaphysically loaded, less obscure, and closer to the bone of actual human lives than what Kantians and other rationalists have offered.

Nonetheless, I do not want to dissent from what the rationalists have said about respect so much as to argue *in favor* of what a sentimentalism that puts empathy at the center of things can say about respect. If concern/caring and respect are both core moral values, then an ethics of empathic caring can accommodate, explain, and justify this assumption. The concept of empathic concern for the welfare of another goes beyond the notion of mere concern for such welfare and, I believe, involves respect for the wishes of or for what is distinctive about the other. I want to argue that this kind of respect is fully adequate both in terms of moral theory and in our lives.[13] But in order to understand how this might be so, I think that we need to say just a bit more about what empathy entails.

In current usage 'empathy' and 'sympathy' mean different things. For example, feeling someone else's pain or suffering is feeling 'empathy' for the person in question, whereas feeling *for* someone else's pain or suffering is an example of feeling 'sympathy' for that person. A great deal more

---

[12] Ronald Dworkin, *Taking Rights Seriously* (London: Duckworth, 1977), 180–83, 272–78.

[13] Seyla Benhabib argues that recognizing the dignity of the "generalized other" necessitates seeing things from the standpoint of the "concrete other." I think this comes very close to the view I am defending here. See Seyla Benhabib, "The Generalized and the Concrete Other: The Kohlberg-Gilligan Controversy and Feminist Theory," in Seyla Benhabib and Drucilla Cornell, eds., *Feminism as Critique: On the Politics of Gender* (Minneapolis: University of Minnesota Press, 1987), esp. 89–92.

can be and has been said about this. (Hoffman's *Empathy and Moral Development* provides a useful discussion). But for present purposes I think that we can work with the idea of empathy in an intuitive way, and, in doing so, we need to recall and refine a point that I made above. Empathy involves seeing or feeling things from the standpoint of others; in some sense, therefore, empathy involves identifying to some extent with another person. But, as numerous writers on the subject have pointed out, empathy *does not* involve losing all sense of one's own identity or merging one's identity with that of another person.[14] Someone who is overinvolved with another person may be unable to feel deep empathy for that person. Rather than respond to what is distinctive in the other individual or what the other individual wants, the overinvolved person may have difficulty separating his own needs and desires from that of the other.

One familiar example of such overinvolvement can be found in the attitudes that some parents have toward their children. Parents with a weak sense of self may seek to live through the successes of their children and have a difficult time separating their own needs from those of their children. Such parents ipso facto have difficulty empathizing with the individual point of view—the needs, wishes, and fears—of their children. This is not because of the absence of an emotional connection with their children: these parents are not like psychopaths, but, rather, they exhibit *too much* connection to their children. Such overinvolvement or overconnection has recently been labeled "substitute success syndrome" (henceforward *sss*).[15] It has been recognized that *sss* involves an inability to empathize with children, an inability to recognize or understand the individuality or wishes of one's children. However, it also seems plausible to say that *sss* parents *fail to respect their children*, since respecting individuals is naturally thought of as requiring respect for their wishes and for what is distinctive about them. So it would appear that an ideal of empathic caring requires one to respect other people and not simply to be concerned with their welfare.

This then raises some important issues about paternalism. After all, there are times when a parent has to overrule or override a child's wishes, desires, or fears and must do so in the interest of or for the welfare of the child. For example, a parent may have to take a reluctant or even unwilling child to the dentist's office, and many people would say that such paternalistic actions can be both morally permissible and obligatory. So if empathy requires us always to go along with what others, including children, want, then an ethics of empathic caring will be very implausible.

But, I do not think that empathy rules out all paternalism. It is both possible and likely for a parent to empathize with his or her child's

---

[14] A point made, e.g., in Hoffman, *Empathy and Moral Development*, 63–91.

[15] On *sss*, see Larry Blum et al., "Altruism and Women's Oppression," in Carol C. Gould and Marx W. Wartofsky, eds., *Women and Philosophy: Toward A Theory of Liberation* (New York: Putnam, 1976), esp. 238.

persistent terror of going to the dentist's office while nevertheless insisting that the child must go. Insisting on the visit may not reflect a lack of empathy for the child, but, rather, a sense of what is good for the child that goes beyond the child's present desires and considers the child's future welfare and desires. So paternalism need not be like *sss*; it need not entail an overinvolvement with and/or an inability to empathize with the distinctive needs and feelings of another individual. We can say that behavior that shows a failure of empathic caring is wrong without thereby having to condemn all forms of paternalism. (Below, we shall see how this distinction affects important political issues of justice.) In addition, we can hold that not every case of overriding a child's wishes involves a failure to respect the child. It is only when overriding stems from a failure of empathy vis-à-vis the child that one can morally criticize the parent for failing to *respect* the child. So I want to say that when one acts from empathic concern for others, one exemplifies both concern and respect for them as individuals, and I believe that this sentimentalist account of what respect amounts to offers us a perfectly plausible and adequate theory of respect.[16]

However, a Kantian may at this point object that the above picture of respect leaves out the important connection between respect and autonomy. Kant may have regarded autonomy as noumenal and thus seen respect as tied to or directed toward a noumenal feature of persons. But autonomy needn't be conceived in such a metaphysically suspect way and nowadays it *is not* seen as something noumenal. Rather, autonomy is conceived as having something to do with rational personhood, with our capacity to think and choose for ourselves, and these ideas are not metaphysically invidious. But then, the objection might go, the sentimentalist who talks of respecting wishes or individuality has not yet touched on what is arguably most central to respect—the fact that, in its deepest ethical embodiments, it is respect for the *autonomy* of the other. The ethics of empathic caring needs to be able to answer this criticism, but it can do so, I think, by showing how such an approach has (or can have) a distinctive way of understanding individual autonomy that is both attractive and plausible in its own right.

Think of the *sss* parent who rides roughshod over the wishes, fears, and desires of his or her own child. If the parent fails to respect these wishes, fears, or desires, or even to acknowledge them, then it will be difficult for the child to respect or acknowledge them too. It is also likely that the child, if not totally self-thwartingly rebellious, will learn to submit in large part to the authority or wishes of the parent. Such children will be

---

[16] However, it can be argued that one may show a lack of respect for someone if one violates deontological obligations to his detriment in an effort to serve the general good or one's own purposes. In this case, an ethics of empathic caring can encapsulate all morally significant forms of respect only if it can succeed (along lines suggested above in the text) in accounting for deontology.

less likely than others to grow up thinking and deciding things for themselves; hence they will lack the kind of autonomy that features so centrally in contemporary discussions. Moreover, this lack of autonomy will
have resulted from what, according to a morality of empathic caring,
counts as *mistreatment* on the part of the parent.

In contrast, parents whose empathy with the growing child allows
them to care about and encourage the child's aspirations and individuality are showing morally required respect for the child by encouraging
the child to think and act for herself. Empathy thus plants the necessary
seeds of autonomy—both encouraging and nurturing autonomy—and in
effect embodies *respect* for autonomy. (I take it that rebellion for its own
sake *is not* a form of autonomy, even when parents' authoritarian or sss
attitudes and actions have "asked for it.")

Recent feminist discussions of autonomy have certainly stressed its
relational, developmental character: that autonomy comes into being only
through personal relationships and social structures that encourage it,
that autonomy is not something we innately possess or inevitably mature
into. But it is also important to stress how (relational) autonomy is and
can be rooted in empathy for us as "second persons" on the part of other
people. Rigid social values or stereotypes clearly deprive girls and women
(and in other ways boys and men) of the fullest autonomous choice in
their lives. The discouragement of individual thinking, especially on the
part of women, and various other forms of coercion also limit autonomy.
Moreover, these various ways of denying autonomy constitute, either
individually or in larger social embodiments, a failure of empathic concern for the individual (girl or woman). Empathy helps to nurture individual autonomy, but if the stereotype of women serving and merely
assisting men prevails at a social level—so that, for example, a young
woman does not even think of trying to become a doctor rather than a
nurse—then social opinions and attitudes represent a kind of mass failure
of empathic concern for what little girls or young women might want for
themselves. I now want to argue that, according to a suitably expanded
ethics of empathic caring, this kind of failure constitutes a form of social
injustice.

IV. Autonomy and Social Justice

If we think of societies roughly as groups of individuals living under or
subject to certain customs, laws, and institutions, then there is an analogy
between the relation that these customs, etc., have to the members of the
society and the relation that individual acts or actions have to their agents.
The customs, laws, and institutions of a given society are, as it were, the
actions of that society: they reflect or express the motives, attitudes, and
the knowledge of the social group in something like the way that actions

express an agent's motives, attitudes, and knowledge, though in a more enduring manner, since societies typically outlast the individual agents in them. So, just as an individual morality of empathic caring regards individual acts as morally good if they reflect empathic concern on the part of their agent and wrong if they reflect a lack of empathic concern, a social morality based on empathic caring will treat customs, laws, and institutions as morally good and just if they reflect empathic concern for (relevant groups of) fellow citizens on the part of those who support and are subject to these customs, laws, and institutions. Conversely, they will be regarded as morally bad and unjust if they reflect a deficiency of such concern (or, worse, the opposite of such concern).[17]

Now this brief statement does not take into account the distinction between citizens and the inhabitants of a country; nor does it consider the extent to which justice requires customs, laws, and institutions to reflect empathic concern for the residents and citizens of *other* countries. But the statement does represent a useful template for use in considering questions of social justice, and I believe it can be applied quite generally to such questions, in particular, to what I said just above about group failures of empathy. Where social attitudes and, consequently, the things people say to one another make it difficult for little girls and young women even to think of becoming doctors, the situation embodies a failure of empathic concern for what little girls and young women might want for themselves, and according to the criterion I have suggested, such a social situation will count as unjust.

Many feminists who have stressed the social/relational bases of autonomy have criticized certain social attitudes and institutions for failing to respect women's individual autonomy. What has not been seen, however, is that such forms of understanding and criticism can be well and attractively grounded in a sentimentalist form of virtue ethics that stresses the moral value of empathy and empathic caring. For example, in *Sex and Social Justice*, Martha Nussbaum complains that, by exalting emotion over reason, caring ethicists like Nel Noddings leave women without the critical apparatus necessary to call into question and change invidious social institutions and attitudes.[18] But it is not *all* emotions that the caring ethicist exalts, and if, in particular, *empathic* caring represents the standard for moral criticism, then such an ethics certainly offers a basis for making criticisms and changes. Empathic concern for women's desires and development will, in almost every case, encourage one to work against and criticize the injustice of social institutions, practices, customs, and opinions that are empathically insensitive or hostile to such desires and development.

[17] For more specific and detailed discussion of how this might work, see Slote, "The Justice of Caring" (though that article discusses caring without explicitly bringing in empathy) and chap. 5 of Slote, *Moral Sentimentalism*.

[18] Martha C. Nussbaum, *Sex and Social Justice* (New York: Oxford University Press, 1999), 74ff.

It should also be clear at this point that a social ethics of empathic caring will take strong issue with typical communitarian views about the (relative) sanctity of social traditions and customs. Communitarianism respects the diversity of the different societies and cultures that actually exist, but it offers no basis for accepting and encouraging diversity where none as yet exists or is well ensconced. If a society is uniform or monolithic, then communitarianism supports *that sort* of tradition and discourages dissent and the diversity it might bring. But because different people have different abilities and temperaments, they tend to *want* different things, and a monolithic community will tend to ride roughshod over such differences and the diversity they might lead to in something like the way that *sss* parents override the desires of their children. A society whose monolithic or rigid character is rigorously enforced exhibits a failure of empathic concern for potential or nascent diversity. It fails to respect individual autonomy in much the same way that *sss* parents fail, and its institutions and the society itself will count as unjust according to a social ethics of empathic caring. So empathic caring may be a relatively simple or compact (dare I say monolithic?) moral ideal, but it strongly encourages social diversity based on individual autonomy and firmly opposes typical communitarian views about social justice.[19]

Note, too, how what we have said about autonomy allows us to address the by-now-familiar criticism that an ethics of caring, by treating as ideal a selfless devotion to others that women are more likely to be susceptible to than men, encourages women to allow themselves to continue being victimized or taken advantage of and is, therefore, both socially and morally counterproductive.[20] But if the moral ideal or standard involved here is that of *empathic* caring, then it is harder to make this criticism. To be sure, the *sss* mother thinks that she is sacrificing herself for the good of her children. However, what she in fact does to them is probably on balance *not* good for them, while she herself gets a kind of primitive, vicarious satisfaction from what she does. (Given her own incompletely formed sense of identity, this serves her needs and welfare more than other things she might do with her life, and, it is likely, this serves her more than she serves the needs and welfare of her own children).

So, if we speak of a caring that *lacks empathy*, it is not at all clear that such an attitude and motivation leave one a victim rather than a victimizer. Perhaps it is better to say, though, that where women (or men) do not

---

[19] While they differ in regard to diversity and social justice, both communitarianism and the ethics of empathic caring oppose the idea that morality can be grounded in reason. Also, both place a greater emphasis on personal interconnection than on the (rights of the) individual in separation or abstraction from others. For an influential (but somewhat atypical) example of communitarianism, see Michael J. Sandel, *Liberalism and the Limits of Justice* (Cambridge: Cambridge University Press, 1982).

[20] There is a version of this argument in Nussbaum, *Sex and Social Justice*, 74ff.

have a sufficient sense of self and where their children suffer the consequences, everyone involved is victimized and unfortunate. This then gives us an argument based on empathic concern for creating social institutions and forms of life that do not so often end up with such invidious situations.

But consider what this means. I maintained above that a sense of autonomy is more likely to develop in children if they are raised with empathic concern, that is, in a way that respects their wishes, aspirations, and individuality. So empathic caring helps to instill and develop autonomous thought and desire, and surely it is the person who can think and plan things out for himself, rather than the person who always thinks and decides on the basis of what others tell him, who is least likely to be victimized by others. Accordingly, if we look at the larger implications of empathic caring, we can see that it would tend to work against rather than maintain the heteronomous selflessness and victimization of women.[21] Thus, for all of the reasons that I have been discussing, social justice conceived in terms of empathic caring would be good for the cause of women.

V. EMPATHIC CARING AND RELIGIOUS TOLERATION

At this point, however, it is time for us to leave behind issues that specifically concern women and to explore some of the wider political implications of the present approach. In particular, it is important for us to consider whether a sentimentalist ideal of empathic caring can do justice, so to speak, to what we ordinarily and intuitively think about individual autonomy and/or liberty in certain areas of political life and thought. Here I am referring to those areas where a sentimentalist approach can seem suspect and appear to have unacceptable, or at least implausible, implications.

One such area—and perhaps the most notable—is that of freedom of religion or religious toleration. For it is often said that sentiments like benevolence, love of one's fellow human beings, and caring can motivate people or societies unjustly to *deny* certain people various important forms of religious liberty. It is said that such sentiments can lead, in effect, to a failure to respect individual and group rights to autonomy within the religious sphere. During the Spanish Inquisition, for example, the religious practices and beliefs of heretics were said to threaten the stability of

---

[21] I am assuming here that the children of empathically caring parents can be raised to be as empathically caring as their parents. In his *Empathy and Moral Development*, Hoffman offers a theory of the development of empathic concern that clearly supports this assumption. I might add that Hoffman's view allows not only for empathic concern vis-à-vis individuals, but also for the kind of empathic concern for whole groups of people (whom one may not be personally acquainted with) that is presupposed in the political applications of empathic caring that I have been and will be making in the text above.

the state, and it was claimed that forced confessions and recantations were necessary to the eternal salvation, and thus to the ultimate well-being, of both those with false beliefs and those whom they might corrupt. This is certainly paternalism, and of a kind that most of us find horrifying. But the paternalism here may seem to spring, and is often said to have sprung, from good sentiments. Many philosophers and others have argued, therefore, that a just social order that respects autonomy and freedom has to go beyond sentiments such as benevolence and concern for others and acknowledge, on rational grounds, an independent order of rights to various freedoms and liberties.

One can find views like this in J. L Mackie's *Hume's Moral Theory*[22] and spelled out at greater length in Thomas Nagel's *Equality and Partiality*.[23] However, I think there is reason to believe that religious intolerance and persecution *do not* arise out of otherwise admirable human feelings or motives in the way that Mackie, Nagel, and so many others have assumed. In cases like the Inquisition, the "dry eyes" (in John Locke's wonderful phrase) of those who persecute and torture others show that such people are not genuinely or primarily concerned with the welfare of those whom they mistreat. Instead, these persecutors have other, egotistical or selfish reasons for doing what they do.[24] And this begins, I think, to give us some reason to suspect that we may not need to go beyond sentimentalist considerations and invoke independently justifiable rights to religious freedom and autonomy in order to explain what is horrifying and unjust about their denial.

But the main reason for believing this can be stated in terms of the notion of empathy. There is something extremely arrogant and dismissive in the attitudes and actions of those who reject out of hand the differing religious beliefs and practices of others and who feel they are justified in suppressing those beliefs and practices in coercive, even violent, fashion. Those who persecute others in this way clearly do not try to understand things from the standpoint of those whom they persecute, and I think that what most strikingly characterizes arrogant attitudes and acts of intolerance toward others is this failure to empathize with their point(s) of view. Just as *sss* parents are criticizable for their failure to empathize with their children as individuals, so, too, are those who practice religious intolerance criticizable as unjust for their failure to empathize with the point(s) of view of those who accept or practice a different religion.

Such forms of paternalism stand in marked contrast with the sort of "benign" paternalism that insists that an unwilling child (eventually) go to the dentist's office. The latter is not plausibly regarded as due to a

---

[22] J. L. Mackie, *Hume's Moral Theory* (London: Routledge & Kegan Paul, 1980), 28.

[23] Thomas Nagel, *Equality and Partiality* (New York: Oxford University Press, 1991), 154–68.

[24] See John Locke, *A Letter Concerning Toleration* (1689), trans. William Popple, ed. John Horton and Susan Mendus (New York: Routledge, 1991), 28.

failure to empathize with the child. Similarly, neither is there a failure to empathize in such presumably acceptable forms of state paternalism as enforcing laws against driving without a fastened seatbelt and against riding a motorcycle without wearing a helmet. Such forms of coercion, even while they override some individuals' desires, need not reflect an unwillingness or inability to see and feel things from the point of view of those whose desires run contrary to the coercion. But this unwillingness or inability is precisely what does typify the religious intolerance and persecution that have erupted so destructively in so many parts of the world during the course of human history. An ethics of empathic caring, therefore, can say that religious intolerance and persecution count as unjust because they show a marked absence of empathic caring.[25] But this then means that, in order to defend religious autonomy and freedom, we do not in fact have to go beyond the moral sentiments in the way that so many philosophers have supposed. Opposition to religious freedom may be compatible with certain kinds and degrees of concern for others, and certainly those who coerce and persecute the adherents of different religions or sects may view themselves as primarily concerned with the welfare of the others. But the "dry eyes" make one wonder about egotism, rationalization, and self-deception here, and the so-called concern, since it is so arrogantly dismissive of the viewpoint of the others, is in any event not of the right type. If it is caring or concern, then it is of a kind that lacks empathy, and it is no wonder, according to the present view, that such a more limited or truncated sentiment should be inadequate to prevent religious intolerance and persecution. An ethics of empathic caring says that it is only a fully empathic relation to and concern for others that can offer a realistic, thoroughgoing, sentimentalist and virtue-ethical basis for individual morality and social justice.

VI. Empathic Caring and Liberalism: Concluding Thoughts

This is not to say, however, that such an ethics provides for and justifies all the sorts of freedom that liberals, for example, have defended. There are, in fact, freedoms that political liberalism would insist upon, but an ethics of empathic caring would question or deny. Thus, an empathic concern for the well-being of others might well lead legislators or officials to bar, say, a march by Nazis on the main street of a small town where many survivors of the Holocaust and their families live. In contrast, a

---

[25] In my *Morals from Motives* (*MfM*, chap. 5), I described a science-fiction case in which a refusal to grant certain religious liberties would be justified and in no way demonstrate a lack of empathy. But it is difficult to think of a single case in actual human history where religious persecutions or intolerance *did not* reflect a failure of empathy; so if we wish to defend religious liberties in the circumstances of actual human life, then our sentimentalist approach may give us what we need.

liberal or libertarian philosophy might insist that the Nazis have a right to be allowed to conduct such a march and use it to express their horrifying political opinions. Such close-to-absolute rights of free speech and assembly might be denied by one who is motivated by an empathic concern for the feelings and wishes of all concerned: not only the survivors and their families but also those who want to march. Such concern might lead one to believe that more damage will be done to the former, if the march occurs, than to the latter, if it does not. Although this assumes that people's lives can be made worse through suffering the taunts of others (thus effectively denying the old adage about sticks and stones), this assumption seems to me to be intuitively quite plausible.[26]

So a political morality of empathic caring might advocate limiting civil liberties in certain circumstances, even though liberals and libertarians would likely reach opposite conclusions.[27] But I do not think this represents much of an objection to the present view and what it has to say about autonomy, because the question of whether to limit civil liberties in situations like the one I just mentioned is such a controversial one today. Since most citizens of democracies are likely to agree that religious persecution is unjust, a sentimentalist theory of justice and autonomy had better be able to agree with and explain this conviction. But because contemporary opinion is so divided about issues like the right to give vent to hate speech in public, the fact that a sentimentalist virtue ethics argues in favor of limiting such speech in some cases is hardly, at this point, a strong objection to the present approach.

Moreover, what has been said here about and in justification of religious liberties can largely be said, mutatis mutandis, about other noncontroversial civil liberties and their exercise. Empathic concern for others will take into account individual desires, such as the desire for freedom of movement and personal association, for example, and our sentimentalist approach can make sense, in its own terms, of what justice clearly or noncontroversially requires in these general areas. But it may be less clear

---

[26] For a feminist defense of the assumption, see Susan J. Brison, "The Autonomy Defense of Free Speech," *Ethics* 108, no. 2 (1998): 312–39; and Susan J. Brison "Relational Autonomy and Freedom of Expression," in Mackenzie and Stoljar, eds., *Relational Autonomy*, 280–99.

[27] Ellen Frankel Paul pointed out to me that a judicial system that allows judges or others to limit civil liberties out of empathic concern for the feelings of certain groups is subject to various forms of abuse. For example, someone might deliberately or unconsciously overestimate the damage that a certain group would do to the feelings of others out of a hatred of that group or a deficient sense of the value of various freedoms. Of course, all legal systems are subject to abuse, but the criteria of justice urged by the sentimentalist arguably yield distinctive possibilities of abuse. Some of these I discuss in *MfM*, chaps. 4 and 5, but more will need to be said about this issue on some other occasion. In any event, and finally, public officials take oaths to uphold the law, and this further constrains the actions they may permissibly take out of empathic concern for one group or another. If, however, and as I suggested above, (the) deontology (of promises and oaths) is itself based in empathic factors, then the present sentimentalism may be able to give a realistic account of the considerations that ought, in justice, to move public officials.

at this point how a sentimentalist approach would or could handle questions of *distributive* justice: for example, issues about economic equality. Since, however, such issues are not directly related to autonomy, I think I should leave them aside for another occasion.[28] My main concern here has been to demonstrate how an ethics of caring or, more generally, a sentimentalist approach to morality and politics can make sense in its own terms of the idea and the ideal of autonomy.[29]

Philosophy, University of Miami

---

[28] I discuss such issues at length in Slote, *Moral Sentimentalism* chaps. 4 and 5.

[29] Since, as I indicated earlier, empathy is evoked less strongly in relation to people we don't know than in relation to those with whom we are personally acquainted, a view that understands individual and social morality in terms of developed human empathy or empathic caring will require different degrees of empathy depending on how closely we are connected to one or another individual or group of individuals. This means that what counts as a failure of empathy toward those who are near and dear might not be criticizable as such in relation to fellow citizens, and it follows, given what has been said above in the text, that what counts as a failure of respect for someone else (for his autonomy) will vary, depending on the degree or kind of relationship that one has to that other person. A state may in all justice be required to show equal respect and equal empathy toward all of its citizens, but have lesser obligations to the citizens of other countries, and what counts as a failure of respect and empathy vis-à-vis one's own children presumably need not count as such in relation to other people's children. So, on the present view, morally appropriate respect for others (for their autonomy) will not always be one and the same thing and will be relative to relationship or connection. However, I do not think this deprives the idea of respect of anything that we need, either as moral theorists or in our lives.

GOD'S IMAGE AND EGALITARIAN POLITICS

By George P. Fletcher

I. Introduction

These days, American politicians are loath to cite biblical passages for fear of being charged with breaching the wall between church and state. There was a time when a presidential candidate could claim that a certain monetary policy would "crucify us on a cross of gold."[1] This kind of rhetoric is now taboo. America's national leaders even avoid quoting the religious phrases from the Declaration of Independence, particularly its references to the "Creator" or "Nature's God." Although in the past some of the greatest American political oratory—Abraham Lincoln at Gettysburg (1863) or Martin Luther King, Jr., at the Lincoln Memorial (1963)—relied unashamedly on biblical sources and imagery, it is no longer considered acceptable to argue publicly in the language of either the Hebrew or Christian Bibles. However religious American society might still be today, political rhetoric is noticeably nonreligious.

This is a peculiar situation, and it is hard to avoid smiling about some of the latent contradictions. Politicians are supposed to go to church or (of late) to synagogue, but they are not allowed to discuss the ideas that are elaborated inside the sanctuary. Their preferred use of these sites is to be photographed coming and going. Politicians are supposed to lead sexually moral lives, but they are not to engage in reflection or discussion about what constitutes the moral life in the Judeo-Christian tradition. Children still pledge allegiance to "one Nation under God, indivisible, with liberty and justice for all" (notwithstanding a bizarre decision by the U.S. Court of Appeals for the Ninth Circuit in the summer of 2002),[2] and yet the New York Board of Regents recently edited a book by Elie Wiesel to eliminate all references to being born in the image of God.[3]

Americans maintain this aversion to public discussion of biblical sources even though it seems apparent that the political energies of the twentieth

---

[1] William Jennings Bryan, "Speech Delivered at the 1896 Democratic National Convention," in *Three Centuries of American Rhetorical Discourse: An Anthology and a Review*, ed. Ronald F. Reid (Prospect Heights, IL: Waveland Press, 1988), 601–6.

[2] *Newdow v. United States Cong.*, 292 F.3d 597 (2002) (holding that the recitation of the Pledge of Allegiance in public schools is an endorsement by the state of religion, and hence unconstitutional).

[3] N. R. Kleinfeld, "The Elderly Man and the Sea? Test Sanitizes Literary Texts," *New York Times*, June 2, 2002, late edition–final, sec. 1, p. 1, col. 1; Evelyn Nieves, "Judges Ban Pledge of Allegiance from Schools, Citing 'Under God'," *New York Times*, June 27, 2002, late edition–final, sec. A, p. 1, col. 1.

century drew heavily on the influence of biblical principles. The fight against "godless Communism" was cast in obvious religious terms. But the better, more persistent case is America's ongoing commitment to egalitarian politics, the constant pressure to include new groups within the inner circle of those regarded as morally equal and entitled to equal benefits under the law, a cause that has only been magnified at the dawn of the twenty-first century. One group after another has asserted its fundamental equality with the group of white American males who were privileged by the original U.S. Constitution to vote and hold office, to own slaves, and to hold sway in patriarchal domestic life. Since the late eighteenth century, and particularly since the Civil War, with a great acceleration in the 1970s, other groups have asserted themselves as being equal in rights to America's founding elite. These newly assertive groups include not only former slaves and women, but also children born out of wedlock, homosexuals, senior citizens, Americans with disabilities, and noncitizens. Other groups have been slow in organizing themselves and generally seem intimidated by the opprobrium they suffer in American society: these include the obese, smokers, prison inmates, and ex-felons.[4] Other groups, such as public school pupils in inner cities, are barely acknowledged as victims of discrimination. However the claims of these various groups are negotiated in the future, there is little doubt that egalitarian politics will dominate the American agenda for a long time to come.

The assumption guiding this political movement is not simply that equal treatment is useful or efficient or that its benefits outweigh its costs. The movement draws on a strong belief that treating people equally is the right thing to do—regardless of the cost. But from where does the moral energy come to assert the equality of groups once considered of lesser status in American society? It is not enough to claim that children born out of wedlock are equal to all other children. One needs a reason. The problem is finding a moral or other nonlegal reason for thinking that human beings are of equal worth and, therefore, should be treated as equal.

What could the reason be? Secular philosophies are hard pressed to provide a reason for their zealous defense of equality. So far as I can tell, Ronald Dworkin has no ideological or moral foundation for the view that the state must treat each person with "equal concern and respect."[5] This is simply a postulate of American academic liberalism. By like token, John Rawls has no case for assuming that in "the original position" all human beings are of equal worth. He just assumes this to be true as a premise of his system of "justice as fairness."[6]

---

[4] On the shocking policy of disenfranchising inmates and felons, see George P. Fletcher, "Disenfranchisement as Punishment: Reflections on the Racial Uses of Infamia," 46 *UCLA L. Rev.* 1895 (1999), and *Richardson v. Ramirez*, 418 U.S. 24 (1974).

[5] Ronald Dworkin, *Taking Rights Seriously* (London: Duckworth, 1977), 275.

[6] Rawls concedes that human equality is simply a postulate of his system. John Rawls, *A Theory of Justice* (Cambridge, MA: Harvard University Press, 1971), 504.

II. Dignity and Equality

There seem to be two approaches to the problem of grounding the duty to treat all people as equal. One is to assume that some single feature of our existence—say our capacity to reflect on our existence or to search for the good—makes us human.[7] But, of course, even if a single standard for humanity could explain why humans are different from animals or machines, it would not follow that all humans are equal. It could be the case that all humans can think and experience conscious self-reflection but, nonetheless, display different degrees of intelligence. If the quality *A* is what makes us human, then—to paraphrase George Orwell's *Animal Farm*—having more of *A* should make one more human, thereby putting one on a higher scale of value.

Single-feature tests of humanity are bound to fail for other reasons as well. Even if some single feature makes us unique, we would still need an account of why this feature has moral worth. Suppose the distinguishing feature of human beings were that we have five toes. So what? It would be hard to generate a moral argument about intrinsic worth from the number of our toes.

The second approach is to proceed by conceding the variance among human beings but to assert that humans share the capacity to recognize and appreciate the humanity that lies beneath our individuality and differences. My favorite literary example is Shylock's speech to the Venetians about why they should recognize him and other Jews as human and equal in moral stature to themselves:

> I am a Jew. Hath not a Jew eyes? Hath not a Jew hands, organs, dimensions, senses, affections, passions?——fed with the same food, hurt with the same weapons, subject to the same diseases, healed by the same means, warmed and cooled by the same winter and summer as a Christian is? If you prick us, do we not bleed? If you tickle us, do we not laugh? If you poison us, do we not die? And if you wrong us, shall we not revenge?[8]

Here there is no single feature that distinguishes Shylock as human. He has the physical constitution of other humans, the same needs, the same vulnerabilities, and the same capacities for joy. Note that there is nothing in this speech about our supposedly higher capacities of thought and self-reflection. The appeal is primarily visual. Shylock's opponents should look at him and see a reflection of themselves.

---

[7] See John E. Coons and Patrick M. Brennan, *By Nature Equal: The Anatomy of a Western Insight* (Princeton, NJ: Princeton University Press, 1999); and Ronald Dworkin, *Life's Dominion: An Argument about Abortion, Euthanasia, and Individual Freedom* (New York: Knopf, 1993).

[8] Shakespeare, *Merchant of Venice*, Signet Classic edition, ed. Kenneth Myrick (London: Penguin, 1965), 3.1.55–63.

Recall the famous teaching that the book of Matthew attributes to Jesus but that is found originally in the Hebrew Bible: "Love thy neighbor as thyself."[9] The Hebrew text *V-avhta et reacha c-mohah* is, in fact, better translated as "Love thy neighbor, for thy neighbor is like you." This is essentially Shylock's appeal: Love (or at least respect) me because I am like thee. The basis of the likeness is purposely kept vague. Resemblance turns on a generalized image of what it means to be human.

Appealing to a generalized image of humanity offers an alternative to the search for a single factor that makes us different from and morally superior to, say, animals and machines. But this appeal suffers from the same flaw as the quest for a single distinguishing feature. So what if we human beings *are* made in the image of each other? Why does that mean that we are all of ultimate or even high moral worth?

In this context we can understand the unusual strength of the argument that we are made in the image of God (Gen. 1:27). The appeal to an image—as in Shylock's arguments—avoids singling out a factor that might be too thin a reed to bear the moral weight of the argument, and bearing some resemblance to the Divine solves the problem of why the resemblance confers dignity. Partaking of the divine image (*imago Dei*) renders human beings of value, arguably of ultimate value. As Immanuel Kant expressed his doctrine of intrinsic human dignity, each human being possesses a dignity that is beyond price, that cannot be traded off against competing values. The arguments in Genesis and in Kant follow if we assume that (1) being in the image of something entails partaking of its value, and (2) God or humanity is of ultimate value.[10] Whether you are a believer or not, these premises lead to the conclusion that humans beings are of overriding value. The troublesome question is, how do we get from the idea of being made in the image of God to Thomas Jefferson's famous proposition in the Declaration of Independence that "all men are created equal"? And if this derivation is problematic, how can we be sure that the principle of human equality derives from the *imago Dei* of Genesis?

The principle that all human beings are of equal dignity is accepted today without serious discussion. No single phrase has moved American politics more than Jefferson's "all men are created equal." After four score and seven years of quiescence, the phrase re-emerged in Lincoln's Gettysburg Address: "[O]ur fathers brought forth on this continent a new nation conceived in liberty and dedicated to the proposition that all men are created equal." One hundred years later, Martin Luther King, Jr., reminded another generation of Americans: "I still have a dream . . . that one day this nation will rise up and live out the true meaning of its

---

[9] Lev. 19:18 (translation by the author).

[10] Kant's argument is not that we are made in the image of humanity but that each person incorporates humanity in himself. See Immanuel Kant, *Groundwork of the Metaphysics of Morals* (1785), trans. Mary J. Gregor (Cambridge: Cambridge University Press, 1998), 37–39.

creed—we hold these truths to be self-evident, that all men are created
equal."[11]

In Supreme Court opinions, this revered creed of the United States has
finally begun to make a lasting impact. Its leading champion is Justice
John Paul Stevens, who first invoked the maxim in a biting dissent to a
decision that denied equal benefits under the law to children born out of
wedlock:

> The reason why the United States Government should not add to the
> burdens that illegitimate children inevitably acquire at birth is radi-
> antly clear: We are committed to the proposition that all persons are
> created equal.[12]

There seems to be little doubt today about the premise that we are all
morally equal and that this radical equality should have some bearing on
our rights under law.[13] But there is less agreement on the historical provenance of this argument and certainly some skepticism about whether its
roots lie in the book of Genesis. I need, therefore, to address this issue.

III. The Relevance of Genesis

There seems to be a widespread view in American academic circles that
because the United States was founded by Christians, the fundamental
values of our legal culture must be Christian in their origin. Thus, the
principle of human equality is attributed to Christian thinking. For example, George Fredrickson comments in his recent book on the history of
racism:

> First came the doctrine that the Crucifixion offered grace to all will-
> ing to receive it and made all Christian believers equal before God.
> Later came the more revolutionary concept that all "men" are created
> equal and entitled to equal rights in society and government.[14]

Paul comes as close as any Christian thinker to articulating a doctrine
of equality within the community of believers: "There is neither Jew nor
Greek, slave nor free, male nor female, for you are all one in Christ

---

[11] See Martin Luther King, "I Have a Dream," speech delivered at the Lincoln Memorial
(Aug. 28, 1963), reprinted in *A Testament of Hope: The Essential Writings and Speeches of Martin
Luther King, Jr.*, ed. James M. Washington (San Francisco, CA: Harper, 1986), 219.

[12] *Mathews v. Lucas*, 427 U.S. 495, 516 (1976) (Stevens, J., dissenting).

[13] Jeremy Waldron, *God, Locke, and Equality: Christian Foundations of John Locke's Political
Thought* (Cambridge: Cambridge University Press, 2002).

[14] George M. Fredrickson, *Racism: A Short History* (Princeton, NJ: Princeton University
Press, 2002), 11.

Jesus."[15] Yet this Christian teaching is a far cry from the Kantian doctrine of intrinsic human dignity, a characteristic of all human beings regardless of their religious commitments. On the contrary, the requirement of faith in Jesus establishes a rather clear barrier to the universal view that all human beings are created equal. Moreover, the tragic history of anti-Semitism in the Catholic Church testifies to the capacity of Paul's teachings to intensify the feeling that some humans, to borrow Orwell's classic phrase, are "more equal" than others.[16]

There is no doubt that Christianity sought to overcome the tribal exclusivity of the Jews as the "chosen people." Indeed, the rhetorical point of Paul's claim of equality "in Christ" is to argue that all Christians are heirs to God's covenant with Abraham.[17] But it is a mistake to confuse a broadening of the criteria of inclusion with a principle of human equality.

Alternatively, some people claim that the principle of equality is rooted in Roman law or in the philosophy of the Stoics. It is true that, though Roman law tolerated slavery, some scholars at the time subscribed to a doctrine of equality as a matter of natural law,[18] but there is no basis for tracing a line of influence from these obscure Roman sources to Jefferson's conceptualization that all men are created equal. The argument that the Stoics originated the normative doctrine of equality also falters for lack of a theory of historical continuity. Also, the Stoic claim seems to have been limited to an argument about the equal rationality of all human beings, a feature that may or may not issue in a normative theory of equality.[19]

The belief that equality derives from Christian thinking is so deeply entrenched that many advance the claim in an obviously self-contradictory manner. Thus, Nicholas Capaldi writes: "Christianity is the origin of the modern conception of equality," but then notes a few sentences later that "Christians drew . . . on the Stoic doctrine" and the Hebrew notion from Genesis that all humans beings, "male" and "female," were made in the image of God.[20] This sounds to me like a recognition that the doctrine is of Jewish origin. Also, there is literally nothing in the Christian Bible that would support a thesis of universal equality. Strikingly, the New Testament fails even to reiterate the basic claim of Genesis that Adam is created in the image of God.

[15] Gal. 3:28 (New International Version).

[16] See James Carroll, *Constantine's Sword: The Church and the Jews: A History* (Boston, MA: Houghton Mifflin, 2001); and Elaine Pagels, *The Origin of Satan* (New York: Random House, 1995).

[17] Gal. 3:29 NIV: "If you belong to Christ, then you are Abraham's seed and heirs according to the promise."

[18] See Ernst Levy, "Natural Law in Roman Thought," 15 *Studia et Documenta Historica et Iuris* 1, 12 (1949) (quoting Ulpian).

[19] Nicholas Capaldi, "The Meaning of Equality," in *Liberty and Equality*, ed. Tibor R. Machan (Stanford, CA: Hoover Institution Press, 2002), 3; available on-line at http://www-hoover. stanford.edu/publications/books/fulltext/equality/1.pdf [accessed May 20, 2003].

[20] Ibid. The Stoic doctrine is, apparently, that "all men posse[ss] the rational capacity to grasp the universal order."

The argument that the idea of equality originates in the book of Genesis, that it represents a Jewish vision of humanity, seems to me well grounded both in the text and in projected channels of historical influence. It is to be assumed, for example, that influential eighteenth-century thinkers such as Jefferson and Kant were familiar with the book of Genesis; the biblical story of creation in the image of God was a given in an eighteenth-century education.

Later debates leading up to the Civil War reveal how crucial the biblical passages were, in fact. When Lincoln said in his Second Inaugural Address that "both sides read the same Bible and pray to the same God," he was right on point. Abolitionists and advocates of slavery read the same passages in Genesis and debated whether all human beings descended from Adam or not. If they believed in 'monogenesis' (i.e., that all humans descend from Adam), then they were likely to be abolitionists. But if they discerned some basis for thinking that there were multiple sources of humanity,[21] then they readily held the view that some human beings belong to a privileged caste while others were properly relegated to a life of serving their superiors.[22]

IV. INTERPRETING A CONTRADICTORY TEXT

Even for those who accept the idea of monogenesis, there is a problem in formulating a principle of human equality. A serious philosophical problem lurks in the transition from "being made in the image of God" to the proposition that "all men are created equal." The Bible itself makes no explicit mention of human equality and, further, the book of Genesis is replete with stories that testify to inequality rather than equality. The most famous of these, of course, is the treatment of Eve and Adam, based on the apparent mistranslation of the Hebrew text that describes Eve as being made from the "rib" of Adam.[23]

---

[21] The thesis of 'polygenesis' (i.e., that God created other human beings besides Adam and Eve) gets some support from anomalies in the story of Cain, one of the sons of Adam and Eve. There is a puzzle about where Cain's wife comes from (Gen. 4:17) and who it is Cain might fear as he sets forth as a wanderer (Gen. 4:14).

[22] See Fredrickson, *Racism: A Short History*, 52 (discussing the origins of the concept of polygenesis in the writings of Giordano Bruno and Christopher Marlowe, where it was suggested that Adam might be the ancestor of the Jews alone), and ibid., 67–69 (discussing Henri de Saint-Simon, Jean-Joseph Virey, and other early nineteenth-century advocates of polygenesis, whose work influenced American pro-slavery writers).

[23] Gen. 2:21–22 AV: "And the Lord God caused a deep sleep to fall upon Adam, and he slept: and he took one of his ribs, and closed up the flesh thereof; / And the rib, which the Lord God had taken from man, made he a woman, and brought her unto the man." There is some dispute about whether the word *tsela* should be translated as 'rib' or 'side'. The reading in favor of male supremacy obviously prefers the former and this translation has entered into the conventional understanding of the text. My view is that 'side' is a more accurate translation.

The Christian reading of the text has furthered the subordination of women. These lines from Corinthians 11:7–9 carry an undying sting:

> A man ought not to cover his head, since he is the image and glory of God; but the woman is the glory of man. For man did not come from woman, but woman from man; neither was man created for woman, but woman for man.

In *Paradise Lost*, John Milton (1608–74) converted this bias against women into beautiful poetry:

> For contemplation he and valour formed, For softness she and sweet attractive Grace, He for God only, she for God in him.[24]

Not only women suffer in the interpretation of Genesis. The narratives of Genesis are replete with implied hierarchies of caste and status. God favors Abel's craft of husbanding animals over Cain's work in the fields. German theologian Claus Westermann reads the resulting conflict as the beginning of class struggle.[25] The tower of Babel leads to the breakdown of the single language that united humanity. With the resulting diversification of languages we encounter the beginning of national differences and the inevitable practice of treating one's own nationals as privileged relative to those of other tribes and nations.

The expulsion of Ishmael from the House of Abraham is possible only because it is implicitly assumed that a hierarchical relationship applies to the wives and concubines of Abraham: Sarah is superior to Hagar and, therefore, can order her expulsion as well as that of her son. Discrimination against homosexuals has its origin in the story of Sodom and Gomorrah: God destroys the cities in "fire and brimstone" because some of the residents clamor to sodomize the visitors whom Lot has brought under his roof. Genesis seems, in fact, to be preoccupied with these distinctions that place some people above others—older children above younger, or women with children above barren women. Indeed, the entire purpose of the book is to describe the emergence of the Hebrews, later called the Jews, as the people chosen by God for a special mission in history.

The only obvious source of discrimination not mentioned in Genesis is race. The idea that people with darker skin are inferior seems to be foreign to the biblical conception of humanity's origins. "I am black, but comely, O daughters of Jerusalem," sings the heroine of the Song of Songs (1:5). Perhaps this line betrays an apologetic tone, but even if skin color

[24] John Milton, *Paradise Lost* (1667), bk. 4, lns. 296–98, in John Milton, *Paradise Lost and Other Poems*, ed. Edward LeComte (Dublin: Mentor Books, 1961).

[25] Claus Westermann, *Genesis 1–11: A Continental Commentary*, trans. John J. Scullion (Minneapolis, MN: Fortress Press, 1994).

matters in the culture of the Bible, I do not believe that race does. There may be a sense that some nations are cursed because of their sins or the sins of their ancestors (e.g., the Amalekites for treachery in warfare, or the Ammonites and Moabites for the acts of incest between Lot and his daughters that resulted in their conception), but the modern biological notion of racial inferiority had to await the development of modern science and its false theories of racial evolution.[26]

Even if we leave aside the tales of inequality in Genesis, we have some trouble understanding why the abolitionist movement put so much faith in the principle that all human beings are made in the image of God. How does one derive a principle of equality from creation in God's image?

So far as I can tell, there are two ways of making the argument. One relies on the prohibition of homicide in Genesis (9:6): "Whoever sheds man's blood, by man shall his blood be shed, for in the image of God [*imago Dei*], God made man." It is worth thinking about the logic of this proposition. Why does *imago Dei* entail a rule against killing? After all, the potential murderer is also made in the image of God. There is a clue, I believe, in a famous discussion in the Talmud about whether it is permissible for *A* to kill *B* if *C* has threatened *A* with death if he does not kill *B*.[27] The answer is no. Even though *A*'s motive may be to save life, namely, his own, choosing between *B*'s life and his own is impermissible. As the rabbinic sages put it: "Why is your blood redder than his?"

The second way of making the argument is to recognize that the claim of dignity implicit in *imago Dei* is, by its nature, ultimate. To partake of God's existence by being made in the image of God is, as Kant expressed the concept of dignity, to be beyond quantifiable value.[28] There is no trade possible against the dignity of a human life, no price that can be put on the existence of a single human being. If human beings are of ultimate value, then it follows that they are of equal value. Were they of finite value, then it would be impossible to avoid a hierarchy based on relative dignity, with some people viewed as having more than others.

The challenge in reading Genesis is to fathom how the same Bible could appeal to both abolitionists and slaveholders, to feminist egalitarians and

---

[26] Admittedly, in the postbiblical period, some commentators argued that Noah's curse of Ham's son Canaan (Gen 9:23–25) expressed the subordination of all Africans who were thought to be descended from Cush, another son of Ham. See Fredrickson, *Racism: A Short History*, at 43–45, 80. For a discussion of the eighteenth- and nineteenth-century "scientific" theories of racial inequality that offered secular support to pro-slavery advocates, see Fredrickson, *Racism: A Short History*, at 56–58, 66–68, and 79–81.

[27] Babylonian Talmud, Sanhedrin 72:1.

[28] Immanuel Kant, *The Metaphysics of Morals* (1797), trans. Mary Gregor (Cambridge: Cambridge University Press, 1991), 230:

But man regarded as a *person*, that is, as the subject of a morally practical reason, is exalted above any price; for as a person (*homo noumenon*) he is not to be valued merely as a means to the ends of others or even to his own ends, but as an end in himself, that is, he possesses a *dignity* (an absolute inner worth) by which he exacts respect for himself from all other rational beings in the world.

to male chauvinists. The beginning of a solution lies in understanding the two stories of creation and the different functions they fulfill in the biblical presentation of the world. Any serious reader of the text will notice striking differences between the two accounts of creation, the first detailed in Genesis 1 and the second beginning in Genesis 2:4. I shall refer to the stories as 'One' and 'Two' as I list the differences:

1. In One, creation lasts seven days; in Two, it takes only one day and there is no mention of a Sabbath on which God rested.
2. In One, the name of God is "Elohim," typically translated as God; in Two, it is "JHVH Elohim," translated as "Lord God." [29]
3. In One, human beings are created in God's image; in Two, human beings are made from the earth.
4. In One, human beings have no purpose other than to celebrate their existence. In Two, human beings have a necessary function in the scheme of creation: nothing could grow because "there was no Adam to till the ground."
5. In One, the origin of humanity lies in a single being called "Adam"; in Two, Adam is bifurcated into male and female beings.

Historically, the difference between these two texts is that the first story, with its emphasis on creation in the image of God, has been a powerful stimulus to an egalitarian political thrust, at least since the late eighteenth century. The second story and other texts have fostered consciousness of the inequalities that we still find all around us. Obviously, the first story resonates more with modern egalitarian sensibilities than does the second. Shall we say that Genesis 1, with its emphasis on creation in the image of God, is right and Genesis 2, with its subordination of women, is wrong? [30] Well, we could do that, but then we would call into doubt the relevance of the biblical text as supporting authority. It is difficult both to

---

[29] The Hebrew here rendered as JHVH is the Tetragrammaton *Yud-Heh-Vav-Heh*. (Orthodox Jews do not pronounce this name aloud, and therefore use a euphemism that means "Lord." Thus the translation in English text of this name is typically "Lord God.") The familiar "Jehovah" represents an attempt to render the Tetragrammaton JHVH in English.

[30] The two creation narratives may be compared by juxtaposing the following excerpts. From the first, or Priestly, version:

So God created man in his own image, in the image of God created he him; male and female created he them. (Gen 1:27 AV)

From the second, or Jehovist, version:

And the Lord God caused a deep sleep to fall upon Adam, and he slept: and he took one of his ribs, and closed up the flesh thereof; / And the rib, which the Lord God had taken from man, made he a woman, and brought her unto the man. (Gen 2:21-22 AV)

and

Unto the woman [God] said, "I will greatly multiply thy sorrow and thy conception; in sorrow thou shalt bring forth children; and thy desire shall be to thy husband, and *he shall rule over thee*. (Gen. 3:16 AV) (emphasis added)

take the text seriously and to make sure the text supports our preferred positions on human dignity and equality.

I have no easy solution to this problem of exegesis, but there is clearly a difference between confronting a contradiction in the biblical text and flatly rejecting a passage simply because it seems "wrong." It is very tempting to argue that it was wrong for God to command Abraham to sacrifice his son Isaac and that Abraham should have resisted and argued with God.[31] But this wholesale rejection of the text implies the superiority of one's own moral judgment. This is much different from wrestling with a contradiction in the text by bringing to bear moral sensibilities.

I also find some solace in the multiple functions of the biblical text. The words of Genesis both teach us normative standards and document our wayward impulse to deviate from these standards. Genesis 1 teaches us a principle of equality that flies in the face of the inequality seemingly endorsed in other chapters of Genesis and in the interpretive tradition that reads into the text words like "rib" and assumes that Eve was created from Adam. A similar bias has entered the reading of the story of Sodom and Gomorrah, which simply takes it for granted that the sin of the local residents was their desire to engage in homosexual *sodomy*. Even our language incorporates the assumption. In fact, the text never overtly refers to anal or same-sex intercourse, and there are other readings that are more faithful to the details of the story, for example, the view that the locals' sin was attempting sex with angels or infringing upon the hospitality that Lot had extended to the visitors.

The problem of interpreting biblical narratives is, of course, one that lawyers and judges encounter all the time in confronting any historic legal text that lends itself to conflicting understandings. In legal cultures there is a point to retaining and, indeed, cultivating contradiction among legal sources. Shall we read the Eighth Amendment to endorse capital punishment simply because it addresses the problem of granting bail in capital cases? Shall we say, as the Supreme Court unfortunately held, that the second section of the Fourteenth Amendment endorses the constitutionality of disenfranchising felons because it creates an exemption for states that disqualify voters "for participation in rebellion, or other crime"?[32]

In my view, the American constitutional culture embodies ongoing contradictions, for example, between the freedoms enshrined in the Bill of Rights and the commitment to equality expressed in the post–Civil War Fourteenth Amendment.[33] The advantage of tensions of this sort is that the legal culture retains its flexibility and adaptability.

---

[31] See Alan M. Dershowitz, *The Genesis of Justice: Ten Stories of Biblical Injustice that Led to the Ten Commandments and Modern Morality and Law* (New York: Warner Books, 2000), 103.

[32] *Richardson v. Ramirez.*

[33] For a book-length argument of this position, see George P. Fletcher, *Our Secret Constitution: How Lincoln Redefined American Democracy* (Oxford: Oxford University Press, 2001).

It is not clear that this is the value to be drawn from the contradictions between the first and second stories of creation; they may simply reflect conflicts between a normative and an anthropological approach to equality. While equality remains the ideal, the entire world continues to witness widespread social discrimination. The biblical text reminds us simultaneously of our ideals and our weaknesses. If we resolve the contradictions in favor of egalitarian principles, if we follow the Declaration of Independence and the Gettysburg Address, we can do so in the conviction that we are still honoring the biblical text as we seek to bring our tradition into harmony with our contemporary values.

V. CONCLUSION

The constitutional separation of church and state has led Americans to disengage from the sensibility that generates our deepest normative commitments. We take for granted equality among human beings, but, in fact, it is not to be so easily assumed. Today there are new voices that raise doubts about whether the least competent or the least moral of human beings should have the same claim to life and human rights as all others.[34] When the equality of human beings is challenged, as it will be from time to time, we must return to the historical origins of our commitments. Even a totally secular society, even one disengaged from biblical study, has much to learn by taking seriously the biblical message and honoring its influence in American culture.

Law, Columbia University

---

[34] See, for example, Peter Singer, *Animal Liberation*, 2d ed. (New York: Random House, 1990).

SHOULD POLITICAL LIBERALS BE COMPASSIONATE CONSERVATIVES? PHILOSOPHICAL FOUNDATIONS OF THE FAITH-BASED INITIATIVE*

BY JOHN TOMASI

I. INTRODUCTION

It is easy and popular these days to be a political liberal. Compared to 'ethical liberals', who justify the use of state power by way of one or another conception of people's true moral nature, 'political liberals' seek a less controversial foundation for liberal politics. Pioneered within the past twenty years by John Rawls and Charles Larmore, the 'political liberal' approach seeks to justify the coercive power of the state by reference to general *political* ideas about persons and society.[1] Since it abandons the debates about personal moral value that have historically dogged liberal theory, political liberalism offers itself as a more latitudinarian, indeed a more liberal, form of liberalism. Being a political liberal is not the only way to be a good liberal, but this approach has become prevalent enough that I shall focus upon it here.

At the same time, it is not so easy or popular these days to be a compassionate conservative. As a presidential candidate in 2000, George W. Bush sprinkled his campaign speeches with references to a new, more compassionate form of conservatism. Unlike some forms of conservative thinking, Bush's stated approach rested not on the ideal of cutting back public spending for welfare, assistance, or schooling programs, with the goal of returning the provision of such goods to the realm of the market and activity among voluntary associations. Instead, Bush emphasized his determination to retain a large public role in the provision of social ser-

* I thank my fellow contributors to this volume for their spirited response to a first draft of this essay. During the past year, I presented versions of this argument at Yale, Duke, Harvard, Brown, the Massachusetts Institute of Technology, the University of Arizona, and the annual meeting of the American Political Science Association in 2002. I am grateful to the participants and organizers of these events. For extended discussions and/or written comments, I thank Charles Larmore, David Schmidtz, Bill Galston, Tom Spragens, Stanley Hauerwas, Stephen Holmes, Martha Minnow, David Estlund, Chris Eisgruber, Luke Swaine, John McCormick, Corey Brettscheider, David Grant, Carmen Pavel, Tony Laden, Leigh Jenco, Patchen Markell, Jacob Levy, Steven Kelts, and, especially, the editors at *Social Philosophy & Policy*. I dedicate this article to the memory of Sir Bernard Williams, teacher and friend.
[1] Charles E. Larmore, *Patterns of Moral Complexity* (New York: Cambridge University Press, 1987). Charles E. Larmore, "Political Liberalism," *Political Theory* 18, no. 3 (1990): 339-60; and John Rawls, *Political Liberalism* (New York: Columbia University Press, 1993).

vices, but to remodel the way in which such services are delivered. The model of delivery that Bush favored would require a substantial rethinking of the official doctrine of church-state relations within the United States. Rather than advocating a policy of strict or 'no-aid' separation between church and state, Bushian compassionate conservatives seek to encourage partnerships between government agencies and faith-based groups. In particular, they argue that government should make public resources readily available to religious groups and other civil society organizations that wish to provide social services. Far from requiring that such groups check their religious or moral viewpoints at the door, the government should guarantee religious groups wide freedom to mix the delivery of their value-laden messages with their provision of services.

A crucial proviso to all such proposals is that secular alternatives for the delivery of social services be available alongside the religiously based ones. Such alternatives are needed to ensure that the religious liberty of recipients of services is fully respected. But where this proviso is satisfied, faith-based organizations should be free to deliver social services in ways that accord with their deeply held religious beliefs, and to do so using public monies.

The rationale underlying the compassionate conservative approach is, in part, prudential. Personal transformation sometimes plays a vital role in people's escaping cycles of addiction and despair, just as Bush credits his own religious conversion in 1986 with enabling him to stop drinking and get his life back on track. Religious groups that provide social services often stress inner change of this sort. But there is also an egalitarian rationale behind Bush's proposal. With the rise of the administrative state in the latter half of the twentieth century, the government increasingly has become involved in areas of social construction where church groups have long been active alongside a variety of secular service agencies. If the government allows secular organizations to receive public funds for the provision of social services, but singles out religious groups for exclusion from such funding, compassionate conservatives argue that this is unfair to religious citizens. On the compassionate conservative approach, therefore, the test for whether some social service organization should receive public funding should not be whether (or how passionately) that group advocates a religious viewpoint. Rather, just as with secular providers, the state merely should ask whether the group in question is objectively successful in providing the good in question.

On these grounds, compassionate conservatives have argued that public funding should be made available to support faith-based practitioners across a broad range of social service issues: drug treatment and criminal rehabilitation programs, initiatives concerning the housing and nutrition of low-income people, daycare for the infants of parents transitioning from welfare to work, after-school tutoring programs, sexuality counseling programs for teens, and even K–12 schooling itself. With public money made available to rally America's religious "armies of compassion," the range of citizen-types that might be enlisted to battle social ills would be widened indeed.[2]

On Bush's inauguration, one of his first acts was to establish the White House Office of Faith-Based and Community Initiatives. With satellite centers in seven of the largest federal agencies, Bush's Faith-Based Initiative became the flagship of compassionate conservatism at the federal level. Bush's plan immediately came under attack from every conceivable ideological direction. Democrats rejected Bush's Faith-Based Initiative as a ploy designed to cut back social services and provide new tax breaks for the rich. Libertarians decried the program as yet another governmental assault on civil society and personal freedom. When the new White House Office of Faith-Based and Community Initiatives and its various satellites began operating in January 2001, Republicans grumbled about the new layers of bureaucracy.

The American Civil Liberties Union, along with Americans United for Separation of Church and State and a wide range of other groups, condemned compassionate conservatism as a violation of the First Amendment guarantee against the establishment of religion. Meanwhile, a number of prominent poverty-fighting evangelicals worried aloud that the governmental oversight attending public funds might corrupt the essentially religious nature of their mission, a concern echoed by many leaders of mainstream churches. From a different direction, Pat Robertson, head of the Christian Coalition, complained that Bush's plan might funnel the money of taxpaying Christians into the coffers of "strange cults." In a particularly embarrassing setback, in June 2001 Bush's own denomination—the United Methodist Church—rejected key elements of Bush's plan, asserting that the plan violated church-state separation, subsidized religious discrimination in employment, and threatened the independence of churches.[3]

The main legislative piece of Bush's Faith-Based Initiative passed in the U.S. House of Representatives in July 2001, but stalled in the U.S. Senate. In December 2002, Bush decided to jump-start the initiative by means of an executive order. Bush's order, now in effect, requires that federal agencies not discriminate against religious organizations in awarding grants to providers of social services. But the order allows religious groups to retain their right to employ religious criteria when making

---

[2] See Marvin Olasky, *Compassionate Conservatism: What It Is, What It Does, and How It Can Transform America* (New York: Free Press, 2000). This book includes a foreward by then-Governor George W. Bush.

[3] For a wide survey of negative reactions to Bush's proposal, see "Faith-Based Folly: Americans Say 'Not So Fast'," Americans United for Separation of Church and State, April 2001, available on-line at http://www.au.org/churchstate/cs4015.htm [accessed February 2003].

employment decisions, and it has come under ferocious attack for that reason.[4]

In this essay, it is not my ambition to offer a defense of compassionate conservatism on constitutional or public policy grounds. Likewise, it is not my ambition to present a foundational defense of the emerging new political form of liberal theorizing. Instead, my aim is merely to suggest that a certain relationship exists between these two systems of ideas. That relationship is this: anyone who is attracted to the form of justification for the use of political power that has been developed within political liberalism should also be attracted to the conception of church-state relations embodied within compassionate conservatism. Some readers, deeply committed to political liberalism, may take this as a demonstration of the virtues of compassionate conservatism. Other readers, deeply opposed to compassionate conservatism, may take this as a reductio ad absurdum of political liberalism. I take no position on such matters. Rather, I mean merely to point out a connection worth pondering: put simply, political liberals should be compassionate conservatives.

Conservatives should hesitate before taking solace in this claim. For if Rawls-style liberals should support Bush-style conservatism, this is only because the Bushians have adopted a form of conservatism that is Rawlsian in its essence. The Faith-Based Initiative—in its rhetoric at least—can be read as a massive capitulation by conservatives to liberal egalitarianism. In the course of this capitulation, American conservatives have abandoned a charge that they once upheld with pride: that of defending a more minimal, classical liberal conception of the American social ideal.[5] So whether the connection I shall describe should be more discomfiting to contemporary liberals or to contemporary conservatives is a question beyond my scope. I mean merely to point out the connection. In America today, the academically dominant version of liberalism and the politically dominant version of conservatism are joined at the hip. If you are going to support one, you ought to support the other. Left-leaning academicians and right-leaning poli-

---

[4] Title VII of the 1964 Civil Rights Act carves out an exemption from antidiscrimination law that allows religious organizations to make employment decisions based on religion. The Welfare Reform Act of 1996 says that this exemption is preserved even for religious organizations that become federal contractors (see 42 U.S.C. § 604a [2001]). For an example of the vehement reaction in some quarters against Bush's executive order, see "Bush Faith-Based Effort Gives Official Blessing to Religious Discrimination: President Circumvents Congress, Allows Tax Dollars to Go to Religious Groups That Discriminate," Americans United for Separation of Church and State, December 12, 2002; available on-line at http://www.au.org/press/pr021212.htm [accessed February 2003].

[5] For example, if the compassionate conservative program is to avoid religious coercion of recipients, secular service providers must be available alongside faith-based ones for all the goods mandated by egalitarian justice. Satisfying this proviso within the contemporary American context would probably require an increase in public spending—and thus in governmental power—far beyond current levels.

ticians have a lot more in common than either side may be happy to admit.

Of course, any complete discussion of compassionate conservatism in the American context must at some point confront the legal questions that I alluded to above. Does a plan such as Bush's, which would channel public funds to faith-based groups, including some that unabashedly advance a particular religious viewpoint as they serve social needs, violate First Amendment guarantees concerning freedom of religion? Can religious groups that provide social services become public contractors yet still make employment decisions based on religious grounds (for example, firing employees on the basis of their sexual orientation)? If the state establishes a program for providing some benefit to citizens generally—for example, a scholarship program for postsecondary education—can religious citizens be singled out for exclusion from such programs, or do religious citizens sometimes have a right to receive public funding?[6]

I note that, while obviously important, these constitutional and statutory questions are not exactly my concern in this essay. These questions assume a given body of rules (namely, the U.S. Constitution, federal statutes, and judicial precedents) and a particular set of policy proposals (here, the Bush Administration's Faith-Based Initiative and various local initiatives under that rubric), and then ask whether the former allows the latter. But political liberalism operates at a more foundational level. Political liberalism offers an *ultima* account of the justification of political power. Rather than assuming, or even itself providing, some particular set of constitutional rules, political liberalism aims to provide a foundational set of moral ideas from which principles of justice might be constructed. The principles of justice, in turn, must be general and powerful enough to guide writers (and interpreters) of constitutions. Because political liberalism operates at this foundational level, there is conceptual space in which my question about the relationship of political liberalism to the Faith-Based Initiative can be asked no matter how the constitutional evaluation of the various elements of Bush's program eventually turns out.

---

[6] See Alan Brownstein, "Constitutional Questions about Charitable Choice," in Derek H. Davis and Barry Hankins, eds., *Welfare Reform & Faith-Based Organizations* (Waco, TX: J. M. Dawson Institute of Church-State Studies, Baylor University, 1999). A test of the employment question at the level of state funding is *Pedreira v. Kentucky Baptist Homes for Children*, 186 F. Supp. 2d 757 (W.D. KY 2001) (employee was fired because her admitted homosexual lifestyle violated the organization's religious values). In the case of *Davey v. Locke*, 299 F.3d 748 (college student denied state scholarship money because he chose to major in theology), the U.S. Supreme Court will consider whether religious citizens sometimes have a right to receive public funding. I am currently writing an article about the issues underlying the *Davey* case, arguing that egalitarian versions of liberalism generate extensive positive religious freedom rights such as those at issue in *Davey*. Egalitarian liberalism thus requires a far more substantial mixing of church and state than do more minimalist, classical conceptions of liberalism. My article is provisionally entitled "Locke v. *Davey v. Locke*."

Of course, this conceptual space comes with a price. There is a great gap between the metapolitical position staked out and defended by political liberals and the particular policy proposals that are being advanced today under the banner of compassionate conservatism in America. I am aware of this gap, and in future articles I hope to examine in detail whether a moral and a constitutional bridge might be built across it in the American context. For now, however, I hope merely to fire a motivational line across this chasm. I shall argue that a constitution written and interpreted on the basis of principles of justice generated within a political liberal framework, whatever the exact form of those principles and that constitution, should be welcoming to programs such as Bush's Faith-Based Initiative.[7] Political liberals, if they are to be true to their own deepest principles, should defend compassionate conservatism as a matter of justice.

II. POLITICAL LIBERALISM

Liberalism, in all its varieties, begins with the affirmation of a principle about the conditions in which the exercise of political power is legitimate. According to liberals, political power is justified only if this power is exercised on the basis of principles derived from ideas that the citizens themselves endorse. This is the 'liberal principle of legitimacy'.[8]

Political liberalism was born out of a crisis in this principle of legitimacy. Liberals have long sought to define the good of political association in terms of a minimal moral conception; that is, a basic value or set of values that most citizens share despite their many important differences.[9] Political principles are neutral—and thus satisfy the liberal principle of legitimacy—insofar as they can be justified with reference to such shared values, without assuming the validity or truth of any particular (controversial) conception of the good life.

In the seminal formulations of Kant (1724–1804) and Mill (1806–73), the liberal commitment to state neutrality was justified ultimately by reference to a particular view of human moral nature: a view championing autonomy (for Kant, a life lived according to rational will) and individualism (for Mill, a life featuring an experimental attitude toward one's projects). Both Kant and Mill, each for his own reasons and in his own

---

[7] Compared to most forms of ethical liberalism, a political conception of liberalism may well "enhance the ability of religious commitment to alter the nature of the state." This phrase is from Stephen Carter, who is skeptical of liberalism's ability in this regard, though Carter does not discuss political liberalism. See Stephen L. Carter, "Liberalism's Religion Problem," *First Things* 121 (2002): 21–32.

[8] My exposition of political liberalism in this section draws from the first chapter of my book *Liberalism Beyond Justice: Citizens, Society, and the Boundaries of Political Theory* (Princeton, NJ: Princeton University Press, 2001), 3–10.

[9] Larmore's exposition of this idea has been especially influential. See Charles E. Larmore, *The Morals of Modernity* (New York: Cambridge University Press, 1996), 123.

way, affirmed the idea that the liberal state should not seek to impose any particular view about the good life on its citizens. Rather, these liberals argued that forms of life have their value to people when, and precisely because, individuals freely affirm these ways of life for themselves. Some contemporary 'ethical liberals'—Ronald Dworkin, Will Kymlicka, and Joseph Raz prominent among them—continue to defend liberal politics firmly within this tradition, though typically by defending ever more expansive or even communitarian conceptions of autonomy.[10]

However, an increasing number of theorists have come to worry that even a broadened ideal of individualism is something over which people may reasonably disagree. Larmore, for example, traces a Romantic movement from Johann von Herder (1744–1803) to Alasdair MacIntyre and Michael Sandel in our day, one central strand of which has been a critique of precisely those moral ideals associated with Kant and Mill. In opposition to the traditional liberal emphasis on reflective individualism as a philosophy of life, thinkers in this Romantic tradition have stressed the values of belonging and custom. For some citizens, Larmore says, "such ways of life (shared customs, ties of place and language, and religious orthodoxies) shape the sense of value on the basis of which we make whatever choices we do." These commitments reach to the foundations of people's nature as moral beings: "They are so integral to our very conception of ourselves as moral beings that to imagine them as objects of choice would be to imagine ourselves as without any guiding sense of morality." [11] From this perspective of human moral nature, the individualistic philosophy of ethical liberalism seems bound to destroy the roots of morality itself.

The problem is not that Romantics reject the importance of critical reasoning and freedom of choice *tout court*. In fact, they typically emphasize that individuals must come to their religious commitments freely. As citizens some individuals may support freedom of choice as a political matter. What Romantics reject, though, is any suggestion that autonomy or open-mindedness captures the essence of human moral nature. Instead, they value such attitudes only instrumentally, as goods having value only insofar as they successfully link a person to truth.[12]

---

[10] For example, Raz and Kymlicka defend conceptions of autonomy that give increasing place to the demands of a person's history or (unchosen) social context of choice. See Joseph Raz, "Facing Diversity: The Case of Epistemic Abstinence," *Philosophy and Public Affairs* 19, no. 1 (1990): 3–46; and Joseph Raz, *Ethics in the Public Domain: Essays in the Morality of Law and Politics* (New York: Oxford University Press, 1994). See Will Kymlicka, *Multicultural Citizenship: A Liberal Theory of Minority Rights* (New York: Oxford University Press, 1995).

[11] Larmore, *The Morals of Modernity*, 129, 130.

[12] Carl Esbeck's defense of political autonomy and his attack on autonomy as a personal ideal is a striking example of this attitude in the context of Establishment Clause jurisprudence: "Unleashing personal religious choice as the core value of the Establishment Clause is not being elevated here as good theology, just good jurisprudence. . . . [F]or observant Jews and Christians, religious liberty consists not in doing what we choose, but in the freedom to do what we ought. . . . [B]elief and practice are understood in terms of truth, not choice." See Carl H. Esbeck, "A Constitutional Case for Governmental Cooperation with Faith-Based Social Service Providers," *Emory Law Journal* 46, no. 1 (1997): 1–42; see esp. note 98.

If these forms of enthusiasm for custom and moral embeddedness are incompatible with any recognizably liberal ideal of human moral nature, then the acceptance of Romanticism as a permanent part of Western culture of life undercuts the traditional justification of liberal politics. Accepting this form of pluralism creates a crisis for traditional accounts of liberal legitimacy.

John Rawls describes the motivational foundations of political liberalism in just this way, though he describes the crisis of legitimacy as arising internally to his own argument for justice as fairness. If state-backed coercion in the name of some set of principles of justice is to be justified, then it must be shown that these principles matter to citizens in a first-personal and moral way. Rawls calls this the 'test of stability'.

In the third part of *A Theory of Justice* (henceforth *Theory*), Rawls describes how people who have once acquired a sense of justice could reasonably be expected to regard justice not as a constraint but as a good in itself. "The desire to act justly and the desire to express our nature as free moral persons turn out to specify what is practically speaking the same desire."[13] Rawls was confident that this congruence would obtain because of the way that the principles of justice were themselves derived. These principles were derived from a device called the original position, a device in *Theory* that is sometimes described as representing an important fact about people: their true moral nature is to be free. An account of justice derived from a particular conception of human nature—if the conception hit upon were true—could then reasonably be expected to be recognized by people as reflecting who they really are. Insofar as people desire to express their true moral nature, and thus avoid giving way to "the accidents and contingencies of the world," they could be expected to recognize those principles as congruent with their own good.[14] Coercive power exercised on the basis of principles derived in this way could thus satisfy the liberal principle of legitimacy.

However, as Rawls came later to see, "*Theory* relies on a premise the realization of which its principles of justice rule out."[15] The premise is that all good citizens must converge on the particular view of human moral nature that the original position was said to model: the true moral nature of people lies in their capacity for freedom. But this particular view of human moral nature—as much as the individualism of Mill or Kant—is something about which many citizens of goodwill, and Romantic "citizens of faith" in particular, disagree. Indeed, Rawls realized, disagreement about the true character of human moral nature is particularly likely in a society that gives central place to associative and deliberative liberties, the hallmarks of a liberal society. Liberal principles of justice support precisely the institutional conditions that undercut (or make unrealistic)

---

[13] John Rawls, *A Theory of Justice* (Cambridge, MA: Harvard University Press, 1971), 572.
[14] Ibid., 575.
[15] John Rawls, "Introduction to the Paperback Edition," *Political Liberalism* (New York: Columbia University Press, 1996), xlii.

the comprehensive form of justification upon which Rawls's argument in *Theory* depended.

No doubt, some citizens who reject autonomy as an ethical ideal do so because they wish to impose their own conception of moral or religious truth on others, for example, by using the power of state institutions to impose their particular view of religious truth on other citizens. Many people who reject the moral ideal of autonomy, however, are firmly committed to taking part in political association with (diverse) others on terms that all can accept. Among this group are religious citizens, many of whom affirm orthodox or literalist interpretations of their religious commitments. How might liberal forms of state coercion be justified to "politically reasonable" citizens such as these?

To justify political coercion in conditions of reasonable value-pluralism, political liberals seek to detach political philosophy from moral philosophy. Leaving aside disputes about human moral nature, they stress the formative role of liberal institutions. People brought up in Western constitutional democracies may share certain political ideas—namely, that society is best conceived of as a fair system of cooperation over time, and that persons should be treated as free and equal for political purposes. Deep principles of justice—of the sort that might guide writers and interpreters of constitutions—might be derived from these shared political ideas rather than from any particular view of moral personality.

Of course, one cannot simply assume a congruence between people's deep moral beliefs and the principles of justice produced by constructivism done in this purely political way. So, once justice has been "politicized" in this manner, further stages of justification must be introduced. These stages test whether people in a society that is diverse in terms of their deep moral principles can affirm a common set of principles of justice, each from his or her own distinctive moral viewpoint. If people can, then an "overlapping consensus" forms and an even further level of justification, "public justification by political society," has been achieved. In this event, the conditions of legitimacy have been met. Political liberal theory has provided us with an argument for a particular conception of justice and an account of how coercion in the name of this conception might be justified, even in a society that accepts citizens of faith as well as autonomous individualists.

Political liberalism attempts to build political life by accepting deep value differences, rather than by attempting to resolve them. In this regard, its impulses are more Reformation than Enlightenment, more Locke than Mill. While still in its infancy, a number of interesting challenges to this paradigm already have been raised. Some critics argue that political liberalism fails on its own terms: when we look closely, we find that political liberalism rests on foundations that are not free from philosophical controversies about moral truth.[16] Other critics argue that the political

---

[16] See especially Raz, "Facing Diversity."

liberal emphasis on "political autonomy" is psychologically indistinguishable from most ethical liberal accounts of "moral autonomy": beneath all the technical camouflage, political liberalism is but a species of ethical liberalism after all.[17] Others, more basically still, argue that even if political liberals can distinguish their view from ethical liberal forms of justification, they should not wish to do so: the life of autonomy and reflective individualism is indeed the good life. Good liberals should stand by their traditional defense of this ideal.

While these are important challenges, a question that interests me far more is one that arises for those who *accept* political liberalism. Political liberals aim to construct a freestanding argument for a conception of justice from purely political ideas of persons and society. This is a conception of justice that they hope can win the first-personal assent not only of the traditional liberal constituency but of Romantic citizens of faith as well. Moreover, political liberals wish to gain such assent while retaining all of their familiar egalitarian ambitions at full strength.[18] The question thus arises: If political liberals move to a broader, more inclusive foundation, what corresponding adjustments might be required in the design of the liberal house?

III. Compassionate Conservatism

To some, the term 'compassionate conservative' may sound like a cynical campaign slogan, or even an oxymoron. In American political parlance, 'compassion' is a term firmly associated with the political Left. A 'compassionate' legislator is one who supports an expansion of governmental services to the least well off. The centralized social welfare programs that were initiated in the 1930s with Franklin Delano Roosevelt's New Deal and that reached their conceptual zenith in Lyndon Johnson's Great Society are paradigms of this professionalized, top-down approach to social compassion. Historically, such programs have sometimes been opposed by conservatives in America on classical liberal terms: such programs violate the property rights of individuals and replace the vitality of civil society with deadening bureaucracies. But American conservatives have also sometimes opposed such programs on Social Darwinist grounds.

---

[17] For an argument that political liberalism conceptually collapses into ethical liberalism on these grounds, see Eamonn Callan, "Political Liberalism and Political Education," *Review of Politics* 58, no. 1 (1996): 5–33. For an argument that the civic educational requirements of the two metapolitical views converge as a matter of practice, see Amy Gutmann, "Civic Education and Social Diversity," *Ethics* 105, no. 3 (1995): 557–59. I offer a defense of political liberalism's distinctness in light of Callan's and Gutmann's critiques in John Tomasi, "Civic Education and Ethical Subservience: From *Mozert* to *Santa Fe* and Beyond," *Moral and Political Education,* (*NOMOS XLII*), Steve Macedo and Yael Tamir, eds. (New York: New York University Press, 2001).
[18] The definitive exegetical statement of this point is offered by my colleague David Estlund. See David Estlund, "The Survival of Egalitarian Justice in John Rawls's *Political Liberalism*," *Journal of Political Philosophy* 4, no. 1 (1996): 68–78.

Generational cycles of poverty, on this strand of conservative thinking, are evidence that some individuals and groups are less worthy and able than others.

In contrast, politicians on the left have stressed the essential goodness of people. When lives go badly, this is not because of an individual's or group's intrinsic inferiority; instead, it is mainly the result of a bad environment (for example, the result of what are described as structural defects in the operation of capitalist markets). To counteract such environmental factors, the government should establish programs that redistribute resources so that every citizen is provided with the material and educational bases of a successful life. Within a pluralist society, such basic resources should be provided neutrally and unconditionally, as entitlements rather than as conditional opportunities. Government respects its citizens when it provides these basic entitlements in a nonjudgmental way, for only in this way can the state help its citizens while at the same time leaving each individual free to live her life according to whatever deep values she herself thinks best.

Public disillusionment with this Great Society approach to social service provision—and especially to fighting severe poverty—grew during the 1980s and early 1990s. Even as more public money was spent, the number of people on the long-term welfare rolls steadily increased. Many problems that government-run programs were meant to solve worsened and seemed ever more intractable, culminating in President Clinton's signing of the Welfare Reform Act of 1996, promising an end to "welfare as we know it."

Compassionate conservatism emerged during this period. Against the Great Society emphasis on people's external circumstances as a cause of their hardships, Marvin Olasky, Gertrude Himmelfarb, and others sought to revive a distinction from American history between poverty and pauperism.[19] Whereas 'poverty' denotes a lack of resources, 'pauperism' refers to a corruption of a person's inner self. Pauperism involves a lack of discipline, self-respect, and sense of commitment to others. The danger of any system intended to alleviate poverty is that the system, if done crudely, may itself inadvertently pauperize people and hold them in this condition. Breaking the cycle requires not only material resources but also inner change. Social service institutions, to be effective, must deliver a complex mixture of material resources and value-laden incentives for inner change. Poverty-fighting, on this view, is thus intimately personal work. It re-

[19] Olasky traces the role of this distinction in America from its roots in colonial times, describing, for example, how Ben Franklin criticized a British welfare act on just this ground when Franklin visited London in 1776. See Marvin Olasky, *The Tragedy of American Compassion* (Washington, DC: Regnery Gateway, 1992), generally; on Franklin, see p. 43. On the wider historical importance of the poverty/pauperism distinction, see Gertrude Himmelfarb, "Welfare and Charity: Lessons from Victorian England," in *Transforming Welfare: The Revival of American Charity*, Jeffrey Sikkenga, ed. (Grand Rapids, MI: Acton Institute, 1997), 27–33.

quires compassion not merely in the Great Society sense of an ever larger and more professionalized cadre of caregivers treating their "clients." Rather, poverty-fighting often requires ethically charged engagement between particular individuals: 'compassion' in the literal sense of 'suffering with'.

Many compassionate conservatives are deeply religious, often but not always in an orthodox or literalist way. Like compassionate liberals, compassionate conservatives see each individual as essentially good: in the compassionate conservatives' terminology, every human life is created in the image of God. However, they believe that each person is also flawed by sin. People have the tendency to put themselves first and shun responsibilities to others. It is only by bonding with others in a transformative way—with family, friends, communities of fellow believers, and ultimately with God—that each individual can realize her or his true moral nature.[20] Explicitly rejecting the ideal of personal autonomy that they see as having been the aim of the Great Society–style programs, compassionate conservatives such as Olasky stress two primary values: affiliation and bonding. Affiliation might take any of a variety of forms: familial, communal, or ethnic. Bonding requires the construction of intimate connections with others that go to the very core of one's identity— especially for volunteers, who sometimes in essence become new family members for those they help.[21] Social service providers should seek not simply to set people free. Rather, they should seek to encumber them— artfully and lovingly drawing each person back, one by one, into communion with family, neighbors, and, most important, God. The fight against poverty, in every case, is a fight to redeem a person's soul.

Compassionate conservatives point to the strong track records of some small grassroots poverty-fighting groups, many of which have an evangelical or religious basis, and they emphasize recent instances where government institutions have actively encouraged such initiatives.[22]

For example, in 1997, when Stephen Goldsmith was mayor of Indianapolis, he established a special office called the Front Porch Alliance. Noting that evangelicals and other "social entrepreneurs" typically attempt to launch their projects on shoestring budgets, Goldsmith assigned full-time city administrators to help cut through red tape (e.g., by expediting applications for building permits, zoning variances, and certificates of occupancy).

Another example of government working with religious groups was an experimental prison pre-release program that George W. Bush launched

---

[20] While this is the true condition of every person in society, average citizens typically have enough material and educational advantages that their flawed condition does not become publicly obvious. This is not so for the worst-off members of society.

[21] Olasky, *The Tragedy of American Compassion*, 101–4.

[22] See Stephen V. Monsma, *When Sacred and Secular Mix: Religious Nonprofit Organizations and Public Money* (Lanham, MD: Rowman & Littlefield, 1996).

in the late 1990s while governor of Texas. Noting that as many as sixty percent of released inmates nationwide return to prison, Bush's program invited any private organization, religious or secular, to set up and run value-based pre-release programs alongside the existing state program. In a Houston prison, Charles Colson's evangelical Prison Fellowship set up one such program called Inner Change, an eighteen-month, Bible-based program that emphasized how God can change hearts. (In Texas, the state made room for such programs but did not fund them.)[23] Prisoners nearing their date of release could participate in the state's secular program or in the religiously based one, as each inmate preferred.

City officials in Cleveland, Ohio, faced with seemingly intractable problems in their system of government-owned schools, experimented with a program of vouchers. Poor students were eligible to receive state-funded vouchers that parents could use to send their children to any participating school, whether public or private, secular or parochial. An overwhelming majority of parents chose to use their vouchers at Catholic schools. Thus, the Cleveland program had the effect of allowing public funds to be used in part to support the teaching of religious beliefs.[24]

Compassionate conservatives argue that partnerships between government and social entrepreneurs—partnerships such as those in Indianapolis, Houston, and Cleveland—should be established and expanded on both the federal and local levels. In particular, compassionate conservatives make three proposals. First, institutions should be established to allow fast-track review of facially neutral government regulations that hinder civil society organizations, whether secular or religious, that have a social service mission. Second, the tax code should be reformed—under the banner of "charitable choice"—to create additional incentives for people to contribute directly to poverty-fighting organizations of their choice.[25] And third, public monies gathered by regular taxation should be made available to religious organizations that provide social services.

As this sketch shows, compassionate conservatism is a complex cluster of proposals. Along with the question of whether these proposals should

---

[23] Olasky describes both of these examples at length. On the Front Porch Alliance, see Olasky, *Compassionate Conservatism*, 61–91; on the Texas pre-release program, see 23–57.

[24] This Cleveland program led to the important Supreme Court case *Zelman v. Simmons-Harris*, 536 U.S. 639 (2002). The Court upheld the constitutionality of the Cleveland school voucher program, which many see as having cleared the constitutional ground for wider aspects of the Faith-Based Initiative. For constitutional analysis, see Ira Lupu and Robert Tuttle, "Sites of Redemption: A Wide-Angle Look at Government Vouchers and Sectarian Service Providers," *The Journal of Law and Politics* (forthcoming).

[25] In a sense, charitable choice merely expands an existing system by which taxpayers subsidize religious groups. Half of all charitable giving from individuals goes to church groups and is tax deductible. Church groups are also generally exempt from sales taxes and local property taxes. According to Olasky, each level of government has long seen merit in such arrangements, and such arrangements have rarely caused conflicts or jeopardized the liberty of churches. "Offering of tax-free status has allowed governments to support the general welfare" (Olasky, *Compassionate Conservatism*, 87).

be implemented on the federal or state level, each proposal might be formulated in less controversial or more controversial ways. For example, there are questions about the *scope* of the programs that compassionate conservatives wish to reform: Are these proposals to apply only to existing governmental programs that minister to the worst-off members of society (e.g., programs providing aid to dependent children), or to programs that identify all citizens as potential beneficiaries (e.g., public schooling)? There are also less controversial and more controversial ways of characterizing the *conditions in which such proposals would kick in*. Do they kick in only when government-run institutions are failing? If so, then the rationale to seek novel ways of delivering services might be derived fairly straightforwardly from the right of the beneficiaries to receive the good at all. Or do the proposals kick in whenever people wish to offer or receive social services in a way that accords with their own deep values? This stronger claim would require a more sophisticated form of justification, one aiming to make out a right of religious liberty held by providers and recipients alike.

The compassionate conservatives' set of proposals also might be interpreted in less or more controversial ways depending on how much *conflict with other values* the proposals involve. Fast-track review, for example, might merely involve speeding up the regular review processes, or it might involve granting social service organizations special exemptions to generally applicable laws and statutes (at least up to the point where such exemptions might begin to conflict with the basic rights and liberties of other citizens).

These proposals also admit of a variety of interpretations concerning the *mode of support* they are seeking. Least controversially, compassionate conservatives might merely be suggesting that the state make room for privately funded programs—as in the evangelical prison pre-release program that then-Governor Bush supported in Houston. If compassionate conservatives are seeking a mode of support that includes funding from public sources, that would be more controversial, but such support might be directed only to recipients via vouchers, thus partly muting its contentiousness. In this way, as in the Cleveland school case, the government's relationship to religious organizations would be insulated by the private choices made by individual citizens. Most controversially, compassionate conservatives might be seeking grants that go directly to religious organizations on the basis of objective, nondiscriminatory criteria, such as the group's proven ability to provide some legislatively identified public good.

While more and less controversial interpretations of the three proposals— fast-track review, tax reform, and public subsidies—have been advanced under the banner of compassionate conservatism, I believe that in each case the weaker, less controversial interpretation has been advanced only for tactical reasons. The essence of what compassionate conservatives are proposing, the conceptual core of the institutional reform they have in mind, lies at the more controversial end of the spectrum of each of these questions. So when I speak of compassionate conservatism, I shall be referring to the strong interpretation of each of the three proposals, as I have identified them above.

A final caveat about the compassionate conservative program is worth mentioning. This concerns the *kinds of restrictions* that might be put on public grants to religious groups. I mentioned earlier that many church leaders originally expressed skepticism about Bush's Faith-Based Initiative. Urban ministries in particular have long agonized over whether to accept direct support from government agencies, fearing the mission-constraining strings that might be attached to such support.[26] Some who have accepted public funds have been forced to walk a delicate legal and spiritual tightrope, for example, by agreeing to remove all religious references from the publicly funded parts of their programs and to offer religious instruction only as optional, privately funded supplements to their programs.

Compassionate conservatives show a new boldness, however, in challenging such restrictions. They want grants without any special religion-limiting strings at all. Olasky describes a conversation that he had with Kathy Dudley, an evangelical poverty-fighter in urban west Dallas, which expresses well the grounds for this boldness. On Olasky's report, Dudley believes in fighting both spiritual and economic poverty, and she rejects governmental restrictions that might force her to choose between these two emphases: "Our mission is discipleship, so if the government gives money to gain one result of the mission, housing, but at the same time tells us we must give up the mission, that makes no sense."[27] Olasky thinks that compassionate conservatism can respond to Dudley's concerns. Provided that there are secular options readily available, government officials with the power to reward or withhold grants should not be allowed to consider the form and frequency of prayers that might be offered by, or even required of, participants in faith-based grant programs.[28]

What explains this new boldness? Compassionate conservatives see evangelical participation in public works projects not as a privilege but as a basic right. Pilot programs such as those in Indianapolis, Houston, and

---

[26] Consider this sentiment from Sister Connie Driscoll, head of a 125-bed shelter for women and children in Chicago: "The only way I would take government funding is over my very cold dead body. We simply don't like the government. We don't like their interference and all their nonsense—you can't do this, you can't do that" (*Pittsburgh Post-Gazette*, January 28, 2001, as quoted by Americans United for Separation of Church and State, "Faith-Based Folly: Americans say 'Not So Fast'" (available on-line, URL provided at note 3 above).

[27] Quoted in Olasky, *Compassionate Conservatism*, 32.

[28] The proviso that secular social service options always be available to recipients of aid is fundamental to the moral and constitutional plausibility of the Faith-Based Initiative. It is the satisfaction of this proviso that enables the initiative to avoid being religiously coercive of recipients. There are difficult questions concerning precisely what it means for the proviso to be satisfied.

Cleveland—where government actively supported religiously based social initiatives—are not instances of a privilege fleetingly granted by administrators who happened to be sympathetic to the concerns of religious
folk. Instead, these programs are early manifestations of a basic right of
citizenship that religious citizens are now seeking to have recognized and
then exercised across an expansive range of social service domains. Olasky
explains, "[T]he aim is not to grant religious preferences but to stop
discrimination against social involvement by churches, synagogues, mosques,
and other faith-based groups of all kinds."[29] Compassionate conservatism rests fundamentally on an assertion of a right to religious liberty. The
social upshot of recognizing this right would be a society very different
from that of contemporary America. This would be a public square where
the domain of the "public" could not be identified in any simple way with
that of the "governmental." Instead, in this society, religious and other
value-laden approaches to the provision of social goods—whether concerning housing, nutrition, reproductive counseling, job training, child-
care, or schooling, and whether considered from the perspective of
providers or of recipients—would be publicly supported on an equal
footing with traditional governmental and publicly funded programs. [30]

IV. A Puzzle for Political Liberals

What should political liberals think of compassionate conservatism? Of
course, we need to distinguish the particular formulations of the Faith-
Based Initiative that the Bush Administration has so far advanced—
formulations that reflect crisscrossing waves of strategic decision-making,
and perhaps unsteady commitment to principle, in a politically charged
environment—from the deeper structure of compassionate conservatism
as an internally consistent ideal. But if we focus on this ideal, what should
political liberals make of it?

Compassionate conservatism appears to require an affirmation of the
political ideas of person and society that are central to Rawlsian liberalism, starting with the acceptance of the fact of reasonable value-pluralism.
After all, compassionate conservatives do not advocate allowing any one
group to use governmental power to force its view of moral value on
other citizens, for example, by demanding a monopoly of social service
provisions under some group's religious banner. While often committed
to religious views as individuals, compassionate conservatives are plu-

---

[29] Olasky, *Compassionate Conservatism*, 192 (emphasis mine).

[30] In this essay I do not consider what means of implementing the compassionate conservative agenda might be constitutionally appropriate in the United States. I note that
Olasky, at least, thinks this should be a matter for the national legislature: "Congress should
draft a law concerning faith-based organizations that bars unconditionally any government
regulation or restriction of religious observance or promotion." Marvin Olasky, "How Much
Risk? Conservative Reaction to Bush's Faith-Based Initiative" [accessed on-line at http://
www.capitalresearch.org/publications/cc/2001/0104.htm, April 2001, p. 5 of 9].

JOHN TOMASI

ralists on the political level: they insist that every individual should be able to choose from a range of social service providers—religious, atheistic, and secular.[31]

Further, compassionate conservatives implicitly accept the core political liberal idea of society as "a fair system of cooperation over time," along with the attendant idea that social justice requires citizens to "share in one another's fate."[32] Compassionate conservatives see themselves as merely asking to be *included* in the project of realizing social justice. Olasky writes, "As members of a community, we have a mutual responsibility for the poor among us and for educational needs, but we have the freedom to carry out that responsibility in a way that accords with our beliefs."[33]

What should political liberals make of the claim that citizens of faith are discriminated against by a public system of social service provision that is conducted solely on a nonreligious basis? The government of a diverse society cannot intentionally promote any one moral or religious viewpoint over any other politically reasonable one. For this reason, government-run programs for the delivery of social services must necessarily take a nonreligious, secular form. But, compassionate conservatives argue, a secular approach to social services, since it must by definition leave out religious values, cannot really be value-neutral. By providing goods and services via mechanisms that are stripped of the particular values of affiliation and bonding that religious citizens hold dear, secular programs in effect promote an approach to life that many politically reasonable citizens reject: a life in which individualism, rather than piety, is valorized as the highest personal value.[34] Neutrality in

[31] Olasky writes, "The compassionate conservative goal is to offer a choice of programs: Protestant, Catholic, Jewish, Islamic, Buddhist, atheist. Some programs may emphasize education, some family, some work. Compassionate conservatives make sure that no one is placed in a particular type of program against his will, but they also try to make sure that religious people are free to communicate their values" (Olasky, *Compassionate Conservatism*, 18–19). They explicitly reject schemes for the establishment, or even for a multiple establishment, of religion (ibid., 98). The aim of compassionate conservatism is to give "all organizations, religious or atheistic, the opportunity to propose values-based . . . programs" (ibid., 55).

[32] Rawls, *Political Liberalism* (hardcover ed., 1993), 15, 303.

[33] Olasky, *Compassionate Conservatism*, 98. Compassionate conservatism is based squarely on the liberal principle of legitimacy—the principle that governmental power is legitimate only if exercised on the basis of principles that are acceptable to those who are subject to it. In asserting their right of religious freedom, they can be understood as demanding that their society be organized according to a conception of justice that adheres to this principle too.

[34] That secular programs promote moral and not just political autonomy is a constant theme among compassionate conservatives. Speaking of the professionalized programs associated with the Great Society, Olasky writes, "Programs that declared themselves 'compassionate' were often the opposite, because most tended to emphasize individual autonomy. Even those organizations that struggled to inculcate moral values accepted the notion that neither marriage nor reliance on family, church or traditional voluntary organizations—which might be dominated by 'patriarchal values'—should or could be encouraged. 'About the only thing you can rely on is your personal feeling about what makes sense for you,' one resource directory declared. . . . Instead of emphasizing affiliation and bonding, many programs stressed bread alone" (Olasky, *The Tragedy of American Compassion*, 201; see also 175, 193, 203, 206, 208, 212, 225).

the delivery of publicly funded social services, from this perspective, is not a property of individual sites for the delivery of such services. Rather, neutrality—or discriminatory bias—is a property that can only be discerned by examining the system as a whole. In a social world committed to treating citizens of faith and secular nonbelievers as full political equals, a public system that mandates that none of its delivery sites may include religious perspectives would fail this test of neutrality.

In an era marked by a vibrant civil society and a small government, the secular bias of government-run programs might not cause any serious problem. Before the rise of the administrative state, as historian David Beito has demonstrated, social services in America typically were provided by charities and a complex system of mutual aid associations.[35] Citizens—whether recipients or providers of social services—would not regularly come into contact with secular governmental agencies. Religious citizens would find ample opportunity to develop themselves and express their concern for one another according to the "Romantic" approaches to value that they affirmed. But as the role of government expands, the effects of the bias inherent in the secular, government-based approach are amplified.[36] For citizens of faith, freedom of religion may become ever more difficult to achieve.

Legal scholar and judge Michael McConnell has made precisely this argument in the context of First Amendment jurisprudence. During the period of American history when the First Amendment was proposed and debated, McConnell notes, the government had little or no involvement with education, social welfare, or the formation and transmission of culture from one generation to the next. Religious freedom was protected naturally, so to speak, by the limited nature of government. But as the size and purview of government grew, especially during the middle part of the twentieth century, the adoption of a strict separationist interpretation of the First Amendment created special burdens for religious citizens. "Religious influences are confined to those segments of society in which the government is not involved, which is to say that religion is confined to the margins of national life—to those areas not important enough to have received the helping or controlling hand of government." In such conditions, a simple separationist or "no-aid" First Amendment jurisprudence becomes oppressive. "More sophisticated and more contentious devices, based on self-conscious religious

---

[35] David Beito, "Fraternal Societies as an Alternative to the Welfare State," in *Transforming Welfare*, 34–49.

[36] Olasky estimates that each taxpaying American family currently pays some $5,600 each year for poverty-fighting programs of various kinds: "[S]o much money is now drained into taxes that many people have little left to give" (Olasky, *Compassionate Conservatism*, 187). In Olasky's view, civil society in America has been so crowded out by Great Society–style programs (especially regarding the service of the most needy) that the natural order will not rebuild itself any time soon. See also the discussion in Monsma, *When Sacred and Secular Mix*, 50–58; and in Stephen V. Monsma and J. Christopher Soper, *The Challenge of Pluralism: Church and State in Five Democracies* (Lanham, MD: Rowman & Littlefield, 1997), 15–50.

pluralism even within the public realm, become essential." Without such devices, the institutions of American government would in effect become "a relentless engine of secularization."[37]

The compassionate conservative program—with its proposals for fast-track review boards, tax code reform, and a greatly expanded system of vouchers and grants—represents a set of sophisticated and contentious devices self-consciously addressed to just the problem that McConnell has in mind. But can a justification for these devices be found? Can a justification be found, not at the level of political calculation, prudent policy-making, or even of constitutional law, but at the most fundamental philosophical level: the level of social justice at which political liberalism operates?

I think that this is a puzzle. But note how high the stakes are for political liberals once this puzzle has been set before them. Political liberals are asking Romantic "citizens of faith" to sign on to principles of justice that have a demanding egalitarian element. Such principles might very well justify Great Society–style programs, the present structure of which these citizens abhor. Without some explicit recognition of their concerns about these state-run programs, they might very well not sign on to these principles. Political liberals want to move to a new, broader foundation, but they do not want their old house simply to collapse. They need to find a way by which the egalitarian elements of their view might survive. How can political liberals accomplish this?

I believe that the move to a political form of justification requires that these liberals go back in and do some creative design work on the egalitarian principles of justice themselves. A detailed architectural model of the adjustments that political liberals must make in the egalitarian model is beyond the scope of this article. Still, I would like at least to sketch what a suitably remodeled liberal house might look like, while tying the discussion to the idea of egalitarianism itself.

V. Egalitarianism and the Worth of Religious Liberty

Classical liberalism—the liberalism of John Locke, for example—mandates an equality of *status* between citizens. The right to hold property, to speak, to vote or to hold public office should not be the prerogative of the members of any particular family, social class, gender, or racial or ethnic group. Rather, basic rights are held equally by all adult members of each liberal political community.

This liberal ideal of equality proved itself a potent solvent against the gummed-up social hierarchies of 17th century Europe. However, even the greatest proponents of this solvent have periodically worried about liber-

---

[37] Michael W. McConnell, "Old Liberalism, New Liberalism, and People of Faith," in *Christian Perspectives on Legal Thought*, Michael W. McConnell et al., eds. (New Haven, CT: Yale University Press, 2001), 21. See also Carl H. Esbeck, "Myths, Miscues, and Misconceptions: No-Aid Separationism and the Establishment Clause," *Notre Dame Journal of Law, Ethics and Public Policy* 13, no. 2 (1999): 285; and Carter, "Liberalism's Religion Problem," 21–32.

alism's ability to seep down and dissolve the deepest, most hardened sources of political inequality. For however potent the classical liberal viewpoint may be against systems of formal inequality, liberal theory seems to have little to say about inequalities in the *actual life prospects* of these (formally equal) liberal citizens. We can put this old worry about liberalism in contemporary terms: the court system of the United States recognizes the very poorest person in America as having exactly the same right to hold and enjoy property as does, say, multibillionaire Bill Gates. With respect to the right to hold property, the two of them are precisely equal. But the value of such a right to a person as wealthy as Bill Gates may be dramatically greater than the value of the right to a person in poverty. Similarly, every American reader of this article has exactly the same right to speak and publish his opinions as does, say, the chairman of Times-Warner Communications. I, too, have exactly the same right to influence the political process as does any citizen born a Rockefeller, a Kennedy, a Gore, or a Bush. But, again, in all such cases, the value of rights held by people as a matter of formal equality may be dramatically unequal.

Egalitarian liberals are liberals who believe that liberalism—against its classical formulations—carries within itself coercively backed guarantees against inequalities such as those described above. The liberal commitment to equal freedom, on its modern reformulation, requires not only equality of status. This commitment also allows, indeed requires, that the liberal state act to rectify inequalities in the *worth* of people's liberties—at least where those inequalities become great enough to threaten people's status as political equals. The worth of people's liberties is now understood to be connected in important ways to those people's ability to command resources. The main thrust of the liberal research agenda for the past thirty years has been to demonstrate that a response to concerns about inequalities in the worth of liberties can be built into liberal theory at the level of justice. In addition to mandating equality of status between citizens, liberal theory is now said to generate far more ambitious principles. These principles require that the state seek to rectify an ever expanding array of inequalities in people's actual life prospects, especially inequalities that result from unchosen circumstances such as differences in people's natural talents or their social starting places. John Rawls's famous "difference principle," which sees liberal justice as requiring that social inequalities be arranged so as to benefit the least well-off members of society—is a paradigm expression of this feature of egalitarian liberalism.[38]

---

[38] Samuel Freeman has coined the term "high liberalism" to describe egalitarian liberalism in the Rawlsian vein. See Samuel Freeman, "Illiberal Libertarians: Why Libertarianism is not a Liberal View," *Philosophy and Public Affairs* 30, no. 2 (2001): 105–51. I offer a response from a libertarian perspective in Tomasi, *Liberalism Beyond Justice*, 108–25. I regret that, through an editing error on my part, the citations to Freeman's work in my discussion are inadequate (especially at 112–12). While standing by my response, I strongly recommend Freeman's fine article.

However, the rise of the administrative state in the pursuit of egalitarian justice may have consequences that were unlooked for by proponents of egalitarianism. In the context of an expanding social role for state agencies, objectionable inequalities in the worth of people's liberties may be generated not only by differences in people's native endowments and social starting places. Inequalities in the worth of citizens' liberties may be generated by activities of the state itself. Because of the great power of the state, both economic and cultural, even state action in pursuit of legitimate egalitarian aims may generate such inequalities. From an egalitarian perspective, such inequalities merit redress, even were they not intended by liberal policymakers.

Political liberals routinely distinguish between two senses of neutrality: (1) 'neutrality of aim', which is the principle that the liberal state should not do anything that is *intended* to favor or promote any one reasonable moral view over any other one; and (2) 'neutrality of effect', which holds that the state should not do anything that makes it *more likely* that individuals accept any particular moral view over any other. While affirming a commitment to neutrality of aim, political liberals reject neutrality of effect as impossible to achieve.[39] Political liberals surely are right to do this: political institutions intimately affect individuals' life prospects, influencing the "ethical background culture" against which each develops his most most basic ways of perceiving the world.[40] To accept a commitment to neutrality of effect would be a recipe for paralysis, making political society itself an impossibility.

But what is the reason behind the liberals' commitment to the other form of neutrality, neutrality of aim? Liberals affirm this principle not as an end in itself but for a deeper purpose: that of respecting citizens as free and equal for political purposes. A government maximizes the freedom of its citizens when it minimizes the unintended effects of its own (legitimately pursued) policies on citizens' personal life plans. While important in the context of any egalitarian society, this idea takes on special significance in the context of political liberalism. Political liberalism avoids collapsing into but another contentious form of ethical liberalism only insofar as the distinction between a state's promotion of political autonomy and its promotion of full-blown ethical autonomy can be maintained. But some reasonable citizens, here citizens of faith, are claiming that the existing system of advancing political autonomy has the effect—even if not intended—of obliterating exactly this distinction in their case. Since this is precisely the group of politically reasonable citizens that political liberalism was designed to include, this is a concern that political liberals must address. Egali-

---

[39] On this distinction and Rawls's rejection of neutrality of effect as a constraint, see Rawls, *Political Liberalism* (hardcover ed., 1993), 193–94; and Larmore, *Patterns of Moral Complexity*, 126 n. 6.

[40] I develop this idea of an "ethical background culture" in my *Liberalism Beyond Justice*, 11ff.

tarian principles of justice may need to be adjusted if they are to fit squarely atop the wider moral foundations that political liberals accept. The arguments of compassionate conservatives, weighed with some Rawlsian insights, may provide the plumb line we need to begin this task.

Rawls's conception of justice as fairness was developed and defended within an ethical liberal framework.[41] The most reasonable conception of social justice, Rawls argued, would consist of two lexically ordered principles, the first setting out equal rights to basic liberties, the second guaranteeing a form of egalitarianism in material goods and opportunities. In our terms, the first principle guarantees citizens a status as equally free, while the second rectifies inequalities in the material holdings on which the worth of those liberties is based.

This conception of justice may be interpreted, or even supplemented, in various ways. For example, Rawls thinks that the political liberties, listed among the basic liberties under the first principle, have a special standing such that they should be guaranteed to citizens at their "fair value"—a more demanding distributional standard than even that of the difference principle.[42]

In light of the concerns raised by compassionate conservatives, might one argue that religious liberties have some special standing akin to that of the political liberties? If so, one technical response to the claims of discrimination we have been considering might be to guarantee citizens' religious liberties at something like this "fair value" standard. Less stringently, one might consider adding a third principle of justice to address these concerns. This principle, positioned lexically posterior to the first two principles, might run roughly as follows: when facing a choice among rival systems for the delivery of social services guaranteed by the first two principles, preference should be given to the system that minimizes any deleterious, differential impacts of the system itself on the worth of citizens' religious liberties.[43]

To determine which, if either, of these strategies would be most appropriate would require a great deal of careful analysis. But however that analysis might turn out, adjustments such as these would be meant to track and express an extremely important idea: in conditions of reasonable value pluralism, respecting citizens means attending not only to what people are owed, but also to the nature of the delivery mechanisms by which that debt is discharged. Citizens are owed this dimension of respect as a matter of justice.

[41] This, at least, is Rawls's view: "*A Theory of Justice* was a comprehensive doctrine of liberalism" (Rawls as interviewed by Bernard O. Prusak, "Politics, Religion, and the Public Good," *Commonweal*, September 25, 1998, 13).

[42] See Rawls, *Political Liberalism* (hardcover ed., 1993), 328.

[43] I discuss ways to formulate such a third principle of justice in Tomasi, *Liberalism Beyond Justice*, 100–4. The seminal exposition of this idea, to which I am much indebted, is Burleigh Wilkins, "A Third Principle of Justice," *Journal of Ethics* 1, no. 4 (1997): 355–74.

I am not suggesting that adjustments such as these should be made merely because I think that many citizens of faith—including, perhaps, compassionate conservatives in America—would find them appealing. This would be to make the principles of justice political in the wrong way. Instead, I believe that these changes, or ones like them, could be justified in a freestanding way from the general ideas of person and society with which political constructivism begins. Implicit in the idea of a public society in which citizens of diverse viewpoints are to be treated as free and equal is the idea that such a society should be as much as possible a *receptive home* to all reasonable citizens, rather than merely being minimally acceptable to them. Principles of justice adjusted along the lines that I have described would require that publicly funded institutions be arranged in a way likely to realize this societal ideal.

VI. CONCLUSION

I mentioned at the outset of this article that there is a great gap between political liberalism (a metapolitical view about the nature of political legitimacy) and compassionate conservatism (a complex set of public policy proposals currently being discussed in the wake of American welfare reform). To safely cross this gap, political liberals would need to work out and defend a more sophisticated conception of egalitarian justice. This conception of justice would be designed to redress not only inequalities in the worth of liberties that result from inequalities in citizens' natural endowments and social starting places, but it would also redress those inequalities that result from governmental action in the pursuit of justice itself. The latter would include inequalities in the worth of religious liberty.

A full account would also need to show how revised principles of justice of this sort might be tied in as justificatory support for forms of constitutional jurisprudence that are hospitable to a mixing of church and state in the delivery of social services.[44] Problems of associational autonomy—including the alleged right of social service organizations to accept public monies and yet continue to use religious criteria in employment decisions—would loom large here.[45]

---

[44] I have in mind the emerging school of "even-handedness" or "neutrality" that seems to be replacing "no-aid separationism" as the core concept of religious liberty. See Ira C. Lupu "The Lingering Death of Separationism," *George Washington Law Review* 62 (1994): 230; Esbeck, "A Constitutional Case"; and Esbeck, "Myths, Miscues, and Misconceptions." For helpful analysis, see Douglas Laycock, "The Underlying Unity of Separation and Neutrality," *Emory Law Journal* 46, no. 1 (1997): 43–74.

[45] For an introductory constitutional defense of the idea that faith-based organizations can become federal contractors and yet retain their right to use religious criteria when making employment decisions, see Carl H. Esbeck, "Isn't Charitable Choice Government-Funded Discrimination?" Center for Public Justice, available on-line at http://cpjustice.org/stories/storyreader$375 [accessed at February 2003]. A fascinating account of the constitutional

My aim in this essay has been far more modest than developing a full, sophisticated account. I have merely attempted to establish a single motivational connection: In the contemporary American context, anyone who is attracted to political liberalism should also be attracted to the Faith-Based Initiative. Political liberals have reason to support compassionate conservatism as a matter of justice.

Political Science, Brown University

---

difficulties with such a position is offered by Laura Mutterperl, "Employment at (God's) Will: The Constitutionality of Antidiscrimination Exemptions in Charitable Choice Legislation," *Harvard Civil Rights–Civil Liberties Law Review* 37, no. 2 (2002): 389–445. More generally, see Martha Minow's fine essay, "Partners, Not Rivals? Redrawing the Lines Between Public and Private, Non-Profit and Profit, Secular and Religious," *Boston University Law Review* 80, no. 4 (2000): 1061–94.

INDEX

Stoicism, 294, 315
Stouffer, Samuel, 238
Subjectivism, 266, 271, 291
Substitute success syndrome (sss), 300–301, 304
Sugden, Robert, 277–79, 284
Summa Theologiae (Aquinas), 216
SVR (Russian intelligence service), 152. *See also* KGB
Sympathy, 272–73, 297, 299–300. *See also* Caring; Empathy

Taking Rights Seriously (Dworkin), 299
Taliban, 10, 103
Talmud, 318
Tanzania, 31, 86
Taxation, 131–32; and tax reform, 334–36
Taylor, Charles, 12–13
Tenth Amendment, 176, 284
Terrorism, 6, 8–12, 105, 120
Teson, Fernando, 32
Thatcher, Margaret, 215
Theoharis, Athan, 163, 164, 165
Theory of Justice, A (Rawls), 267, 329–30
Theory of Moral Sentiments, The (Smith), 270
Thompson, Dennis, 39
Tiberius, 87
Tiersma, Peter Meijes, 196
Tocqueville, Alexis de, 56, 58, 99, 236, 243
Tolerance, 212, 223, 225, 251, 261–62, 263
Tomasi, John, 223n11, 231n34
Treatise Concerning the Correction of the Donatists (Augustine), 216
Treatise of Human Nature, A (Hume), 297
Trepper, Leopold, 152–53
Truman, Harry, 149
Truth, 78, 178, 328; and half-truths, 169
Turgot, Baron, 226

United Kingdom. *See* Great Britain
United Nations: charter, 16, 17–26, 27, 28–30; Security Council, 14–16, 17, 18–19, 21–22, 26, 27–28, 29, 31, 36
United States, 41–42, 86; and the American creed, 110–11, 314; Articles of Confederation, 84; Bill of Rights, 97, 320; Civil War, 100, 101, 142, 311, 316; Congress, 48–49, 80, 86, 168; Constitution, 83, 263, 291, 311, 326; Supreme Court, 81, 195, 280, 285, 314
United States Code, 192, 193, 194, 197
United States v. Carolene Products (1938), 285–86
Universal Declaration of Human Rights (1948), 18
U.S. Court of Appeals for the Ninth Circuit, 310

USSR. *See* Soviet Union
Utilitarianism, 122, 123, 136–38, 139–40, 189, 190, 298, 299; act-, 32–34, 37, 295; indirect, 271–76; rule-, 32–34, 122, 138, 275

Values, 12–13, 123, 266, 268, 327; social, 206, 213–14, 220
Veil of ignorance, 68–69. *See also* Rawls, John
Venona decryptions, 141, 155, 156, 158, 159, 160, 162, 163–64, 165, 166
Verba, Sidney, 109, 236–37
Virtue, 270; government promotion of, 96, 212–13; intellectual, 244–62; moral, 256–57, 258–59; and vice, 269
Virtue ethics, 294–95
Voluntary associations, 236–37
Voting: and gerrymanders, 89; and low-information rationality, 79–80; and suffrage, 89; value of, 79. *See also* Ignorance: problem of public
Voucher programs, 334–35

Walker, John, Jr., 155
Walzer, Michael, 9, 31, 110
War, 34–35; conventions, 2; just, 10–12; and treatment of noncombatants, 2, 8–11, 33
Watergate scandal, 203
Wealth: and political power, 90; redistribution of, 122, 136–38, 332; and savings, 131–32, 139
Welfare, 78, 268, 286–87, 331–32; and *British Poor Law Report*, 268
Welfare state, 130–31, 139
Welfarism, 87, 96, 299
Well-being, 14–15, 57, 121, 122, 123, 124–27, 140
Westermann, Claus, 317
White, Harry Dexter, 156, 160–61, 162
Wiesel, Elie, 310
Williams, Bernard, 136
Wittgenstein, Ludwig, 113
World War II, 164, 212
WorldCom, 86, 290
Wright, Charles, 242, 259

"Yale argument," the, 175–76. *See also* Lying
Yardley, Herbert, 149
Yugoslavia. *See* Kosovo

Zagzebski, Linda, 224, 256, 258
Zubilin, Vasili, 153